D1546001

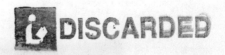

THE ENGLISH COURT
IN THE REIGN OF
GEORGE I

THE ENGLISH COURT
IN THE REIGN OF
GEORGE I

BY

JOHN M. BEATTIE

Assistant Professor in the Department of History
University of Toronto

CAMBRIDGE
AT THE UNIVERSITY PRESS
1967

Published by the Syndics of the Cambridge University Press
Bentley House, 200 Euston Road, London N.W.1
American Branch: 32 East 57th Street, New York, N.Y. 10022

© Cambridge University Press 1967

Library of Congress Catalogue Card Number: 67–10776

Printed in Great Britain
at the University Printing House, Cambridge
(Brooke Crutchley, University Printer)

To my Parents

CONTENTS

PREFACE

This is a study of the royal household, the organization that provided for the personal needs of the monarch and created the social setting in which he lived. How was the household organized? What kinds of men staffed its departments? How much did it cost and how was the money provided? How were posts obtained and how much were they worth? Such matters form the core of the book. In the last two chapters I have sketched in some aspects of the social and political importance of the court and, since administrative and social-political matters are not entirely distinct, some parts of the earlier chapters also bear on these wider themes. But to deal fully with them would have required a full-scale political study and I have not attempted this. I have placed the weight and focus of the book on the 'domestic' aspects of the subject in the belief that this institution—which has not been studied at all for the eighteenth century or in much detail for the previous two centuries—deserves extended study in its own right; and also that its study will throw some light on eighteenth century financial and administrative practices, the control and distribution of patronage and the rewards of office-holding.

This book grew out of an interest in the reign of the first Hanoverian king of England, but it is in no sense a history of the reign or a study of the monarchy. It is hoped, however, that it might help to dispel a few of the myths that still cling tenaciously to George I. The picture of the king as a dull and ignorant man who came to England with a small army of hungry retainers and abandoned himself to vice and his new country to his friends is happily passing away. But milder myths remain: that the king knew nothing and cared little about England; that he abdicated his prerogative to his ministers; that his court was an uninteresting and unimportant backwater of English life, with the king living alone in two rooms and never seeing company. There is truth in some of this, but it all needs drastic qualification. It is hoped that, as well as exploring the workings of a vast and important institution, this book will also help to make some of those necessary qualifications.

The book is a revised version of a Ph.D. dissertation submitted to the University of Cambridge in 1963. In the preparation of both the

Preface

dissertation and the book I have been fortunate to have the advice of Professor J. H. Plumb and it is a great pleasure to express my deepest appreciation to him. I shall always be thankful that I have had the benefit of his vast knowledge of the period and grateful for his support and encouragement. I also benefited for two terms in Cambridge from the advice of Miss C. B. A. Behrens and it is a pleasure to express my thanks to her. I am grateful, too, to Professor John M. Norris of the University of British Columbia, who was kind enough to read my dissertation and make many suggestions about how it might be improved. Professors Archibald S. Foord and Richard J. Helmstadter and Dean Willard Piepenburg read the book in typescript and improved it in many ways. It is a very great pleasure to have an opportunity to thank them and all the people who have helped me; it need hardly be added that I am responsible for the errors and shortcomings that remain in my book.

Acknowledgments are due to the owners and custodians of manuscripts who gave me permission to consult their papers and to quote from them. I am grateful to H.R.H. Ernst August, Prince of Hanover, for his kind hospitality and for permission to consult his papers in the Niedersächsisches Staatsarchiv in Hanover; to His Grace the Duke of Marlborough, for permission to use the manuscripts at Blenheim Palace; to His Grace the Duke of Devonshire, for permission to consult the manuscripts at Chatsworth; to the Marquess of Cholmondeley for permission to quote from the papers of Sir Robert Walpole on deposit in the Cambridge University Library; to the Marquess of Lothian for permission to use the Melbourne Manuscripts; to Earl Cathcart for permission to consult the Cathcart Manuscripts; to Lady Monica Salmond for permission to publish material from the Panshanger Manuscripts and to the Hertfordshire County Record Office where they are deposited. I would like to thank the Trustees of the British Museum for permission to quote from the Additional Manuscripts, the Stowe Manuscripts and the Egerton Manuscripts; the Controller of H.M. Stationery Office for permission to reproduce unpublished Crown-copyright material in the Public Record Office; the Lord Chamberlain for similar permission with regard to the Lord Chamberlain's and Lord Steward's papers; and the Huntington Library, San Marino, California, for permission to reproduce material from the Stowe Manuscripts among the Huntington Collections.

Preface

The staffs of Cambridge University Library, the British Museum, the Public Record Office, the National Register of Archives, the Niedersächsisches Staatsarchiv, the Huntington Library and numerous County Record Offices have been unfailingly courteous and helpful. I particularly remember with gratitude Mr E. K. Timings of the Public Record Office and Hugh Murray Baillie of the National Register of Archives who both gave so generously of their time and knowledge.

I acknowledge with thanks my debt to the Provost and Fellows of King's College, Cambridge, to the Research Board of the University of Toronto and to the Canada Council for the financial assistance which made my research possible.

Part of Chapter 8 has appeared in a rather different form in an article in the English Historical Review. I am grateful to the editor of that journal for permission to reproduce it here.

Finally, I wish to thank my wife, Susan, for her assistance and support. She has lived with this book for many years and has contributed to it more than she realizes. I owe my greatest debt to my parents. I have dedicated the book to them with affection and gratitude.

Toronto   J.M.B.
12 December 1966

ABBREVIATIONS

Add. MSS.	Additional Manuscripts, British Museum.
C(H)MSS.	Cholmondeley (Houghton) Manuscripts, Cambridge University Library.
Coxe, *Walpole*, II	William Coxe, *Memoirs of the Life and Administration of Sir Robert Walpole*, (1798), vol. II (correspondence).
C.T.B.	*Calendar of Treasury Books.*
C.T.P.	*Calendar of Treasury Papers.*
C.T.B. & P.	*Calendar of Treasury Books and Papers.*
H.C.J.	*Journals of the House of Commons.*
H.M.C.	*Historical Manuscripts Commission.*
Household Ordinances	*A Collection of Ordinances and Regulations for the Government of the Royal Household...from King Edward III to King William and Queen Mary* (The Society of Antiquaries, 1790).
HM, Stowe MSS.	Papers of the duke of Chandos in The Huntington Library, San Marino, California.
LC	Lord chamberlain's department papers, Public Record Office.
LS	Lord steward's department papers, Public Record Office.
N.S.A.	Niedersächsisches Staatsarchiv, Hanover.
P.H.	Cobbett's *Parliamentary History of England* (36 vols., 1806–20).
Plumb, *Walpole*, I	J. H. Plumb, *Sir Robert Walpole. The Making of a Statesman* (1956).
Plumb, *Walpole*, II	J. H. Plumb, *Sir Robert Walpole. The King's Minister* (1960).
S.P. Dom.	State Papers, Domestic, Public Record Office.
Stowe MSS.	Stowe MSS., British Museum (see also above, HM).
Suffolk Correspondence	Croker, J. W. (ed.). Letters to and from Henrietta Countess of Suffolk and her second husband, 2 vols., 1824.
T 1, T 30, etc.	Treasury Papers, Public Record Office.

1

INTRODUCTION

I

By the reign of George I the royal household had not played a significant role in the government of England for almost two centuries. Before the administrative reforms of the first half of the sixteenth century the household had occupied a central place in the government of the country. Not only was it the source of political authority but also its departments, the chamber and the wardrobe, had rivalled and from time to time had replaced as agencies of national administration those departments that had 'gone out of court' in the twelfth century, the chancery and the exchequer. As Dr Elton has argued, it was characteristic of 'medieval' government that 'the institutions of government depended for their vitality and force on the existence of an active king with an active household, often formally duplicating the work of out-of-court offices'.[1] Historians are currently debating the scope and significance of this involvement of the household in national administration and the nature of 'the Tudor revolution in government'. But whether or not the fundamental changes that mark the turning away from 'medieval' government and the construction of a modern, bureaucratic government took place in the fourth decade of the sixteenth century and under the guidance of Thomas Cromwell, as Dr Elton insists, it is beyond dispute that whereas in the reigns of Edward IV and Henry VII the household was the most active agency of national administration, after the 1530's even the palest version of this 'chamber' administration was never duplicated. The rise of the privy council, the emergence of the secretary as a national officer, the elaboration of new revenue courts and, in mid-century, the reorganization of the exchequer, together thrust the household aside as an instrument of national administration and restricted it to a purely domestic role. Indeed, it was itself reorganized in the 1530s in order that it might assume effectively this

[1] G. R. Elton, 'The Tudor Revolution: a Reply', *Past and Present*, no. 29 (December 1964), p. 43.

more modest task.[1] The household became then simply the institution which supplied the daily necessities of the king's court and created the ceremonial background of the monarch's life. It retained this essential character thereafter.

There remained until the nineteenth century some slight blurring in the separation of the household, and especially of the chamber, and the central government. A number of men, particularly at lower levels, remained nominally in the household and were paid by a household treasurer, though their work made them part of the central bureaucracy. To take one example of several, the messengers of the chamber were on the establishment of the lord chamberlain's department and were paid by the treasurer of the chamber, but they were primarily diplomatic couriers who worked mainly for the secretaries of state. Such minor exceptions as this do not, however, lessen the force of the fundamental distinction that had been made in the sixteenth century between the administration of the king's household and the administration of the country. Whereas previously the treasurer of the chamber, the cofferer and other officers of the chamber and of the household below stairs had often worked in national as well as purely 'domestic' affairs, after the administrative reorganization of the first half of the sixteenth century the vast majority of them were concerned entirely with personal service to the monarch or in service in some way connected with his court. The great officers of the household continued to be important men in politics into the eighteenth century, but the household itself played very little part in national affairs.

The separation between the household and the departments of the central government had not, however, deprived the king's household of social and political importance. So long as the king remained at the centre of the political and social life of the country, in the eighteenth century as in the sixteenth, his household continued to be an institution of more than merely 'domestic' importance. In the reign of George I the court was no longer the only focal point of administration, politics and social life, but it was still the most obvious source of patronage and political power, and the centre of the upper-class social world of London and the country.

In contemporary usage 'the court' was more than an idle and tradi-

[1] G. R. Elton, *The Tudor Revolution in Government. Administrative Changes in the Reign of Henry VIII* (1959), ch. VI.

tional synonym for 'the government' because the king continued to dominate the political world. Of course the necessity of dealing with Parliament imposed limitations on him, but the king continued to exercise with a good deal of freedom the duty of choosing the ministers who would direct the policy and, to some extent, control the patronage of the government. So long as this, his most vital prerogative, remained intact and unchallenged, the king's views about policy and patronage could not be ignored. The court was thus still Mecca for the place-hunter. And while the king retained his freedom of action, and while the doctrine of responsibility had not advanced far enough in fact or in theory to allow ministers to control 'unofficial' advisers and to insist that he accept advice only from those who had to bear the responsibility for his actions in Parliament, those who had access to him and were his constant companions could still hope to exercise some influence on the government. Most of the greater household officers enjoyed such access to the king, though some had much more opportunity to speak to him than others. A distinction must be made between officers like the master of the great wardrobe who were of high enough rank to have the *entrée* to the drawing-room but who in the course of business would not have much occasion to visit the king privately, and those men whose duties brought them frequently into the royal presence. Whether anything was made of such access to the king would depend, of course, on the talent and ambition of the courtier. Contemporaries, for example, expected that a politician like the duke of Argyll might be able to take advantage of the privileges that the court offices he accepted in 1714 and again in 1719 gave him. At the beginning of the reign, Peter Wentworth thought that Argyll was 'very wise in accepting the Key to the Prince [that is, the office of groom of the stole] for it will give him frequenter access to court that the junto men care for'.[1] And when he became lord steward to the king in 1719 (after being forced out of the prince's household in 1716) it was said, in a newsletter sent to Hanover, that Argyll's great rival in military affairs, Lord Cadogan, was very unhappy that the duke was 'in a position where he has the ear of the King'.[2] But not all courtiers were capable of or interested in playing a large part in

[1] J. J. Cartwright (ed.), *The Wentworth Papers 1705–1739, selected from the private and family correspondence of Thomas Wentworth, Lord Raby, created in 1711 Earl of Strafford* (1883) p. 426.

[2] N.S.A., Cal. Br. Arch., Des. 24, England 131 (newsletter of 10/21 February 1719).

I-2

politics, even behind the scenes. The typical courtier who had no ambition to be anything but a courtier, like the 'professional' man-of-business, undoubtedly yearned for stability and security and these were not normally to be gained by dabbling in politics. The court was full of men like the duke of Grafton, who spent thirty-three years of his life as lord chamberlain (1724–57), and who was content to play very little part in politics. His post gave him a seat on the Cabinet—as did normally the other three great household offices: lord steward, master of the horse and groom of the stole; and though this did not mean very much when, as happened by the fourth decade of the century, a small, efficient 'inner cabinet' developed which excluded all but the handful of ministers with departmental responsibilities from the governing circle, in Anne's reign and in George I's, membership in the Cabinet could still bring a man to the centre of government.[1] Even so Grafton, and many like him, were content to be docile followers and this undoubtedly explains Grafton's longevity in the court post.

As a permanent career, of course, the household could offer an ambitious man only a very limited field. But, on the other hand, a politician who found himself stuck momentarily in the household was not necessarily excluded from affairs. It was in any case possible in the early eighteenth century to move from the court to a more active place. The household and the offices of 'public business' had been clearly separated two hundred years earlier, but men were not yet divided and fixed for all time, except perhaps by temperament, into 'courtiers' and 'men of business'. The duke of Newcastle moved from the lord chamberlainship to be secretary of state; his brother went from a court post to the treasury board; Lord Hervey from vice-chamberlain to lord privy seal. Service at court could still, that is, open the way to posts concerned with the 'public business'; if it was no longer the only path to the top, the household had not yet been displaced as one ladder to success. Some household posts were more suitable than others if one's object was to escape to a place of greater consequence: a well-paying sinecure like the treasurership of the chamber would better suit a politically inclined man than a working post like the vice-chamberlainship. But the man counted for more than the post. Hervey, and other active members of the inner, personal household like gentlemen of the

[1] J. H. Plumb, 'The Organisation of the Cabinet in the reign of Queen Anne', *T.R.H.S.* 5th ser. VII (1957).

Introduction

bedchamber, found the holding of such a post no barrier to concurrent or subsequent work in a place of 'public business'.[1]

For those without such ambitions court office offered simply honour and profit. It was a considerable distinction to be an officer of the king's household. This was true of many posts in the government, of course. As Lady Mary Wortley Montagu told her husband, a seat on the treasury board, which he was hoping to get in 1714, 'looks well' and 'will be an addition to your figure and will facilitate your election'.[2] But the household was the most obvious place for a gentleman seeking honourable employment, for there were many posts at court that were both prestigious and financially attractive. At George I's court, for example, there were about thirty posts worth over £1,000 a year, and almost another 100 worth over £200 a year, most of which would have been acceptable to a gentleman conscious of his honour.

In addition to the honour and the salary, an appointment to one of the greater posts at court, and especially to those of the first rank that brought the holder into the private apartments and into frequent contact with the king, was a clear demonstration of royal favour; and the prospect of its future exercise on his friends' behalf was likely to increase a man's own galaxy of hangers-on and dependants, to inflate his 'connection' and his status. An officer who, like the vice-chamberlain, spent his days 'near the sun'—a place-hunter's phrase—with frequent opportunities to speak to the king, was obviously in a good position to help his friends. His influence did not work quite as effortlessly as Lord Hervey suggests when he remembered how, as vice-chamberlain, he had taken his father's chaplain, Robert Butts, 'out of obscurity and had by his interest (since he was vice-chamberlain) first made him Dean of Norwich and three years after Bishop [of Norwich]'.[3] But courtiers like the vice-chamberlain obviously had opportunity enough to beg favours for friends and relatives from the king and his ministers; and there were many ways in which a friend at court could help, from a recommendation for an appointment down to getting a man freed from the burden of serving his turn as sheriff.[4] If a man was so inclined,

[1] See below, pp. 250-1.
[2] Lady Mary Wortley Montagu, *Letters* (1893), I, 214-16.
[3] John, Lord Hervey, *Some Materials towards Memoirs of the Reign of George II*, ed. R. R. Sedgwick (3 vols., 1931), p. 532.
[4] For courtiers being requested to get their friends relieved of this duty see *H.M.C. Cowper MSS.* III, 50, 51, 66-7.

such natural interest could be of considerable value in furthering his own and his family's position. When Lady Mary Wortley Montagu said that a seat on the treasury board would facilitate her husband's election, presumably she meant that a man who was so close to the sources of patronage would prove to be an irresistable candidate. Courtiers, or some at least, could have the same appeal. Thomas Coke, who was vice-chamberlain, 1706–27, and member of Parliament for Grampound in Anne's reign, kept up a considerable correspondence with his electors, most of which dealt with his response to their frequent requests for favours.[1]

Even if he was innocent of political ambition, a leading courtier's contact with the king, his proximity to those sources of patronage that upper-class society so genuinely depended on for the employment of their sons, could only raise a man in the eyes of the world. It gave him importance and distinction in the eyes at least of that large segment of upper-class society that regarded the king's drawing-room at St James's not only as the centre of the social world but also as the place where family ambition could be most easily gratified.

II

The king's drawing-room had become by the eighteenth century the focal point of the court. In most palaces it was the central and the largest room of the state apartments and the place where the king most often met court society. In both size and function it had been a comparatively recent addition to the king's apartments; and, since its development had important effects on the pattern and character of court social life it may be worthwhile tracing briefly the changes in the room pattern of the royal palaces and the functions of the various rooms over the previous two centuries.

In the eighteenth century the state apartments consisted in all palaces of a series of rooms on the first floor which were approached by way of a courtyard and the grand staircase. At the head of the stairs the visitor entered the guard chamber—so called because the yeomen of the guard were on duty there—and then, leading off from it, two smaller rooms in succession, the presence and privy chambers. The privy chamber led in turn into the largest room of the wing and the usual place of assembly,

[1] See, for example, *H.M.C. Cowper MSS.* III, 107.

the drawing-room. Beyond that were the sovereign's private apartments, consisting of a smaller drawing-room, one or more bedchambers and several writing closets.

This room pattern had begun to emerge clearly from an original single chamber by the fifteenth century, for by then the king's bedchamber and another private room had been separated from the great hall. Under the early Tudors a further step in the elaboration of the state apartments was taken with the separation and naming of the presence and privy chambers.[1] As the names imply, the Tudor monarchs gave audiences in the presence and retired for privacy into the privy chamber, beyond which was the bedchamber. In the household ordinances promulgated at Eltham in 1526, access to the presence chamber was granted to 'lords, knights, gentlemen, officers of the King's house, and other honest personages', that is, in effect, to anyone of birth or position.[2] Entry to the privy chamber, however, was closely guarded. It was ordered by these same regulations that 'Noe person, of what estate, degree or condicion soever he be, from henceforth presume, attempt, or be in any wise suffered or admitted to come or repaire into the King's privy chamber' except the servants on duty there and others invited by the king himself.[3] The strict privacy of this room, even if established then, was not, however, maintained in the seventeenth century. In the reign of Charles I the right of entry to the queen's privy chamber was granted to the nobility, and it is likely that at the same time the king's privy chamber was open to all courtiers generally.[4] At the Restoration, Sir Richard Leveson reported that the 'Court is modelling itself as it was in the late King's time, that is, that persons are to come near the King's person as they are in quality'. But he goes on to say that 'persons that do effectually wait for business' could enter the privy chamber, and this was confirmed in Charles II's own household regulations.[5]

The privy chamber had thus become only slightly less public than the presence by the seventeenth century and its place as a private room was taken by a smaller 'withdrawing' room, between the privy

[1] A. R. Myers, *The Household of Edward IV* (1959), p. 14; E. K. Chambers, *The Elizabethan Stage* (4 vols., 1923), I, 142.

[2] *Household Ordinances*, p. 152.

[3] *Ibid.* p. 154.   [4] *Ibid.* p. 248.

[5] *H.M.C. MSS. of the Duke of Sutherland*, p. 199; *Household Ordinances*, p. 361.

chamber and the bedchamber. Such a room was in existence as early as 1627 in the queen's apartment and, like Henry VIII's privy chamber, entry to it was gained only by invitation.[1]

Considerable changes were made in the state apartments after the Restoration, both in the room pattern and in the rules governing the right of *entrée* to various rooms. From about the middle years of Charles II's reign into the eighteenth century the state apartments in all the royal palaces were rebuilt. This was to an extent no doubt in imitation of Louis XIV's vast building enterprises and also in response to a heightened taste for polite society; and perhaps more fundamentally, because the existing rooms were simply too small to accommodate the numbers of people who now thronged the court. The result of this rebuilding was to produce a court strikingly different from that of the Tudors and early Stuarts.

The main innovation was the building of a large room between the privy chamber and the private rooms. This was first called a withdrawing room, like the one already in existence, and later an audience chamber or drawing-room. Such a room was built at Whitehall as early as 1670; and early in James II's reign when the queen's lodgings on the river side of Whitehall were rebuilt by Christopher Wren they included a new large drawing-room.[2] But the new room is most clearly to be seen at Hampton Court, where, in the extensive rebuilding undertaken for William and Mary, Wren made the drawing-room the central and largest room of the royal apartments, approached through the guard chamber, presence and privy chambers, and leading into an ante-room and the bedchamber.

In the eighteenth century this new drawing-room was the main room of assembly, and the first three rooms became simply ante-chambers to it. These functions were recognized by a further change of names at Hampton Court in George I's reign; the privy chamber, having long ago lost its original function, now lost its name and was called simply the second presence and the large central room became known as the audience chamber.[3]

[1] *Household Ordinances*, p. 342.
[2] L.C.C. *Survey of London*, xiii, 71, 76; *Publications of the Wren Society*, vii, pl. xv.
[3] Ernest Law, the historian of Hampton Court, dates the present nomenclature (i.e. two presences, an audience chamber and a drawing room) from 'about 1720' (*A Catalogue of the Pictures at Hampton Court*, p. 34).

Introduction

At St James's, though the same names were not employed, the same development of a larger 'public' court is evident. St James's was not really an adequate replacement for Whitehall when that palace was burned down in the fire of 1697. It was a maze of small and, Defoe said, 'mean' rooms and was in general, as a contemporary wrote in 1734, 'so far from having one single beauty to recommend it, that 'tis at once the contempt of foreign nations, and the disgrace of our own'.[1] It seemed obvious to many people that Whitehall would have to be re-built. There was no dearth of plans, but, though a grateful government built a palace for the duke of Marlborough, money was never made available to rebuild Whitehall and British monarchs were content for some time to put up with a building that was in every way inadequate as their main residence.[2] Some attempt was made in Anne's reign to improve and enlarge the state apartments. The Hampton Court model was followed as closely as possible for the central feature of the new apartments was a large drawing-room.[3] But because of the restrictions of space even these new apartments at St James's were not so regular in design as they were at Hampton Court. Instead of a majestic sweep of rooms, one leading directly to the next from the great staircase to the private lodgings, at St James's the state apartments were in the form of a letter T: the guard chamber, presence and privy chambers forming

[1] G. D. H. Cole (ed.), Daniel Defoe, *Tour Through the Whole Island of Great Britain* (1927), I, 357; James Ralph, *A Critical Review of the Public Buildings...in and about London and Westminster* (1734), p. 48.

[2] It might be said in passing that all the facilities proved to be inadequate in 1714. There was difficulty accommodating both the king and the Prince and Princess of Wales under its roof and in fact very few of even their closest servants could be lodged there. Only a handful of English and German servants had apartments at St James's. Most of them were scattered around Whitehall and in Somerset House or, in the case of the Hanoverian ministers and courtiers, in hired lodgings in the area surrounding the palace. In the first few years after the king's arrival there is evidence of considerable and frantic rebuilding and new building going on 'below stairs', providing new kitchens, cellars, sculleries, a new confectionery, a new charcoal house, etc. (LC 5/156, p. 229; LC 5/157, pp. 102–3; LS 13/176, p. 63; LS 13/115, fo. 81). It must indeed have been something of a relief to those who laboured in the royal kitchens and allied departments when the prince and princess were turned out of the palace in December 1717, for the removal of their separate and independent household must have eased considerably the strain on the physical resources of St James's.

[3] *Publications of the Wren Society*, VII, *The Royal Palaces of Winchester, Whitehall, Kensington and St James's*, 207–29 and pl. XXXI.

9

the stem, with the large drawing-room and the council chamber on the one side and a small drawing-room (the old withdrawing room) and the bedchamber on the other, forming the bar of the letter and separated by the privy chamber at the junction. The new large drawing-room was thereafter the main room of assembly.

Similar developments can be traced at Kensington. Wren's proposals for an extension to the house bought by William III from the earl of Nottingham included a new wing of state rooms in which a large drawing-room would separate the privy chamber and the bedchamber.[1] This proposal was not, however, carried out, and a similar plan to build a new drawing-room in Anne's reign was also cancelled.[2] Under George I the royal apartments were finally rebuilt, at first in 1718 by Benson, who succeeded Wren at the board of works, and (because his work was discovered to be structurally unsound) again in 1723-4.[3] The new room distribution followed the now familiar pattern: a guard chamber, presence and privy chambers followed by a large drawing-room, a small private room and the bedchamber.[4]

III

By the early eighteenth century, then, the state apartments had come to consist of three groups of rooms: the outer, or public, rooms; the private rooms; and a large room in between these two groups that was still essentially private but which was open to visitors at stated times during the week when the king entertained at a drawing-room.

The development of the large drawing-room not only provided a more splendid setting in which the king could meet company, it also helped to make a clear separation between the public and private rooms of the state apartments, and in particular to maintain the privacy of the royal bedchamber. This was clearly intended when the new apartments were built at Whitehall in Charles II's reign. In January 1683 Sir Charles Lyttelton wrote:

There is another thing which is now as much talked on: the new orders about the bedchamber, since the King is come into these new lodgings. Nobody except the Duke [of York], Lord Ormond, and I think Hallifax, the two

[1] *Publications of the Wren Society*, VII, pl. XIX.
[2] *C.T.P. 1702–1707*, p. 441. [3] *Wren Society*, VII, 189–96.
[4] LC 5/157, pp. 284-5.

Introduction

Secretaries of England and the Secretaries of Scotland are to come into the bedchamber without leave first asked; nor are they to ask leave, if the King be in the closet. None under the degree of nobleman or privy councillor may ask leave at all, unless he says he has business with the King.[1]

Previously the bedchamber had been much more accessible to ordinary courtiers. On numerous occasions John Evelyn speaks of being in the king's or queen's bedchamber as though it had become, after the Restoration, a normal room of assembly.[2] The building of the new drawing-room and Charles II's new orders about *entrée* to his bedchamber in 1683 produced therefore a considerable alteration in the style of court life, for together they helped to make possible a clearer separation of the private and public characters of the monarch. William III repeated with even greater strictness Charles II's rules about the right of *entrée* to the bedchamber. After 1689 only servants on duty there and the Prince of Denmark, the king's ministers and great household officers, and a few others whose names were kept by the pages guarding the door could enter the bedchamber without permission.[3] To some extent Queen Anne reverted to an earlier pattern, for she occasionally entertained in her bedchamber instead of in the drawing-room, and Swift, in 1711, spoke of talking to Lord Rochester 'when I was in the bedchamber'[4] as though the bedchamber had once more become rather more accessible to courtiers than Charles II or William III intended.

George I went firmly back to the practice established by these monarchs. Though William III's ordinances governing his bedchamber were not formally reaffirmed, they were clearly enforced in George I's reign.[5] The king found them very much to his taste. He hated ostenta-

---

[1] E. M. Thompson (ed.), *Correspondence of the Family of Hatton...1601–1704* (2 vols., Camden Society, 1878), II, 21.

[2] E. S. de Beer (ed.), *The Diary of John Evelyn* (6 vols.), III, 261, 322, 463.

[3] Stowe MSS. 563, fos. 14–15 (Orders for the government of the bedchamber, 1689).

[4] H. Williams (ed.), *Journal to Stella* (1948), p. 451.

[5] They were certainly in force in the Prince of Wales's court. On one occasion even his grooms of the bedchamber were refused admission, an insult for which the groom of the stole had to apologize (Cathcart MSS. A/11, 5, 6 August 1715). William III's bedchamber orders were probably still in force in George II's reign. Among the Blenheim MSS. (F 1/13) there is a notebook containing a copy of William III's ordinances with this note inside: 'Taken from an examined with an Authentick copy in the custody of the Right Honourable Henry Earl of Pembroke, Groom of the Stole to his Majesty. 31 Jan. 1738/9 by William Hetzler.'

tion and display and people making a fuss. In England he kept in the background as much as possible and guarded the privacy of his bedchamber, so that in his reign the tendency towards a separation of the private and public aspects of the monarchy was strongly reinforced. He saw his ministers, and others who desired an audience of him, not in the bedchamber but in the closet, a private room at the other side of the bedchamber from the public rooms and reached by means of the back stairs. Normally the king spent two or three hours every day before dinner receiving visitors in this room. Admittance was gained only through an introduction by the gentleman of the bedchamber in waiting or a secretary of state. This applied to everyone, including peers; and even the king's German ministers did not introduce people to him directly, but arranged for the gentlemen of the bedchamber to do so.[1]

At other times the king met court society in the drawing-room. On several evenings a week he entertained at an assembly, usually called a 'drawing-room', which had a major place in the upper-class social life of London. Attendance there helped to distinguish the 'ins' from the 'outs', in the social as well as political sense. These drawing-rooms were held both in the winter, at St James's, and in the summer at a country palace, for the court followed, and thus reinforced, the pattern well established among landed society of spending the summer in the country and the winter in town.

George was normally in residence at St James's from October or November until the middle of May or early June. Except for the six occasions during the reign when the king went to Hanover for the summer (when he followed roughly the same time schedule), the court normally left London for Kensington Palace in May and then went on to Hampton Court or Windsor in July or August, returning to London in October or November. To some extent the dates of this movement were determined by the weather—London was very hot and smelly in the summer—and by the meeting of Parliament. But also in the reigns of the first two Hanoverians the dates of this seasonal movement of landed society from town to country must have been partly determined, for those who took attendance at court seriously, by the dates of the kings' birthdays. The celebration of the king's birthday was one of the

---

[1] Blenheim MSS. D 2/2; Edmund Calamy, *Own Life*, pp. 380–1; A. Clark (ed.), *Memoirs of Nathaniel, Lord Crewe* (1893), p. 34.

great court occasions; the rooms were always particularly crowded and by courtiers who traditionally expressed their devotion to the sovereign by wearing new and especially splendid clothes.[1] For the habitual courtier not to appear at court on such an occasion would have been a calculated insult, and so the fact that George I's birthday fell on 28 May and George II's on 30 October must have kept many of the nobility and greater gentry in town later than they might have wanted in the father's reign, and brought them back earlier in the son's. Certainly in 1718 the Dutch Resident in London, l'Hermitage, noticed that many people had 'deferred going to the country until after' 28 May;[2] and in 1736, when George II stayed in Hanover into November, Lord Hervey noted that the London tradesmen were unhappy 'as they thought the King's absence prevented people coming to town, and particularly for the Birthday'.[3]

For those who frequented the court, the great court 'showdays', the king's birthday and the anniversaries of the coronation and of the accession, were very special occasions. But there were of course many other opportunities to bow to and perhaps to speak to the king. In most reigns the king held a *levee* for the gentlemen of his court in the private apartments in the morning; and on several evenings a week it had become customary by the early eighteenth century for the sovereign to meet both men and women at an assembly in the drawing-room.

George I, however, did not encourage visitors *en masse* to his private apartments and he very rarely invited the gentlemen of the court to a *levee*. Nor at first did he hold a drawing-room in his own apartment. For the first two years of the reign he gratified his decided preference for privacy and quiet by allowing the Prince and Princess of Wales to act in his place. It was in the princess's drawing-room at St James's, not in the king's, that the royal drawing-rooms and occasional balls were held. This continued until 1717 when, for a combination of personal and political reasons, the king was forced to exert himself and to displace his son as the leader of court and London social life. After 1717, and especially when, in December of that year, the prince and princess were thrown out of St James's and set up a rival court, the king appeared in his own drawing-room on two or three evenings a week.

[1] See below, p. 206.   [2] Add. MSS. 17677 KKK 2, fo. 620.
[3] Hervey, *Memoirs*, p. 609.

13

In addition, after 1717 he also joined the company on Sundays after chapel.[1]

Queen Anne had often held her drawing rooms in the early afternoon instead of the evening and, when there was little company, in her bed-chamber. At the best of times a drawing-room could not have been a very lively affair (though a man was thrown out of one in 1718 for fighting and being 'drunk and saucy').[2] But, if one can trust Swift, Anne's seem to have been particularly dull. In 1711 Swift wrote to Stella from Windsor

There was a drawing room today at Court; but so few company, that the Queen sent for us into her bed-chamber, where we made our bows, and stood about twenty of us around the room, while she looked at us round with her fan in her mouth, and once a minute said about three words to some that were nearest her, and then she was told dinner was ready, and went out.[3]

The privacy of George I's bedchamber was never infringed in this way. When he began to meet company in his own apartments, the assemblies were invariably held in the drawing-room. At these assemblies the king sometimes played cards, but most often he stood or sat at one end of the room and chatted to those visitors nearest him who could speak French.[4] Normally the company would form a semi-circle round the king—the institution was, indeed, often called a 'circle'—and though George I does not seem to have wandered about very much, in the next reign his son seems to have delighted in moving along the 'circle' and around the room, carefully choosing those to be honoured with a word and those to be snubbed.

Drawing-rooms in the early eighteenth century thus do not seem to have been as formal as they later became. If the room was very crowded,

[1] See chapter 8. William Byrd, a Virginian who spent several years in London and went frequently to the drawing-room, records several visits to court on Sunday afternoons in 1718 and 1719 (William Byrd, *The London Diary, 1717–21*, ed. L. B. Wright and M. Tinling, 1958). The court was often more crowded on Sundays than for the evening drawing-rooms. A Swiss visitor who was taken to St James's on a Sunday in 1725 found so many 'noblemen and officers' at court to see the king on his way to and from chapel that he was unable to get into the drawing-room to watch the procession 'on account of the crowd' (Cesar de Saussure, *A Foreign View of England in the reigns of George I and George II*, 1926, pp. 38–9).
[2] Lady Cowper, *Diary*, p. 98.   [3] H. Williams (ed.), *Journal to Stella*, p. 328.
[4] *H.M.C. Portland MSS.* v, 541, 546, 549; Saussure, *A Foreign View of England*, pp. 43–4.

the king could talk to only a few people and the rest of the company chatted to one another and moved around. Apart from paying respect to the sovereign, this must have been a compelling reason for going to the drawing-room, to meet friends. Swift wrote in 1711, 'I was at Court at noon, and saw fifty acquaintances I had not met this long time; that is the advantage of a Court...'; and again, 'the Court serves me for a coffee-house, once a week [he went to the drawing-room every Sunday] I meet acquaintances there that I should not otherwise see in a quarter'.[1] Others must have gone hoping to make new friends, especially among the 'great men', for both the English and German ministers in George I's reign often attended his drawing-room. In general, as Lady Bute said in 1761, attendance at the king's drawing-room was 'a means of introduction into the world'.[2]

Invitations were not issued for drawing-rooms; nor, so far as is known, were regulations ever formulated in the eighteenth century to define who had the right to attend.[3] The vagueness of social distinctions would have confused the attempt. There were obviously some people whose attendance was not only unquestioned but expected, either because of their birth or their position—the king's ministers, the great court officers and generally, as the Dutch Resident called them, 'people of the first quality and consideration of both sexes'. It is the lower limit of court society that is hard to define. Of household servants, only those holding positions of dignity and honour—the heads of the four main departments, a few sub-department heads, the vice-chamberlain, the bedchamber servants, the equerries and the more important personal servants generally—were courtiers in the social sense. Lady Chetwynd, the daughter of a viscount, was allowed to continue going to the drawing-room when she was appointed sempstress to George II. But George III considered this a particular favour given to her by his grandfather and, though she obviously did little sewing, he refused to receive so undignified a servant in his drawing-room.[4]

For the rest of society, except naturally for the great mass of people who had neither interest in nor hope of going to court, there were two

[1] *Journal to Stella*, pp. 421, 522.

[2] J. W. Croker (ed.), *Letters to and from Henrietta, Countess of Suffolk...* (2 vols., 1824), II, 259.

[3] Tickets were issued for a ball in 1715, but even this seems to have been unusual (A. R., Heinsius Correspondence, 1925).   [4] *Suffolk Correspondence*, II, 258–62.

primary factors which limited the numbers of those who went to drawing-rooms. The first, obvious but important, was desire. Not everyone who might have qualified wanted to go, either because they despised the court and courtiers or, more narrowly, because they were out of favour or out of sympathy with the administration. A second factor which helped to confer or deny access to the court was the necessity of wearing fashionable clothes. Proper clothes were the only necessary ticket of admission to court, and especially on ordinary drawing-room nights. The footmen and ushers on duty on the staircase and in the public rooms must have known large numbers of courtiers by sight, of course, but the factor that decided whether others gained entrance must have been the quality and style of their dress. Dudley Ryder, who became Attorney-General in the next reign, but who was in 1714 simply a student at the Middle Temple without obvious social connections, had no difficulty getting into the drawing-room on ordinary evenings; he records several occasions in his diary on which he clearly entered the drawing-room quite freely; and on one such occasion he was accompanied by his cousin who had borrowed a coat and wig. He found it a little more difficult however, to get into the drawing-room on court 'showdays'. When he went on the first anniversary of George I's accession —dressed in his 'best clothes and laced ruffles'—he got past the ushers at the door between the guard and privy chambers only by pretending to be with some important person in front of him. On another occasion he found he could only get into a ball at court by bribing one of the servants.

When I came to St James's [he writes in his diary] I attempted to get upstairs but was repulsed. Upon that I went to the coffee house and stayed a half-hour and came back again and resolved to try again. And I attempted and was repulsed, but I immediately put one shilling into his hand [the hand, no doubt, of a footman] and he let me go. Now I was among a vast crowd of nobility and gentry waiting for the opening of the door into the dancing room. And about a half-hour after the door was opened, we all rushed in as fast as we could go and got in among the rest and got into a pretty good place.

It seems clear that while court society was dominated by the aristocracy and the greater gentry, entry to at least its outer fringes was not impossible for many less exalted people who cared to make the effort and who could afford it.[1]

[1] W. Matthews (ed.), *The Diary of Dudley Ryder, 1715–16* (1939), pp. 55, 62, 66, 76–7, 221, 356.

Introduction

IV

The structure of the household of George I's reign had been well established by the late fifteenth century and perhaps earlier. The only major development in the intervening period had been the establishment of a separate bedchamber department by James I, a department whose head, the groom of the stole, had very quickly gained independence of the lord chamberlain who was the leading officer of the court 'above stairs'. The end of purveyance in 1660 and its replacement by a system of contracting with merchants, and also the rise of the Treasury to a position of dominance over the spending departments, had brought changes in the administrative and financial practices of the household. But in structure, apart from the development of the bedchamber, the household remained in the eighteenth century what it had been two centuries and more before. It consisted of four main departments: the lord chamberlain's department; the household below stairs under the lord steward; the stables under the master of the horse; and, by the late seventeenth century, the bedchamber.

Except for the lord chamberlain's department, each had a clearly defined and unified purpose. The gentlemen and grooms of the bedchamber under the groom of the stole were personal servants to the king in the private apartments; the stables department looked after the king's horses and carriages, though its leading officers, the master of the horse, the equerries and pages of honour, were also personal royal servants, and generally speaking took the place of the officers of the bedchamber when the king went out of doors; the household below stairs was a supply department, a vast catering establishment that acquired, prepared and distributed food, fuel, drink, candles and the like.

While its structure had changed little over the previous two centuries, the household had been decreased considerably in size. By 1714 it contained many fewer servants than it had a hundred or even fifty years earlier. Rising costs in the seventeenth century brought great periodic pressures for retrenchment. In the course of the seventeenth century whole sub-offices as well as many individual offices were abolished or simply not filled. In James I's reign there had been departments of the tents, of the beds, a chandlery, a boulting house, and a wafry; these were no longer in existence in 1714. William III abolished a number of offices, including that of esquire of the body; and a number of other posts—especially 'sporting' posts, huntsmen and keepers of dogs, and the like—were simply not filled by Queen Anne and George I. Of forty-six posts in the Hall in Charles I's reign, only five survived in 1714, and four of these were abolished by George I. There were drastic reductions in many other departments in the course of the century. There had been 200 yeomen of the guard in the early seventeenth century: there were just over 100 in 1714. There had been ninety-seven grooms in the stables in Charles I's reign and only twelve remained in George I's. In the same period the number of servants in the household below stairs had been decreased from about 300 to about 160.[1]

Altogether, between Charles I's reign and George I's, the king's household was reduced from about 1450[2] to about 950. In George I's reign these 950 royal servants were distributed as follows:

Lord chamberlain's department and offshoots (including gentlemen pensioners (40); yeomen of the guard (*c.* 100); the artisans of the great wardrobe (*c.*30); the jewel office) .... *c.* 660
Bedchamber .... *c.* 30
Household below stairs .... *c.* 160
Stables .... *c.* 100

Total *c.* 950

Not all of these men were 'domestic' servants; and even of those whose work was essential to the running of the household, only a proportion were in waiting at a time. On the other hand there were

---

[1] A list of royal servants dating from 1607–8 is printed in *H.M.C. MSS. of Lord Montagu of Beaulieu*, pp. 51–67; and see G. E. Aylmer, *The King's Servants. The Civil Service of Charles I, 1625–1642* (1961), appendix, pp. 472–4. There are printed lists of the household servants of George I in John Chamberlayne, *Magnae Britanniae Notitia: or, the Present State of Great Britain*, of which there were five editions during the reign: in 1716, 1718, 1723, 1726, and 1727. There are other published lists in *The Present State of the British Court . . .* (1720); *A New Exact and Methodical List of all the Officers Civil and Military since King George's accession to the Throne* (1715). In MS. sources the servants above stairs are included in the Establishment of the chamber among the lord chamberlain's papers (LC 3/6–8); the Establishment of the household below stairs (LS 13/44) includes the names of the more important officers of the lord steward's department and the stables. Minor servants in these departments are named in entry books of warrants of appointment (LS 13/260–1 for George I's reign). There is a useful comparison of the establishment of the treasurer of the chamber's office in the reigns of James II, William III, Anne and George I at T 38/523.
[2] G. E. Aylmer, *The King's Servants*, p. 27.

Introduction

many more men working at court than the total of official servants indicates. All of the greater and many minor household officers had personal servants, some of whom did their masters' work, and some of whom were paid a small wage by the king, though they were not his sworn servants and do not appear on the household establishment. There is no way to discover exactly how many such servants' servants worked at court, but a conservative estimate would suggest at least 200–300, and quite possibly there were more like 400.

The household was smaller than it had been but it was by far, of course, the largest domestic organization in England. The day had long since passed when great magnates could afford to maintain hordes of domestics and retainers in numbers rivalling the king's. The servants employed at court far outnumbered those employed by even the most grandiose subjects. During the eighteenth century the households of the greatest noblemen seem to have consisted of between thirty and fifty servants—those for example of the dukes of Somerset and Newcastle—though the duke of Chandos employed ninety-three at Canons at one time, including a private orchestra. But few Englishmen could match the domestic splendour of Canons. Most of the nobility and gentry had fewer than thirty servants, and only the wealthiest commanded the services of as many as twenty.[1]

There were well over 1,000 men connected in some way with the royal household. Their contributions to the king's domestic service varied enormously. There were many whose services were essential to the proper working of this vast domestic organization; there were others whose work had once been important but no longer was; and, because the household retained some small connection with departments of the central government, there were still others whose work was of 'national' rather than of 'domestic' importance. The work particularly of the men in the first category and the structure and organization of the four household departments in which they served, forms the subject of the following two chapters.

[1] J. J. Hecht, *The Domestic Servant Class in Eighteenth Century England* (1956), pp. 5–6; C. H. Collins Baker and M. I. Baker, *The Life and Circumstances of James Brydges, first Duke of Chandos* (1949), p. 176.

PART I

2

THE DEPARTMENTS OF THE
HOUSEHOLD

I. THE CHAMBER AND THE BEDCHAMBER

I

The lord chamberlain's department was the largest by far of the four
main court departments. It centred on, but its officers were by no means
exclusively concerned with, the public rooms of the court above stairs.
Its main concern might be described as ceremonial, for under the head
of the department, the lord chamberlain, were the ushers and grooms
of the presence and privy chambers and other officers like the gentlemen
pensioners, the sergeants-at-arms and the yeomen of the guard who
worked in and added ornamentation to the public rooms at court. In
addition, the lord chamberlain's department included the master of the
music and the musicians, the chaplains and the choir of the chapel royal,
and many others who contributed to what might be broadly defined as
the public and ceremonial side of court life. But the chamber was much
more shapeless and much less unified than this might suggest. There
still remained some residual connections between the court above
stairs and the central government, and as a result, the lord chamberlain's
department included a number of men whose work was only partly—
and in some cases, not at all—concerned with service to the king or
the court. It included, for example, a number of tradesmen and craftsmen who worked for and supplied goods to departments of the central
government and the Houses of Parliament as well as court departments;
and it included the messengers who have previously been described as
diplomatic couriers. The chamber included also a number of sub-
departments that can only be regarded as offshoots of the main department, for, while they were part of the court above stairs they were
largely independent of the lord chamberlain's authority. One of these,
the bedchamber under the groom of the stole, had gained sufficient
independence of the lord chamberlain to have become an entirely

separate department, while others—the great wardrobe and the jewel office particularly—remained within the general framework of the chamber but occupied a position on the fringes of the department and, in some respects, on the fringes of the court itself.

The court above stairs was not then a centralized and tightly organized department under its leading officer. There was a central core of servants in the public rooms of the court, but around this core, and acknowledging only in varying degrees the authority of the lord chamberlain, were numerous individuals and sub-departments some of whose work was only partly 'domestic' in character. The work of most of these officers and servants was co-ordinated, rather than controlled, by the lord chamberlain, and his general oversight of the department could be accomplished with the help of a very small administrative staff.

The post of lord chamberlain was perhaps that of greatest honour and dignity at court. Like the three other great court posts, the office was firmly in the hands of the peerage by the eighteenth century, and, indeed, George I's four lords chamberlain were all dukes.[1] This ensured that they had little to do with the day-to-day work of the chamber; the routine tasks of the office were most often performed by the vice-chamberlain, the lord chamberlain's secretary and two clerks. But the post was no sinecure. Few lords chamberlain perhaps were concerned with the detailed work of their office, but all had to spend a good deal of time in attendance at court. Even when the court was in the country during the summer, the lord chamberlain was expected to be in attendance and to do his share of entertaining by keeping an open table.[2] In practice either the lord chamberlain or the vice-chamberlain had to be in residence all year round, for there were many occasions (such as the reception of ambassadors and the great court celebrations like the sovereign's birthday and the anniversaries of the accession and coronation) when orders had to be issued to the numerous servants of the department, orders which, as Vice-Chamberlain Coke[3] was once re-

[1] Dukes of Shrewsbury, 1710–15; Bolton, 1715–17; Newcastle, 1714–24; Grafton, 1724–57.

[2] J. M. Graham, *Annals and Correspondence of the Viscount and the First and Second Earls of Stair*, (1875), I, 399; D. N. Smith (ed.), *The Letters of Thomas Burnet to George Duckett 1712–22* (1944), pp. 139–40.

[3] Thomas Coke (1674–1727), member of Parliament Derbyshire 1698–1710, Grampound 1710–14. Son of a gentleman usher to Queen Catherine (1684). Vice-chamberlain 1706–27.

minded when he was lingering away from court, could not be given by anyone else.[1]

This work, as well as the normal administrative work of the office, fell most heavily on the vice-chamberlain. With the help of the lord chamberlain's secretary,[2] the vice-chamberlain had to deal with a host of problems both important and trivial. The lord chamberlain's office was in charge of the distribution of lodgings. It was on lord chamberlain's warrants—duly endorsed by the Treasury—that the great wardrobe and the jewel office delivered furniture, furnishings and plate for the use of the king and the court.[3] Similarly, the work done at court by the board of works, extensive new building as well as minor alterations, was initiated by a warrant from the lord chamberlain. Doubtless much of this work was mere routine and could be dealt with by a clerk; but there was much that was not routine. At times of great ceremonial it was the lord chamberlain's duty to see that there were sufficient servants in attendance, to see to the entertainment of the guests, the placing of the guard, to make sure that the musicians practised and then appeared on time. When the court was to move to the country, or when George I went to Hanover, the lord chamberlain's office informed the other court departments, specified the number of servants needed, arranged the transport and, through the harbinger, a chamber servant, arranged lodgings en route.[4] Beyond that, the lord chamberlain and the vice-

[1] *H.M.C. Cowper MSS.* III, 181.

[2] Sir John Stanley, Bt. (of Grange Gorman, Dublin), was secretary from at least 1689 (and perhaps earlier) until c. 1719, when he resigned and took a pension of £400 so that Newcastle, the lord chamberlain, could appoint his distant relation James Pelham (G. Webb and B. Dobree (eds.), *The Complete Works of Sir John Vanbrugh*, 1927–8, IV, 124). Stanley was also a commissioner of the customs (1708–44) and his wife (Anne Granville, sister of Lord Lansdowne) was housekeeper of Somerset House, an office created in 1719 (perhaps as part of the arrangement when Stanley resigned as secretary) and worth £200 a year (LC 3/53, pp. 162–4). James Pelham (1683–1761) was member of Parliament for Newark 1722–41, and Hastings 1741–61.

[3] Copies of the lord chamberlain's warrants are in LC 5/156–8 (for 1714–27); since Treasury approval was necessary for the execution of a warrant involving expenditure there are copies of warrants to the jewel office and the great wardrobe among the Treasury papers. They are included in the *Calendars of Treasury Books* (henceforth cited as *C.T.B.*) indexed under Royal Household: Lord Chamberlain. And see *H.M.C. Cowper MSS.* III, 110, 115, 185–6, 187.

[4] LC 5/156–8 and *C.T.B. passim* (Lord Chamberlain's warrants); *H.M.C. Cowper MSS.*, III, pp. 78, 99–100, 107–8, 181, 185, 196. For the musicians see, for example, LC 5/158, p. 250.

chamberlain were frequently called upon to arbitrate disputes among court servants, disputes about perquisites, or duties, or about who had the right to consume what at which table.[1]

In addition, the lord chamberlain claimed a general supervisory power over theatres. This power was, however, only vaguely defined in George I's reign, and it remained so until the Licensing Act of 1737 made clear the extent of his right to control the theatres and to license plays. The difficulty before 1737 was that while 'the Lord Chamberlain and his subordinates, particularly the Master of the Revels, had at least from the time of the Tudors exercised a measure of control over the theatrical companies of London',[2] the situation had been confused and complicated by Charles II's grant of patents to two managers of theatres in 1660. From then until the Act of 1737 successive lords chamberlain and managers had disputed the extent of their conflicting jurisdictions, the lords chamberlain claiming an overriding and prior right from which the managers insisted that their patents freed them. One of the bitterest of these disputes occurred in George I's reign between the duke of Newcastle, lord chamberlain, and Sir Richard Steele, one of the managers of the Drury Lane Theatre. Newcastle was not the first lord chamberlain to dispute the managers' claims to independence, but this quarrel was particularly bitter because Steele was at odds with the ministry of the day on many issues, and he had especially made enemies at court with his bitter attacks on the Peerage Bill of 1719. The result was that early in 1720 the managers' patent was withdrawn and a new one issued which omitted Steele's name. The lord chamberlain's right to control and censor the theatre, though still very vague, was thus vindicated. His powers were immeasurably strengthened in 1737.[3]

One of the lord chamberlain's and vice-chamberlain's duties at court was to keep the king informed of and seek his approval for even trivial departures from routine (especially if extraordinary expenditure was

---

[1] See, for example, *H.M.C. Cowper MSS.* III, 80, 117, 185; *H.M.C. Townshend MSS.* p. 331; LC 5/157, p. 210 ('orders concerning the gentlemen ushers' table', 6 Ap., 1719).

[2] John Loftis, *The Politics of Drama in Augustan England* (1963), p. 20.

[3] Loftis, *op. cit.*, especially chh. II and IV; John Loftis, *Steele at Drury Lane*, pt. III; John Loftis (ed.), *Richard Steele's 'The Theatre', 1720* (1926), introduction; Phyllis Hartnoll, 'The Theatre and the Licensing Act of 1737', in Alex Natan (ed.), *Silver Renaissance* (1961).

required), as the following letter to Coke from the lord chamberlain's secretary, Sir John Stanley, illustrates. The letter is not dated, but it can be placed in September 1717. Stanley is replying to a suggestion that the tennis court at Hampton Court could be converted into a temporary drawing-room to accommodate the crowds of visitors that thronged the court that summer.

I received the favour of yours last night, and have given directions that the card tables at St James's and the four dozen of cane chairs should be sent to Hampton Court as soon as they can be. As to the Tennis Court I dare give no directions, till the King is apprised of the charge; for the putting up sails as you propose will cost at least £200. The boarding it up will cost as much more, and I am sure will not be done in two months; nor will the room be lighted under £10 a night, which I believe the King will think too great a charge, to turn a good tennis court into a bad barn, that will endanger the lives of everybody that sits in it. I therefore desire that you will represent this to his Majesty for his commands; for without it it will not be fit for me to send a letter to my lord chamberlain to sign for what may be thought a great and unnecessary expense.[1]

But though the lord chamberlain's subordinates seem to have been kept busy by such problems, they did not attempt to exercise a constant and minute control over the entire department. The nature of the chamber organization in any case precluded such direction from above. Unlike the household below stairs, in which the sub-offices were firmly controlled by the lord steward and the administrative committee known as the board of green cloth, the chamber was more nearly a confederation of equals. The leading officers of the sub-offices of the chamber were usually peers and this in itself helped to ensure that they remained more independent of the head of the department than were the sub-officers below stairs. But also the historical development of the chamber towards the autonomy of its parts had been confirmed and strengthened by the financial arrangements of the department for there was no central treasurer under the lord chamberlain.

In the first place, the office of the robes, the gentlemen pensioners and the great wardrobe each had a paymaster who was entrusted with the

---

[1] *H.M.C. Cowper MSS.* III, 186. The king decided that the tennis court should be used and it was converted by the board of works. Melbourne (Coke) MSS. packet 70 (Stanley to Coke, 14 September 1717); LC 5/157, pp. 102–3.

bulk of their financial affairs. But more serious than that had been the curtailment of the work of the treasurer of the chamber in the sixteenth century. In the last flowering of 'chamber administration' under the Yorkists and first two Tudors the treasurer had been at the centre of the national financial administration. But as a result of the administrative reforms of Henry VIII's reign which created new agencies of national finance outside the household, the treasurer of the chamber fell from this lofty perch and became once again simply a household officer.[1] At the same time, however, the household too had come under scrutiny, and a series of reforms were carried out in order to give it a coherent and self-sufficient administrative system. One of the main planks of these reforms of 1539–40, Dr Elton has shown, was an attempt to 'break down to some extent the separation of Chamber and Household'[2] by making the board of green cloth the business centre of the whole court. To this end some household payments formerly made by the treasurer of the chamber were transferred to the cofferer's account, to the treasurer, that is, of the lord steward's department. The cofferer thereafter made no further encroachments, but in fact most of the treasurer of the chamber's business had been taken away from him. In the eighteenth century he paid few salaries; indeed, most of the officers of the chamber—including the lord chamberlain himself, the vice-chamberlain and the ushers and grooms of the state apartments— received their basic salaries not from the treasurer of the chamber but from the cofferer. The treasurer's remaining business was only to reimburse the physicians, the watermen, the messengers and a number of other chamber servants who submitted bills for their services.

The treasurer of the chamber's financial responsibilities were not even co-extensive therefore with that part of the chamber that remained immediately under the lord chamberlain's direction, and this splintering in the financial structure had undoubtedly helped to confirm the fragmentary nature of the lord chamberlain's own authority. The treasurership itself nevertheless remained one of the major court posts. It was often held by a peer, and it often served an ambitious man as a stepping-

---

[1] On this matter I have followed G. R. Elton, *The Tudor Revolution in Government*, ch. III, sect. 2 and ch. VI.

[2] *Ibid.* p. 393; and see pp. 388–94, 403–6. 'Household' here refers to the lord steward's department. These reforms are discussed at greater length below.

stone to better things.[1] Though it was not as desirable as many posts of the first rank, it was, at over £2,000 a year, more profitable than many of greater honour. And there was the further attraction that the work of the office was done entirely by the treasurer's two clerks, the more senior of whom was in effect, and sometimes in name, his deputy.[2] James Brydges, who had made a fortune as paymaster of the forces in Anne's reign and did not thereafter have to worry about a post's emoluments, said in 1714 that the treasurership of the chamber was the only office he would consider accepting because it would trouble him so little.[3]

The administrative staff at the centre of the department was very small, for besides the lord chamberlain, the vice-chamberlain and the treasurer of the chamber, there were only a secretary and four clerks on the establishment.[4] To the department whose work these men attempted to direct and co-ordinate we will turn now, dealing first with the servants in the public rooms at court, then the more miscellaneous servants, and, finally, with those 'offshoots' that were still part of the chamber, the jewel office and the great wardrobe.

II

The public rooms at court in the eighteenth century—the guard chamber and the presence and privy chambers—were in the care of separate staffs of servants as they had been when they first emerged from the single chamber in the sixteenth century. By 1714, however, the changes in the functions of these rooms described earlier had altered considerably the work and the status of their servants. The privy chamber, once the sovereign's principal private room, was by the eighteenth century as open to the well-born and fashionably dressed as the presence and guard chambers. All three rooms were open daily to visitors and, except on drawing-room nights when a further room was opened, it was here

---

[1] It was held during George I's reign by the earl of Radnor (1714–20), Henry Pelham (1720–2), who moved on to a seat on the treasury board, and by Charles Stanhope (1722–7) who accepted this post as a comfortable resting place after being forced to resign as secretary to the Treasury after the South Sea scandal.

[2] *C.T.B.* XXI, 222.

[3] H.M. Stowe MSS. 57, vol. II, pp. 37–9.

[4] The Treasury had also forced the chamber to accept a new officer in 1690 whose duty was to help check the expenditure. For this man, the comptroller of the accounts of the treasurer of the chamber, see below, p. 121.

that the gossips and newsmongers and place-hunters gathered. For all practical purposes there were no longer any distinctions among these public rooms, but they still retained separate and distinctive staffs. The withdrawal of the monarch to a private apartment beyond the drawing-room had of course affected their work, especially of those in the privy chamber.

There were fifty-six officers attached to the privy chamber at the beginning of George I's reign, forty-eight gentlemen and four each of gentlemen ushers and grooms. Only the ushers and grooms, however, had any remaining duties. The gentlemen of the privy chamber had been deprived of their original purpose when a separate bedchamber staff had been created in the early seventeenth century. At the same time they had also been deprived of their salary. James I increased their number, from the fourteen of Henry VIII's reign, to twenty-four and gave them quarterly terms of waiting during which they were allowed 'diet' at a court table.[1] Even this was taken away after the Restoration,[2] and by the end of the century their number had doubled again, to forty-eight. In George I's reign nothing was required of these gentlemen of the privy chamber. They played some part in the coronation and in other great ceremonies,[3] but they no longer had any real duties at court though George II seems to have expected one or two of them to appear on drawing-room nights.[4]

Though it was unpaid, the post of gentleman of the privy chamber was nevertheless eagerly sought in the eighteenth century. The honour derived from holding a post in the royal household was not entirely dependent on the size of the emoluments or the significance of the office, and doubtless appointment as one of the gentlemen of the privy chamber was valued by many simply as evidence of royal favour. But the honorific aspects of the post do not fully explain its peculiar attrac-

[1] Nicholas Carlisle, *An Enquiry into the Place and Quality of a Gentleman of the Privy Chamber* (1829), p. 90.

[2] *Ibid.* pp. 196–7.

[3] Six of them attended at coronations and royal funerals, and gentlemen occasionally assisted the master of ceremonies at the public audience of new ambassadors (LC 5/3, pp. 7–10 (extracts from the papers of Sir Clement Cottrell Dormer); Carlisle, *Enquiry*, pp. 321–53). The dukes of Aquitaine and Normandy were represented at coronations by two gentlemen of the privy chamber, for which duty the gentlemen were always knighted (*ibid.* pp. 300–20).

[4] LS 13/116, fo. 77 v.

tion. The gentlemen of the privy chamber derived important and practical benefits from a post that involved them in no troublesome attendance, for they were considered in law as menial servants of the Crown. This meant in the first place that they could not be compelled to serve in the militia or on a jury or in a local public office[1]—a great boon to a man who wished to avoid being chosen as sheriff. Further, and perhaps more significant, no household servant could be arrested for debt or on any civil charge without the leave of the lord chamberlain. This privilege, derived from the royal prerogative, was intended to work for the convenience and dignity of the sovereign—who might find it inconvenient to have his coachmen arrested while performing his duty—and not for the protection of the servant. Privilege against arrest, Coke had said, was only to extend to those household servants who were constantly in attendance.[2]

In the seventeenth and eighteenth centuries menial servants of the Crown were freed from parish and other offices, and their immunity from arrest was tested and verified several times in the courts.[3] By Coke's

[1] An order in Council to this effect was issued at the beginning of each reign (see PC 2/85, pp. 134–5; 6 December 1714) and was duly noted by the household departments; copies of the order of 6 December 1714 are to be found, for example, in the record book of the board of green cloth (LS 13/176, pp. 16–18). That of 1760 is printed by Carlisle, *Inquiry*, pp. 282–3.

[2] 2 Institutes, 631.

[3] For royal servants claiming privilege to free them from parish office see S. Pegge *Curialia* (1791), pt. III, 78; *S.P. Dom.* 35/11, fo. 14. For immunity from arrest see Charles Petersdorff, *A Practical and Elementary Abridgment of the Cases argued and determined in the Courts of King's Bench, Common Pleas and Exchequer...from 1660 to 4 Geo. IV* (15 vols., 1825–30), II, 295–9, where a dozen cases involving royal servants' immunity from arrest are listed. In *The King vs. Moulton* (Easter term, 1665, King's Bench (English Reports, 84: 2 Keble 3) the court delivered the opinion that none of the king's servants in ordinary could be arrested without notice being given to the lord chamberlain. But the lord chamberlain could not 'privilege any person perpetually, but only for a convenient time' and 'after the expiration of a reasonable period his Majesty must either remove the involved party or make him pay his debts'. The lord chamberlain up to the end of the seventeenth century seems to have dealt in person with many of the petitions he received from creditors seeking permission to proceed against royal servants. Between 1626 and 1697 these applications were recorded in 'petition' books (LC 5/183–192) along with the lord chamberlain's decision in each case. Permission was either granted immediately or both parties were called to the lord chamberlain's lodgings where presumably he tried to force a settlement. There are no petition books extant for the period after 1697 and if the

definition, however, the gentlemen of the privy chamber should not have benefited from these privileges for by the end of the seventeenth century they had no duties at court at all. But for some reason—perhaps as compensation for their loss of salary and diet—they had been specifically granted to them. In a warrant appointing a gentleman of the privy chamber in 1662 it is set out that 'His person is not to be arrested or detained without leave first had and obtained, neither is he to bear any public office, nor to be impanneled on any Inquest or Jury, *nor* to be warned to serve at Assizes or Sessions'.[1] In the eighteenth century their warrants of appointment ran only in general terms—the place was held with all the rights and advantages thereunto belonging and previously enjoyed[2]—but the gentlemen of the privy chamber continued to benefit from these legal privileges. Their right to immunity from arrest on a civil charge was not challenged until 1818, when, in the Court of King's Bench, a gentleman of the privy chamber, arrested for debt, was not discharged on his plea of royal service as had been the custom.[3] This judgement was repeated in 1822 when it was decided that Coke's definition must be enforced; that is, that only those servants actively employed at court were entitled to the benefits of exemption from arrest.[4]

In the eighteenth century the gentlemen of the privy chamber enjoyed these privileges without question, and they were of great potential value. The post was not considered a menial one, yet in law it was treated as such; a gentleman could, therefore, hold it with honour—and do nothing—while enjoying as many legal benefits as those in daily attendance. Lord Macclesfield, the lord chancellor,

lord chamberlain continued to deal with these cases, the evidence—the petitions and decisions—has been lost. According to an eighteenth-century law dictionary the lord chamberlain could permit an action against a royal servant (Giles Jacob, *A New Law Dictionary*, 1729, 7th ed. 1756: under 'arrest') but this is not prominent in cases at least later in the century and it seems likely that the lord chamberlain was appealed to less and less, and that royal servants' privileges against arrest became unconditional. There is a seventeenth century treatise on this matter of household servants' rights and privileges (Fabian Philipps, *Regale Necessarium, or the legality, reason and necessity of the rights and privileges...claimed by the King's servants*, 1671).

[1] Samuel Pegge, *Curialia*, pt. 1, pp. 46–7.
[2] *Ibid.* p. 46; Carlisle, *Enquiry*, p. 255.
[3] *Luntley vs. Battine*, Mich. term, 1818, King's Bench, 2B and A, 234.
[4] *Tapley vs. Battine*, Hilary term, 1822, King's Bench, D and R, 79.

doubtless had these advantages in mind when, in thanking a lord chamberlain for appointing Peter Desmaizeaux to the privy chamber in 1722, he said that 'it will give him a little ease with respect to a small pension he has in Ireland'.[1] And such advantages also perhaps explain the presence among the gentlemen of the privy chamber of a number of prominent merchants. Of the ninety-one men who held this post during the reign of George I, at least nine were prominent in the London business community,[2] and another six were sons of such men who had set up as landed gentlemen.[3] There are also soldiers,[4] minor

[1] Add. MSS. 32686, fo. 219. For Desmaizeaux (who was Macclesfield's son's tutor) see below p. 34. His pension, granted in 1710, was worth 3s. 6d. a day (C.T.B. XXIV, 258–9).

[2] Nathaniel Hickman, a member of the Court of Assistants of the Royal African Co., 1710, 1716; Peter Delaport, a thread merchant; a director of the South Sea Co., 1715–21; Robert Chester, goldsmith and West India merchant, director of the South Sea Co., 1715–21; Richard Lewing, a director of the South Sea Co. in 1726; Hon. Horatio Townshend, younger brother of Charles, 2nd Viscount Townshend; director of the South Sea Co., 1715–18, a director of the Bank of England several times between 1722 and 1736, deputy-governor 1723–33, governor 1733–5; member of Parliament for Great Yarmouth, 1714–22; Moses Raper, a director of the Bank several times between 1716 and 1742; Sir Jonathan Andrews, Kt., East India merchant, assistant of the Royal African Co., 1701–10, deputy-governor, 1711, sub-governor, 1712; a director of the East India Co.; Richard Lockwood, member of the Court of Assistants, Royal African Co., 1722; member of Parliament for Hendon, 1713–15, London, 1722–7, Worcester City 1734–41; Sir Jeremy Sambrooke, Bt., a chairman of the East India Co.

[3] Sir Brook Brydges, Bt., of Goodneston, Kent (1679–1728), son of a director of the Bank who purchased Goodneston; like his father (who died 1718) he was an auditor of the imprest; Sir Ceasar Child, 2nd Bt. of Claybury Essex (c. 1678–1725), son of Sir John Child, an East India merchant, who left him a fortune; Sir Ceasar also got a fortune through his wife, the daughter and heir of Sir Stephen Evance, a goldsmith; Sir James Robinson, 3rd Bt. of Cranford, Northampton (c. 1669–1731), 2nd son of Sir John Robinson, master of the clothmakers company 1658 and an alderman, sheriff and lord mayor of London; Sir William Leman, Bt., of Nin Hall, Hertford, son of a fishmonger and alderman succeeded in the title by his cousin, a London apothecary; Sir Anthony Sturt, Kt., of Heckfield, Hants., son of Anthony Sturt a London meal man and commissioner of the excise; Owen Buckingham (d. 1720) son of Sir Owen Buckingham, a manufacturer of sailcloth and alderman of London, 1696–1713, who bought land near Reading in 1700; Owen jnr. was a commissioner of victualling and, like his father, member of Parliament for Reading 1708–13, 1716–20.

[4] Wriotesly Betton (d. 1731), lt.-col. in 1719; Gervase Parker, lt.-col. in 1715, rose to be lt.-gen. and C.-in-C. Ireland, 1748; John Trevanion, a captain of Foot in 1726

literary figures,[1] a physician,[2] and men who held another post at court or in an administrative department,[3] to be found among the gentlemen of the privy chamber. The majority of the holders of this post in the early eighteenth century were men of landed families, among whom were a number of members of parliament and many who were related to parliamentary families.[4] Almost all of them, that is, were part of the political establishment.[5]

Member of Parliament for Tregony 1705–8, Bodwin 1708–10, Cornwall 1713–22; Molton Lambard, lt.-gov. Tilbury, February 1715, knighted in 1727; Henry Hawley, (c. 1685–1759) col. of Dragoons, 1717, rose to be lt.-gen. and C-in-C. Scotland 1745–6; John Ligonier, (1679–1770) lt.-colonel of Horse 1716, col. 1720, brig.-general 1735, general of Horse 1746, field marshal 1757, created an Irish viscount, 1757, and an English earl, 1766; member of Parliament for Bath 1748–63.

[1] Peter Desmaizeaux (?1673–1745) a scholar who published several works on and translations of the classics, as well as collections of the works of Locke (1720) and Toland (1726) and a life of Bayle (1734). John Chamberlayne, the author of *Magnae Britanniae Notitia: or the Present State of Great Britain*, was also a gentleman of the privy chamber during this reign.

[2] Gideon Harvey (1669?–1754) son of a physician of the same name who died c. 1700. He followed his father in the lucrative sinecure of physician to the Tower; Fellow of the College of Physicians, 1703.

[3] Humphrey Brent, commissioner of the customs 1723–30; Stephen Poyntz, the diplomatist; Sir Thomas Read, Bt. (member of Parliament for Cricklade 1715–47), clerk of the green cloth to George II, as Prince of Wales and as king; Sir Edward Lawrence, gentleman usher, ?1703–19; Sir Godfrey Kneller, principal court painter.

[4] Sir Richard Lockwood (p. 33, n. 2); Sir Thomas Read (n. 3, above); Owen Buckingham (p. 33, n. 3); Sir Brian Broughton, Bt., of Broughton, Staffs. Member of Parliament for Newcastle-under-Lyme 1715–24; Richard Swynfen, of Swynfen, Staffs., member of Parliament for Tamworth 1708–10, 1723–6, were all members of Parliament while holding the post of gentleman of the privy chamber. In addition, a number of men were in the House either before or after they held the post. It is interesting to note that Trevanion (p. 33, n. 4), and Townshend (p. 33, n. 2) both ended their parliamentary careers in 1722 and were both appointed gentlemen of the privy chamber in the same year; this would seem to confirm that the post was highly valued for the privileges it conferred. Apart from those included in the notes above, the following men who held the post during the reign of George I have been identified: William Forester of Dothill, Shropshire, member of Parliament for Wenlock 1715–22, 1734–41, 1754–8 (son of William Forrester, a clerk of the board of green cloth c. 1689–1717); Sir Robert Fagg, Bt., of Wiston, Sussex, member of Parliament for Steyning 1734–40; Sir Charles Buck, Bt., of Hamby Grange, Lincs.; Henry Greswold of Malverne Hall, Warwick; Sir George Bridges Skipworth, Bt., of Metheringham, Lincs.; Benjamin Moyer, of Low Leyton, Essex; Sir John Werden, Bt., of Leyland and Cholmeaton, Chester (son of Sir John Werden

The peculiar advantages to be derived from so untroublesome a post also doubtless help to explain why, instead of its declining into insignificance, the place was highly valued and why the number of gentlemen of the privy chamber continued to rise. There were forty-eight by the end of the seventeenth century. Anne too, had had forty-eight, but in George I's reign the number rose again. This was not apparently a conscious decision—the establishment was simply exceeded. There was probably no strong objection since the gentlemen of the privy chamber received neither diet nor salary. At any event, while forty-eight were appointed in 1714, there were sixty on the establishment by 1720 and sixty-five in 1723. These numbers were maintained, and George II began his reign with seventy-two.[1]

The development of the bedchamber staff as personal attendants to the sovereign which had taken away the functions of these gentlemen of the privy chamber, had similarly deprived some of the servants in the presence chamber of their work. The carvers, cupbearers and sewers, of whom there were four each in 1714, had originally assisted the king at dinner but this function had also been taken over by the gentlemen and grooms of the bedchamber. They had not been deprived of their wages, but the sixteenth-century fee of £33. 6s. 8d.[2] had not been increased, and unlike active court servants they were not entitled to either board-wages or 'diet'. They sometimes formed part of the king's retinue on special occasions,[3] and Charles II had expected them 'to be in ready attending in the Presence Chamber...that so strangers

the diplomatist and secretary to James II as duke of York); Sir William Russell, Bt., of Chippenham, Cambs.; Sir Richard Sherrard; Thomas Brocas of Wokefield, Reading; Richard Jackson of Wesenham Hall, Norfolk; Courtney Croker of Lineham, Devon; Sir John Chester, Bt., of Chickeley, Bucks.; Lisle Hackett of Moxhill, Warwick; Sir Thomas Aston, Bt., of Aston, Chester; Sir Edward Coke of Langford, Derby; Sir John Statham, Kt., of Wigwell, Derby, member of Parliament for St Michael 1713–15; Sir Gilbert Pickering, Bt., of Tickmarsh, Northampton and West Leyton, Leicester, member of Parliament for Leicester 1708–10; John Crew (?John Crewe, member of Parliament for Cheshire 1705–10, 1722–7?).

[5] I would like to thank Dr J. H. Plumb, from whom I borrowed this phrase, for giving me much information about the political connections of these gentlemen of the privy chamber.

[1] LC 3/7; LC 3/8; LC 3/13; J. Chamberlayne, *Magnae Britanniae Notitia* (1723), pp. 540–1.   [2] *Household Ordinances*, p. 250. (An account of fees, etc., c. 1578.)

[3] George I was attended by a sewer, a carver and a cupbearer when he was entertained at the Lord Mayor's banquet a month after his arrival (LC 5/156, p. 35).

and men of quality, that shall have occasion to resort to Our Court, may not finde it empty'.[1] But carvers, sewers and cupbearers were only seldom in attendance and these sinecures, like those in the privy chamber, were often held by men with other jobs at court or in the administration. Doubtless they valued them for similar reasons for they would provide similar privileges; and also these places would ensure them a small income, a form of pension, after retirement from the more active place. Caspar Frederick Henning, who had acted as keeper of the privy purse during the last two years of the reign of William III[2] and who was re-appointed (though probably as a cover for a German) under George I, was also a carver; Charles Delafaye, an under-secretary of state was a sewer, as was Grey Longville, the first herald of the revived Order of the Bath (1725). John Evans who was a clerk in the lord chamberlain's office under Anne and George I, was also a cupbearer (1722–34). These chamber posts may also have been valued as a first step to a more active and lucrative office. Robert Tripp, appointed a carver in 1720, became an usher two years later (without relinquishing his former post) and Charles Chester Eyres resigned as a cupbearer in 1713 to become a groom of the removing wardrobe.[3]

The eight sewers of the chamber similarly may not have had any duties in the eighteenth century, but this is not absolutely clear. They had originally served at the lord chamberlain's table when he had dined in the great chamber[4] and they were certainly not doing this in 1714. There are other suggestions that, like the 'gentleman sewers' these places were sinecures: they are not mentioned in Charles II's household ordinances; no provision for travelling wages was made for them and they do not seem to have attended at court in the country;[5] nor, in town, had they the right to dine at a court table. On the other hand,

---

[1] *Household Ordinances*, p. 355.

[2] C.T.B. xv, 86. Henning was born in Holstein and naturalized in England in 1693. (*Publications of the Huguenot Society*, xviii, 1911, 288.)

[3] For MS. and printed lists of court servants in this reign see p. 18. Changes among servants in the chamber are best followed in the 'appointment books', which record copies of the warrants of appointment, among the lord chamberlain's papers (LC 3/63–4, for George I's reign). Where no other reference is given, these have been used whenever appointments or changes in the chamber are discussed in this chapter.　　　　[4] S. Pegge, *Curialia*, pt. III, p. 62.

[5] C.T.B. xxx, 322–3 (list of travelling charges 1716); LC 5/157, pp. 88–90 (servants on duty at Hampton Court in 1717).

they are described in a contemporary list of court posts as messengers who attended in the guard chamber and 'take directions from the gentlemen ushers to fetch necessaries'.[1] And the fact that two of the eight sewers in 1714 were Protestant refugees[2] and that another three were appointed during the reign,[3] suggests that there were some duties to be performed. Sinecures were most often held by more important men than these as an extra source of income, and Protestant refugees if given charity were more likely to be given a small pension on the 'French pension list' for which a sum of £15,000 was set aside.

Of course not all the posts in the presence and privy chambers became sinecures when the sovereign withdrew to more private apartments. The public rooms in the eighteenth century were often crowded with visitors and they had to be cleaned, fires and candles had to be attended and the doors guarded against intruders. This work was performed by the regular staffs of the rooms, which consisted of four gentleman ushers and four grooms in the privy chamber, and four gentleman ushers daily waiters and an assistant usher, eight ushers quarter waiters, four pages of the presence, and a chamber keeper, in the presence chamber. In the guard chamber, the outer room of the state apartments, ten grooms of the great chamber were in attendance. Though there were no longer any important distinctions among these rooms, their staffs of servants remained separate. There was a certain amount of promotion within each—grooms of the privy chamber occasionally became ushers, and, in the presence chamber, quarter waiters rose to be daily waiters[4]—but there was no movement between them. But the ushers of each room were of equivalent 'degree' or rank, as were the grooms of the privy chamber and the quarter waiters,[5] and it is most profitable to consider them all at once simply as the staff of the public rooms.

[1] *The Present State of the British Court* (1720).
[2] Paul Garnier and James Grassineau (naturalized in 1684 and 1706, respectively: *Pub. Huguenot Soc.* XVIII, 165.
[3] Charles Nezeareau, Peter Quantiteau and Crispen Wissell, appointed in 1715, 1716 and 1720 respectively.
[4] Joseph Ashley appointed groom of the privy chamber in 1714 was promoted to gentleman usher in 1719. Henry Gardie was promoted from quarter waiter to daily waiter assistant in 1727 and subsequently to full daily waiter. There are a few other cases but such promotions were not regular; in the chamber, men most often stayed in the post to which they were appointed.
[5] The equivalent 'ranks' of court servants are not always easy to distinguish. The

No regulations governing the work of chamber servants in the eighteenth century have been discovered. Up to the end of the previous century ordinances had been issued regularly, but as far as the chamber is concerned those of James II appear to have been the last. These differ only slightly from Charles II's regulations to which it will be most convenient to refer here since they are in print.[1] Lacking these detailed ordinances it is difficult to discover exactly what the responsibilities of the ushers, grooms and other servants of the public rooms were in the eighteenth century. On the other hand, it is unlikely that by 1714 their duties had changed much from those laid down in the Stuart ordinances; indeed the fact that no further regulations were formulated in the eighteenth century seems to be a clear indication of this. Further, the lord chamberlain in 1722 reminded the ushers that it was their responsibility to see that all servants under them 'constantly wait in their respective places, according to the Ancient Orders of the House'.[2] The most recent statements of 'ancient orders' were those of Charles II and James II and it seems fair to assume that the regulations concerning the chamber outlined in them were still in force in the reign of George I. Occasionally they can be checked by more contemporary evidence, but these Stuart ordinances provide the basic source of information about the work of chamber servants.

There was, of course, very little actual work to be done. The four

'titles' of posts—squire, knight, gentleman, groom, page and so on—were often of medieval origin and no longer always reflected the relative value of posts in the eighteenth century. There is, however, a contemporary ranking of some chamber servants. This is the schedule of 'travelling wages', the extra daily allowance made to those servants who attended at court in the country. These allowances were a relatively modern development and, unlike the regular fee attached to each office, were easily adjusted because they lacked the force of custom. Most important of all for our purposes the amount of this extra salary is a clear guide not only to the value but also to the status or rank of chamber posts. In George I's list of travelling allowances, 2s. 6d. a day is granted to the pages of the presence 'or any office of that degree' (C.T.B. xxx, 322). In 1711 William Lowndes inquired of the comptroller of the treasurer of the chamber's office (William Vanbrugh) what travelling charges were allowed 'to the officers of like rank with the Exons of the Yeoman of the Guard and also what is reasonable to be allowed to the said Exons in that case'. Vanbrugh in reply named the gentlemen ushers of the privy chamber and the gentlemen ushers daily waiters as 'the officers of like rank' (T 1/134/30).

[1] James II's ordinances are at LC 5/196; for Charles II's see *Household Ordinances*, pp. 325 ff.   [2] LC 5/158, pp. 68–9.

Departments of the Household, I

pages of the presence, who waited in pairs,[1] cleaned the rooms and made the fires.[2] These pages were distinctly inferior servants to the ushers and grooms. Their meagre salary of £25 a year was supplemented by fees and by a right to all candle-ends (valued at £20 later in the century),[3] and they were allowed diet when in waiting. But their social inferiority was underlined by the fact that they were not allowed to dine at the main table with the other chamber servants and the equerry and the corporal of the yeomen in waiting, a right which from time to time they tried to establish by physical force.[4]

The only other ordinary work in the public rooms, the lighting and replenishing of candles, and the guarding of doors, was the responsibility of the grooms in the privy chamber and the quarter waiters in the presence, but much of this may have been performed by their personal servants.[5] These men and their superiors, the ushers, were in no sense menial servants, but they came regularly into waiting in rotation and seem to have worked long hours. The ushers and grooms in the privy chamber and the daily waiters and quarter waiters in the presence each worked a monthly shift in turn, their schedule being determined by the lord chamberlain. In addition, the gentleman usher assistant also attended daily (apparently every day of the year)[6] so that there should have been always three officers on duty in the presence and two in the privy chamber. According to Charles II's ordinances, the normal working day for the ushers and grooms was 9.00 in the morning until 9.00 at night with two or three hours off during the afternoon for dinner,[7] but this may have been modified when the 'drawing-room' became an established institution, for this meant that on two or three nights a week visitors were at court until midnight or later.[8]

---

[1] *Household Ordinances*, p. 355.

[2] The king's necessary women cleaned all the rooms of the state apartments except the presence and privy chambers (*C.T.B.* xxx, 321–2). A 'firemaker' in the presence chamber was appointed in 1714, but since in 1723 he had not yet appeared to do his duty we must assume that the pages were still responsible for the fires in the public rooms (LS 13/200, 8 February 1723).

[3] Blenheim MSS. F 1/65.   [4] See, for example, *H.M.C. Townshend MSS.* p. 331.

[5] E.g. *H.M.C. Cowper MSS.* iii, 80.

[6] *Household Ordinances*, p. 355. The assistant usher was in waiting every day of the court's four month stay at Hampton Court in 1717, while two gentlemen ushers divided their work (LC 5/157, pp. 88–90, 98).

[7] *Household Ordinances*, p. 355.   [8] For the 'drawing-room', see chapter i.

The work of the grooms and quarter waiters must have been more demanding in the sixteenth and early seventeenth centuries than in the eighteenth for strict regulations had then been in force about *entrée* to the presence chamber and particularly to the privy chamber. There was less necessity to guard the doors in the eighteenth century when these rooms had become essentially ante-chambers. The grooms and quarter waiters became perhaps more decorative than functional but that is not to say unnecessary. These rooms were after all the most frequented at court, and dukes did not open doors for themselves. It was necessary, too, to keep out anyone who was, in the words of Charles II's regulations, 'not meete or worthy' to be there, which meant in practice anyone not properly dressed. The gentlemen ushers were charged with this duty in the seventeenth century and in the eighteenth they continued to be the guardians of court etiquette and decorum.[1] The ushers in waiting also formed part of the king's procession when he went to chapel on Sundays, and part of his retinue when he went out in state; they accompanied him to Hanover and to Kensington or Hampton Court.[2] In addition the gentlemen ushers also had the minor, though lucrative, administrative function of swearing in all chamber servants below those of the first rank.[3] From time to time they were asked to certify that bills received by the treasurer of the chamber—from the barge-master, for example—were correct; and they had the more regular and troublesome task of presiding at the gentlemen waiters' table to make sure that no food was stolen and that only those entitled to dine there did so.[4]

In 1736 William Wentworth, a gentleman usher to Frederick, Prince of Wales, complained to his uncle, Lord Strafford, that his place 'was the lowest office for a gentleman' in the prince's service and, on another occasion, that he was 'but one remove from a footman and indeed many slights are put on me as Gentleman Usher that would not be as your nephew'.[5] But his main complaint was not that he lost dignity as

---

[1] *Household Ordinances*, p. 355. Prince Eugene, on his arrival in England in 1711 wondered whether he could go to court in his military wig, a long wig being customary. He was assured that 'it was a thing of no consequence, and only observed by gentlemen ushers' (Swift, *Journal to Stella* (ed. H. Williams), 1948, pp. 456–7).

[2] LC 5/156, pp. 35, 67; LC 5/157, pp. 88–90; LC 5/202, p. 295; Stowe MSS. 227, pp. 336–8.   [3] LC 5/63–4 (entry books of warrants of appointment, 1714–27).

[4] LC 5/157, p. 210 ('orders concerning the gentlemen usher's table', April 1719).

[5] Add. MSS. 22229, fos. 144–5, 199.

the nephew of an earl, but that his post was so removed from the inner circle of the prince's court, the private rooms. 'If I stick here', he said, in urging his uncle to get him a better job, 'I shall be but little the better for serving a Prince who has been taught that he is not to speak to so low a servant.'[1] In the previous reign, the earl of Bristol thought that he might encourage his son Henry to work harder at the University if he was told that 'without a good stock of learning', his brother Carr, Lord Hervey,[2] would not 'be able to recommend him to anything in a Court above a gentleman usher's place'.[3]

Posts that required attendance in the public rooms for at least three months a year far removed from the sovereign were not attractive to the ambitious courtier. But the financial benefits, though not enormous if compared to posts in the bedchamber, were reasonably attractive. The ushers in the privy chamber received £200 a year and those in the presence £150 a year, both of which sums were increased by fees.[4] To this must be added the benefit of lodgings, and diet when in waiting. The grooms and quarter waiters earned perhaps £100 with fees and also dined at court. There was one further significant advantage attached to the post of gentleman usher daily waiter. The senior usher always held in addition the post of gentleman usher black rod attending the House of Lords, estimated at the beginning of the reign of George III to be worth £1,800 a year.[5] By 1760 it was noted that the senior usher had not 'of late years taken his turns of attendance' at court,[6] and though in George I's reign he frequently accompanied the king to Hanover,[7] he may not have come regularly into waiting in this period either. The ordinary daily waiters' total emoluments may not have been much greater than £250 a year, but they had at least the prospect of rising by seniority to the first ushership, a very comfortable income and normally, a knighthood. This may have done something to allay any suggestions of social inferiority associated with such service at court, and in the early eighteenth century several of the ushers, and even grooms and

---

[1] Add. MSS. 22229, fos. 144–5.
[2] A gentleman of the bedchamber to the Prince of Wales.
[3] *The Letter Books of John Hervey, first Earl of Bristol* (3 vols., 1894; Suffolk Green Books. no. 1), II, 118–19.
[4] For the wages and fees of chamber servants see chapter 6, appendix.
[5] Blenheim MSS., F 1/65.   [6] *Ibid.*
[7] Sir William Sanderson, black rod, went to Hanover in 1719, 1720, 1723, and 1725. LC 5/202, pp. 291, 301–5, 309–15, 357.

quarter waiters, were drawn from gentry families: for example, Sir William Sanderson and Sir Charles Dalton, who were daily waiters;[1] Sir Edward Lawrence and Brownloe Sherrard, ushers of the privy chamber;[2] Thomas Hutton, Sir Clement Clerk and James Ede, quarter

[1] Sir William Sanderson (d. May 1727) of Combe, Greenwich; son of Ralph Sanderson and, like his father and his three sons after him, a naval officer; gentleman usher assistant 1698–1710, daily waiter 1710–27; he became first gentleman usher and black rod in November, 1718 and in July 1720 he was created a baronet. Sir Charles Dalton (1660–1747) was the sixth and youngest son of Sir William Dalton, Kt., of Hawkswell, Yorks; assistant usher 1710–15, daily waiter 1715–47; gentleman usher black rod May 1727, at which time he was also knighted. His five brothers dying before him, he inherited the family estate at Hawkswell from his niece. The other gentlemen ushers daily waiters in George I's reign were: Jeremy Chaplin 'of St Anne's Westminster, Esq.' (d. March 1716); usher 1694–March 1716. Sir William Oldes Kt. (d. 1718); usher ?1702–18; knighted June 1710. Francis Aston 'of Whitehall Esq.' (d. 1715); held land at Maplethorp, Lincolnshire, though apparently did not reside there: usher 1692–1715; he was elected F.R.S. in 1678. Sir Thomas Brand, Kt., 'of Clarges Street, Middlesex' (1669–1761); held an appointment as daily waiter extraordinary ?1715–16 and a full appointment after 1716; knighted January 1718; he was also embellisher of letters to eastern princes which involved a little work (see for example, *C.T.P.* 1708–14, pp. 174, 210, 601)—a curious post for a man who could not sign his name to his will. Mark Anthony Saurin (d. 1763) assistant usher 1715–18, daily waiter 1718–27, usher to the queen 1727–37; he was born at Nismes, in France, the son of Jean Saurin; naturalized 1707; he was an army officer, entering a regiment of Foot as a lieutenant a month after being naturalized; on half pay 1712–24; entered the Life Guards in Sept. 1724 and rose to be lt.-colonel of the Royal Dragoons in 1746. Henry de Sauniers, assistant usher 1718–May 1727, usher May–June 1727; usher to the queen 1727–37; born at La Rochefoucaud the son of Peter de Sauniers (or Desaunieres), he was the nephew of Rene de Sauniers, Sieur de L'Hermitage (1653–1729) the Dutch Resident in London after 1692; de Sauniers was naturalized in 1706.

[2] Sir Edward Lawrence (d. 1749) usher of the privy chamber ?1698–1719; knighted in 1701 and created a baronet in 1749 a few months before his death. He was the son of the Rev. Paul Lawrence of Tangmere, Sussex, a member of a cadet branch of the Lawrence family of Huntingdon. His father and subsequently Sir Edward inherited the main family estate in Huntingdon and he lived at St Ives. He also held the post of collector of customs at Shoreham. Brownloe Sherrard (d. 1736), usher of the privy chamber 1697–1728, was a younger son of a Lincolnshire family; in 1730, after he had given up the post, he inherited the family estate at Lobthorpe and a baronetcy from his brother. He was a gentleman of the privy chamber in Anne's reign, and again after 1729. The other ushers of the privy chamber under George I were: Henry Sands (or Sandys) (d. 1728), usher ?1702–28, had been a colonel in the army under Anne, but was out of the army by 1714; John Anderson (d. 1728), usher ?1702–28; Joseph Ashley (d. 1712), groom of the privy chamber 1714–19, usher 1719–32.

waiters,[1] and William Whitmore, one of the grooms of the privy chamber.[2]

One other group of chamber servants should be mentioned briefly: the grooms of the great chamber. The ten grooms, who were sometimes called 'lord chamberlain's footmen',[3] were essentially court messengers working both within and without the palace, on duty in monthly shifts in groups of five. They carried messages to individuals, or, if the king wished something to be widely known, to whole groups of people. After the quarrels in the royal family in 1717 and 1737, for example, the king announced that anyone who frequented the prince's court would not be welcome at his; this message was delivered to the houses of all peers, privy councillors and great court officers living in London by the grooms of the great chamber.[4] The grooms also did duty as footmen in the guard chamber and on the great staircase when there was a drawing-room or a ball at court.

Of the gentlemen, ushers, grooms and pages attached to the public rooms—of whom there were roughly 100–120 in George I's reign, depending on the number of gentlemen of the privy chamber on the establishment at any time—only thirty-one had any substantial duties remaining. And of these, only twelve—two ushers and an assistant, a groom of the privy chamber, a quarter waiter, two pages of the presence and five grooms of the great chamber—were normally in waiting at a time. (Of course these men might not always have been physically present for the ushers and grooms of the presence and privy chambers had personal servants who did much of their work.)[5] But three other groups of officers also attended in the public rooms. These were the gentlemen pensioners, the sergeants-at-arms and the yeomen of the guard; their duties must be briefly noticed.

[1] Thomas Hutton (d. 1725) eldest son of Sir Thomas Hutton, Kt., of Nether Poppleton, Yorks. (d. 1704). He was at Gray's Inn; quarter waiter 1707–25 and also under-housekeeper of Somerset House. Sir Clement Clerk, 3rd Bt. (d. 1715), eldest son of Sir Talbot Clerk, 2nd Bt. of Launde Abbey, Leicester (who d. 1708) usher 1711–15. James Ede, of Cudworth, Surrey (d. August 1722); quarter waiter June 1714–August 1722.

[2] William Whitmore (1649–1719) son of William Whitmore of the Haywood, Herefordshire; described in his will as 'of Whitehall'; groom of the privy chamber, 1695–1719.   [3] LC 9/376, pt. III, p. 2.

[4] Melbourne MSS. packet 71; *H.M.C. Cowper MSS.* III, pp. 116–17; LC 5/202, p. 436.

[5] *H.M.C. Cowper MSS.* III, 80.

The establishment of the band of gentlemen pensioners had been first proposed in 1509 but it was not until 1539 that the band had any permanence. It was conceived as a personal mounted bodyguard to the sovereign, composed of three officers—a captain, lieutenant, and standard-bearer—and fifty gentlemen of good family, with a clerk of the cheque, and a harbinger to provide lodgings when the band followed the king.[1] One of the purposes behind the foundation of this royal guard was doubtless to add to the visual splendour of the Tudor court, a purpose clearly acknowledged when, soon after 1539, the pensioners assumed duties in the presence chamber.[2] But there was another, and more practical aim: that of training gentlemen in the military arts and the use of weapons. As late as 1684 the value of the band 'as a Nursery to breed up the Nobility and Gentry in military discipline' was emphasized in royal orders concerning the recruitment of pensioners.[3] But their military character was not very pronounced, at least not in the early eighteenth century; a number of pensioners at the beginning of George I's reign were army officers, but there does not seem to be a very close connection between service in the band and service in the army.[4] In the early eighteenth century the pensioners' attendance was limited to ceremonial duty in the presence chamber on Sundays and such festival days as Christmas, Easter and the sovereign's birthday.

[1] J. B. Curling, *Some Account of the Gentlemen at Arms* (the Band of Gentlemen Pensioners) (1850), p. 6; Samuel Pegge, *Curialia*, pt. II; G. R. Elton, *The Tudor Revolution in Government*, pp. 387–8.

[2] Curling, *Account*, pp. 7–20.   [3] Pegge, *Curialia*, pt. II, pp. 114–18.

[4] William Seymour, 2nd son of Sir Edward Seymour (speaker of the House of Commons and treasurer of the navy under Charles II; a lord of the Treasury 1691–4; comptroller of the household 1702–4), was the lieutenant of the band of pensioners under Anne and George I; a lt.-general in 1707 and colonel of a regiment of Foot; he retired in 1717 and died in 1727. Other army officers serving in the band of pensioners in George I's reign were Jeffrey Saunders, John Mohun, George Bellamy and William Lancaster, and there may have been others.

The duke of Montagu, the captain of the band, proposed, in 1733, a complicated scheme to turn the pensioners into another guards regiment when his ambition for military rank—he had wanted the command of the Blues—had been disappointed. The captaincy of the band was, he thought, 'undoubtedly a military post', and his grandiose schemes, which came to nought, were designed to give him military rank and a position 'which tho' it be nothing in reality might sound honorable'. Letters on this subject from Montagu to Walpole and ?Newcastle are at C(H)MSS. Corresp. 2008, 2011, 2120.

On Sundays, an officer and twenty gentlemen[1] in their crimson uniforms with gold braid and gold lace, and carrying their axes, formed a guard in the presence to meet the sovereign at the drawing-room door and then follow next after him in the procession to chapel; on festival days the whole band attended.[2]

The eight sergeants-at-arms performed similar ceremonial duties in the presence chamber, waiting quarterly in pairs on Sundays and festival days. They were mace-bearers, and, like the pensioners, their main duty seems to have been to form part of the sovereign's escort to chapel, carrying their maces before him.[3]

Both the pensioners and the sergeants-at-arms helped to control the spectators who crowded the court on Sundays but this was incidental to their main purpose. They were for display; and these posts could be purchased only by those whose attendance upon the king in public added to the dignity and splendour of the monarch. By a special order of 1684 the pensioners were to be drawn exclusively from the families of the nobility, 'gentlemen of blood' and men who had distinguished themselves in army service.[4] From the emphasis placed on the quality of the applicant's family and the size of his estate in petitions for appointment as a gentleman pensioner or sergeant-at-arms in the early eighteenth century, it is clear that the social qualification was still paramount.[5]

These men performed essentially a decorative function and came into waiting only on special occasions. The efficient internal court guard—

[1] The band had been reduced from fifty to forty gentlemen in 1670, when, also, their wages were fixed at the level obtaining throughout the eighteenth century: £1,000 a year to the captain, £500 to the lieutenant, £310 to the standard-bearer, £100 each to the forty gentlemen and the clerk of the cheque, and £70 to the harbinger (Curling, *Account*, pp. 126–7; *C.T.B.* xxx, 157).

[2] Saussure, *A Foreign View of England*, pp. 38–41; *Household Ordinances*, p. 357.

[3] Saussure, *A Foreign View of England*, pp. 38–41; *H.M.C. Cowper MSS.* iii, 186.

[4] *Household Ordinances*, p. 357; Pegge, *Curialia*, pt. ii, p. 124.

[5] James Brydges, earl of Carnarvon, wrote to the duke of Shrewsbury, lord chamberlain, in June 1715, to 'request [a favour] in the behalf of the bearer Mr [Joseph] Nicolls. It is to desire Your Grace will give him leave to surrender his post as one of the sergeants at arms to a gentleman (as I am informed of a very good character and Estate)...The Gentleman's name is [Mark] Delves and his Estate is represented to me about £800 per an' (H.M. Stowe MSS. 57, vol. 12, pp. 45–6). A similar request from the duke of Montagu to Walpole on behalf of a man who wished to purchase the place of standard-bearer to the pensioners emphasized that he was a 'gentleman of very good family and estate' (C(H)MSS. corresp. 2396e).

as distinct from the foot guards on duty at the palace gate—was provided by the corps of the yeomen of the guard. This consisted in George I's reign of a hundred yeomen under a captain, a lieutenant, an ensign, and four corporals. Their particular duty centred on the guard or outer chamber, the first of the public rooms, at the head of the stairs, but they also provided an escort whenever the king left the palace. Forty yeomen and a corporal attended daily; and two of their number slept in the guard chamber at night.[1]

III

The servants attached to the public rooms at court account for less than half of the 660 or so officers and servants of the court above stairs. They formed the core of the department under the lord chamberlain but that department also contained numerous other men, and a few women, with diverse and often unrelated functions. Some of these were entirely 'domestic' servants in the sense that their work was entirely household work, devoted in some way to the well-being of the king or his court. They included, for example, the housekeepers and wardrobe-keepers who, with their staffs, were responsible for the cleaning and upkeep of the royal palaces and for their furniture and furnishings.

Most palaces had only a very small permanent staff since the court was constituted only where the sovereign was in residence. No large domestic organization was permanently attached to any one palace; when the king left St James's for Kensington or Hampton Court he took with him the bedchamber staff, the ushers and grooms, and kitchen, stable and other essential servants. Four necessary women, who cleaned the royal apartments and the public rooms, also followed the court.[2] But when the king was not in residence, cleaning and general upkeep was entirely the responsibility of the housekeepers[3] who were

---

[1] R. Hennell, *The History of the King's Body Guard of the Yeomen of the Guard*; S. Pegge, *Curialia*, pt. III; *Household Ordinances*, pp. 353–4.   [2] *C.T.B.* xxx, 318.

[3] Housekeepers were appointed at Kensington, Hampton Court, Windsor, Whitehall, Newmarket and, after 1719, at Somerset House. There had been in Anne's reign a sinecure office of housekeeper of St James's; it was valued by Oxford, who held it from 1703, not so much probably for the emoluments of £92. 3s. 4d. a year but for the land and house adjoining the palace that Anne also gave him with the post. He had a grant for thirty-one years, but George I purchased the office and house from him in 1717 for £7500 (Add. MSS. 17677 KKK 2, fos. 289–90; *H.M.C. Portland MSS.* v, 588; Blenheim MSS. D 2/4.).

given an annual grant (varying between £200 at Newmarket and £320 at Hampton Court) for their own salary and for the wages of their servants.[1] The small permanent staffs—there were only nine at Kensington for example[2]—were thus the housekeeper's own servants and were not officially part of the chamber establishment. There were also under-housekeepers appointed at several palaces,[3] but apart from them the only other official royal servants permanently on duty when the court was not in residence were the keepers of the standing wardrobes.

The wardrobe organization, which provided furniture and furnishings for the state apartments, was complex and fragmentary. Two wardrobe offices remained under the direction of the lord chamberlain: the removing and the standing wardrobes. (The great wardrobe and the office of the robes, which were also part of the general wardrobe organization, were effectively independent of the lord chamberlain, as will be seen.) The removing wardrobe, which was staffed by a yeoman, two grooms and three pages, who had a permanent office in Whitehall, was simply a distributing office. It received furniture from the great wardrobe and arranged for transport to its destination.[4] Once installed, the furniture came under the care of the keepers of the standing wardrobes, who like housekeepers, were appointed at the main royal residences—St James's, Kensington, Hampton Court and Windsor—as well as at Somerset House and Whitehall.[5]

Not all those under the lord chamberlain, as has been said, were permanently at court or came regularly into waiting, for the department included a host of men who were not in a strict sense 'domestic servants'. The lord chamberlain's general authority extended over the

[1] *C.T.B.* xxx, 318.
[2] The housekeeper's personal servant, a necessary woman, a sweeper, two watchmen, a bell-ringer, a man to pump water, a locksmith and a joiner.
[3] At St James's, Hampton Court, Richmond, Newmarket and Somerset House.
[4] The lord chamberlain's warrant to the great wardrobe usually specified that the articles were to be delivered to the 'yeomen of the removing wardrobe'.
[5] There was a move in 1709 to abolish the keeperships of the standing wardrobe at Whitehall, Windsor and St James's and to put the care of the furniture there in the hands of the removing wardrobe (*C.T.B.* xxiii, 348). Nothing came of this, but by an order at the beginning of George I's reign, the post at Whitehall—obviously a sinecure since the royal apartments had been lost in the fire of 1697—was to lapse upon the death of the holder, Daniel Child (*ibid.* xxx, 318).

king's two personal physicians, his two surgeons and two apothecaries as well as those appointed to attend the household servants. He commanded the services, when necessary, of the watermen, the musicians, the chaplains; by his directions the harbingers—a knight, a gentleman and six yeomen harbingers—arranged lodgings when the court travelled.[1] These harbingers also occasionally arranged lodgings in London for visiting diplomats,[2] but normally this was the responsibility of other chamber servants, the master of the ceremonies, the assistant master and the marshall.

These officers of the ceremonies maintained the formal links between the court and foreign diplomats in London. The master conducted ambassadors into the king's presence for their audiences of presentation and departure; he was the channel by which messages to foreign diplomats—and presents from the king on their departure—were delivered; and he and his assistants were the court's experts in the complex problems of diplomatic ceremonial and privilege, and the arbitraters of any disputes.[3] Such expertise was only acquired by long experience and by the study of the precedents upon which the intricacies of the ceremonial were based, and this perhaps explains in part why the office of master was for so long in one family, the Cotterell, later Cotterell-Dormer family.[4]

The fact that three officers concerned with the ceremonies, who were really part of the diplomatic service, were still in theory under the lord chamberlain is one of many instances of the blurred division between the civil service proper and the king's domestic and private service. There are a number of other examples in the lord chamberlain's department. The decypherer, the latin secretary, the embellisher of letters to foreign princes, all on the chamber establishment and all paid by the treasurer of the chamber, were employed exclusively by the secretaries of state.[5] But perhaps the clearest instance in the chamber of the blurring of the line between 'domestic' service and the public

---

[1] LC 5/157, p. 10; LS 13/115, fo. 65; *H.M.C. Cowper MSS.* III, p. 78; Pegge, *Curialia*, pt. II, p. 98.

[2] LC 5/156, p. 52.

[3] LC 5/2–3 (papers of the masters of ceremonies, 1660–1758); *C.T.B.* XXX, 197, 226, 342, 372, 375, 553; *C.T.B.* XXXI, 570, 616; D. B. Horn, *The British Diplomatic Service, 1689–1789*, p. 212.

[4] *D.N.B.* (sub. Cotterell); and see below p. 157.

[5] *C.T.P.* (1714–1719), p. 312; *C.T.B.* XXIV, 438.

service was the case of the forty messengers. These men were under the authority of the lord chamberlain and he was often engaged in an attempt to make them attend their duty. On occasion he suspended a messenger for a short period for dilatoriness following complaints from a secretary of state.[1] He was also vigilant to prevent them hiring deputies to do their work.[2] Their wages and their bills for journeys undertaken, which were based on distances travelled and—since they also arrested and detained suspected persons—the number of days they had kept a prisoner, were paid by the treasurer of the chamber after being checked by two clerks, who were also chamber servants.[3] But again, they worked almost exclusively for the secretaries of state. Their services could be commanded by the lord chamberlain or by the privy council, but their main concern was carrying the diplomatic mail.[4]

There were, in addition, a number of other messengers still on the chamber establishment who worked for the Treasury, the chancellor of the exchequer and the lord chancellor. They were in practice, like the ordinary messengers, part of the staffs of officers of the central government. This was also true of three sergeants-at-arms who were on the lord chamberlain's establishment but who worked for the Treasury, the lord chancellor and the House of Commons.

Similarly there was not yet a clear-cut distinction between public service and private service to the monarch in the work of many of the tradesmen and craftsmen who were on the lord chamberlain's establishment. The king's stationer, for example, supplied books and stationery to the offices of the secretaries of state and other government departments as well as to household offices, and the cost was borne on the treasurer of the chamber's account.[5] The locksmith was also paid by this treasurer for work done in many offices outside the court; and the rat-killer, to name only one more of many such servants, plied his trade in the Houses of Parliament as well as St James's Palace.[6]

The lord chamberlain's department thus embraced numerous men who were not in practice court servants at all, or who were only partly court servants. A similar confusion of functions can be observed in the

---

[1] LC 5/156, p. 305; LC 5/158, pp. 101–2.   [2] *Ibid.*

[3] For the problems that these messenger's bills caused, see below p. 120–1.

[4] D. B. Horn, *The British Diplomatic Service, 1689–1780* (1961), pp. 219–25.

[5] *C.T.B.* xxx, 321.

[6] LC 5/156, p. 151.

two offices referred to earlier as offshoots of the chamber, offices that were part of the court above stairs but were essentially independent of the lord chamberlain—the jewel office and the great wardrobe.

IV

The jewel office was a minor sub-department. It had only a small staff, consisting of the master of the office, a yeoman, a groom and a clerk. The mastership, though perhaps to be counted as a post of the first rank, was the poorest office that could be held by a peer at court; it was not, one man complained later in the century, 'a place of particular dignity, nor of much profit'.[1] The main business of the office was to order articles made in plate from the goldsmith as directed by a warrant from the lord chamberlain and to distribute them to those named in the warrant.[2] Part of this plate went to the household below stairs for the king's own use, but a number of officers were also entitled to receive plate from the jewel office. The secretaries of state, the speaker of the House of Commons, the four great court officers and the treasurer and comptroller of the household all received 1,000 ounces of plate (valued at about £400) when entering office; ambassadors received plate to the value of £2,500 when going abroad, and secretaries to embassies plate worth £112.[3] This was on loan only, but in practice at the termination of the appointment office holders were usually made a present of it, or if not, simply failed to return it.[4]

The jewel office was thus a storage and distributing office whose work was by no means confined to the narrow limits of the household. Nor was the great wardrobe simply a court office, though the bulk of its work was in the provision of furniture for the state apartments, and, in this reign, for the apartments of some of the king's German courtiers.[5] This office also provided the livery of those servants—the yeomen of the guard and the watermen, for example—who wore a distinctive uniform, and a money payment or clothes to a large number of other

[1] *Chatham Correspondence*, I, 188.
[2] Warrants to the jewel office are at LC 5/107–14; since Treasury approval was needed for the execution of these warrants notice of them is also among the Treasury records and is included in *C.T.B.* (see index, under 'Jewel House').
[3] See, for example, *C.T.B.* XXIX, 120, 149, 801; T 1/260 fos. 113–14.
[4] *C.T.B.* XXIX, 26; XXX, 49, 77; XXXII, 19.
[5] *Ibid.* XXIX, pp. 368, 375, 377, 379, 388, 445, 510, 518, 528; and see below p. 127.

court servants.[1] Special hangings, and new clothes worn by livery servants at times of mourning or on festive occasions, were also supplied by the great wardrobe.[2] All this was household business, but this office also provided ambassadors going to take up appointments abroad with footstools, surplices, a Bible and Prayer Books,[3] and also provided the regiments of guards with colours and standards.[4]

The mastership of the great wardrobe was a very valuable post— perhaps the most valuable at court[5]—and it was the only major post in the household in this period that was held for life. It was so held from 1671 to 1749 (except for a few years under James II) by the first and second dukes of Montagu.[6] Besides being financially attractive, it was also a sinecure, for the master had the right to name a deputy for whose salary he received an annual allowance of £200 along with his own salary of £2,000.[7]

The deputy, assisted by a clerk, was the effective head of the office. Both posts in this reign were monopolized by one family: Thomas Dummer was deputy master, and his brother Edmund was the clerk until 1730 when he was succeeded by Thomas's son, Thomas Lee Dummer.[8]

[1] *C.T.B.* xxix, p. cxcii.
[2] *Ibid.* pp. cxcvii–ccix; *C.T.P.* (1708–14), pp. 329, 486.
[3] *C.T.B.* xxix, 150, 801.
[4] LC 5/156, pp. 76–8, 97, 126.   [5] See below p. 191.
[6] Ralph Montagu, later earl and duke of Montagu, bought the office in 1671 and obtained a grant for life; this was suspended by James II, but he obtained it again in 1689 (John Macky, *Memoirs*, 2nd ed., 1733, p. 43). His son held it, also for life, from 1709 to 1749, the reversion to it having been procured for him in 1704 by his mother-in-law, the duchess of Marlborough, as part of her daughter's marriage portion (*H.M.C. Buccleuch and Queensbury MSS.* I, 352; *Memoirs of the Duchess of Marlborough*, 1930, p. 304).
[7] *C.T.B.* xv, 206.
[8] Thomas and Edmund were the sons of Edmund Dummer who was surveyor of the navy and who had a contract to conduct a postal service between England and the West Indies (D. M. Clark, *The Rise of the British Treasury*, 1960, pp. 22 n., 63 n.). Thomas Lee Dummer, clerk of the great wardrobe 1730–65, was member of Parliament for Southampton 1737–41 and Newport 1747–65.

V

The court above stairs was only loosely organized therefore under the lord chamberlain. Around the relatively tight core of posts in the public rooms there were several different levels or layers of chamber servants. Some of these were purely 'domestic' servants and worked regularly at court; others worked at court, but irregularly; still others were not 'domestic' servants at all, but were employed entirely by a department of the central government; and a few worked both at court and in the central government. It should be added perhaps that there were some who did not work at all. Apart from those noted among the posts in the public rooms, there were a number of sinecures in the lord chamberlain's department, two of the most attractive of which were the posts of sergeant porter and groom porter.[1]

Because the department was concerned with the ceremonial aspects of court life—its main function being the provision of a suitable backdrop for the sovereign's public life—it included many posts of what might be called the 'middle-rank'; that is, places that were not enormously profitable nor attractive to the politically ambitious or to a man conscious of holding a high social position, but which were well enough paid and sufficiently honorific to be filled by men on the fringes of the landed class or even well within it. There were numerous middle-ranking places in the 'core' of the department, among the servants attached to the public rooms, as has been seen. But there were many others too. The officers of the ceremonies were naturally men of some social position since they had to deal with foreign diplomats, but so too were holders of other and less obvious places. The mastership of the jewel office was often held by a peer, and it may be looked upon as one of the lesser posts of the first rank. But the places of yeoman and groom

---

[1] The post of sergeant porter at the gate was held between 1705 and 1743 by Philip Cavendish (member of Parliament for Beeralston 1721, St Germans 1722–7, Portsmouth 1734–43), a naval officer who attained flag rank in 1727 and who was a lord of the Admiralty 1742–3. The post of groom porter was an office that combined 'oversight of common Billiards Tables, common Bowling Grounds, Dicing Houses, Gaming Houses and common Tennis Courts and power of Licensing the same within the Citys of London and Westminster or Borough of Southwark' (LC 5/156, p. 49) with the right to judge gaming disputes at court and also with the right to purvey all fireplace equipment in all court apartments (*H.M.C. Cowper MSS.* III, 113–14). For Thomas Archer who held the post in George I's reign see below p. 156.

of that office were not very inferior. The yeoman had a salary of £106 which was more than doubled by fees;[1] and the post was held under Anne and George I by Edward Pauncefort, who was also receiver-general of the Excise.[2] Indeed the rank of yeoman and groom had in general a much superior status in the chamber than in the department below stairs. The post of yeoman of the removing wardrobe, for example, was held in George I's reign by Grey Maynard, son of the third and brother of the fourth Baron Maynard. He held it from 1710 until 1741 when he inherited the title.[3] The post of clerk of the robes was another attractive post of the middle rank; it was held between 1700 and his death in 1722 by William van Huls who had been private secretary to William III (who had given him this post for life)[4] and later in the reign by Charles Brumpstead who was at the same time cashier of the salt duties.[5] The posts of housekeeper and of deputy master and clerk of the great wardrobe, and the sinecures of groom porter and sergeant porter at the gate, may also be included among the good middle-ranking places of the chamber.

It may be suggested, indeed, that as many as a fifth of all chamber posts came into this category; and this does not include those posts—like gentlemen of the privy chamber, sewer, carver and cupbearer—that were valued for reasons other than their monetary value. This proportion of such posts was exceeded among court departments only in the bedchamber, the department under the groom of the stole.

VI

The royal bedchamber was also an offshoot of the larger chamber department. In the early sixteenth century the private servants of the Crown were the officers of the privy chamber, but in the early seventeenth century a separate staff of bedchamber servants was created when the privy chamber became a more public room. At first the bedchamber staff remained part of the chamber, but gradually during the century,

---

[1] See chapter 6, appendix.

[2] Appointed May 1710 (*C.T.B.* XXIV, 304) and re-appointed joint-receiver general with Lord Delawarr, November 1715 (*ibid.* XXIX, 842).

[3] G.E.C. *Complete Peerage.*

[4] *C.T.B.* XIV, 310; XVI, 169; Luttrell, IV, 304; he was member of Parliament for Bramber for just a few months before his death in 1722.

[5] *C.T.B.* XXIV, 244.

and especially after the Restoration, the groom of the stole as first gentleman of the bedchamber, established his position as a department head independent of the lord chamberlain.[1] In 1714 the bedchamber and the rest of the king's private apartments were entirely in his charge. The department included the gentlemen of the bedchamber—generally twelve, though the number varied—each waiting a week in turn; eight grooms, who also attended in turn; six pages of the bedchamber; several necessary women who cleaned the rooms; and two coffer-bearers. In the court of a queen or princess, the gentlemen and grooms were replaced by ladies and women of the bedchamber.

The duties of the gentlemen and grooms could be extremely formal. They dressed the king according to an elaborate ritual, and, when he dined in public, they served him on bended knee. The preciseness and formality of the dressing ceremony may be seen in this description by Lady Masham of the duties of a bedchamber woman: when Queen Anne was dressed

the bedchamber Lady being by, the bedchamber woman gave the shift to the Lady without any ceremony and the lady put it on [the queen]. Sometimes likewise the bedchamber woman gave the fan to the Lady in the same manner and this was all that the bedchamber Lady did about the Queen at her dressing.

When the Queen washed her hands the Page of the Back-stairs brought and set down upon a side table the basin and ewre, then the bedchamber woman set it before the Queen and knelt on the other side of the table over against the Queen the bedchamber Lady only looking on. The bedchamber woman poured the water out of the ewre upon the Queen's hands.

The bedchamber woman pulled on the Queen's gloves when she could not do it herself. The page of the back-stairs was called in to put on the Queen's shoes.[2]

A similar formality attended upon the dressing of a king.[3] But, whereas George II (at least when Prince of Wales) was dressed in form

---

[1] In the reign of Charles I, for example, the lord chamberlain successfully claimed the right to appoint to some bedchamber places on the grounds that they were is his department. (Aylmer, *The King's Servants*, p. 70). According to William III's bed-chamber ordinances of 1689, however, all posts in the private apartments not in the gift of the king were to be disposed of by the groom of the stole (Stowe MSS. 563).

[2] J. W. Croker (ed.), *Suffolk Correspondence*, I, 292–4.

[3] See, for example, William III's bedchamber orders (Stowe MSS. 563) which were still in force in the reign of George II.

by his bedchamber servants,[1] George I was not. In a later chapter dealing with the social life at court and George I's participation in it, the king's domestic arrangements and the importance of his German court in London will be discussed in more detail. Here it may be said briefly that George brought with him to England a number of bedroom pages and his two Turkish *valets de chambre*, Mehemet and Mustapha, who had served him in Hanover for over twenty-five years. The presence of these personal servants naturally curtailed the activities of the English bedchamber staff. But, further, as well as his preference for his accustomed servants, George I had such a strong aversion to formal etiquette that even without his German valets it is doubtful whether he would have submitted to the morning rigours that his son enjoyed. Especially during the first two years of the reign, the king lived as private a life as was possible. The bedchamber places of gentleman and groom were filled of course, and the men doubtless came into waiting—they were certainly doing so in 1717—but their activities were limited to introducing men into the king's presence in his closet and accompanying him when he went out of his apartments. Even when George dined in public, which he did for the first time in 1717, the bedchamber gentlemen did not serve him on bended knee in the traditional attitude required of his attendants by the Prince of Wales.[2]

The office of groom of the stole, the first gentleman of the bedchamber was, at least in name, of older origin than the other bedchamber places. The title was transferred from the privy chamber, for in the sixteenth century one of the gentlemen of the privy chamber had also been known as the groom of the stole.[3] With the creation of a separate bedchamber staff the new groom at its head had much greater influence

---

[1] Charles Cathcart, one of the prince's grooms of the bedchamber, on several occasions in his journal describes his part in the prince's dressing ceremony. (E.g., Cathcart MSS. A/11, 21, 22 November 1714). On one occasion when the gentleman of the bedchamber was absent he had 'l'honneur de donner la chemise au Prince' (*ibid.* 9 July 1715).

[2] See chapter 7.

[3] *Household Ordinances*, p. 156. In William III's establishment of 1689, the groom of the stole is listed with the servants of the privy chamber; also the fact that the groom still received a basic fee of £33. 6s. 8d. at the cofferer's office (plus boardwages) suggests that the office was of older origin than those of ordinary gentlemen of the bedchamber who received a salary of £1,000 a year at the Exchequer.

and prestige than the old had had; in the seventeenth and eighteenth centuries he was usually the closest court officer to the king. William III, unfettered by the provision of the Act of Settlement of 1701 that was later to prohibit a foreigner holding public office in England,[1] appointed his Dutch friend William Bentinck groom of the stole and created him earl of Portland. And in 1689 he also issued detailed ordinances for the organization and conduct of the servants in the bedchamber and private apartments that were in essence a statement of the rights of the groom of the stole to order all things in these apartments independent of the lord chamberlain.[2] This put to rest, if it was still in doubt, any question of the autonomy of the bedchamber department.

The groom enjoyed the right of access to the king at any time; if the king was dressed in form it was the groom's privilege to put on his first shirt. Of all court officers the groom of the stole was the closest to the king and in constant waiting and it was in consequence the post usually held by a great favourite: Portland under William III, the duchess of Marlborough under Anne, Lord Bute under George III. It is not surprising therefore that George I did not at first make an appointment to the office. Apart from the fact that he did not desire the services of an English courtier to help dress him, George could not have known many members of the peerage well, and a title was a necessary qualification for the post. It was rumoured early in the reign that Marlborough had asked for it and had been refused because the king 'is informed that whoever he gives it must from the duty of the place be always near his person, and therefore he is resolved to know the man very well on whom he shall confer it'.[3] It is also likely that Baron Bernstorff and Baron Bothmer, the king's leading Hanoverian advisors in London, urged the king to keep the post open. Bothmer's letters to Hanover during the weeks between the death of Queen Anne and the departure of George I for England were filled with recommendations and suggestions for filling posts at court and in the administration, most of which were acted on.[4] He explained the duties of the gentlemen and grooms of the bedchamber and forwarded the names of many of those

[1] 12 and 13 William III, c. 2.
[2] Stowe MSS. 563.
[3] Sir John Perceval to Bishop Berkeley, November 1714 (Add. MSS. 47027, fos. 355–6).
[4] Stowe MSS. 227. For Bothmer and Bernstorff see chapter 7; and for Bothmer's influence in the filling of court posts in 1714, see chapter 5.

eventually appointed; and it is perhaps significant therefore that he never mentioned the place of groom of the stole or suggested a candidate. It was of course in the German ministers' interest to have this post unfilled, for an able English politician near the king might have quickly deprived them of their monopoly of the royal confidence and checked to some extent their enormous influence in English affairs. If it was their influence that kept it open in 1714, it was perhaps an indication of Bernstorff's failing power and a foretaste of his repudiation by George I in the following summer when, in February 1719, the king made Lord Sunderland his first groom of the stole, a post he held in conjunction with his place at the head of the Treasury.[1]

The appointment was also an indication of Sunderland's personal standing with the king and was to be of the greatest importance to him in the future. For when, in April 1721, he was forced to resign from the Treasury during the outcry over the South Sea Company scandal (in which he was deeply implicated and only aquitted at the House of Commons inquiry by the vigour of Walpole's defence),[2] he retained his post in the royal bedchamber and with it the benefits of access to the king and a place in the Cabinet. This post did not make him an important political figure, of course: he was that already. But undoubtedly as groom of the stole he was able to remain more easily at the centre of affairs. As the earl of Hardwicke was to say later in the century, Sunderland moved 'from one office to another, still retaining the character and influence of prime minister'.[3] That he retained the court post was certain evidence too of the king's continued favour; and while he enjoyed this favour his great rival in the ministry, Robert Walpole, found it expedient to secure Sunderland's acquittal from charges of corruption in the South Sea affair, when it might have seemed to be in Walpole's interest to let him be convicted and punished. Walpole would have benefited in Parliament and in the country by Sunderland's disgrace, but not at court, and as Sir John Vanbrugh predicted, this was sufficient to force Walpole to defend the man with whom he was engaged in a struggle for power behind the scenes. Vanbrugh wrote to Lord Carlisle on 18 February 1721:

[1] See chapter 7.
[2] J. H. Plumb, *Sir Robert Walpole. The Making of a Statesman* (1956), I, 344–7; J. Carswell, *The South Sea Bubble* (1960), pp. 226–44.
[3] Yorke, *Hardwicke*, II, 96.

By all I can learn, I incline to think Lord Sunderland will not be dropt.
I believe he still has the King, which, with the consideration of his great
ability in Parliament, may probably induce Lord Townshend and Mr Walpole
to think it for their own service to draw with him.[1]

The appointment of Sunderland's friend, Lord Carteret, to the post of
secretary of state and the bestowal of a Garter upon Lord Lincoln, the
brother-in-law of another of his staunch supporters, the duke of Newcastle, were clear proof that 'Lord Sunderland stands on firmer ground
than people in general fancied'.[2] He not only weathered the South Sea
crisis, but also maintained and even strengthened the position of his faction
in the ministry during the last year of his life; he died in April 1722.[3]

George I waited a year before appointing his successor. There was a
struggle for the post between the Walpoleans and the Sunderland
faction. Rumours that it would be given either to the duke of Devonshire, a follower of Walpole, or to Sunderland's political heir, Lord
Carteret, were current in London in May, 1722. And some thought
that the Hanoverian ministers would again endeavour to prevent the
post being filled at all.[4] After a year, however, the king gave it to a
court peer of famous name but few attainments, Francis, 2nd Earl
Godolphin, son of the lord treasurer. He was Marlborough's son-in-law,
and was attached to the Sunderland faction, but he had not inherited
his father's talents and was unlikely to use his post near the king against
the interests of any group in the ministry. Chesterfield said of Godolphin
when he became lord privy seal in 1735 that he was 'like an old piece of
family plate never made use of but to fill up a gap in a great entertainment'.[5] He usefully filled a gap in 1723, but in his hands the post of
groom of the stole was simply a place of great honour and profit.[6]

[1] *H.M.C. Carlisle MSS.* p. 30; and see Plumb, *Walpole,* I, 344–6.
[2] *H.M.C. Carlisle MSS.* p. 31 (also printed in Vanbrugh, *Works,* IV, 130, where it is
dated 20 February).
[3] For the struggle between Walpole and Sunderland see in particular Plumb, *Walpole,*
I, chh. 9 and 10, and C. B. Realey, *The Early Opposition to Sir Robert Walpole* (1931),
chh. 1–3.
[4] Newsletter (written by Ambrose Philips for Lord Cowper) 7 May 1722, Panshanger
MSS. Letterbooks, VI, 88; *H.M.C. Portland MSS.* VII, 345.
[5] Lady Finch to the countess of Burlington, 17 May 1735, Chatsworth MSS. 230/3.
[6] Both of George I's grooms of the stole had extra allowances of £4,000 making a
total gross salary of £5,000 which was reduced to about £4,010 when all fees and
taxes were paid; see chapter 6, appendix.

Below the groom of the stole in the bedchamber hierarchy came the gentlemen of the bedchamber, usually eleven or twelve, though Charles II had occasionally increased the number, and James II had as few as eight.[1] Their duties, like those of the Tudor gentlemen of the privy chamber they had replaced, were mainly concerned with personal attendance on the king in his private apartments. Each man waited a week in turn. The precise nature of their work depended of course on the temperament of the sovereign, and as has been said, George I demanded little of his gentlemen. George II both as Prince of Wales and as king required their attendance both at his dressing and at a morning *levée*, and the personal servants of his princess and queen had an extremely full day.[2] George I's reluctance to participate in the ceremonial aspects of court life, public and private, did not mean that these posts became sinecures during his reign, at least in the sense that no attendance at all was expected of them. Especially in the years following 1717, after the split in the Whig party and the quarrel in the royal family, when life at court brightened up considerably, the gentlemen of the bedchamber were the king's constant companions in the public if not always in the private rooms.[3] And at all times they were in attendance to introduce petitioners to the king in his closet. But the reduction of the private aspect of their duties might at least in part explain the increase in their number during the reign. The customary eleven were appointed at first, but by the end of the reign there were seventeen.

The earl of Dorset, who had taken the news of the queen's death to Hanover, and the earl of Berkeley, who commanded the fleet accompanying the king's yacht from Holland, were both made gentlemen of the bedchamber on 18 September, before the king arrived in England, the first at Bothmer's suggestion.[4] Within a month nine others were added,[5] with another—the distinguished soldier, Lord

---

[1] It was expected that there would be eleven named in 1714. Peter Wentworth wrote in October: 'There's but ten lords of the Bedchamber named so there wants one lord and the Groom of the Stole' (Add. MSS. 31144, fo. 528).

[2] See J. J. Cartwright (ed.), *Wentworth Papers*, pp. 468–9, for Peter Wentworth's description of a typical day of one of the queen's equerries at Hampton Court in 1731.

[3] See chapter 7.   [4] *H.M.C. Portland MSS.* v, 495–6; Stowe MSS. 227, fos. 317–19.

[5] The dukes of Kent, Richmond and Grafton, earls of Lincoln, Selkirk, Manchester, Orrery and Stair, and Lord Carteret (LC 3/7, lord chamberlain's establishment book). For details of the careers of peers I have relied mainly on Collins, *Peerage* (1812 ed.), and G.E.C. *Complete Peerage.*

Orkney—named as a supernumerary, that is with the honour of the place but no salary until a vacancy should occur. But their number rose steadily during the reign. On 9 May 1719 four new gentlemen of the bedchamber were appointed[1] and in July 1720, upon the reconstruction of the ministry after the re-entry of Walpole and Townshend, two more.[2] There were seventeen gentlemen—and in 1726 another supernumerary—for the remainder of the reign, a number rarely equalled again during the century.[3]

These posts which brought the holder so much in contact with the king were naturally considered to be very honourable. They were generally the preserve of the nobility. It was not unknown in other reigns for sons of peers bearing only courtesy titles and sitting in the House of Commons to be appointed. When George II succeeded to the throne, his gentlemen of the bedchamber included Lord William Manners, second son of the 2nd duke of Rutland (and member of Parliament for Leicestershire), Lord Herbert, son of the earl of Pembroke, and Lord Paget, son of the earl of Uxbridge. They had all served him in a similar capacity as Prince of Wales—for which post the requirement in 1714 seemed to be that the holders be earls' sons at least[4]—and doubtless George II felt some commitment to them in 1727. George I had no such commitment to an existing bedchamber staff in 1714 and the rule laid down by Baron Bothmer during the great rush for jobs at the beginning of the reign that only peers of the realm could be gentlemen of the bedchamber[5] was adhered to faithfully. Three eldest sons of living peers were appointed but they had been previously called to the House of Lords in their fathers' baronies.[6]

---

[1] Marquess of Lindsey and the earls of Warwick, Bridgewater and Holdernesse.

[2] Duke of Queensbury and Lord Harold.

[3] Eighteen gentlemen and thirteen grooms were appointed in 1760 at the beginning of George III's reign. But this was an unusually large number and quite untypical. See below p. 255.

[4] Cartwright, *Wentworth Papers*, p. 431.   [5] Stowe MSS. 227, fos. 437–40.

[6] Peregrine Bertie (eldest son of the duke of Ancaster) was created Baron Willoughby d'Eresby, March 1715, though he was known as the marquess of Lindsey (his father's second title); gentleman of the bedchamber 1719–27; succeeded as duke of Ancaster 1723. Anthony Grey, known as Lord Harold (eldest son of the duke of Kent) created Baron Lucas, November 1718; gentleman of the bedchamber July 1720–July 1723. Charles Townshend (eldest son of Viscount Townshend) created Baron Lynne, May 1723 and immediately made a gentleman of the bedchamber.

The gentlemen of the bedchamber held places of great honour but the holders were not all simply courtiers, if by that is meant a man whose sphere of action and whose ambitions lay wholly within the framework of the court. Many, probably most, of the peers who held bedchamber posts were men of this type, but not all were. For these honorific posts were often held in conjunction with a place of 'business', and movement in both directions between such court posts and posts in the administration was not uncommon.[1]

The grooms of the bedchamber, of whom eight were appointed in 1714, were also servants to the king's person. In former reigns (there had been none of course in Anne's reign, or rather their place had been taken by women of the bedchamber) they had given rather more constant attendance than the gentlemen of the bedchamber, whose personal service seems to have been limited to the formal dressing ceremony in the morning and at meals only when the king dined in public. The grooms seem to have been more normal servants. In March 1715, while the 'establishment' of the new court was being considered, the board of green cloth asked the lord steward to determine 'whether a diet may be granted to the grooms of His Majesty's Bedchamber they having formerly had half the king's diet in regard to their constant attendance on his royal person as well as in dressing and undressing as at each meal'.[2] Such devoted attendance was not required by George I, and the grooms were given neither dinner nor supper at court until, in common with the gentlemen of the bedchamber, they were given a table when the king went to Hampton Court in 1717.[3] They came into waiting throughout the reign,[4] but more for public show than private use.

Their salary was half that of the gentlemen—£500 a year, paid at the Exchequer. The holders were all gentlemen of good families, a requirement emphasized by Bothmer in his letters to Hanover in August and September 1714. Four sons of peers and two baronets were among the thirteen men who held the appointment during the reign.[5] Besides social

---

[1] See below pp. 250–1.   [2] LS 13/115, fo. 11.   [3] LS 13/115, fo. 62.

[4] See, for example, *H.M.C. Polwarth MSS.* I, 217. Sir Gustavus Hume, a groom of the bedchamber, to Lord Polwarth, 16 April 1717: 'I am now at a place from whence I cannot write to your Lordship very correctly (being in waiting at Court attending the King's coming out to Council)...' and also pp. 320–1, 378–9.

[5] William Ker (groom 1714–27) was the 3rd son of Robert, 3rd earl of Roxburgh and brother of the 5th earl and 1st duke of Roxburgh, secretary of state for Scotland,

respectability, the grooms of the bedchamber appointed in 1714 had one other thing in common: army service. William Breton, Envoy to Prussia as well as a groom of the bedchamber, was also a brigadier and colonel of a regiment of dragoons when he died in February 1715.[1] Henry Cornwall and George Fielding were both serving in the Horse Guards in 1714.[2] Phillip Honeywood, James Dormer, James Tyrrell and William Ker had all seen service in the late war as colonels of regiments, but by 1714 they had either been deprived of them for political reasons or their regiments had been broken.[3] Ker's regiment of dragoons was restored to him early in 1715, and in July of that year, when thirteen regiments of dragoons and eight of foot were raised in the face of the prospective Jacobite rising, Honeywood, Dormer and Tyrrell were each returned to service and given regiments of dragoons.[4]

Six pages of the bedchamber, often called 'pages of the backstairs', were also under the authority of the groom of the stole. Working in pairs, their main task, apart from attending to the fires and candles in the private apartments,[5] was to attend the doors which led from the backstairs to the ante-room and the closet, and to knock—or rather, in Anne's reign at least, to scratch[6]—on the closet door when someone came to wait on the sovereign. Though the salary was a mere £80 they were extremely valuable places—the purchase price in Anne's reign was 1,000 guineas[7]—the increase in the emoluments of the post, which

1716–25; Charles Cornwallis (groom 1714–22) eldest son of Charles, 4th Lord Cornwallis. He succeeded to the title at his fathers' death in January 1722, continued as groom of the bedchamber for a few months and gave it up when he was appointed chief justice in eyre South of Trent in May 1722. He was created Earl Cornwallis in 1753; Robert Herbert, 2nd son of the earl of Pembroke, was groom of the bedchamber May 1723–7; Charles Howard, 3rd son of Henry, 5th earl of Suffolk, groom 1714–27; succeeded as 9th earl in 1731.

Sir Wilfred Lawson, 3rd Bt. of Isell, Cumberland was groom of the bedchamber June 1720–May 1723; Sir Gustavus Hume, 3rd Bt. of Castle Hume, Fermanagh in Ireland, was a groom June 1715–27.

[1] Dalton, *George I's Army*, I, p. 185.   [2] *Ibid.* pp. 96, 101, 102 n. 3.
[3] Honeywood was deprived of his regiment of Foot in 1710 for drinking a toast damning the new ministry and praising the old.
[4] The details of their army careers can be found in Dalton, *George I's Army*; for the regiments raised in 1715 see J. Fortescue, *History of the British Army*, II, 5–6.
[5] Stowe MSS. 563 (Bedchamber Ordinances).
[6] Panshanger MSS. Letterbooks, II, 112.
[7] *Ibid.* p. 90.

must have been substantial, coming largely, it may be surmised from tips.[1] Besides this, some of the pages enjoyed other posts too. Edward Brown for example was under-housekeeper of St James's as well as a page of the bedchamber; and in 1724 he 'surrendered' (that is to say he probably sold) the former place to another page, Lambert de Grave.[2] The pages of the bedchamber did not clean the private apartments; this was done by the king's two necessary women.[3]

Two other servants, the coffer-bearers, were in practice attached to the bedchamber staff, though they worked only when the king travelled. It was then their duty to collect sufficient wagons from the ordnance office at the Tower and to load them with the king's personal baggage and that of all officers above stairs.[4] For this they were paid a flat rate plus travelling charges, sometimes by the treasurer of the chamber and at other times by George I's personal treasurer, or keeper of the privy purse, Mehemet.[5] Whatever the reason, there are numerous bills from the coffer-bearers paid by Mehemet, and it is perhaps worth noting that he was not prepared to be generous to the coffer-bearers with the king's private money. They received ten shillings a day for travelling charges from the treasurer of the chamber, but Mehemet gave them only five, noting on one of their bills as if in justification, 'Le Green-cloth ne donne que 5 shillings par jour quand leur cartaker voyage.'[6]

VII

There was one other office, another 'offshoot' of the chamber—actually an offshoot of an offshoot, for it had originally developed out of the great wardrobe[7]—whose work was so intimately concerned with private service to the monarch that it is best considered with the bedchamber department: the office of the robes. This consisted of a master,

[1] See below p. 198.
[2] LC 3/63. The pages had other occasional duties. On 23 March 1726 the board of green cloth ordered 'that two loaves per week be allowed to the Gentlemen [i.e. pages] of the back stairs to feed the Ducks' (LS 13/116, fo. 3).
[3] *C.T.B.* xxx, 32.
[4] See, for example, LC 5/157, pp. 21, 317; LC 5/158, p. 226.
[5] N.S.A., K.G., Cal. Br. 22, xiii, Anhang 3, vol. xix (4 June 1715; 10 June, 19, 30 July 1717), vol. xxi (November 1719).
[6] *Ibid.* vol. xix (30 July 1717). For Mehemet's work as a private treasurer see chapter 7.
[7] Chambers, *Elizabethan Stage*, i, 52.

a yeoman, three grooms and four other minor servants whose main function was to make or to have made and to store the king's clothes and especially his robes of state. For this purpose the master made contracts with tradesmen and craftsmen—a linen draper, a laceman, tailors and embroiderers and so on—who were also sworn servants of the crown. In William III's bedchamber orders, the master of the robes was given privileged access to the bedchamber, and both the master and the yeomen played a part in the daily dressing ceremony.[1] In the reign of a queen, both posts were held by women. The mastership was a place of honour and like the post of groom of the stole it was usually held by a particular favourite; indeed in Anne's reign the two posts were held together by the duchess of Marlborough and by the duchess of Somerset, who succeeded her. The mastership of the robes was not, however, always held by a peer. George II installed a Hanoverian courtier, Augustus Schutz, in the office when he came to the throne, dismissing Walpole's son-in-law, Lord Malpas.[2] For most of his reign (to 1726) George I's master of the robes was William Cadogan,[3] a protegé of Marlborough who had been given the post soon after the king arrived in England. But Cadogan was also Ambassador to Holland,[4] and apart from that conclusive evidence, there is no indication that he or the yeoman, Charles Hodges, found their court offices time-consuming. George I did not require at his dressing the services of his gentlemen and grooms of the bedchamber, and he undoubtedly also dispensed with those of his officers of the robes. On top of that, the king's clothes were made during this reign by his own German tailor

[1] Stowe MSS. 563.

[2] Augustus Schutz came to England in 1714 as one of the prince's Kammerjunken or gentlemen of the bedchamber (N.S.A., K.G., Hann. 9, Secreta Domus, III, 6). Since he had been born in England while his father was in London as the Hanoverian envoy extraordinary (1693–1710), Schutz was able to hold a post in the English court. He became a groom of the bedchamber to the prince (*S.P. Dom.* 35/70, fo. 5) and in 1727, master of the robes.

[3] William Cadogan (1672–1726) served with distinction under Marlborough in whose support he resigned in 1713. Member of Parliament for Woodstock 1705–16. Colonel of the Coldstream Guards 1714–22; general of all the Foot Regiments 1717–26; colonel of the First Regiment of Foot Guards, 1722–6; master of the robes 1714–26; master general of the ordnance, 1722–6. Created baron (1716) and Earl Cadogan (1718). Envoy to Hanover 1706, to The Hague 1707–10 and October 1714; envoy and ambassador to the United Provinces, 1714–20.

[4] D. B. Horn (ed.), *British Diplomatic Representatives* (Camden Soc., 1932), p. 161.

who accompanied him from Hanover and they were paid for, in part at least, out of the privy purse.[1] The business of the office of the robes was therefore much curtailed during this reign. A few court servants received mourning clothes from this office, but its main concern seems to have been to make and take care of the king's state robes, the Coronation and Garter robes and so forth,[2] and its nine places must have been virtual sinecures under George I.

[1] See below p. 260.
[2] *C.T.B.* xxix, clxii–clxiv (Declared Accounts, 1714–21).

3

THE DEPARTMENTS OF THE HOUSEHOLD

II. THE HOUSEHOLD BELOW STAIRS AND THE STABLES

I

The household below stairs—or, simply, the household—under the lord steward, was a highly organized and unified department both administratively and financially. Its main business was the collection and preparation of food and the distribution of wine, beer, bread, fuel and candles to all those court servants entitled to receive them. It was a vast catering establishment, divided, like the chamber, into a number of sub-offices each with its own separate task and staff of servants. But whereas above stairs the historical development of the chamber had been towards the greater independence of its parts, the offices in the lord steward's department had never been allowed a similar freedom. The offices below stairs had to work together to some extent if the department was to function at all, and from as early as the fifteenth century they had been subordinated to the central controlling committee of the department, the board of green cloth.

This board was made up of the leading officers of the department: the lord steward, the treasurer, the comptroller, the master of the household, the cofferer and four clerks.[1] The board supervised the work of the whole department. They made contracts with the purveyors; they checked the accounts of the receiving offices and the kitchens and, through the cofferer, paid the bills; they were responsible for discipline;

---

[1] There were actually two clerks and two clerks comptrollers, but though the terminology persisted, by George I's reign there was in practice no distinction among them as there had been in the sixteenth century when their duties had been quite separate. Since they all performed the same duties in the eighteenth century—each waiting a month in turn—they will be referred to here simply as the clerks of the board.

only on their authority could the establishment of the department be exceeded in any way. Since these and other matters involved them continuously in petty details, the board of green cloth met regularly twice a week at St James's. Not that these meetings were well attended. The clerks carried the burden of the work. Two or three, and even all four, were usually present at these meetings, and one of them was daily in attendance to check the accounts and to supervise the whole department. During the reign of George I the attendance at board meetings was recorded in the minute book on 364 occasions, and the attendance figures for those meetings are as follows:[1]

Lord steward	present on 54 occasions
Treasurer	present on 7 occasions
Comptroller	present on 32 occasions
Master	present on 26 occasions
Cofferer	present on 22 occasions
1 clerk	present on 4 occasions
2 clerks	present on 102 occasions
3 clerks	present on 165 occasions
4 clerks	present on 93 occasions

The lord steward was one of the great court officers. He ranked in dignity and importance with the lord chamberlain, and like the latter, George I's four lord stewards were all dukes.[2] He usually sat at the board of green cloth only when the purveyors' contracts were settled—to lend weight to the side of the household negotiators and dignity to the final settlement. But the lord steward's record of attendance at the board is not a true measurement of his concern with household affairs. He was often called upon to settle one of the numerous minor problems that the board of green cloth struggled with, and especially problems connected with the establishment of the department: whether the footmen should have a 'diet' allowed them; whether a servant should have

---

[1] Based on the minutes of board meetings (1714–26) in LS 13/115. The board rarely met in full session in August, September or October. In those months a clerk was in waiting but there were few board meetings. See, for example, LS 13/116, fo. 20: 'Mr Wynn being the officer [i.e. clerk] in waiting at Hampton Court for the Month of August 1728, and he for the most time alone there, nothing occurred but the ordinary way of service and therefore no minutes were taken that month.'

[2] Dukes of Devonshire (1714–16), Kent (1716–19), Argyll (1719–25) Dorset (1725–30).

5-2

one or two bottles of wine; whether the widow of a kitchen servant should have a pension. Such questions are to be found on almost every page of the minute books of the green cloth meetings, and many of them were referred to the lord steward.[1] His authority in such matters was absolute. 'My Lord Steward', it was recorded in the minutes in 1727, 'sent orders by Mr Wynn [one of the clerks] that the allowance of Dyett hitherto served to Mrs Purcell shall be continued till further order, notwithstanding My Ld. Chamberlain's Warrant to the Contrary'.[2] Such edicts from the lord steward to the board of green cloth were more usual than occasional and it seems clear that he must have been resident in town during much of the year.

Indeed the lord steward was more often concerned with the details of household administration than the other leading officers immediately below him. The treasurer of the household was a financial officer in name only and the post was a sinecure in the eighteenth century. The Whig earl of Cholmondeley, who held the post from 1708 to 1713 (when he was dismissed for opposing the peace settlement)[3] and again from 1714 to 1725, was not even required to be normally in attendance at court, as the lord steward undoubtedly was. In 1710, when the changes in the ministry were not to his liking, Cholmondeley explained to Matthew Prior his desire to stay in the country and also why his post made this possible:

The uncertainties in the public affairs of the world [he wrote] and the uneasiness that naturally belongs to them does in good earnest still more and more fix my inclinations upon the quiet of my garden and a country life, from which I shall be with great difficulty drawn. However, my most hearty and sincere wishes are that everything may be done for the honour, glory and safety of the Queen; and though I own this is but a very impotent way of serving Her Majesty, yet a Treasurer, as I am, without cash and little or no credit, hath nought else that I know but wishes.[4]

Only on seven occasions during the reign was the presence of the treasurer recorded at meetings of the board of green cloth. The third

---

[1] See, for example, LS 13/115, fo. 11 'queries prepared for the lord steward' about the establishment. Even such a minor matter as the addition of a pension of a shilling a day to the establishment was referred by the clerks of the green cloth to the lord steward, who sought the necessary royal signature (LS 13/115, fo. 55).

[2] LS 13/116, fo. 13.

[3] Swift, *Journal to Stella*, p. 656; Add. MSS. 17677 HHH, fo. 423.

[4] *H.M.C. Bath MSS.* III, 442.

of the senior officers, the comptroller of the household, attended board meetings more often, but still not more than three or four times a year, and like the lord steward himself, usually only when contracts were being negotiated.[1] The post of comptroller was not, however, a sinecure. Though he had long since ceased to perform his original task of checking the accounts of the household, the comptroller seems to have had some duties that kept him at court. The precise nature of these is not clear, but they seem to have included some supervisory duties on great court occasions; and they may have been political in character. At any event they were sufficiently onerous to deter at least one man from accepting the post. At the beginning of the reign of George I, when the new court and ministry were being formed, the comptrollership was offered to James Brydges who had secured a considerable fortune as paymaster of the army in the previous reign and had used it to gain the ear of the most important of the king's Hanoverian advisors.[2] The offer came through de Kreienberg, the Hanoverian Resident in London,[3] probably from Bothmer with whom Brydges was on friendly terms. Brydges decided not to accept the post because it would keep him in town too much. His 'great objection to it', he explained to a friend, was

the attendance that Post, and also the expense it requires...Everyone who has had it yet, as I remember have [sic] not only attended constantly at Court in town but likewise at Windsor, and wherever the Court happens to be, which will by no means agree with my temper; besides the hurry one must always be in upon great days at Court.[4]

And to de Kreienberg, in refusing, he said that he wished to spend the remainder of his life 'a little more to myself than I fear the Comptroller's staff would have permitted me'.[5] The fact that Hugh Boscawen,[6] comptroller of the household, 1714–20, was the only important English courtier to accompany George I to Hanover in 1715[7] seems to be further indication that the comptroller, if no longer a financial officer, had at

[1] See below p. 90.   [2] See below, pp. 145–6.
[3] HM, Stowe MSS. 57, vol. 11, p. 37.
[4] *Ibid.* pp. 34–5.   [5] *Ibid.* p. 37.
[6] Hugh Boscawen (*c.* 1680–1734), 1st Viscount Falmouth (1720); groom of the bedchamber to the duke of Gloucester, 1698–1700, and to the Prince of Denmark, 1702–8; comptroller of the household 1714–20; joint vice-treasurer of Ireland, 1717–34; member of Parliament 1705–20.
[7] Lady Cowper, *Diary*, p. 118.

least some duties at court. And promotion from comptroller to treasurer was quite common: Cholmondeley was comptroller before 1708; and Paul Methuen,[1] who succeeded Boscawen as comptroller in 1720, was promoted to treasurer in 1725. Since the emoluments of both posts were the same (£1,200 a year) the escape from a comparatively busy post to a sinecure must have been the real advantage in such a change.

The absence of the three senior household officers from the meetings of the board of green cloth had been expected even in the sixteenth century, and it had been provided for in the reforms of 1539–40 by the creation of a new post, master of the household.[2] Originally four masters had been appointed; but they were reduced to two in 1554, and by the end of the seventeenth century only one remained. The post had been in part conceived as a link between the chamber and the board of green cloth.[3] But this function was never fully developed, and the masters were soon seen simply as useful officers of the department below stairs, and particularly as replacements for the three senior officers in the work of the department. In James I's ordinances they are instructed to be daily in the 'compting house' (where the green cloth met) 'in the absence of the Great Officers' to review the previous day's accounts.[4] However, by the end of the seventeenth century the master had also ceased to attend the board regularly, and in George I's reign the post was a sinecure, worth about £1,000 a year.[5]

The remaining officers of the board of green cloth carried the burden of the work. The financial business was in the hands of the cofferer— or at least of his deputy and the clerks of the office; and the four clerks of the green cloth were mainly responsible for the supervision of the sixteen offices of the department.

The cofferership had been in the sixteenth century the highest post in

---

[1] Paul Methuen (1672–1757) son of the diplomatist; lord of the Admiralty, 1709–10; lord of the Treasury 1714–17; acting-secretary and then secretary of state 1716–17; comptroller of the household 1720–5; treasurer of the household 1725–9; member of Parliament, 1708–10, 1715–47; and a diplomat.

[2] Elton, *The Tudor Revolution in Government*, pp. 392–3.

[3] *Ibid.* p. 393.   [4] *Household Ordinances*, p. 310.

[5] The mastership of the household was revived as an office of real business after 1782 when the clerkships of the board of green cloth were abolished by Burke's Economical Reform Act, and the master, according to one of the under clerks of the household at the time, 'had the management of the whole Household under the Lord Steward put into his hands' (Bray MSS. Guildford Muniment Room, 85/2/3).

the household obtainable by promotion, the cofferer normally being chosen from the clerks of the green cloth, who in turn rose from the lower offices of the household.[1] Not only therefore as the treasurer of the department below stairs, but also as the most senior of the 'career' servants under the lord steward, the cofferer had had a position of considerable importance in the everyday conduct of household business. After Cromwell's reforms of 1539–40, he was required to attend at the green cloth office every morning to advise the clerks in their check of the previous day's expenditure.[2] And in this same period his financial duties were considerably enlarged; for, as part of an attempt to make the board of green cloth the business centre of the whole court, many of the officers of the chamber whose salaries had previously been paid by the treasurer of the chamber were to be paid in the future by the cofferer.[3] This linking of the two departments was maintained into the eighteenth century. The cofferer continued to be responsible not only for all the charges arising in the household and stables—all the wages and board-wages and the expense of food, wine, fuel and candles and so on for the entire court—but also for many of the salaries of officers above stairs. To this extent what Dr Elton has seen as a deliberate attempt by Cromwell to break down the separation between the two major departments, the chamber and the household below stairs, was successful.[4] But, though the cofferer continued to pay some of the charges of the chamber, the linking of the two departments had become simply a formality by the eighteenth century. And it is clear that it was abandoned in theory, for when a new office was created in the chamber, that of assistant gentleman usher, it was put on the treasurer of the chamber's establishment though the other gentlemen ushers remained on the cofferer's. But also, the board of green cloth—which, as Cromwell saw, was the only household authority capable of imposing its will on both departments[5]—had ceased by the eighteenth century to discuss the affairs of or to interfere in the lord chamberlain's department.[6]

---

[1] A. P. Newton, 'Tudor Reforms in the Royal Household', in *Tudor Studies*, ed. R. W. Seton-Watson (1924), pp. 254–5.

[2] Cromwell's ordinances are in *Household Ordinances*, pp. 228 ff. There is a valuable discussion of their contents and importance in Elton, *The Tudor Revolution in Government*, ch. 6.

[3] *Ibid.* pp. 393, 405.   [4] *Ibid.*   [5] *Ibid.* pp. 379–80.

[6] LC 5/156, p. 162. That it could not have interfered very effectively was proved, if proof were needed, early in the reign of George III when the lord steward of the

The cofferer's account remained the largest of all household paymasters but the degree of co-operation between the two major departments that the reforms of Henry VIII's reign had inspired had become fossilized by 1714. The board of green cloth in the eighteenth century was mainly concerned with the regulation of the department below stairs.

The cofferers themselves were strikingly different in the eighteenth century from those of the sixteenth. Once filled by promotion from below, the post in the eighteenth century was held by men, often peers, who paid little attention to the work of the office.[1] The cofferership had become an 'honourable sinecure',[2] and the work was done by a deputy and one or more clerks.

The deputy cofferership was probably first created in George I's reign. The place was simply that of cofferer's clerk and it was so called until William Pulteney, who was cofferer 1723-5, brought in John Merrill to help him in the office. Merrill had had considerable experience in the army pay office, and Pulteney seems to have had a high regard for his talents in financial matters. It seems likely that Merrill (and William Sloper who succeeded him, probably in 1725, and who also had had a good deal of administrative experience) actually did the cofferer's work.[3] And it was perhaps out of a desire to increase the emoluments of the office for a man like him, and an unwillingness to do this out of his own salary and fees, that Pulteney got his clerk's income increased. In February 1719 the board of green cloth had disallowed an appeal by the cofferer's clerks to be allowed to take fees;[4] in February 1725 Mr Edwards, a clerk in the cofferer's office, was given a flat sum of £200 'in full satisfaction of all fees on the account of money impressed in His Majesty's service from the time of His Majesty's

household, Lord Talbot, began a serious reform of the department. It was later said, in justification of the fact that this reform was not more extensive, that he had no control over and no authority to change those parts of the household establishment that related to chamber and stables salaries (J. Secker to ?, 24 February 1780, Bray MSS. 85/2/3).

[1] It was held in George I's reign by the earl of Godolphin (1704-11, 1714-23), William Pulteney (1723-5) and the earl of Lincoln (1725-8).

[2] Quoted by Wiggin, *A Faction of Cousins*, p. 257.

[3] For Merrill and Sloper, see below p. 154.

[4] LS 13/115, fo. 88; in Anne's reign the clerks had taken a fee of 1 per cent on purveyor's bills, but this right had clearly been withdrawn before 1719 (LS 13/175, p. 107).

accession to the time Mr. Pulteney was made cofferer',[1] that is to say just over £20 a year. At the same time, however, the board authorized John Merrill, 'cofferer's clerk', to take a fee of 1 per cent of all money paid on the cofferer's account, which 1 per cent should have been worth roughly £900 a year, though it was valued at only £500 to £600 by a cofferer in 1754.[2] At any event it was a considerable increase in the emoluments of the office; and at about the same time the increase was matched by the inflation of the title of the office from clerk to deputy cofferer.[3] It is an interesting comment on Pulteney's political influence and on personal influence in general, that this came in a period when an effort was being made to eliminate fees in the household and set salaries 'at a certainty'.[4]

As the cofferer had previously been chosen from among the clerks of the green cloth, so the clerks themselves were most frequently recruited up to the end of the seventeenth century from the clerks of the three principal household offices, the kitchen, the spicery and the avery, the latter being the office concerned with stable supplies. Clerks were also employed in six other offices below stairs: in the acatry (one of the offices of supply below stairs), the poultry office, the bakehouse, wood-yard, the scullery and the pastry office. And they were in that order of importance. In the old promotion system, a vacancy among the clerks of the green cloth was filled by the senior of the three principal clerks (those of the kitchen, spicery and avery), his place being taken by the clerk of the acatry and all the other clerks moving up one place. The vacancy at the other end of the scale, in the clerkship of the pastry office, was filled by a clerk assistant.[5] Promotion to the board of green cloth may not always have worked smoothly, but it was still possible up to the end of the seventeenth century for a man to begin as a lowly clerk assistant and work his way up to a seat on the governing committee of the department. In William III's reign this ceased entirely. In

[1] LS 13/115, fo. 130.

[2] Dickens, *Eighteenth Century Correspondence*, p. 230, quoted by Wiggin, *A Faction of Cousins*, p. 149.

[3] The first mention I have seen of this title in official documents is in the cofferer's declared account for October 1724–June 1725.

[4] See ch. 6.

[5] This system of promotion is outlined in detail (before 1701) in the ordinances contained in the household 'establishment' books; see, for example, William III's 'establishment', *Household Ordinances*, pp. 420–1.

1691 a clerk of the kitchen, Charles Isaac, was appointed a super-numerary clerk of the green cloth[1] and he was a full member of the board by 1694. But he was the last household clerk to be so promoted. Thereafter clerks of the green cloth were brought in from outside the household, and the clerkships of the kitchen, spicery and avery became the highest posts obtainable by promotion in the department below stairs. To some extent the post of clerk of the green cloth required a certain social qualification by the reign of George I. The change is underlined by the case of Henry Lowman. It was rumoured in 1714 that Lowman, who had been a clerk in the household since 1689 and first clerk of the kitchen since 1709, and who, since he had been born in Brandenburg, was thought to be highly favoured, would become a clerk of the green cloth. It was also suggested, however, that there might be 'objections as to his genteelity'. He was not appointed; nor was his petition to the king in 1723 begging to be promoted to the board successful. He died in 1742 still first clerk of the kitchen.[2]

In the reign of George I, eleven men held the post of clerk of the green cloth and they were of distinctly higher social standing than the clerks of the household offices beneath them. Most of them belonged to established landed families. Two were baronets,[3] and six of the others were related to peers either by blood or marriage;[4] indeed William

---

[1] Add. MSS. 40791, fo. 21 (lord steward's book of the earl of Devonshire).

[2] Cartwright, *Wentworth Papers*, p. 422; *S.P. Dom.* 35/45, fo. 158.

[3] Sir John Walter, 3rd Bt. of Sarsden, Oxford. (d. 1722) clerk, 1711–16; member of Parliament for Appleby 1694–5, 1697–1701, Oxford City 1706–22; Sir Robert Corbet, 4th Bt. of Addersley, Shropshire (?1670–1740); clerk 1720–35; commissioner of the customs, 1735–40; member of Parliament for Shropshire 1705–10, 1714–22.

[4] William Feilding, 2nd son of the 3rd earl of Denbigh (d. 1723) clerk 1716–23; member of Parliament for Castle Rising 1705–23. Sir William Forester of Dothill Park, Shropshire (1655–1718) clerk ?1690–1717, member of Parliament for Wenlock 1679–81, 1689–1715: married *c.* 1680, a daughter of the 3rd earl of Salisbury. Charles Godfrey (d. 1715) master of the jewel office, clerk 1704–11, 1714–15; married Arabella Churchill, (sister of John, duke of Marlborough), who had been James II's mistress. Richard Sutton (*c.* 1674–1737) brother of Sir Robert Sutton the diplomatist and cousin of Lord Lexington; clerk 1724–7, entered the army 1690 (major-general 1727); envoy to Prussia 1726–32; member of Parliament for Newark 1708–10, 1712–37. Robert Bristow (1688–1737) of Micheldever, Hants.: son of a merchant who purchased Micheldever; married (1709) daughter of Sir John Ward (a director of the Bank of England and governor, 1701–3); his sisters married the 1st earl of Buckingham and the 1st earl of Effingham. Robert the clerk of the green cloth

Coventry, who was appointed a clerk in 1717, inherited the earldom of Coventry from his cousin, the sixth earl, in October 1719 while he was performing the duties of a clerk of the green cloth in attendance on the king in Hanover. He resigned from the board in the following March, however, when he was appointed lord lieutenant of Worcestershire. Nine of the eleven clerks in George I's reign were also members of Parliament while they were in office.[1]

Of the clerks, only Charles Godfrey and John Charlton had had any previous experience of court administration, both of them having been master of the jewel office before holding the clerkship of the green cloth. Apart from Giles Earle, who had had experience of army administration,[2] and Robert Bristow, who was a merchant and had been previously both a director of the Bank of England and of the East India Company, none of the other clerks entered office in any sense trained for detailed administrative and accounting work, a training which had distinguished the clerks of an earlier period who had worked up through the ranks of the household clerical staff. Such a situation was made possible not by the total withdrawal of the clerks of the green cloth from household work—which would have eliminated the problem— but by two other circumstances. In the first place, the men who did have clerical experience below stairs and who, under the old system, would have eventually risen to the board of green cloth, were retained as clerks to the clerks of the board. They were four in number,[3] and like

---

(1724–37) was also a director of the Bank of England 1713–20, and of the East India Co. (1711–17); member of Parliament for Winchelsea 1708–37. William Coventry (?1688–1751) eldest son of Walter Coventry, a London merchant, and cousin and heir male of Gilbert, 6th earl of Coventry who died childless in October 1719; clerk 1717–20; member of Parliament for Bridport 1708–20.

[1] See p. 74, nn. 3–4. The remaining three clerks were: Robert Wroth (d. 1720) of Burpham, near Guildford, 2nd son of Sir Henry Wroth; clerk 1715–20, member of Parliament for Guildford 1705–8, 1717–20; John Charlton (d. September 1720) master of the jewel office (?1707–10), clerk 1714–March 1720, joint-cashier of the excise, March–September 1720; Giles Earle (c. 1678–1758) clerk 1720–7, member of Parliament for Chippenham 1715–22, Malmesbury 1722–47.

[2] See below p. 155.

[3] In 1714 the under-clerks were; Edward Parsons, clerk of the woodyard, scullery and pastry; John Shaw, clerk of the poultry and bakehouse; John Price, clerk of the acatry; and Luder Spiesmaker, yeoman of the accounting house. This latter office was simply the place where the board of green cloth met. Its yeomen and grooms had always been available to the board as junior clerks.

the clerks by whom they were appointed, they were each on duty for a month and were daily in the green cloth office performing the task for which they had training—keeping accounts. The second and more fundamental circumstance which had allowed the withdrawal of the clerks of the green cloth from the detailed work of household accounting (though as shall be seen they had by no means withdrawn from the task of general and constant supervision of the whole department) was the changing household administrative system.

At the time of Cromwell's reforms in 1539–40 provisions for the household were obtained by the ancient method of purveyance whereby the Crown, by a right deriving from the royal prerogative, sent into the counties 'purveyors' who bought supplies at a discount and commandeered carts to transport them to court. In Elizabeth's reign a system of 'composition' was developed, by which counties 'compounded' with the Crown's agents for a certain quantity of goods at a fixed price. The courts of the first two Stuarts were provisioned by both composition agreements and purveyance.[1] In relation to the uncertainties of supply under these systems the elaborate ordinances of 1539–40, the multitude of checks and counter-checks which they proposed, assume greater meaning. Much of the responsibility for the proper functioning of the household was, by these ordinances, given to the clerks of the green cloth. Among their many other duties, they were expected to be in daily attendance to check the previous day's accounts in each office and to inspect the provisions received from the purveyors.[2] But this system of purveyance was superseded in 1660. Charles II gave up the royal prerogative of purveyance in return for a parliamentary grant for life and an entirely different method of supply was developed. The court now bought from established merchants at a price agreed on in a contract negotiated annually. Since the merchant purveyors were known, there was perhaps less necessity for a daily inspection of the household by a senior officer. In theory at least any irregularities in the supplies could now easily be detected by the clerks of the various offices, reported to the board of green cloth, and the offending merchant could

---

[1] Allegra Woodworth, 'Purveyance for the Royal Household in the Reign of Queen Elizabeth', *Transactions of the American Philosophical Society*, n.s. xxxv (1945), 1–90. G. E. Aylmer, 'The Last Years of Purveyance, 1610–60', *Econ. Hist. Rev.*, 2nd ser. x (1957), 10–40.

[2] Elton, *Tudor Revolution in Government*, pp. 390 ff.

be brought to account. Further, not only the supplies but also the expenses of the household were better regulated after the Restoration. After 1662 lists of fixed charges and allowances, 'establishments', were regularly issued at the beginning of every reign or when, during a reign, major changes were made.[1] Every expense which could be predicted was included: the number of dishes to be served at each table and the amount of ingredients to be used, as well as all salaries and board-wages paid on the cofferer's account. In this way, since the price of supplies contracted for was known, an ordinary, established annual expenditure was settled. The fact that there was now a much greater certainty and regularity in the methods of supply in the department below stairs perhaps encouraged and allowed the withdrawal of the clerks of the green cloth from the detailed work of household administration. But this is not to say that these posts were sinecures in the reign of George I. A new kind of clerk was being recruited, and they left the drudgery of the office to their assistant clerks, but it would be a mistake to assume that they were themselves totally unconcerned with household affairs. Later in the century they seem to have withdrawn a little, but they certainly had not in George I's reign. The clerks of the green cloth were still in this period the real administrators of the department below stairs.

The meetings of the board took place in the green cloth office wherever the king was in residence.[2] They met twice a week, generally on Wednesday and Friday, and the meetings were usually well attended, at least by the clerks. Two distinct kinds of business were transacted, one judicial, the other administrative. Part of their judicial work stemmed from the fact that all cases arising within the royal household and the verge (an area extending twelve miles around the court, but excluding the City of London and other liberties) fell within the jurisdiction of the Palace Court, which had been formed in 1625 by an amalgamation of the courts of the Marshalsea and of the verge.[3] All the

---

[1] The household establishments are among the lord steward's papers, beginning LS 13/30.

[2] The main green cloth office up to 1715 was in Whitehall, but in that year it was removed to St James's Palace (LS 13/115, fos. 12, 23; LS 13/176, p. 23). Offices were also maintained in other palaces when the king was in residence, but since the board met only infrequently during the summer the centre of their work remained at St James's.

[3] W. S. Holdsworth, *A History of English Law* (5th ed., 1931), I, 208–9; Aylmer, *The King's Servants*, p. 45.

officers of the board of green cloth, including the clerks, a number of other great household officers and a number of judges acted as judges in this court.[1] It seems to have been called into session only infrequently, however, and important cases tended to be removed immediately to the Courts of King's Bench or Common Pleas.[2] But the main judicial work of the clerks of the green cloth arose because of a duty closely associated with the jurisdiction of this court: the board also had to deal with cases involving infractions of the peace within the verge. In practice the board was mainly concerned with cases of debt, for no one could execute a writ upon a debtor within the verge without its permission.[3] And though the board seems to have always given permission automatically to all who applied for 'the liberty of the law', the clerks of the green cloth had to devote a good deal of time to these petitions from creditors.[4]

The clerks of the board of green cloth were also invariably sworn as justices of the peace in Middlesex and Westminster,[5] and this reinforced their authority in the immediate neighbourhood of St James's. They were particularly concerned to remove all evidence of vice from within the vicinity of the court. They exercised their right to license public houses, for example,[6] and, in 1716, the board ordered the marshal's men[7]

to apprehend pickpockets and common women who daily walk and pick up men in St James's Park and pick pockets in the same, and shelter in the said Park and disorderly houses within the Verge... [and to bring them] before us, if then sitting, if not before the next Justice of the Peace.[8]

On another occasion, the marshals were told to remove 'divers women with their kine' who had invaded St James's Park to sell milk

---

[1] LS 13/88 (records of the court).   [2] Holdsworth, *History*, I, 209.

[3] For two cases, of 1691 and 1703, in which this right was disputed and upheld, see LS 13/174, fos. 35–6 and LS 13/175, fos. 24–6.

[4] In the early years of the reign some of the judgements on these petitions are recorded in the minute books of the board (LS 13/115), but the bulk are in the 'petitions book' (LS 13/122).   [5] See, for example, LS 13/176, p. 144.

[6] LS 13/259, fo. 47, (a warrant from the lord steward, 23 May 1712, dismissing Francis Ford, a child of the kitchen, for keeping a public house in St James's Park 'without any licence or leave from the board of green cloth').

[7] The knight marshal, and his six men, were officers of the household below stairs who were available to the board of green cloth to carry out its decisions in debt and other cases; they also helped to keep order within the court.

[8] LS 13/176, p. 51.

there, and who had 'offended and disturbed many persons of quality'.[1]
The board of green cloth also had to deal with any threats to the good
order of the court. They several times, for example, ordered the hackney
chairmen, who preferred to jostle for fares at the foot of the great
staircase leading to the state apartments, to wait for business outside
the palace gate.[2]

Their main work, however, continued to be the regulation of the
offices of the department below stairs. In George I's reign, in theory at
least, the board of green cloth devoted one of its two weekly meetings
to petitions from creditors and the other to household business.[3] To
judge from the minute books, however, they were rarely able to arrive
at so orderly a procedure, for the affairs of the household were their
constant preoccupation and the business of the offices below stairs seems
to have obtruded at most meetings. All aspects of the work of the
department fell within their province.

At the beginning of a reign, the board set out the household establishment. The king's orders about his own table and those allowed to
servants in waiting were transmitted to the board by the lord steward,[4]
and the first clerk of the kitchen was then required to work out from
these 'diets' the total amounts of ingredients needed to prepare them
and, from the contracted prices, the established charge of the tables.[5]
The board declared the total expenditure to be allowed for such things
as table linen, bottles and glasses, and fuel and candles.[6] With the
salaries of the servants of the department below stairs and those of the
chamber and stables who were paid by the cofferer, the board was able
at the beginning of the reign to set out the ordinary, predictable expenditure of the cofferer's office which, when approved by the king,
became the household establishment.

Of course the establishment could not be fixed for all time and
throughout the reign the board of green cloth spent a good deal of time
deciding trivial questions that affected it: whether the household confectioner should dine at the ewry office; whether the scourer's assistant
should be given an allowance for his attendance at the gentlemen
waiters' table at St James's; whether the gentlemen of the bedchamber
should be allowed candles for their dining table. Such problems were

[1] LS 13/174, fo. 7.   [2] LS 13/176, p. 12.
[3] LS 13/116, fo. 11.   [4] LS 13/115, fo. 11.
[5] *Ibid.* fo. 15; LS 13/116, fo. 11.   [6] LS 13/115, fo. 16.

their constant preoccupation. They were particularly vigilant to regulate and control the allowances of fuel and candles. James Dickson, for example, 'was ordered to burn 300 billets daily during the five winter months in the Presence and Privy Chambers, and no less and no more, the allowance being so much made'; in October 1715, however, they had to decide to allow him to burn another fifty billets a day 'by reason of the cold weather'.[1] For an extra 'drawing-room' or a ball at court the board worked out the number of extra candles needed;[2] and, conversely, so exacting was their control that when the king went out in the evening to the playhouse or elsewhere, the board withdrew the normal allowance of lights for the drawing-room.[3]

The regulation of the 'livery' of allowances of bread and beer, of candles and fuel made to court servants was another of their constant concerns. At the beginning of his month in waiting the clerk on duty issued to each of the offices concerned—the pantry, cellar, buttery and spicery—a list of the servants entitled to receive the livery that month and the amounts due. This was supposed to be within the limit set in the establishment of the department; but household servants seemed to find it very easy to invent reasons why their allowances should be increased, and their petitions to the board were both frequent and troublesome.[4]

The control of the expenditure of the offices below stairs was a particularly difficult problem. In theory any expenditure not included

[1] LS 13/116, fo. 13; LS 13/115, fo. 29.
[2] Ibid. fos. 79, 80.   [3] Ibid. fo. 100.
[4] No court servant, it might be said, was as frequent—or successful—a petitioner with regard to these allowances as the two ladies who came to England with George I, Madame Schulenberg and Madame Kielmannsegge. Both ladies were given generous allowances of food, beer, wine, candles and fuel at their arrival, but with every year their appetites grew. Kielmannsegge, for example, had two gallons of beer a day for herself and servants in 1714. In June 1715 she requested and was given four and a half gallons; by April 1717 she had twelve barrels a month, increased on 17 April to fourteen, and on 6 June to sixteen. Her allowance of sherry, claret, bread, and candles grew correspondingly. Schulenberg did not lag behind (LS 13/115, fos. 20, 54, 58, 59). In 1718, as part of the retrenchments of that year (for which see below pp. 127–8), it was thought less expensive to give each of the ladies £3,000 a year and a kitchen in lieu of food and all allowances (LS 13/115, fos. 76, 81). Madame Schulenberg (by then, duchess of Munster) was, however, allowed candles and fuel on top of this because the king habitually took his supper in her apartment. For these ladies see chapter 7.

in the establishment had to be authorized by the clerk of the green cloth in waiting before it could be allowed in the accounts. At the end of every month the offices of the department had to account to the board for their expenditure under the two heads of established charges and extraordinary charges; and the latter had to be submitted in a separate 'creditor' along with the vouchers showing the authorization.[1] But extraordinary and incidental expenditure was, in this as in all departments, very difficult to control in practice. The opportunities for peculation in the household below stairs were still vast. The system of purveyance itself provided unlimited opportunities; as will be seen presently, many of the purveyors to the household were servants in the department, and not a few were in such a position that no one could check what they said they delivered into their own office.

The clerks of the board of green cloth were faced with an immense task in trying to restrain household expenditure and regulate the work of the offices of the department. It is obvious from their minute books that they were taking their duty seriously and were trying to govern the department; orders and decisions streamed from the green cloth office after their meetings. One case in particular seems to illustrate clearly their devotion to the king's interests. This was their decision on a petition from the man who attended the green cloth table at St James's. This table was maintained by the clerk in waiting, at the king's expense, when the court was in the country, especially for the entertainment of distinguished guests who had not received an invitation to dine with the king or at another court table. In the winter of 1717–18 a green cloth table was, most unusually, kept at St James's; indeed, it was so unusual that no provision had ever apparently been made for a table attendant in town. The man naturally petitioned for an allowance, but the board refused him on the grounds that there was 'no president of that kind'.[2] They assured him that he might always count on their friendship, but the officers of the green cloth were reluctant to create a precedent even for a pittance and in a case which so nearly concerned them—an attitude that suggests a good deal both about the rigidity of the system and the zeal with which the board of green cloth tried to maintain it.

[1] LS 13/115, fo. 12; LS 13/177, fo. 42; for the board dealing with extraordinary diets see LS 13/115, fos. 46, 47, 54, 62, 64, 75, 79.
[2] LS 13/115, fo. 22.

Apart from the control of expenditure, every aspect of the work of the department below stairs came within the province of the board. When the court moved to the country, the board, having received notification of the move from the lord chamberlain, made the arrangements. They designated the household servants who were to travel, ordered necessary supplies and arranged for carts and wagons to transport them, and they dealt with all the new problems about the daily allowances of fuel and candles and so on that a move to a new palace created, problems that were especially troublesome at a palace like Hampton Court where there was a good deal more entertainment—more drawing-rooms, more balls and plays—than in town. Every such entertainment meant more work for the clerks of the green cloth.[1]

It was also the duty of the board to see that only sworn servants worked in the department and to prevent—or at least to control—the use of deputies. In 1730 they discharged all the apprentices in the kitchen because 'they had not been allowed to work by the Board'; and they ordered that for the future only six apprentices were to be admitted to office, and only when they had the approval of the clerks of the green cloth.[2] The board regularly dealt with petitions from servants who wanted to bring in a deputy from outside the household. This was a favour granted only with reluctance, for they were 'of opinion that none ought to wait for another but a sworn servant';[3] but it sometimes could not be avoided in the case of old and infirm servants who had not been able to get a pension to enable them to retire from office.[4] The board also frequently dealt with petitions from men who wanted to go into the country, for only with their permission could a household servant leave London, whether he was in waiting or not.[5]

All the servants of the department below stairs were subject to the discipline of the green cloth officers. Not infrequently they suspended men for 'misbehaviour' and neglect of their work; and the more senior servants were not exempt. In January 1716 Henry Lowman, the first clerk of the kitchen, was suspended from his office 'for behaving him-

[1] LS 13/115, fos. 54, 61-2; LS 13/176, pp. 43, 46, 102, 164.
[2] LS 13/116, fo. 31.
[3] *Ibid.* fo. 21.
[4] LS 13/115, fo. 71; LS 13/116, fos. 21, 29, 38; for pensions, see below, p. 199.
[5] LS 13/115, fos. 12, 23, 74, 119.

self disrespectfully to the Board', and he was only restored to it when, a week later, he 'made his submission' to their authority.[1] On another occasion one of Lowman's clerks refused to obey a green cloth order, and 'thinking himself only accountable to his master [Lowman] denied the authority of the Board'. After his salary was 'suspended until further order', he too soon apologized and was re-admitted to office.[2] At least four other servants during the reign were suspended or dismissed by the board of green cloth for similar offences or for not performing their duties.[3] Similarly they occasionally called merchants and purveyors to account for delivering inferior goods to the offices below stairs. In 1715, after the board received complaints about the 'extreme badness of the beer', the brewer was made to promise that the quality would be improved in the future.[4]

II

The sixteen sub-offices over which the green cloth presided each had clearly defined tasks and a separate staff of servants. There were two levels of posts within the department, clerical and non-clerical. As has been seen, clerks were employed in the kitchen and the spicery (and these men, along with the clerk of the avery in the stables, were considered to be 'senior' clerks) and in the acatry, the poultry, the bakehouse, the woodyard, the scullery and pastry offices. The clerks had their own system of seniority and promotion. On the non-clerical side, the highest ranks were sergeant, gentleman and in the kitchen, master cook—all of these equal in status; then came yeoman, groom and child (this was a rank, not an age group), page, scourer and turnbroach. Not all these ranks were represented in all the sub-offices of the department, but yeomen and grooms were common to most, and if they did not have a clerk at their head, the larger of them especially would by led by a sergeant or a gentleman.

The organization of the department into sub-offices had been established as early as the fifteenth century and, however necessary all of the offices had been earlier, by the eighteenth century a number of

[1] LS 13/176, p. 48.
[2] LS 13/116, fo. 23.
[3] LS 13/115, fos. 29, 48, 73; LS 13/200 (8 February 1722/3).
[4] LS 13/115, fo. 24.

developments had brought a considerable reduction of the work of some of them. There had been a substantial decrease in the number of servants in the seventeenth century—from about 300 in Charles I's reign[1] to about 160 in George I's—and two entire offices, the chandlery and the wafery, had been abolished. But these reductions had not perhaps been extensive enough in view of the fact that the work of the department as a whole, and of some offices in particular, had been greatly affected by the new system of purveyance introduced after 1660. To explain this it is necessary briefly to review the work of the household sub-offices.

The largest by far was the kitchen, or rather kitchens: for normally there was a clear division between the privy kitchen, which served the king, and the household kitchen, which prepared the food for all court tables other than the king's. This division, which had operated in Anne's reign, was not at first maintained when George I came to the throne. In his first household establishment all the kitchen servants are listed together, and they are all described as belonging to the privy kitchen.[2] But in fact the preparation of the king's dinner was immediately taken over by the kitchen staff that he brought from Hanover; and it was large enough for the job, for it consisted of a kitchen master, two clerks, three master cooks and an under-cook, a tasting master, a warder of the kitchen tackling, six kitchen boys, and a kitchen girl, three roasting boys, a confectioner, a master of the cellar, three silver servants, a servant of the fire, two watchmen and other servants—a total of thirty-one in all.[3] One of the consequences of the king's bringing his own kitchen staff to England was the dismissal in July 1715 of the man who had served Anne as first master cook, John Faverall.[4] The place was thereafter kept vacant, probably to prevent bad feeling about the Hanoverian cooks preparing the king's dinner, for the first master cook had customarily received a daily fee above his salary for doing so,[5] and a first master cook in office might have been unwilling to stand by with

[1] Aylmer, *King's Servants*, p. 27.

[2] LS 13/44.

[3] N.S.A., K.G., Hannover 9, Secreta Domus III, 6.

[4] The English master cooks apparently served the king's dinner until 1 February 1715 but not thereafter (LS 13/115, fo. 3). The post of first master cook was 'determined' on 26 July 1715. LS 13/260 (royal warrant of 26 July 1715; LS 13/44).

[5] LS 13/115, fo. 9.

good grace and lose his perquisites. The distinction between privy and household kitchens in the English establishment was revived in 1717, however, when the court moved to Kensington and Hampton Court.[1] It is likely that the king had left most of his own kitchen servants in Hanover in 1716—he certainly left many of his bedchamber servants there after his first return—and that by 1717 as a consequence the privy kitchen was at least partly staffed by English servants; hence the revival of the names privy and household kitchens. On the other hand, the Hanoverian cooks themselves were retained and indeed they were increased to six in 1719.[2] The king's privy kitchen also prepared Madame Schulenberg's and Madame Kielmannsegge's dinner and supper until, in 1718, they were each given £3,000 a year with which to maintain their own private kitchens. The Hanoverian ministers, including Bernstorff and Bothmer, had had their own kitchens from the start.[3]

The household kitchen, or 'the English kitchen' as it was sometimes called in this reign, prepared the food for about thirty servants who were entitled to dine at court. Most servants by 1714 were given an allowance of money—boardwages—instead of food,[4] but some, and especially those in constant attendance in the state apartments, were still provided with a table. The number varied from reign to reign, and during a reign it was different at Hampton Court than at St James's, but normally in town there was a 'gentleman waiter's' table for the

[1] There are references to the 'privy' and 'household' kitchens in the green cloth minutes in May 1717, and later in the summer (LS 13/115, fos. 59, 63).

[2] *Ibid.* fo. 101. On 24 March 1719 'Mr Lowman [clerk of the kitchen] Master Cooks, Hanover Cooks attended [the board of green cloth meeting] in relation to the kitchen goods and the kitchens being dirty. The Hanover Cooks complained that the saucepans made use of for the King's diet was [sic] used by other cooks. It was ordered that a set of goods be appropriated for His Majesty's diet only' (LS 13/115, fo. 89).

[3] For the German ministers, see chapter 7. In 1719 Bernstorff asked the board of green cloth to allow his cook to work in the king's kitchen 'to learn of one of the Hanover cooks' (LS 13/115, fo. 88).

[4] See below pp. 181–3. At the Restoration numerous great officers and servants dined at court, including the groom of the stole and lord chamberlain and all the officers of the board of green cloth (LS 13/31). This was clearly very expensive and in the retrenchment of 1663 all but a few court tables were suspended (Baxter, *The Development of the Treasury*, pp. 69–70), and by 1668 only four court tables were maintained for servants. The great bulk of court servants were on boardwages (LS 13/35).

ushers and grooms of the state apartments, the equerry in waiting, the pages of honour and the corporal of the yeomen of the guard;[1] this was the table of the *élite*. In addition, separate tables were provided for the pages of the back stairs, the chaplains, the yeomen of the guard, the clerk of the kitchen and the cooks.[2] Queen Anne had also provided her ladies in waiting with a table at St James's, but George I, having dispensed with the services of his gentlemen and grooms of the bedchamber, did not at first feel himself obliged to pay for their dinner. They were never given a table when the court was in London, but while George I was at Hampton Court, in 1717 and 1718, and at Windsor in 1724—opportunities for dining outside the court being limited—many more royal servants, including the gentlemen and grooms of the bedchamber, dined at the royal expense.[3]

The household kitchen thus prepared food for six or more tables every day. It had a much larger staff than the other sub-offices below stairs: in George I's reign it employed two clerks, two master cooks, six yeomen, five grooms, six children, two scourers, eight turnbroaches and two doorkeepers. The yeomen, grooms and children were concerned, along with the master cooks, with the actual preparation of food, for they were responsible for soups, boiled meats and roasted meats respectively.[4] And they were of higher status than the scourers, turnbroaches and doorkeepers who did the menial work, for they were serving an apprenticeship, and were on a ladder of promotion that led up from child to master cook.[5]

Over the whole office the two clerks of the kitchen, who waited monthly in turns, had entire authority. The clerks of George I's reign, Henry Lowman and James Eckersall, had the assistance of two under-clerks, one of whom in practice took Lowman's place after 1722 when

---

[1] LC 5/156, p. 68 (lord chamberlain's warrant listing those entitled to dine at the waiter's table 13 January 1715). And see chapter 6.

[2] LS 9/115–22 (Books of Fare, 1714–27).

[3] LS 9/117, fos. 118, 121. When the king went to Hanover no officers or servants dined at court except the chaplains—for services in the chapel royal continued—and the yeomen of the guard who continued to attend in the guard chamber. On Sundays when the court rooms were open to the public, the gentlemen ushers and servants on duty were also given a table. All these tables were provided by an officer of the kitchen under a contract for so much each (LS 13/115, p. 48).

[4] *The Present State of the British Court* (1720), pp. 6–8.

[5] For household promotion see below pp. 169–171.

he retired from the business though not the title of clerk.[1] The clerks
and their assistants kept the kitchen accounts; and, in addition, they
were also responsible, as will be seen, for the accounts of the pantry, the
buttery and the cellar. Their main responsibility was to make up daily
a bill of fare, within the established limit, for the next day's service for
all the tables and to take it to the clerk of the green cloth in waiting for
his approval.[2] The clerk of the kitchen also calculated the amounts of
food and ingredients needed to prepare these 'menus' and entered this
into the 'diets' book which was the main record of the expenditure of
the office.[3] He then ordered the necessary provisions from the purveyors or from the offices of supply below stairs. The clerks of the
kitchen also kept the records of servants in receipt of boardwages,[4] and
they issued the debenture by virtue of which the boardwages were paid
at the cofferer's office. They received a fee for each debenture issued,
and this was just one of the numerous legal perquisites that helped to
make theirs a valuable office worth, at least £250 a year plus lodging
and a 'diet'.[5] And its attraction was enhanced considerably by the
opportunities it provided for an activity that most servants below stairs
seem to have indulged in freely—theft. Obviously the clerks who were
responsible for the ordering and distribution of all the food received
into the kitchen were in a good position to ensure that the table they
were allowed was provided with the very best the king could offer.
And if they did not sell the food and wine they helped themselves to,
and charged to the Crown, they certainly lived very well. Their friends
did too. Eckersall's 'snug house at St James's', Swift said, was one of
the favourite dining places of a man 'who is a true epicure'. Swift
himself dined there and with Lowman on several occasions. Once, at
Eckersall's he 'had the Queen's wine and such very fine victuals, that
I could not eat it'.[6] In 1760 a man who was in a position to know, one
of the under-clerks of the green cloth, offered this explanation of why
the clerks of the kitchen lived so well:

[1] LS 13/260 (royal warrant to the lord steward, 17 November 1722); and see below
p. 170.
[2] LS 9/114–22 ('Books of Fare,' 1714–27); for the 'bill of fare' going to the green
cloth office daily see LS 13/115, pp. 29, 54.
[3] LS 9/37; LS 9/41–5 (1714–27).   [4] LS 9/73–7 (1714–29).
[5] See chapter 7.
[6] Swift, *Journal to Stella*, p. 202; and see pp. 365, 375.

It is the business of the clerks of the kitchen constantly to attend to inspect the provisions before it goes to the kitchen and to give proper allowances of the different ingredients according as the service may require, it being in their department to order the whole provisions for the kitchen service. It gives great opportunity for fraudulent practices which have been constantly made use of, they taking for themselves and friends great quantities of different articles which they charge as used to his Majesty.[1]

The kitchen did not prepare all the household food. The confectionery office, staffed by two yeomen and a groom, was responsible for preparing the desserts of fruit served at the king's and the household tables. The confectioners acted partly as independent tradesmen as well simply as household servants, for they were the purveyors of the fruit served at the king's table whereas for the ordinary household tables they simply prepared and arranged fruit received from the grocer who was under contract, or from the household gardens.[2] When the court moved to Hampton Court or Windsor and more tables were required for courtiers and distinguished guests, the confectioners entered into a contract with the board of green cloth to provide the extra service at a set price per dish.[3]

The pastry office was employed in the making of bakemeats, of pies and tarts and some sauces. It consisted in the early eighteenth century of two yeomen, two grooms, a 'furner' who did the heavy work, and a 'salsaryman' who was responsible for sauces. Up to the reign of William III this office had also had a separate clerk—it was the lowest post of the clerical hierarchy—to receive and account for the flour and other necessities the pastrymen used. But in the reign of William III the clerkships of the pastry and of the scullery were combined with that of the woodyard. This was probably a form of compensation for these clerks of the ending of the normal household promotion system under which they could expect to advance to the board of green cloth; the combination of posts would of course give them a much higher salary. And undoubtedly it was thought to be possible to combine the clerkships both because these offices must have had much less business in the eighteenth century than they had had in the sixteenth, when many more servants dined at court, and also because of the change in

[1] Bray MSS, 85/2/3 (not paginated consecutively).
[2] LS 13/115, fos. 13, 62.
[3] *Ibid.* fos. 63, 129; LS 13/22 (book of contracts).

the system of purveyance after 1660 that had also allowed the clerks of
the green cloth to withdraw from the detailed accounting work of the
department. The result was that the accounts of the pastry were made up
in the eighteenth century by a man who, as likely as not, knew nothing
about it; by a man who, as William Bray, an under-clerk of the green
cloth, said in 1760, had 'neither direction or inspection' of the office.[1]
It is not certain that this removal of authority had had a deleterious
effect on the working of the office by 1714. It certainly had by George
III's reign. In 1760, according to Bray, the pastrymen made much more
in the office than was needed for the service of the king's and the household tables and they had made it 'a shop from which they sell to all the
neighbouring nobility and gentry round about at the expense of his
Majesty'.[2]

The bakehouse, which employed a yeoman and two groom bakers
and a bread-bearer, whose duty it was to carry the bread into another
office, the pantry, provided the bread for the household under contract
for so much a loaf and manchet.[3] The bakers were no longer, that is,
simply salaried household servants but rather they acted essentially as
tradesmen who bought their own necessities and held the contract to
supply the needs of the household. The pantry, which was in the charge
of a gentleman and also employed two grooms, received the bread
from the bakers and delivered it out to the king, to the household tables
and to all those servants in receipt of a daily allowance of bread as part
of their livery.

A number of the other offices below stairs were responsible for the
collection and distribution of food and supplies. The cellar and the
buttery, like the pantry, served the king's and household tables and
also delivered out the daily allowance of beer and wine respectively to
those in receipt of them. It was undoubtedly because of this work—
the distribution of the daily livery—that the clerk of the kitchen was
so intimately connected with the pantry, the cellar and the buttery.
These offices were without their own clerks—their senior officer was a
gentleman—and the clerks of the kitchen kept their accounts, verifying
in the process that the deliveries accounted for were within the limits
stated in the establishment.[4]

---

[1] Bray MSS. 85/2/3.   [2] *Ibid.*
[3] Copies of the contracts are at LS 13/22 (1715–27).
[4] Bray MSS. 85/2/3.

The main task of the scullery was to take care of the plate, the dishes and covers, to lay them out before dinner, to collect and wash them afterwards. But even this office was also concerned with supply, for the scullery was responsible for the ordering and distribution of the charcoal used at court, and one of its officers had a contract to supply herbs and root vegetables to the kitchen.[1] Another servant, one of the children of the scullery, seems to have had a right to provide under contract a number of the lamps used around the palace; at least two of the men who enjoyed this right sub-contracted it in this period, with the permission of the board of green cloth, to yet another scullery servant, the pankeeper.[2]

Most of the other offices were concerned more purely with supply. The acatry, which was under two joint-clerks and a sergeant, and had a staff of yeomen and grooms, received meat, fish, salt, bacon and a number of other things. After receipt these were sent into another office, the larder, which, though it had its own staff of two yeomen and three grooms, was essentially part of the acatry. From the larder supplies were delivered into the kitchen upon the orders of the clerk of that office. The spicery was another supply office with its own clerk. It received and distributed wax and tallow candles as well as the goods purveyed by the grocer and the 'oylman'; the latter supplied a long list of delicacies, including Westphalia hams, olives, pickled cucumbers, mangoes, caviar, parmesan cheese, oysters, truffles, asparagus and ketchup.[3] The scalding house received, killed and cleaned the fowl, which it delivered into the poultry office. This latter office also had a clerk at its head, but the post, like the three clerkships previously mentioned and doubtless for similar reasons, was always held in conjunction with another clerkship, that of the bakehouse. The woodyard was another office of supply, largely concerned with the distribution of wood and coal; and the ewry, another, kept and cared for the table linen.

The food and other commodities received and distributed by these offices was supplied by purveyors who entered into a contract signed annually with the board of green cloth between November and January.[4] There were two kinds of purveyors: tradesmen, and men who were

---

[1] LS 13/22 (contracts); LS 13/115, fo. 109.
[2] LS 13/175, fo. 76.   [3] LS 13/22 (contracts).
[4] *Ibid.* The contracts were usually signed after the service began, for the contract year began on 1 October.

servants of one of the offices below stairs. In the reign of George I tradesmen supplied meat, fowl, groceries and special delicacies, bacon, salt cod, beer, table linen, and wax candles. The contracts for fish and tallow candles were shared between several purveyors some of whom were tradesmen and some servants, the latter being the yeomen of the salt stores in the acatry (fish) and a yeoman of the poultry (tallow candles). Many more things were supplied entirely by household servants. As was seen earlier, the bread was supplied by the servants of the bakehouse, the yeomen and grooms of the office sharing the contract. In addition, the yeomen and grooms of the woodyard purveyed the coal and firewood distributed by their office; the grooms of the scullery similarly had the contract for charcoal; the servants of the poultry supplied fruit for the pastry office, as well as peas, beans and other green vegetables; the flour used in the pastry and also the vinegar used for sauces was furnished by a yeoman of that office; the contract for cider, mead and strong beer was held jointly by the gentleman and the other servants of the buttery; and a page of the scullery supplied herbs and root vegetables under contract.[1]

This system of purveyance for the royal household, developed after 1660, had affected the work of some household offices. Under the earlier system, for example, the acatry had received cattle to slaughter, and had been responsible for hanging and cutting the carcasses. After 1660, however, meat was received from a butcher under contract, in joints, and the work of the acatry was obviously very much reduced.[2] Similarly the bakehouse was no longer a working household office in

[1] The information about contracts is taken from the book of contracts LS 13/22; and from references in the green cloth minutes: e.g. LS 13/115, fos. 2, 4, 5, 7, 20, 33, 41, 46, 109. For a discussion of the methods of supply to the royal household between 1660 and 1812 see Sir William Beveridge, *Prices and Wages in England from the Twelfth to the Nineteenth Centuries* (1939), I, 319–41.

[2] In 1739 a report of the surveyor general of Crown lands disclosed that the clerk of the acatry then in office enjoyed the benefit of a piece of ground in Whitehall which had once been used by the acatry as a slaughtering place. ' ...when the King's Household came to be supplied with provisions another way', he reported, 'the use of the Slaughter House consequently ceased, and from that time the ground and building standing thereon came into the hands of some of the officers of the Acatery [and] were converted into a sort of yard or warehouses for the sale of coal and wood' (*C.T.B.&P.* 1739–41, pp. 55–6). In George I's reign cattle continued to be slaughtered at Hampton Court, perhaps because of the difficulties of supplying joints of meat from butchers in London (LS 13/176, p. 164).

the way it had been when, under the old purveyance system, the bread had been baked at court from wheat received from various counties.

As a consequence of this new method of supply, and of the resulting changes in the work of some of the offices below stairs, there seems to have been some change in the kinds of men who held posts of the middle rank in the department, particularly the posts of clerk, gentleman and sergeant. The method of recruitment of these officers and the old system of promotion will be discussed at greater length in a later chapter,[1] but it should be noticed here that whereas under the strict system of promotion by seniority which seems to have been in operation until the late seventeenth century, these middle-ranking servants had worked their way up through the department after beginning in very humble posts, by the early eighteenth century there is some evidence that the breakdown of the system, which had allowed clerks of the green cloth to be recruited from outside the household, had also extended lower down the scale. In George I's reign some of these clerks and gentlemen of offices came into their posts without any previous service in the department, a circumstance made possible no doubt by the reduction of the work of some of the offices below stairs. And these new men, or some at least, tended to be of distinctly higher social standing than previous holders of the posts. Earlier, clerks of offices had been called 'esquires', but this seems invariably to have represented a rise in social status through office holding; in the early eighteenth century a number of men of gentle birth can be found in such posts. Sir Anthony Wescombe, Bt., was one of the joint-clerks of the acatry in George I's reign, a clerk, that is, of an office whose business had been much reduced; and Peter Campbell, a member of Parliament and Colonel of Horse (and in 1735 a brigadier-general), became gentleman of the buttery in 1721.[2] These cases were as yet untypical of the department as a whole: most of the clerks and other servants in charge of offices below stairs had gained experience in the department before rising to these posts. But it was perhaps inevitable that if some offices ceased to be places of real business the way would be open for the entrance of influential outsiders and the previous system of promotion by seniority would break down.

[1] See chapter 5.
[2] Campbell was member of Parliament for Buteshire 1722–7, Elgin Burghs 1728–34 and Buteshire 1734–41. For his army career see Dalton, *George I's Army*, I, 98.

Departments of the Household, II

Perhaps the most striking aspect of the method of supply developed after 1660 was the fact that many of the purveyors were also in charge of offices. This, along with the fact that five separate clerkships of the offices below stairs were combined in two men in the early eighteenth century, meant that in some of the offices the purveyor was also effectively the accountant who checked the quality and quantity of the goods supplied. That is to say, there was no check at all. The opportunities this afforded for fraud may be seen in the case of the man who imported the king's wine. The wine was imported by an officer of the cellar under the direction of the board of green cloth. James Heymans, who had served William III before 1689, became keeper of the ice and storekeeper of the wine in England and carried on this service in William's reign[1] and again from 1714 to 1719. He was directed each year how much to buy,[2] but the choice was left entirely to him, and he employed his own agent in France. But Heymans was also a private wine dealer, and when he died in 1719 an inspection of the cellars disclosed that he had not kept his private affairs and the royal service entirely separate. The cellar was found to contain a good deal of inferior wine and much of the king's wine, paid for by the cofferer, had apparently been sold, doubtless to Heyman's great profit.[3]

It is very clear that there were a great number of such abuses practised below stairs, abuses which the board of green cloth struggled to control. One of their most difficult tasks was to prevent the abuse of the right to take fees and perquisites which most servants in the lord steward's department enjoyed. The clerks of the board and the master of the household had themselves, at Anne's accession, given up their right to take fees in return for twenty-four shillings a day each. This it was hoped would 'encourage them to execute their offices with care and frugality',[4] for they would no longer have a financial interest in seeing the household expenditure maintained at as high a level as possible. But few other servants below stairs had had their allowances reduced 'to a certainty'; almost all depended on their share of fees and perquisites to

---

[1] LS 13/174, fos. 4, 14.   [2] LS 13/115, fos. 9, 21, 29, 50, 51, 67, 103.

[3] *Ibid.* fo. 99; in 1721 new orders for the storekeeper of the wine were issued in which it was emphasized that the storekeeper must not be a private wine dealer; and every three months he was to present an account of wine in the cellar to the board (LS 13/176, p. 155).

[4] LS 13/258, fo. 17.

supplement a stipendary allowance. The master cooks, for example, claimed every lamb's head; the clerk of the spicery had a fee of one ounce in seventeen of the wax delivered into his office and a percentage of other things; the servants of the ewry shared the old and worn-out linen; the clerk of the acatry claimed a fee (in money—it was included in his account) on meat received in the office; and so on.[1] Not unnaturally, these rights were often abused, and the board of green cloth frequently dealt with offenders. That the ewry servants were often premature in condemning linen tablecloths and napkins as useless is clear from the repeated reprimands given them by the board for the great losses from the office. On one occasion, indeed, a yeoman of the ewry was caught selling large quantities of new linen.[2] And theft was not confined to this office. Saucepans—especially silver saucepans— disappeared with alarming frequency from the kitchen;[3] indeed the kitchen seems to have been particularly easy to pilfer. The household ordinances, doubtless in an attempt to limit the number of people who had access to it, repeat with telling insistence that the posts of turn-broach, porter, scourer and doorkeeper—all of them menial kitchen places—are not to be sold, and that none of these servants is to be allowed into waiting except by a certificate signed by two or more clerks of the green cloth.[4] Swift may have had the possibilities of theft in mind when he wrote of a man:

> I give you joy of the Report
> That he's to have a Place at C[our]t
> Yes and a Place he will grow rich in
> A Turn spit in the R[oyal] Kitchen.[5]

As was suggested earlier, the clerk of the kitchen himself seems to have set an example to those he was supposed to supervise that was hardly to the advantage of the Crown.

The opportunities for fraud in the lord steward's department and the abuses that the fee system gave rise to were both amply illustrated in 1707 when the board of green cloth investigated two of the offices below stairs, the scalding house and the larder, after receiving repeated com-

---

[1] LS 13/115, fos. 13, 14, 20, 21, 28, 32, 41, 42, 68, 76.
[2] LS 13/115, fo. 59; LS 13/116, fos. 24–5.   [3] LS 13/115, fos. 47, 88.
[4] LS 13/44; *Household Ordinances*, p. 420.
[5] 'Upon the horrid plot discovered by Harlequin, the Bishop of Rochester's French Dog' (1722).

plaints about the poor quality of the food served to court tables. The butchers and the poultry contractors were called before the board and they revealed under oath that the servants of these offices had devised various schemes that had both defrauded the king and affected the quality of meat and fowl served at court tables. The officers of the scalding house, for example, had encouraged the poulterer to deliver fowl of poorer quality than the establishment allowed (and the king paid for) and had pocketed the difference; and they had made, the poulterers thought, close to £10 a month in this way. The officers also indulged in a variety of other fraudulent practices; sometimes, in a more straightforward way, they charged things to the accounts that had not been used and then got a 'kick-back' from the poulterer. To increase their fees, they encouraged the poulterer to deliver very large— and undoubtedly very tough—rabbits into the office, for they had rabbit skins as a perquisite. And because they claimed the fat of the fowl as a fee, they cut off as much as they could as they prepared them, 'by which means', the poulterers explained, 'the fowl when at the fire sink [and] become dry and unsightly'. When the butchers were examined, they told a similar story of disorder and corruption in the larder.[1] On this occasion the servants of both offices were suspended for periods of one to three months and they lost one quarter's wages. And the board drew up new orders for the conduct of the offices.[2] It seems reasonably clear, however, that unless the board of green cloth devoted some time to seeing that their orders were observed in the offices below stairs such abuses as those practised in the scalding house would soon creep back.

In trying to govern such a department, the clerks were faced with an enormous, perhaps an impossible, task. The fee system could not but encourage corruption and an unnecessary increase of expenditure, especially in offices in which the clerkship had been effectively reduced and in which many servants were also purveyors. But in the early years of the eighteenth century the board of green cloth was at least actively trying to maintain its control; the clerks frequently reminded those in charge of offices of their duties, and from time to time they examined the accounts to see that the allowances being delivered out, especially in connection with the daily livery, were within the established limit.[3] On occasion too, they inspected the offices below

---

[1] LS 13/175, fos. 54–5.   [2] *Ibid.* fos. 55–6, 58–60.
[3] LS 13/115, fo. 10; LS 13/116, fo. 16.

stairs; in September 1715 they met at the ewry, 'to examine the quantity and condition of the table linen'.[1] It may well be that the frequency of their exhortations to the offices in their charge is a measure of their failure to prevent numerous abuses, but it seems clear on the other hand that the board in George I's reign was more successful and more conscientious than they became later in the century.

When George III came to the throne, his lord steward, Lord Talbot, set out to reform the department and as a necessary prelude, an under-clerk of the board, William Bray, conducted a detailed inquiry into the state of the offices below stairs.[2] This revealed a state of disarray that seems much worse than anything in George I's reign. Bray describes many posts below stairs as sinecures; many officers attended only occasionally, he discovered, and then only to look after their fees and perquisites; they left the work of the office either to deputies or to the purveyor and his private servants. As a result of this survey, four offices, the acatry, bakehouse, scalding house, and poultry office, were entirely abolished; their work was given to other offices and their servants were pensioned off. At the same time, a new and much stricter set of rules regulating the conduct of the remaining offices and the accounting procedure below stairs was drawn up.[3] In their insistence on personal attendance and on the proper drawing up of accounts, these new orders suggest that the department was in considerable chaos in 1760. Of course there were numerous abuses below stairs in George I's reign, but Bray's analysis and the language of these new orders together suggest that the measure of control over the department that the board had previously exercised had been allowed to slip under George II.

This would seem to be verified too in the minute books of meetings of the board. As has been seen, in George I's reign the board of green cloth met regularly twice a week for most of the year, and after each meeting there are several pages in the minute books of decisions taken and orders sent out. After about 1732 the recorded decisions of the board become much sparser and less detailed. A page count gives a rough indication of this: in the ten years 1726–35 green cloth decisions occupy 120 pages of the minute books; but in the succeeding ten years they occupy only forty; thereafter they are even sparser. Indeed in the 1750s only about twenty meetings are recorded;[4] in George I's thirteen-

---

[1] LS 13/115, fo. 25.   [2] Bray MSS. 85/2/3.
[3] LS 13/193.   [4] LS 13/116.

year reign, by contrast, there were 364 meetings. A falling off in vigilance on the part of the clerks of the green cloth might seem to be indicated too by the fact that in 1760, as part of Talbot's reforms, their numbers were increased from four to six. And there is other, and more substantial, evidence of this. In March 1782 the lord steward reminded the clerks that one of their number had to attend daily to issue necessary orders and to conduct the general management of the department, and 'to prevent', he went on to say, 'the irregularities which had been practised in the late reign, when inferior persons issued such orders'.[1] The 'inferior persons' he was referring to were undoubtedly the clerks to the clerks of the board. There is not the slightest suggestion in George I's reign that these men were anything more than clerks who did the drudgery of keeping accounts. If by 1760 they had largely taken over the work of their superiors—and besides Talbot's remark, the fact that Bray refers to them once as 'deputy clerks of the Green Cloth' suggests that they had—there could hardly have failed to have been a loss of weight and authority in the control of the household offices. George III himself was dismayed by the board. 'I am sorry to see', he wrote to John Secker, the secretary to the lord steward, in 1781, 'whenever the business is to be done by the Green Cloth that it requires triple the number of servants than when they are not employed.'[2]

Only a more detailed study of the period after 1727 could reveal the extent to which the board had relaxed its control over the household. But it seems certain that the board that Burke spoke of with such contempt later in the century bore little resemblance to that of George I's reign. The clerkships were abolished by Burke's Economical Reform Act in 1782, and no one sprang eagerly to their defence. This is perhaps the strongest comment on their ineffectiveness by then. But it would be a mistake to date their decline much before the middle of the reign of George II. This is not to say that the household of George I was run economically and efficiently—far from it. But the clerks in 1714 were by no means idle. It is clear from the frequency of their meetings and the range of matters discussed that the clerks in George I's reign took their duties seriously. They did not eliminate every abuse and malpractice; these were inherent in a department which laboured under an administrative system inherited from the sixteenth century and earlier,

[1] LS 13/117, fo. 56.
[2] LS 13/281 (household notebook of John Secker; not paginated).

and into which a new method of purveyance had been introduced without being accompanied by any administrative reconstruction and rearrangement. Nor could they be expected to prevent all the evils that flowed from the fact that some of the purveyors were also servants in the offices below stairs, or from the more fundamental problem that the fees of servants in the department varied directly with the amount of business done in their office. These things were not conducive to producing in those in positions of responsibility in the household careful and economical administration. The board of green cloth, none the less, was attempting to impose control from above in George I's reign. They were deeply concerned with household administration, as they clearly were not later in the century.

III

The officers and servants of the stables under the master of the horse fell into two distinct categories. On the one hand, the leading officers—the master himself, the gentleman of the horse, the equerries and the pages of honour—were personal servants of the king, companions to him out of doors where they took the place of the gentlemen and grooms of the bedchamber; these were therefore posts of great honour. On the other hand, since it was the business of the department to take care of the horses and carriages, there were also a large staff of menial servants, and of coachmen and postilions and the like. The whole department, including the small sub-department of the stud, totalled a little over a 100.

It was a smaller and much less complex department than the household below stairs to which it was to a great extent tied financially. The salaries of all those under the master of the horse, and all ordinary or fixed charges (for fodder as well as some fixed amounts for repairs to the equipage) were included in the household establishment and paid by the cofferer.[1] Only extraordinary charges—for unforeseen repairs, for buying horses, for providing new liveries for servants[2]—were paid on a separate stables account with money received from the exchequer in the ordinary way and for which the master submitted a declared

[1] LS 13/44.
[2] The master of the horse won the right to provide liveries for servants in the stables—i.e. mainly for the coachmen, footmen, postilions and chairmen—after a legal battle with the master of the great wardrobe in 1694 (*C.T.B.* x, 495).

account. The administrative staff was very small. Besides the master, it consisted of the avenor, the clerk of the avery and the clerk of the stables. For a few months in 1716 there was also a separate office of clerk of the extraordinaries, but this post, created in April, and one of a number of small alterations then made in the department,[1] had been abolished by November and the work returned to the clerk of the stables.[2]

The post of avenor, the head under the master of the horse, of the administrative staff, was not apparently in the early eighteenth century a place of much business; it was held in this period as an added perquisite by one of the leading officers, the gentleman of the horse or a commissioner of the office of master. The avenor still paid some charges,[3] and he, or the clerk of the office—the clerk of the avery—swore in new servants, issued the debenture for wages paid by the cofferer and prepared the stables establishment for the board of green cloth.[4] But the main financial work that remained in the stables, paying and accounting for extraordinary expenditure, was done by the clerk of the stables. He prepared the necessary creditor for this expenditure, and when it was passed by the board of green cloth,[5] he made up the declared account. The clerk of the stables also paid the numerous small charges incurred on royal journeys, money for which came out of the privy purse.[6]

The leading officers of the stables were the holders of the honorific posts: the master, the gentleman of the horse, the six equerries and the five pages of honour. The master was the third officer of the royal household, taking precedence over all except the lord chamberlain and the lord steward. Like these other great court posts, the mastership of

[1] LS 13/260 (royal warrant, April 1716).   [2] LS 13/115, fo. 51.

[3] LS 13/260 (royal warrant of 29 September 1714 directing the avenor to pay £1,000 a year to the keeper of the 'running' horses at Newmarket).

[4] LS 13/115, fo. 27; C.T.B. IX, 36.   [5] LS 13/116, fo. 20.

[6] Whenever the court moved to Hampton Court or Windsor or elsewhere, the master of the horse (through the clerk of the stables) distributed small sums of money in all the towns through which they passed: 10 guineas to the poor prisoners in Guildford, 5 guineas to the bell-ringers, 'to women who strew the ground with flowers in various places', etc.; also when the king visited a nobleman in the country, as he did at various times in 1717, for example, the musicians and domestic servants of that nobleman were also tipped by the master of the horse. Numerous accounts for such outlays—money paid by the king's personal treasurer, Mehemet, to the master— are among the papers of George I in Hanover (N.S.A., K.G., Cal. Br. 22, XIII, Anhang no. 3, vols. XIX, XX).

the horse was in the eighteenth century always held by a peer, and often, as in the case of Scarborough under George II, by one particularly close to the king. It was a very lucrative as well as honorable post—'the handsomest employment in Britain', according to one contemporary.[1] If this was true it was the perquisites of the office rather than the salary that made it so, for the latter was but £1,266, which, while handsome enough, was not enormous for great court places.[2] The perquisites were more promising. All masters received gold plate to the value of £400 on entering office; and the master in office at the death of a sovereign could claim the royal coaches and coach-horses as his fee. This was obviously valuable for some at least, and it was an expensive item for court finances at the beginning of a reign. And the master of the horse enjoyed further benefits. He was allowed the use of twelve horses (whose upkeep alone cost the king over £500 a year);[3] and four footmen, six grooms, a coachman, a postilion and a stable-helper were provided for his own use on the establishment of the department. Some masters seem to have drawn on servants beyond this number for their own private service.[4] It may have been these extra expenses that led Anne in 1712 and George I in December, 1715, to put the office into commission. Anne granted the office to her two commissioners, Conyers Darcy[5] and George Fielding,[6] with all the rights, profits and advantages that the master of the horse enjoyed. But they were at least persuaded to accept a money payment in lieu of their right to the equipage at the queen's death,[7] and Bothmer was able to report with some relief to

[1] Cathcart MSS. corresp. c/2, James Cathcart to Lord Cathcart, 20 March 1716.
[2] For salaries and fees see chapter 6.   [3] LS 13/44.
[4] '...there were 24 footmen waiting at table, and as he is Master of the Horse to the King 16 of them in the King's livery and the rest in his own...' (John Collis, Mayor of Hastings, describing a dinner at the duke of Richmond's (c. 1735): Earl of March, *A Duke and his Friends*, p. 304).
[5] Conyers Darcy (1685–1758) second son of John Darcy of Aske, Yorkshire; grandson of 1st earl of Holdernesse, brother of 3rd and uncle of 4th earl. Member of Parliament for Yorkshire 1707–8, Newark 1715–22, Richmond 1722–47, Yorkshire 1747–58; avenor 1711–17, gentleman of the horse 1712–17; commissioner for the office of master of the horse 1712–14, 1715–17. Dismissed in June 1717 but returned to court in 1719 as master of the household (1719–30); comptroller of the household 1730–55.
[6] George Fielding (c. 1674–1738) second son of John Fielding, a canon of Salisbury, and grandson of the earl of Desmond. Page of honour to William III (?1694–1702); equerry (?1702–14); commissioner for the office of master of the horse 1712–14; groom of the bedchamber 1714–27.   [7] C.T.B. xxx, cxci.

Hanover in August 1714 that carriages would be available for the king's entry.[1] George I appointed a master of the horse at the beginning of his reign. The duke of Somerset, who had held the post before 1712,[2] was given it again but when he resigned in October 1715 in protest against the arrest of his son-in-law, Sir William Wyndham, for suspected Jacobite activities,[3] the commission was reconstituted. Darcy had retained his stable posts of avenor and gentleman of the horse at the change of reigns, and he was reappointed to the commission. Fielding had become a groom of the bedchamber in 1714, however, and his place in the commission was taken by Francis Negus, who had been surveyor of the stables and had the added advantage of being a Norfolk neighbour and friend of Robert Walpole's.[4]

George I restricted the rights of his commissioners much more than had Queen Anne. They were granted £800 a year each, but this was 'in lieu of', and not as well as, all fees, profits and advantages enjoyed by the master of the horse. The result was a saving of at least £1,179 for the salaries, liveries and horses of the footmen and other servants normally provided for the master; and between 1717 and 1727, when Negus was the sole commissioner, there was a further saving of £800 in salary.[5] It is possible that George I was himself responsible for the changed terms under which the office of commissioner was held, for there are among the State Papers copies of the warrants appointing the commissions of 1712 and 1715 both translated into French.[6]

The gentleman of the horse, who was the next to the master in the

[1] Stowe MSS. 227, fos. 366–71; Bothmer to Robethon 24 August/4 September 1714.

[2] Charles Seymour, 10th duke of Somerset (1662–1748); gentleman of the bedchamber 1685–7; lord president of the council and a lord of trade 1702; master of the horse 1702–12, September 1714–October 1715.

[3] Coxe, *Walpole*, I, 71; *H.M.C. Fortescue*, I, 53–4; Lady Cowper, *Diary*, pp. 51–5.

[4] Francis Negus (d. 1732), member of Parliament for Ipswich 1717–32; served under Marlborough and attained rank of lt.-colonel. Surveyor of the stables and surveyor of the highways under William III; commissioner for the office of master of the horse 1715–27; avenor 1717–27; master of the buckhounds 1727–32. Negus was sole commissioner from 1717 (when Darcy was dismissed) until 1727 when George II made the earl of Scarborough master of the horse.

[5] Both of these savings appear in the household accounts (e.g. C(H)MSS. 45/5) which, without entirely discrediting them throws some doubt on the contemporary rumours that George I gave part of the emoluments of the office to his Hanoverian master of the horse, Baron Kielmannsegge, or to Madame Schulenberg.

[6] S.P. Dom. 35/68, fos. 168, 169–72.

department, was in effect the first equerry, in the same way that the groom of the stole was also the first gentleman of the bedchamber. He received a smaller annual stipend (£256 as against £300) than the equerries, but he found compensation in pluralism; the gentleman of the horse seems always to have held the post in conjunction with an equerryship or another place in the department, such as avenor.[1] The six equerries, as well, of course, as the gentleman, were always men of good family and connections, as might be expected of places that brought the holder into close attendance on the monarch.[2] They waited a month in turn, the nature of the duties, as with all personal servants, depending entirely on the wishes of the sovereign. There is nothing to indicate that George I demanded much more of his equerries than of his gentlemen and grooms of the bedchamber, though he loved to hunt and they must have accompanied him then. In some reigns, however, the life of an equerry could be a very full one, especially during the summer when the court was in the country.[3]

Of course it was a mark of considerable distinction to be one of the king's equerries, but the monetary rewards were not great. The salary of £300 was reduced almost to £250 by taxes and fees, and, unlike many far less honourable posts, it was not increased by any perquisites beyond lodging and the right to dine at court during their month of waiting. The equerries may well have valued the post, and the *entrée* it provided to the inner circle of the court, as a springboard to better things. Many of them found their reward in the army. As Peter Wentworth pointed out to his brother in 1726, 'the rest of my brother Querrys [*sic*] have all posts in the Army excepting Lord Elmore [Aylmer]'.[4] Wentworth had been trying since 1714 to get another court post (he wanted to be a groom of the bedchamber), or a com-

---

[1] Darcy held it with the post of avenor; and Henry Berkeley held it with an equerryship.
[2] George I's equerries were: Henry Berkeley (and after 1717, gentleman of the horse), brother of the earl of Berkeley; Peter Wentworth, brother of the earl of Strafford; Henry Pulteney, brother of William, later earl of Bath; Henry Aylmer, son of Admiral, Lord Aylmer; William Cecil, son of John Cecil of Salton. Wilts.; Thomas Panton.
[3] See Peter Wentworth's description of a typical day at Hampton Court in 1731 in J. J. Cartwright, *Wentworth Papers*, pp. 468–9.
[4] Add. MSS. 22227, fo. 58. For the army careers of Henry Berkeley, Henry Pulteney, William Cecil and Thomas Panton see C. Dalton, *George I's Army*, I, 130, n. 3; I, 291, n. 3; II, 35–8; I, 103, respectively.

mission in the army and the command of a troop of horse. In 1714 he had spoken of his 'hard fate only to continue' as an equerry;[1] and in 1731, still trying to improve his position at court, he observed at the conclusion of a letter describing his full life at Hampton Court, 'if I don't make something of it at last, I shall have hard Fate'.[2]

Some equerries were promoted to better posts. George Fielding and William Breton became grooms of the bedchamber in 1714, for example, and as Wentworth pointed out, most of them found compensation for their hard work and low salary in an army post. In a much more obvious way the post of page of honour provided an opening to better things, and especially to the army. In 1723 Walpole recommended a young man, Sir William Irby—'the remains of a worthy family fallen into decay'—for the post of page of honour as a means of perhaps repairing his family's fortune.[3] It was a post given to young men of good family and normally held for only a few years. They gave some limited attendance on the monarch,[4] but they were also expected to learn the arts of horsemanship at the riding academy—which was conducted by two other officers of the department, the equerries of the crown stable[5]— in preparation for entry into the army. It was common for the pages to be commissioned after a few years at court, and to be given a pension to make up the difference between the salary of a junior officer and a page.[6] Unlike the equerries, they usually then left the court, though

[1] Cartwright, *Wentworth Papers*, p. 416.

[2] *Ibid.* p. 469, For Wentworth's search for favour see below pp. 172–3.

[3] *S.P. Dom.* 35/46, fo. 86.

[4] For example Queen Anne was attended by a page of honour when she went to the Sacheverell trial (Panshanger MSS. Letterbooks, II, 104–5).

[5] George I's equerries of the crown stable were Henry Foubert and Peter Rechaussé. Their main task was to care for the king's own riding horses. The salaries of the pages of honour were increased—'for their better education and encouragement'— from £200 to £260 in 1716. Part of this was for 'exercises at the Academy' (LS 13/260, royal warrant of April 1716).

[6] The following held the post in this reign: Guildford Killigrew, Thomas Murray, Thomas Bloodworth, John Mordaunt, John Hampden, Emmanuel Howe, Archibald Carmichael, Sir William Irby, Walter Villiers. Of these Killigrew, Murray, Blood- worth, and Hampden got army commissions and gave up their court posts; they were each given a pension of £150 a year (LS 13/260, royal warrants of 29 February 1724, 25 October 1726, 26 May 1717); Mordaunt was promoted from page of honour to be gentleman of the horse to Princess Anne in 1718; in 1726 he too got a commission in the horse guards (Dalton, *George I's Army*, I, 197).

some, Sir William Irby, for example, made this post the beginning of a more permanent court career.[1]

Besides these administrative and honorific posts, the department included another eighty or so men who were concerned with the upkeep of the buildings, the care of the carriages and of the upwards of 100 horses the king required. Two surveyors of the stables—one for the Great Mews at Charing Cross, the main stables establishment, and one for the stables at Hampton Court, a post held after 1714 by Sir Richard Steele and described by him as a virtual sinecure[2]—were only required to report to the master of the horse about the state of the buildings and what repairs might be needed. Six purveyors shared the contract to provide hay and straw, oats and beans to the stables in London and at Kensington, Hampton Court, and Windsor. The department also included the king's twelve footmen, five coachmen, five postilions and four chairmen. Most of the other servants of the stables were engaged in necessary menial work: they were farriers, saddlers, stable keepers, grooms and the like. Finally, there were two sub-departments of the stables; the stud at Hampton Court under a master who, though he received money separately from the exchequer, presented his accounts to the master of the horse;[3] and a small establishment at Newmarket which looked after the king's ten 'running' horses, to a total cost of £1,000 a year.

IV

This concludes the survey of the main departments of the royal household. It was a vast establishment, and it cost a great deal of money. Not as much in proportion to the total national expenditure as it had a hundred years earlier when, it has been estimated, the household consumed 40 per cent of Charles I's annual expenditure in peace-time.[4] The other expenses of government had risen considerably since then, but still George I's civil list accounted for close to 15 per cent of the government's normal annual expenditure, and the household took more

[1] Sir William Irby, 2nd Bt. (1707–75); page 1724–8, equerry to the Prince of Wales 1728–36; vice-chamberlain to the Princess of Wales 1736–51; lord chamberlain to the dowager Princess of Wales 1751–72; member of Parliament for Launceston 1735–47, Bodmin 1747–61; created Baron Boston 1761.
[2] R. Blanchard (ed.), *The Correspondence of Richard Steele* (1941), p. 106.
[3] T 1/222, fo. 190.
[4] Aylmer, *The King's Servants*, p. 27.

than a third of that; it was still, therefore, a significant item in national finances. The household money was distributed by a number of paymasters, all of them to some extent under the authority of the Treasury though independent of each other. It remains now to see how this financial system worked, how much the household cost, and how the money was provided and distributed. This is the subject of the following chapter.

4

FINANCIAL PROBLEMS AND THE
COST OF THE COURT

I

George I was the first English king to have a fixed income guaranteed by Parliament. After the Restoration Charles II had been granted an annual revenue of £1,200,000, a sum that was thought by Parliament to be adequate for the normal peace time expenses of government. Charles was not guaranteed this revenue, but only the yields of certain specified branches of the revenue, mainly customs and excise, which, it was calculated, would produce this sum. His annual revenue therefore varied from year to year and it was most often lower than the total figure Parliament had intended the king should have. In 1685 similar arrangements were made for James II. Though he was rather better treated than his brother in that the sources from which annual revenue was derived were increased, James had no more guarantee than had Charles that the sum that Parliament had granted would be collected.

After the Revolution of 1688 this approach to national financing was considerably modified. Partly because of Parliament's reluctance to make the king a grant for life, partly because of the immediate and vast expenses of the war, the financing of William III's early years bears a certain hand-to-mouth character. But during the reign a distinction began to be made between the military and naval expenses of the state on the one hand and the ordinary costs of civil government and the household on the other. That is, the concept of a Civil List began to emerge; and in 1697 the first Civil List Act granted William III a revenue for his life of £700,000 a year 'for the service of his Household and family and for other his necessary expenses and occasions'. The responsibility for all military costs was henceforth assumed by Parliament and dealt with by annual provisions.[1]

[1] 9 and 10 William III, c. 23. For the beginnings of separate Civil Lists, the produce of the revenues and the expenditure of the households of William III and Anne, see William A. Shaw's introduction to C.T.B. vols. XI–XVII, XVIII, XIX, XXIII and XXV.

The Civil List was to be raised out of customs revenues, the hereditary and temporary excise, the revenues of the Post Office, and the few remaining hereditary revenues of the Crown.[1] As in 1660 the king was not *guaranteed* £700,000 a year from these sources but his income was limited to this sum; if it exceeded it the surplus could only be disposed of with the consent of Parliament. In fact William III's Civil List revenues seem never to have approached this figure, and the possibility that they might was considerably lessened by an Act of 1700 which appropriated £3,700 a week (£192,000 a year) out of the excise for the 'use of the public', a reduction that was made perpetual early in Anne's reign.[2]

At Anne's accession the same revenues were granted to her and it was hoped that she, too, would have £700,000 a year for Civil List purposes.[3] However, this was made even more unlikely than it had been in William's reign by a number of further restrictions on and appropriations from the sources that were to supply this sum. In 1705 Anne relinquished the First Fruits and Tenths of the clergy and this reduced the hereditary revenues by about £13,000 a year.[4] And in 1710 another appropriation from the Civil List revenues was made by Act of Parliament—over £28,000 being taken from the revenues of the Post Office for 'public uses'.[5] By 1713 the Civil List was in debt almost £1 million, partly as a consequence of these reductions. This debt was partially paid off when Parliament gave Anne the right to raise £500,000 by means of a lottery financed out of the hereditary revenues.[6] But this further reduced these revenues, and the Civil List, by £35,000 per annum for thirty-two years. Thus a debt which had arisen partly at least because the Civil List revenues had been reduced by Parliament was removed only at the cost of further reducing them.

In William III's reign and in Anne's, therefore, the sources from which the Civil List revenues were drawn were considerably encumbered, and in no year before 1714 was the £700,000 envisaged by the Acts of 1697 and 1702 available to the Crown. It has been calculated that William III's Civil List income between 1695 and 1702 averaged

---

[1] For these revenues see J. E. D. Binney, *British Public Finance and Administration, 1774-1792* (1958), pp. 21, 34-5, 76-85.

[2] 12 and 13 William III, c. 12; 2 and 3 Anne, c. 3.   [3] 1 Anne, c. 7.

[4] 2 and 3 Anne, c. 11. For the amount of the reduction see T 1/190, fo. 28.

[5] 9 Anne, c. 10; T 1/190, fo. 28.   [6] 12 Anne, c. 11; see *C.T.B.* xxvii, 492-4.

only about £397,000 a year, and that even though special grants were made him, he left a Civil List debt at his death of over £800,000.[1] Under Queen Anne the customs and excise revenues were more productive, but even so her Civil List income was only about £590,000 a year on average between 1702 and 1712;[2] the debt of 1713 and the lottery to raise £500,000 to relieve it were the inevitable result.

George I was also granted £700,000 a year from the same revenues three weeks after his accession but the inadequacy of the sources from which this was to be drawn was at last recognized. Baron Bothmer, the Hanoverian minister in London at the time of Anne's death, expressed his confidence, in August 1714, that Parliament could be made to see the sense of an enlargement of the Civil List funds.[3] In March 1715, in his speech to the new Parliament, the king pointed out that he would have to provide £100,000 a year for the support of the family of the Prince of Wales, and that the revenues had been considerably reduced since 1697.[4] Two months later, William Lowndes, the secretary to the Treasury, provided the House of Commons with the evidence. Papers were laid before the House showing the net income from Civil List revenues between 1699 and March 1715, and how much the sources had been restricted since 1697.[5] On the basis of these figures the ministry sought an extra grant of £120,000 a year so that the £700,000 that Parliament still accepted as a reasonable sum for Civil List purposes might be available to the Crown. This was voted in May 1715[6] and in itself it made it tolerably certain that £700,000 would for the first time be provided for the Civil List each year. But, in addition, by this Act the king was *guaranteed* this sum. An Aggregate Fund (out of which the £120,000 was also to come) was created, and extra grants from it would be forthcoming to make up any shortcomings in the Civil List revenues. On the other hand, as in the 1697 Act, any surplus over £700,000 was not to be used for Civil List purposes but was to be returned to the Aggregate Fund.

[1] *C.T.B.* Introduction to vols. XI–XVII (1695–1702) by William A. Shaw, p. xl.

[2] *C.T.B.* Introduction to vol. XXV (1711) by Shaw, p. xxviii; slightly different figures (for 1702–12) are given in *H.C.J.* XVII, 433–5.

[3] Bothmer to Robethon, 24 August 1714, Stowe MSS. 227, fo. 366.

[4] *H.C.J.* XVIII, 18; English and French versions, in Jean Robethon's hand, are in Stowe MSS. 228, fos. 28–9, 36–8. (For Robethon see below chapter 7).

[5] *H.J.C.* XVIII, 75, 78, 79–83; and T 1/190, fos. 27–8.

[6] 1 Geo. I, c. 12; *P.H.* VII, 57–60.

George I was thus given a more generous and a more certain Civil List provision than either of his two predecessors. Though £100,000 was designated by Parliament as for the support of the Prince of Wales and this was beyond the king's grasp[1]—George I still had £600,000 a year guaranteed for his own expenses. And in this reign the funds set aside for the Civil List, strengthened by the grant from the Aggregate Fund, did in fact produce the sum that Parliament intended the king should have. Over the whole reign the annual revenue from these two sources was a little over £760,000 on average.[2] Nevertheless, George I was as troubled as William and Anne had been with an insolvent Civil List. The Civil List was rarely out of debt in the reign and on three occasions appeals had to be made to Parliament to relieve an accumulated deficit amounting in each case to close to a year's revenue.[3] In this reign, however, the cause of this debt will clearly have to be sought elsewhere than in a deficiency of the revenues, which Shaw blames for the debts of George I's two predecessors.[4] In examining this problem the first task in this chapter will be to establish what the cost of the household was—for it is only with this portion of the Civil List that we are concerned—how the debts arose and how they were dealt with. Following this the attempts of the Treasury to control and to reduce the expenditure of the household will be examined.

II

The Civil List revenues supported a good deal more than just the royal household. Military and naval expenses had been financed separately since William III's reign, but the cost of the 'civil service' was still borne out of the £700,000 granted for the Civil List. The king still paid the salaries of judges, of the lords of the Treasury, secretaries of state, the lord privy seal, and numerous other officers and servants in the departments of the central administration, as well as the entire cost of the diplomatic service, pensions, royal bounties and secret service. And even the money issued to household treasurers was not entirely for household purposes; one of the largest items on the treasurer of the chamber's account, for example, was always the cost of messengers who were essentially part of the diplomatic service. The household,

[1] See below p. 269. [2] C(H)MSS. 46/36. [3] See below pp. 115-17.
[4] See, for example, *C.T.B.* xxvii, 492 ff.; and xxiii, li.

indeed, accounted, for only about a third of the Civil List expenditures. The 1697 Act, that is, represented only a stage in the evolution of a Civil List that would be devoted entirely to the Crown's personal expenses. The Civil List in 1714 was still 'mixed'—corresponding perhaps to the uncertain constitutional position of the monarch—at a stage at which the Crown had been relieved of responsibility for the provision of some of the national expenses but left with others.

For the service of the household several paymasters received money separately from the exchequer and were personally responsible for it. Money was imprested 'upon account' from the exchequer to the following officers: the cofferer (for the household below stairs and the ordinary expenditure of the stables); the treasurer of the chamber; the master of the great wardrobe; the master of the robes; the master of the horse (for the extraordinary expenditure of the stables). The paymaster of the gentlemen pensioners and the keeper of the privy purse also received money from the exchequer though they were not required to submit to the same accounting process as these imprest accountants. In addition several household officers, including the gentlemen and grooms of the bedchamber, received their salaries at the exchequer, and the king's goldsmith also received payment there for the goods he delivered into the jewel office.

The household accountants were financially independent and equal, for there was within the household no supreme authority and no unified control over the expenditure. The only such control that was exercised came from outside, from the only department with the authority and competence to provide oversight over the entire household expenditure, the Treasury. But before considering the nature and effectiveness of the Treasury's control over the household, it will perhaps be most valuable to establish what the annual expenditure was and how the debt arose.

The main departmental expenses can only be obtained from the declared accounts. These were the formal accounts of money received and paid out which the main departmental paymasters submitted to the auditor of the imprests, before whom they also swore as to their accuracy. The auditor then read the account before the treasury board, or, in the case of the cofferer's account, before the barons of the exchequer in full court. The account was 'declared' when it was read by the auditor and when the bills and vouchers upon which it rested were examined. If it was approved the account was sent on to be enrolled in three different offices, ending in the pipe office, and the accountant was given his discharge.[1]

The declared accounts are not entirely satisfactory as records of the annual expenditure of the household for they record only the money that was paid out, not the debts incurred. One case will illustrate this. Between 3 December 1714 and Christmas 1719 the treasurer of the chamber's declared accounts show that he received £184,741 from the exchequer and that he spent £184,448; thus he had £293 in hand. But three months after the end of this period, on 25 March 1720, the Civil List was declared to be in debt by a little over £550,000, and part of this was a debt of £40,662, or one year's expenditure, in the treasurer of the chamber's office. When an extra grant was arranged to pay off this debt, the treasurer's expenditure increased accordingly. In the nine months following 9 June 1720 he declared expenses of £71,849, almost twice the amount he normally issued in a year. Thus a good part of what he paid out in 1720–1, and of what is included in that year's declared account, was for expenses incurred in previous years. Which is simply to say that though the declared accounts may represent faithfully the year's business, they do not represent the year's expenditure, the debts incurred.

The declared accounts pose a further problem in that departmental periods of account rarely coincided.[2] The cofferer's and the master of the great wardrobe's accounts ran from Michaelmas to Michaelmas; the treasurer of the chamber's from Christmas to Christmas, or from Lady Day to Lady Day; the master of the horse's generally 1 April to 31 March. On top of that several years' accounts were occasionally declared together and are impossible to separate. Still the declared accounts are for some departments the only records of expenditure. And even in those departments in which annual accounts are preserved— in the household below stairs, for example—these are also accounts of money issued and their totals duplicate exactly the totals in the accounts as declared.[3] The declared accounts must be used, therefore, but since

[1] S. B. Baxter, *The Development of the Treasury, 1660–1702* (1957), pp. 111–12.
[2] The period of account was usually, though not necessarily, one year; the accounts were often submitted several years after the period accounted for had ended.
[3] The 'declared accounts' of the cofferer have been checked for several years against the account books called 'pedes parcellarum' (LS 4.) which record the monthly, half-yearly, and annual expenses of each sub-office and of the whole department

the different periods of account as well as the nature of the accounts make it impossible to get from them the real annual cost of the household, an annual average for each department has been calculated for George I's reign by dividing the total expenditure declared in the accounts during the reign by the number of months accounted for, and multiplying by twelve. This gives some indication of the annual expenditure of the major departments. The annual expenditure for the gentlemen pensioners, the privy purse, the goldsmith and for salaries paid at the exchequer has been similarly calculated from the records of exchequer issues. The average annual expenditure of the household of George I thus obtained is summarized in Table 1:

TABLE I

Household below stairs	£87,252
Chamber	39,996
Great wardrobe	23,112
Robes	3,564
Stables (extraordinaries)	10,908
Works and buildings (and gardens)	33,966
Salaries paid at the exchequer	29,040
Band of pensioners	5,760
Privy purse	30,324
Goldsmith	8,532
Total	£272,454

To know only the average expenditure is not, of course, entirely satisfactory. It conceals the fact that the expenses of some departments varied from year to year, and in some steadily increased during the reign. The work of the great wardrobe, for example, was always heaviest in the first year or two of a reign because the office bore much of the expense of burying one monarch and crowning another; and there was also inevitably a lot of new furniture bought at the beginning of a reign.[1] The expenditure in the household below stairs was also

below stairs; against the accounts of the comptroller (LS 1.) which contain an account of board-wages paid by the cofferer and some incidental expenses; and against the 'creditors' (LS 8.), the accounts of extraordinary expenses (these are also incorporated into the 'pedes parcellarum').

[1] In George I's reign this initial heavy charge is to some extent shown in the great wardrobe declared account for the year ending 29 September 1715 but variations in expenditures do not always show up so clearly in the declared accounts.

variable, especially perhaps under the first two Georges, for they were frequently out of the country, and the cost of their visits to Hanover was borne by the electoral treasury. When George I left England many court tables besides his own were discontinued, and there were other savings for such things as candles and fuel. Altogether the king's absence reduced the expenditure in the household below stairs by about £600 a week.[1] Also in this reign there was a great variation in the amount of entertaining at court. George I normally lived very quietly, but in some years, as will be seen in a later chapter, he was forced to entertain lavishly, especially when the court was at Kensington and Hampton Court.[2] It was calculated in 1720 that such a summer's entertainment added about £15,000 to the cofferer's account—a considerable addition to the 'establishment' of the household below stairs.[3] The expenditure on salaries paid at the exchequer, to take another example, rose during the reign as the number of gentlemen of the bedchamber was increased. The bedchamber staff cost £15,000 at its minimum, in 1714, when it consisted of eleven gentlemen and eight grooms. After Sunderland's appointment as groom of the stole (at £5,000 a year) in 1719, and the addition of six more gentlemen (four in 1719 and two in 1721) the bedchamber salaries had risen to £26,000 a year.

But if the statement of average expenditure conceals such variations during the reign, it does at least serve to indicate the general distribution of household expenditures. It also suggests that the household contributed considerably towards the mounting Civil List debt, for it seems clear that this total of over £272,000 was rather more than it should have been if the Civil List was to stay within £700,000 a year. This may be deduced from several calculations made by the Treasury after 1718 of the Civil List debts and of anticipated future expenditures. Among Sir Robert Walpole's papers, for example, there is a forecast drawn up in 1720 of expected expenditures in the year beginning at Michaelmas, 1720.[4] It is based partly on the 'establishments' of departments, together with any known additional charges, and partly on calculations of average expenditures during the previous three years. According to this the total Civil List charge for the year would be over £832,000, that is to say, a deficit of over £132,000 was anticipated. Of this total expenditure the household portion was expected to be as follows:

[1] C(H)MSS. 45/5, p. 1.   [2] See chapter 8.   [3] C(H)MSS. 45/5, p. 1.
[4] C(H)MSS. 45/5.

TABLE 2

Household below stairs	£94,326
Chamber	36,781
Great wardrobe	13,000
Robes	2,480
Stables	9,364
Works (and gardens)	17,300
Salaries paid at the exchequer	34,930
Band of pensioners	6,000
Privy purse	30,000
Goldsmith	4,000
Total	£248,181

If this is compared with the figures for the average expenditure of the household in Table 1 it would seem that the estimate of the coming deficit in 1721 was perhaps too low. For while the expected expenditure of the household below stairs is slightly higher than the normal actual charge—largely because it includes the cost of a summer's entertainment, though the king in fact went to Hanover in 1721—this is more than offset by the artificially low estimates for the great wardrobe and the board of works. These were both wished-for rather than anticipated expenses,[1] and they were together perhaps £25,000 below what these offices normally spent. If the household forecast was too low for 1720–1, the Civil List debt in that year might well have been even greater than £132,000. This may have been a little more than in most years, but debt was certainly its normal condition. It had been estimated at Michaelmas 1718 that the debt was then £396,206.[2] It had grown, that is, at the rate of almost £100,000 a year from the beginning of the reign; the annual deficit may well have been closer to £130,000 a year by 1721, as the Treasury estimate suggests.

If the annual deficit on the Civil List was between £100,000 and £130,000 in the first half of the reign of George I, it was a greater debt than Anne had accumulated on a slightly lower income. How much greater the Treasury discovered in 1720 when the estimate for the coming year was compared with the average expenditure on the various heads of the Civil List in Anne's reign.[3] This comparison revealed that in the household below stairs George I's expenses for the coming year were

---

[1] See below p. 128.   [2] C(H)MSS. 46/17.   [3] *Ibid.* 46/20/2.

almost £13,000 above the average of Anne's reign; of course the household figures for 1720-1 are rather inflated, as has been mentioned, but even so, George I's *average* expenditure in this department was almost £6,000 more than Anne's (£87,252 compared to £81,477). The difference can be largely accounted for in the cost of their respective 'diets', their own tables; Anne's was established at £2,800 a year, George I's at £7,665.[1] Similarly, the treasurer of the chamber's expenditure was up almost £8,000 a year in George I's reign over Anne's; the stables cost slightly more; and the total for salaries paid at the exchequer—partly because of the size of George I's bedchamber staff—showed a substantial increase. If the Treasury had been more realistic about the expenditure of the great wardrobe and the board of works, these too would have appeared in 1720-1 as higher than Anne's, but in both cases they compared the average expenditure in the previous reign with the total they *hoped* to keep George I's to and they were able, in this way, to show the expenditure decreasing in these offices. In fact, the average expenditure by the board of works in George I's reign was £1,000 a year more than in Anne's and that by the great wardrobe over £4,000 more.[2]

By 1718 the Treasury was well aware that expenses were increasing and that the Civil List was going into debt at a rate of rather more than £100,000 a year. A retrenchment was attempted.[3] But in 1720 the annual deficit seemed to be becoming even greater, and by then the problem was sufficiently acute for the government to raise the matter in the House of Commons. On 4 May 1720 Aislabie, the chancellor of the exchequer, acquainted the House with the existence of the debt and read a message from the king in which a solution was suggested. Two groups of men had been trying for some time—against the objections of the South Sea Company—to get charters of incorporation as insurance companies; they were now, indeed, willing to pay £300,000 each for them.[4] Nothing could be easier, it was suggested, than to grant the charters and to use the £600,000 to pay off the accumulated

[1] LS 13/44.
[2] The fact that some of the Hanoverian courtiers were given liberal allowances in the great wardrobe and the household until the retrenchment of 1718 helps to account for the increased expenditure of these offices. See below, p. 127.
[3] See below, pp. 127-9.
[4] For the rather shady dealings of these syndicates see J. Carswell, *The South Sea Bubble*, pp. 138-40.

8-2

debt on the Civil List.[1] A Bill was brought in immediately to enable the king to grant the charters. Sir William Wyndham moved that the king be asked to present an account of the Civil List debts, but this was swept aside—it was still widely believed that it was inconsistent with the king's honour to have the expenses of the household looked into[2]—and instead the Commons voted their thanks to the king for discharging the debt without raising new taxes.[3] The Bill passed the House of Commons on 31 May, and the London Assurance and the Royal Exchange Assurance Companies were incorporated in June 1720.

Unfortunately only £300,000 was collected from this source,[4] and on 11 July 1721 the Commons was informed that no more could be expected. The debts on the Civil List had not been discharged—they stood at £555,178 at Lady Day 1721 according to the accounts laid before the House by William Lowndes—and another method of raising money had to be found.[5] The king now proposed to raise £500,000 by selling annuities at 5 per cent and to finance them by taxing salaries and pensions paid out of the Civil List at the rate of 6*d.* in the pound.[6] A Bill to impose this tax was passed through all its stages by 21 July, and became law shortly thereafter.[7]

[1] *H.C.J.* XIX, 355–6; *P.H.* VII, 647.

[2] Oppositions often insisted on Parliament's right to inquire into the reasons for Civil List debts (see, for example, *P.H.* VIII, 455, 459–60), but Queen Caroline would have found general agreement when she said that 'the Civil List was given to the king with a discretionary power to do what he thought fit with it; and that the Parliament, since it made it his property without conditions, had no more business now to meddle with it, than they had to meddle with the private property of any other man in the kingdom' (Hervey, *Memoirs*, p. 684). Most men would have agreed with this sentiment in general, even though there may have been some doubts about its application to the case Caroline then had in mind—George II's refusal to grant the Prince of Wales £100,000 a year from the Civil List. Even Shippen, in a typically outspoken speech at the beginning of George II's reign in which he charged the previous administration with corruption, was very far from the spirit of Burke. He would have liked George II to be more economical than his father, but he did not claim that Parliament had the right to regulate the household if the Civil List did go into debt (*P.H.* VIII, 601–4).

[3] *H.C.J.* XIX, 356, 357; R. Chandler, *Debates*, VI, 214–15; Plumb, *Walpole*, I, 291.

[4] Carswell, *The South Sea Bubble*, p. 197.

[5] *H.C.J.* XIX, p. 628; the account is printed p. 629.

[6] *Ibid.* p. 628; *P.H.* VII, 856, 858.

[7] 7 Geo. I, c. 27; a clause in the Act discharged the Insurance Companies from the obligation to pay more than £150,000 each into the Exchequer.

Since £300,000 had been received from the sale of the charters, the Civil List had accumulated a total debt of £855,178 by 25 March 1721. This was at a rate, from the beginning of the reign, of about £125,000 a year. The rescue operations of 1720 and 1721 eased the immediate burden, but they had done nothing, of course, to solve the basic problem—the fact that expenditure exceeded the income by a considerable margin each year—and, inevitably, the Civil List went into debt again. By Michaelmas 1724 the debt totalled £508,364, having accumulated at just under £130,000 a year since 1721.[1] Again the problem was laid before the House of Commons,[2] and another plan was devised—a variant on that used in 1721 and using the same fund raised from Civil List salaries—to raise another £500,000 for Civil List purposes.[3]

The proportion of these Civil List debts that related to the household is not easy to calculate, especially from the figures presented to the House of Commons, because some of the Civil List categories— 'salaries paid at the exchequer', for example—are not separated in the accounts and are not easy to separate into their household and non-household components. A rough estimate is that in the statements of debt in 1718, 1720, 1721, and 1724, the household portion had accumulated at between £30,000 and £45,000 a year.

To summarize: the Civil List revenues during George I's reign produced the intended sum of £700,000 a year, but the expenditure exceeded this by £120,000 or £130,000. Out of the total expenditure of over £800,000, the royal household cost roughly £270,000, of which perhaps £30,000 to £45,000 went unpaid and accumulated as part of the larger Civil List debt. On three occasions during the reign, Parliament was acquainted with the existence of the debt, and with parliamentary approval a total of £1,300,000 was raised to pay it off. George I

---

[1] After the £500,000 had been raised in 1721 there was still remaining a debt of £55,178. The debt declared at Michaelmas 1724 was £508,364 (*H.C.J.* xx, 477) which meant that the accumulation in the period 25 March 1721 to 29 September 1724 was £453,186, a rate of £129,481 a year.

[2] *H.C.J.* xx, 477; *P.H.* VIII, 433 ff.

[3] The king was allowed to raise £1 million at 2*d*. per day per cent and to use half to pay off the annuities sold in 1721 and the other £500,000 for the Civil List debt. (11 Geo. I, c. 17). The deduction of 6*d*. in the £ was calculated in 1725 to be producing about £32,217 a year (*H.C.J.* xx, 477—but see C(H)MSS, 32/6 for a slightly lower figure) which was sufficient to pay the interest at the above rate on £1 million.

reigned for only a few weeks short of thirteen years, so that in effect he received an extra annual sum of £100,000, that is a total of £800,000 a year. But this was still not quite sufficient.[1]

The cause of the constant debt is clear: the Civil List grant was too low; or—and this explanation was most likely to appeal to Parliament—the expenditure was too high. The ministry could do nothing about the first, or at least there was never an attempt to do anything about it directly. But a curtailment of expenditure was a possible solution. The only authority capable of exercising control over spending departments and limiting their expenditure was the Treasury. To see what attempts were made to eliminate the household debt—for only that part of the larger Civil List debt is within our scope—it is now necessary to examine briefly the nature and extent of Treasury control over the household.

III

By the early eighteenth century the lord treasurer, or the lords of the Treasury, had gained sufficient authority over spending departments, including those in the household, to be able to exercise more than just a general supervision over their activities. The household paymasters received their money from the exchequer, but it could only be issued to them at the instruction of the Treasury. Treasury permission was also necessary before the money could be spent.[2]

The treasury board also regularly requested accounts from the household paymasters of what had been issued to them and for what purpose, and how it had been disbursed. Such departmental accounts were not called for with unvarying regularity, but they were not uncommon. After 1718 the Treasury also gathered in estimates of future expenditure. In September 1710 the household paymasters had been called upon to present an estimate of what they expected their expenditure to be in the coming year.[3] This seems, however, to have been an isolated case in Anne's reign; it came in a period when the Treasury was making a special effort to watch the Civil List closely, calling for weekly accounts

---

[1] At George I's death the Civil List was again, and inevitably, in debt—according to one estimate, by £491,156.

[2] S. B. Baxter, *The Development of the Treasury 1660–1702* (1957), pp. 68–71; for the complicated process by which money was issued see J. E. D. Binney, *British Public Finance and Administration, 1774–1792*, pp. 172–6.

[3] *C.T.B.* XXIV, 451.

of expenditure and making a weekly distribution of the available cash.[1]
This vigorous impulse did not last into George I's reign, but the practice
of asking for forecasts of future expenditure was revived in 1718, soon
after Sunderland became first lord of the Treasury. On 24 March, four
days after Sunderland's appointment, the spending departments were
asked to send to the Treasury an estimate of their expenditure to the
following Christmas; and in September an estimate of the coming
year's business was called for.[2] From these the expected expenditure of
the Civil List for the year beginning Michaelmas 1718 was calculated.[3]
Henceforth in this reign, estimates of future as well as accounts of past
expenditure were regularly requested.[4]

These estimates provided the Treasury with an up-to-date establishment of each office, and the control of expenditure depended on the
extent to which it could be 'established'. Extraordinary and incidental
expenditure could easily proliferate and get out of control. The departmental establishments were made up at the beginning of the reign,
largely by the officers of the department concerned, but they had to be
approved by the king.[5] George I obviously took some interest in them;
in 1716 the newly formed treasurer of the chamber's establishment
contained 'alterations made by his Majesty's special directions'. When
the king had signed them they were sent to the Treasury for the board's
approval. They could be changed at any time by the Treasury or by a
royal warrant.[6] Some of the establishments contain a good deal more
than wages and board-wages. The establishment of the household below
stairs, for example, included the amounts of ingredients needed and
allowed for each court table, including the king's, from which the

---

[1] *C.T.B.* xxiv, pp. 43, 52, 67, 84.

[2] *Ibid.* xxxii, 28, 576.

[3] There is a copy of this in C(H)MSS. 46/17.

[4] *C.T.P.* (1720–1728), pp. 78, 191, 434. Estimates of expenditures in the household
below stairs for the years commencing Michaelmas 1719, 1720, 1721, 1722, 1723,
and 1724 are in LS 13/176, pp. 131–2, 149–50, 172, 191, 205, 217.

[5] LC 5/156, p. 291.

[6] LS 13/115, fos. 3, 16; *C.T.B.* xxix, 298. The establishment of the household below
stairs for George I's reign is at LS 13/44; that of the treasurer of the chamber at
C.T.B. xxx, 317–23; an establishment of the fixed charges in the great wardrobe
for salaries and liveries at the beginning of George II's reign is at C(H)MSS.
45/18/8. The establishment of the robes was changed by the Treasury in 1716,
C.T.B. xxix, 780, xxx, 342; the establishment of the stables was changed in several
particulars by a royal warrant in April 1716 (LS 13/260).

annual cost of each could be calculated; and it listed the totals of bread, beer and fuel—the liveries—allowed to the household servants. But not all establishments were as finely drawn as this, and not all could be, for much court expenditure was irregular and could not be accurately planned for. Even in the household below stairs, there were 'extraordinary' expenses not foreseen in the establishment, such as those occasioned by a special entertainment or reception. But in this department such expenses, though sometimes substantial, were accounted for separately, were carefully controlled by the board of green cloth, and were not a great problem. Indeed they rarely amounted to more than one-tenth of the annual expenditure.

In other departments, however, a much higher proportion of the yearly charge could not easily be foreseeen. Of the expenses in the treasurer of the chamber's office, for example, only the wages paid there could be fully 'established' and they accounted for only about half of the annual expenditure. Most of the treasurer's business was to meet demands made by bills for goods delivered and work done. Only those named in the establishment could submit bills, but the amounts could not be foreseen with precision. This sort of expenditure was obviously hard to control. Some idea of its normal range was gained, of course, by experience; and in a sense the Treasury was trying to set an establishment for this expenditure when it asked for estimates of a coming year's business, for the treasurer of the chamber could provide this only by taking an average of the previous three or five years' totals for bills. But even with such a guide an establishment of payments could not easily be enforced, for they were so various and so variable. The treasurer of the chamber, for example, paid the bills of the stationers who supplied the secretaries of state's offices, as well as some household offices, with paper, pens and ink; and he paid the occasional bills of those numerous chamber servants, like the apothecaries, the locksmith, the instrument makers and many others, who, as well as receiving small fees, were paid for work performed.[1] But the largest such charge in this office arose out of the work of the forty messengers. Their bills for journeys and for arresting and keeping prisoners at the behest of the secretaries of state were very complex, for their charges were based on the distance travelled and a number of other variables.[2] Their bills had to be signed by six privy councillors or by the lord chamberlain or a

[1] C.T.B. xxx, 321.　　　　　　　　[2] Ibid. p. 320.

secretary of state and an account of them was kept by two chamber servants, the clerks of the cheque. But there was here, as with all bills, considerable opportunity for fraud, as was discovered when, between 1699 and 1701, a thorough investigation into messengers' bills and the work of the clerks of the cheque uncovered the existence of systematic cheating and the inflation of charges which had been connived at by the clerks.[1] As a result both clerks were dismissed and new rules were drawn up for the checking of messengers' bills.[2] The most important and practical improvement in the system, however, came in 1701, when the salaries of the clerks was doubled and their right to take fees from messengers was withdrawn.[3] Previously their own income had grown in proportion as the messengers' bills were inflated; with this inducement removed there was some chance that the clerk might attempt to act as a 'check' on the messengers. As will be seen presently, the situation in which men were expected to limit expenditure when their material interests were dependent to some extent on its growth was not uncommon, and was clearly a barrier to any long-term retrenchment.

The high proportion of expenditure on bills in the treasurer of the chambers' office and the difficulties of controlling it had led the Treasury in 1690 virtually to impose a new official on the department, the comptroller of the accounts of the treasurer of the chamber, whose duty it was to check the validity of the bills submitted.[4] The place was still filled in George I's reign and there is some evidence that he was still active;[5] but, as so often happened—as Burke was to say, the household was full of cheats watching cheats—he seems to have been as interested in his own profits as in saving the Crown's money.[6]

In the two sub-departments of the chamber that were spending offices, the jewel office and the great wardrobe, there was in George I's reign no provision for even this check, and in these offices, in which expenditure on bills made up a good part of their charge, the limitations of Treasury control over household expenditure were the most glaring. Both offices performed their tasks by virtue of the lord chamberlain's warrant to the master ordering plate from the jewel office and furniture and furnishings from the great wardrobe. In theory the Treasury con-

---

[1] *C.T.B.* XIV, 17, 40–2, 57, 58; XV, 10–12, 13–14.
[2] *Ibid.* XIV, 58, 275, 278, 327.   [3] *Ibid.* XVI, 80–1.
[4] *Ibid.* IX, 759; and see Baxter, *The Development of the Treasury*, p. 71.
[5] LC 3/53, fos. 124–5; *C.T.B.* XXX, 45.   [6] *Ibid.* XXVI, 44–5.

trolled their expenditure because the master of the office was required to send an estimate of its cost to the board before a warrant could be executed; and no work could be performed until the warrant had been counter-signed by the board.[1] However, the expenditure in both offices was out of control in practice. In the jewel office, which was the least serious case, the expenditure was always greater than that anticipated by the master's estimates because those who received plate were entitled to have it made up into such cups and bowls as they desired and, though the amount of plate used was strictly limited, the master had no authority to limit the amount spent on workmanship. In 1727 the master, James Brudenell, reported to the Treasury that between 1714 and 1724 the actual costs had been a quarter as much again as that estimated in the warrants (£39,957 as opposed to the estimated £31,700).[2]

The great wardrobe presented much more serious problems of control. At least in the jewel office the price of plate was fixed and known; in the great wardrobe the price of the materials and workmanship needed to execute the lord chamberlain's warrants was left entirely to the master. In George I's reign the great wardrobe was, and had been for some time, almost entirely independent of any superior authority. An investigation of the office by the Treasury in 1728 revealed that numerous attempts to impose some Treasury control on the master had all failed and he had continued to be a law unto himself.[3] The investigation of 1728 revealed that at no point in the great wardrobe system— between the receipt of the lord chamberlain's warrant and the final declaration of the master's accounts—was there any outside check or control. The estimated costs of work to be done on lord chamberlain's warrants that had to be sent to the Treasury might or might not be accurate, but they were never examined by anyone, and the warrants were counter-signed by the treasury board without any investigation.[4] Indeed there is some evidence that the Treasury did not bother to give even its formal authorization. In 1729 it was discovered that few warrants were counter-signed, and that the great wardrobe and other offices (sensibly enough) never waited for an authorization to come before proceeding with the work. The result was that of £9,734 spent by the

[1] *C.T.B.* xv, 209, xviii, 313; the warrants (and a note of permission for them to be executed) are included in *C.T.B.*

[2] T 1/260, fos. 113–14.   [3] T 1/266, fos. 223–31.

[4] *Ibid.* fo. 224.

great wardrobe on meeting the demands of lord chamberlain's warrants in the year prior to June 1729, the Treasury had authorized only £1,072.[1]

The investigation of 1728 revealed further that the master or his deputy were left to order whatever materials and workmanship might be needed, but they never did so by a written contract. Indeed not all materials were supplied even under a verbal contract, for, in many cases, materials were ordered simply with the instruction that they should be supplied 'at the cheapest price possible'.[2] As a result, and hardly surprisingly, the great wardrobe was paying from a third to a half more than the market price for materials.[3] The Treasury investigation further revealed that there was not even a check by the office itself on the quality of the work done in the royal palaces or on the quality and quantity of materials delivered into the office. Occasionally, the deputy master testified, a note was taken of deliveries but it was not normal practice.[4] The bills of the tradesmen and craftsmen were simply accepted as true and entered into the account, and the account—and this was the crux of the 'system' and the real explanation for the independence of the office—was accepted by the auditors of the imprests as it stood; the master of the great wardrobe enjoyed the unique and striking privilege of presenting his account without any accompanying bills and vouchers. There was no way that it could be checked therefore, and it was passed virtually automatically.[5]

It is difficult to know exactly how harmful this independence was in practice, that is, how wasteful of the king's money, but it is clear that the cost of materials was far higher than the market price, and doubtless the cost of labour was too. Also it can be noted that among the other departments, the wardrobe had the reputation of being wasteful as well as slow to do its work, and it seems to have been circumvented whenever possible.[6] It was probably much worse than other offices of the household. And the poorness of the great wardrobe system was particularly noticeable because the bulk of its expenditure was for work ordered by warrants and there was no attempt made to check on the fairness of the tradesmen's bills. But the abuses prevalent in this office were to some extent inherent in the other household offices.

[1] C(H)MSS. 46/46/1.   [2] T 1/266, fo. 224.
[3] *Ibid.* fo. 225.   [4] *Ibid.* fo. 224.
[5] *Ibid.* fo. 227.   [6] *H.M.C. Cowper MSS.* III, 109.

In 1718 the Treasury attempted to impose some control over the great wardrobe. This was not, it should be said, the first time that the Treasury had tried to regulate its affairs. In Charles II's reign, when other spending departments were coming under the close supervision of the Treasury, the great wardrobe had even then presented special problems; in April 1683 the Treasury had had to issue regulations for the office when it was discovered that the master had simply ignored their directions about how his money should be spent.[1] In 1699 an attempt was made to bring the wardrobe under stricter control by requiring the master to send an estimate of the cost of any work to be done in his office to the Treasury, and to wait for their approval before proceeding with it.[2] This check, if it had ever been effective, was no longer so in George I's reign. Towards the end of Anne's reign the Treasury again became very interested in the affairs of the wardrobe, and especially its curious privileges in the matter of accounting. Lord Oxford had in fact asked the auditors of the imprests to report to him on 'the present method of making up and passing the accounts of the Great Wardrobe'; and having read the report it seemed to him that many of the rules governing the office 'are fit to be renewed and others added'.[3] He ordered the auditors to draw up a new set of regulations. Eighteen months later, however, the secretary of the Treasury was pleading with the master, Montagu, to send the lord treasurer a much more detailed account of the debt in his office than the one he had submitted.[4] The wardrobe had escaped reform again. Then, in 1718, as part of a general retrenchment scheme, the Treasury moved once more to regulate the affairs of the office.[5] The fact that it failed again, and the extent of its failure, is perhaps a good measure of the difficulties of curbing the waywardness of an office headed by so important a figure as the duke of Montagu. The first decision in 1718 was to set an arbitrary limit of £18,000 a year on the expenditure of the office. In the following year, in an attempt to enforce this order, a new set of rules was drawn up for the office which were designed to bring a measure of Treasury control over its activities.[6] In particular, contracts were to be regulated. The Treasury created two new offices for the wardrobe, a comptroller

---

[1] Baxter, *The Development of the Treasury, 1660–1702*, p. 69.

[2] *C.T.B.* xv, 209.   [3] *Ibid.* xxvi, 390, 398.

[4] *Ibid.* xxvii, 446.   [5] *Ibid.* xxxii, 535.

[6] T 1/266, fo. 228.

and a surveyor, whose job it was to sign written contracts with the purveyors and see to it that they kept to them. But these orders were still-born; for some reason the great wardrobe was allowed simply to ignore them. Perhaps the political influence of the master, Montagu, was sufficiently powerful—and it must be remembered that the ministry was under considerable pressure in 1719, for Stanhope and Sunderland were facing both the hostility of the Germans at court and the opposition of Walpole and the Prince of Wales in Parliament.[1] Whatever the reason nothing more was heard in George I's reign of the comptroller and the surveyor of the great wardrobe. The idea was not forgotten, however, and in what may have been more favourable circumstances—at the beginning of a new reign, and with Walpole securely entrenched at the head of the Treasury—the full-scale investigation of the great wardrobe referred to earlier was undertaken in 1728. This uncovered with a wealth of evidence abuses previously known or guessed at but never fully documented, and the Treasury was now able to appoint a comptroller who reported to the board on the justice of tradesmen's bills. For a while at least the new system produced the desired results. In 1729 the new comptroller, John Hutt, reported to the Treasury on a group of bills submitted to the great wardrobe. He found that the cabinet maker's demand for £512 for work done at St James's and Kensington should be reduced by £316 because most of the work had not in fact been done; similarly, he thought a chairmaker was guilty of grossly overcharging and that his bill should be reduced from £240 to £132.[2] It was claimed in 1740 indeed that the rates now being charged by the tradesmen employed by the great wardrobe were so much lower than in George I's reign that the office was saving £5,000 a year on average.[3] This may well have been true, but if so the office was considerably busier than it had been in the previous reign, for its average annual expenditure was over £3,000 a year more.[4] The likelihood is that either the tradesmen had discovered ways of fooling even the Treasury nominee working in the great wardrobe, or and even more likely, the comptroller's vigilance had slackened with the years. New rules and new checks were the Treasury's normal response to such difficulties as they faced in the wardrobe. But the Treasury had previously failed to insist on its perfectly sensible rule that no work should

---

[1] See below, chapter 7.   [2] T 1/272, pp. 89–90.
[3] C(H)MSS. 45/28.   [4] *Ibid.* 45/29/1.

be performed by the wardrobe until it had been authorized. This slackness, coupled with the failure of the comptroller of the accounts of the treasurer of the chamber to bring that office's incidental expenditure under control, suggests that what was needed 'was not a better set of rules but adequate enforcement of any set of rules', as Professor Baxter has said of similar problems in an earlier period.[1]

No other household department was as independent of outside control in George I's reign as the great wardrobe. But its vices were different only in degree from those of other offices. It is clear that the control of incidental expenditure was a formidable problem for the Treasury, but there were many other difficulties too. In the household below stairs, for example, though written contracts were made with the purveyors, and though the Treasury occasionally asked to see them,[2] the board of green cloth acted quite independently in this matter. And the fact that numerous household purveyors were servants in the department, and often servants who were obliged to check the quantities and qualities of supplies coming into their offices, was hardly calculated to protect the king's interests. In the office of the robes—and doubtless in all offices that employed purveyors—merchants commonly paid the master, or mistress, for the privilege of serving the Crown, and then added something on their prices to make up for it.[3] This points to a further weakness in the system that was common to all offices: a substantial part of court servants' salaries, as will be seen in a later chapter, came from fees; and fees of poundage—a percentage of the money issued out of an office—were common to most paymasters. The fact that fees were taken on money paid to merchants and purveyors had two serious effects: the bills were increased to take it into account; and, what was much worse, the paymasters and others who benefited, had nothing to gain by trying to lower the expense of their office, for by so doing they would lower their own income. Some small steps had been taken towards remedying this situation by withdrawing the right to take fees in return for a fixed salary. The case of the clerks of the cheque for the messengers was noted above; and the clerks of the green cloth, the commissioners for the office of master of the horse, and the master of

---

[1] Baxter, *op. cit.* p. 70.
[2] *C.T.B.* xv, 51; xvi, 109.
[3] [Nathaniel Hooke], *An Account of the Conduct of the Duchess of Marlborough* (1742), p. 324.

the great wardrobe himself had also accepted fixed salaries.[1] But even if this reform was effective in their cases, it was not yet in George I's reign very widespread; the incomes of the cofferer and the treasurer of the chamber, to name only two major offices, were still dependent on fees taken on the money they handled.[2]

IV

By 1718 the Civil List debt had grown to such proportions that the Treasury took steps to effect some retrenchment. One obvious source of increasing costs was attacked immediately: the German courtiers. In the early years of the reign the expenditure of both the great wardrobe and the household below stairs was considerably increased by the demands made on them by some of the Hanoverian ministers and courtiers. They had food, fuel and candles from the household, after a ruling by the attorney-general that such grants did not infringe the clauses in the Act of Settlement forbidding grants of land, honours or offices to foreigners.[3] These allowances were substantial and they grew every year, especially Madame Schulenberg's and Madame Kielmann-segge's.[4] These ladies and other Hanoverians, including the Prince and Princess of Wales until 1717, were also allowed to furnish and repair their apartments at the king's expense, and lord chamberlain's warrants to the great wardrobe and to the Board of Works on their behalf were particularly frequent and particularly expensive.[5] The first step in the campaign to cut costs in 1718 was to curb the demands that the Hanoverian courtiers were making on the household departments. The king was persuaded to grant the two ladies a fixed sum of money instead of their previous allowance of food and supplies from the household below stairs;[6] in the following year they were also given money in lieu of furniture out of the great wardrobe.[7] This placed a ceiling on and eliminated the uncertainty of these grants, and it also reduced the possibility of fraud and wastage.

At the same time the expenditure of the great wardrobe was fixed

[1] See pp. 191, 196.　　　　[2] See below pp. 189–91.
[3] LS 13/115, fo. 36 (note of the attorney-general's report).
[4] See above, p. 80.
[5] See, for example, *C.T.B.* XXIX, 289, 388, 543, 752, 856; and vols. XXX, XXXI, XXXII *passim.*　　[6] See above, p. 80.　　[7] E.g. LC 5/157, pp. 296, 328, 426.

at a maximum of £13,000 a year and that of the Board of Works at
£14,400.[1] This was only the first step. In September 1718 as has been
seen, the Treasury called for estimates of the coming year's expenditure
and on the basis of these and the known deficit it was able to predict
the indebtedness of the Civil List a year hence. In conjunction with this
calculation an analysis was made of the Civil List expenditures and of
the ways in which it might be reduced.[2] These 'observations upon the
present state of the Civil List' are most revealing of the attitudes of the
Treasury towards reform and of the limits within which any reforms
would be restricted. It was suggested that £87,209 might be saved on
the Civil List account by various retrenchments, but there was much
more wishful thinking than there were concrete proposals in the
method outlined in the report. For example, it was stated that the
expenditure of the household below stairs should not exceed the average
of the establishments in force in the reigns of Charles II, James II,
William III and Anne. Since the estimate for 1718–19 was £20,441
higher than that average, it was announced that the household expenditure should be reduced by that amount. There was no inquiry as to
what the necessary expenses of the household were. But worse than
this, even if one grants the assumption that the household requirements
were unchanging (that what had once served Charles II was still sufficient) and that prices had not changed, even if that is granted, what is
missing from the Treasury report of 1718 is some indication of *how* this
reduction of £20,000 a year was to be made in the cofferer's account.
As for the treasurer of the chamber's establishment, it was to be reduced
by nearly £4,000. But how? All that the author of these 'observations'
could offer was the suggestion that the lord chamberlain should be
called on to exercise 'more care and good management with respect to
Bills', that is with respect to the warrants he signed ordering goods and
services for the chamber.

There were, however, a few realistic proposals in the report. Pointing
out that the great wardrobe could not be expected to keep its expenditure within the limit of £13,000 set for it under the present system,
the author made two suggestions. First, that a great saving would result
if the king stopped the lavish grants of furniture to the Hanoverian
courtiers; this was acted on in 1719 as has been seen. The second
proposal, the most radical of the whole paper, struck a jarring and alien

[1] C.T.B. xxxii, 535.   [2] C(H)MSS. 46/17.

note. It was nothing less than the total abolition of the great wardrobe on the grounds that it was so wasteful of money and so costly in salaries. This idea was not, however, to receive sympathetic hearing until 1782, when the office was abolished by Burke's Economical Reform Act and its business transferred to the lord chamberlain.

Some reduction of household expenditure—especially the burden of the Hanoverian courtiers on the great wardrobe and the household below stairs—may have resulted from the retrenchments of 1718. There is plenty of evidence that after this the Treasury at least remained closely in touch with the problems of the Civil List.[1] But the hard results of the retrenchment were obviously of minor importance, for the Civil List debt continued to mount. And without more radical changes than those suggested in the Treasury paper of 1718, it would have been difficult to effect the saving of upwards of £100,000 a year which alone could have kept the Civil List solvent. Apart from the proposal to abolish the great wardrobe, there was nothing in the report to suggest that the Treasury wished to undertake a fundamental attack on the system; there was no mention of the problems caused by fee-taking, by sinecures, by incidental expenditure. This was not because these were not understood to be fundamental problems. From the late seventeenth century on there had been enough fruitful reforms to suggest that there was a good deal of awareness that the difficulties of controlling incidental expenditure and the unwillingness to reduce expenses that fee-taking encouraged bedevilled any long-term retrenchment. As has been seen, a number of household officers had had their right to take fees withdrawn and their incomes set at a 'certainty'; in addition, some servants who had once submitted bills for their services had been given fixed salaries instead; and a number of minor offices had been abolished.[2]

---

[1] The annual estimates of forthcoming expenditure indicate this. And there are masses of papers among Sir Robert Walpole's manuscripts—surveys and analyses of revenues and expenditure, both retrospective and current, statements of debt, etc.—to attest to his continual interest in and battle with Civil List problems (C(H)MSS. 45 and 46).

[2] See p. 17; for some cases in 1685 see Baxter, *Development of the Treasury*, p. 205. In 1701 the master of the barges and the housekeeper of Hampton Court, among other servants, were deprived of their right to submit bills and were given a fixed salary; and by 1716 when the treasurer of the chamber's establishment was formed, a large number of chamber servants, including most of the housekeepers and surgeons, had had their income 'reduced to a certainty' in this way in the interests of economy (C.T.B. xxx, 317–19).

Reforms of this nature, minor in extent, but none the less effective and lasting, had been in progress slowly from the late seventeenth century. But it was one thing to recognize the value of such reforms in principle; it was quite another to apply them in a general way. The difficulties of effecting any large-scale reform of the system cannot be overestimated. Anyone who attempted changes had to overcome the inertia of the system; the self-interest that officials had in the *status quo* was a formidable obstacle. Henry Pelham put it clearly in a letter to his brother, the duke of Newcastle, in 1750:

The Civil List you know is much in debt...I have endeavoured to lessen the expenses at home as much as possible, and have succeeded as far as relates to my own Office, but a long series of uninterrupted extravagance to call it by no worse name, having got into all the great offices of the Kingdom, makes it very difficult, if not impracticable for the best intentioned to get the better of habit and custom.[1]

There were other besides human barriers. A proper reform of the Civil List could not have progressed very far without causing a fundamental change in the whole administrative and financial system. To consider only the financial problem, it would have required a considerable increase in the royal income, and therefore in taxes, to have abolished fee-taking and substituted salaries throughout the household and the departments of the central government.[2] Such rigidity was not to be shaken in an age searching for political stability, and an age that was not in any case faced with a crisis because of the financial and administrative system. Only when the system faced a widespread and widely felt breakdown, in the reign of George III, did the general application of such radical reforms as the abolition of useless offices at court and in the central administration and the conversion of fees to salaries become possible.

In the circumstances of the early eighteenth century perhaps only a larger income could have solved the problem of the Civil List debt. The author of the 'observations' on the Civil List of 1718, after reviewing the possible means of retrenchment, saw this, realistically enough, as the crux of the problem. If the king were allowed to keep the surplus revenue then being produced by the Civil List funds, instead of return-

[1] Add. MSS. 32721, fo. 355, quoted by J. W. Wilkes, *A Whig in Power* (1964), p. 172.
[2] For the fees taken in the household see chapter 6.

ing everything over £700,000 to the Aggregate Fund, the problem of the debt, he suggests, would be largely solved.[1] This solution commended itself to Walpole, among whose papers—even though he was out of office at the time of its composition—a copy of the 1718 analysis is to be found. In 1727 Walpole not only managed to get George II a guaranteed income of £800,000 a year, he also persuaded Parliament to allow the king to retain and use the surplus revenues of the Civil List funds.[2] Since these funds were then producing over £800,000 a year, and since George II refused for some time to give the Prince of Wales £100,000 a year as Parliament had expected, the problem of the Civil List debt was for the moment solved.

It was a short-term solution which only covered up the basic problems of the Civil List. These were to be tackled in a fundamental way only when, in the 1780s, the whole financial and administrative system was called into question following the disasters and humiliations of the American War.

[1] C(H)MSS. 46/17.   [2] 1 Geo. II, c. 1.

5

APPOINTMENT, PROMOTION, AND
TENURE OF COURT SERVANTS

I

To discover how men got jobs at court it is necessary to ask two questions: first, who had the right of appointment; and secondly, how was their choice determined?

The right of appointment was divided between the king and the heads of departments, though some middle-ranking officers appointed their subordinates. Generally speaking, the king appointed to all the major posts and some of the middle rank, and left the great mass of middle and lower posts to the great court officers, but the extent of the king's rights varied from department to department and was surprisingly uneven. Thus in the department below stairs, he exercised extensive rights over appointments; all the members of the board of green cloth, from the lord steward down to and including the clerks, and all the clerks and sergeants of the various offices that made up the department, were appointed by royal warrant.[1] The lord steward appointed the yeomen, grooms and pages,[2] while the lowest menial servants in the kitchens were appointed by the clerks of the board of green cloth.[3] Similarly, in the bedchamber department the king appointed the leading servants, the groom of the stole and the gentlemen and grooms of the bedchamber, while all the lesser posts—the pages, the laundress, and so on—were in the gift of the groom of the stole.[4] In the department under the lord chamberlain and in its offshoots, the king's rights were more circumscribed, at least in theory. Only the heads of the depart-

---

[1] LS 13/260; Add. MSS. 20101, fo. 55; Stowe MSS. 306, fos. 92–7.
[2] LS 13/261; Add. MSS. 20101, fo. 55; Stowe MSS. 306, fos. 92–7.
[3] LS 13/200 (notes of appointments at end of volume).
[4] This division was clearly defined in William III's bedchamber ordinances (Stowe MSS. 563). Earlier in the century the lord chamberlain had successfully claimed the right to appoint to places in the bedchamber since it was an office above stairs (Aylmer, *The King's Servants*, p. 70).

ment and sub-departments were Crown appointments, that is the lord chamberlain and the vice-chamberlain, the captains of the yeomen and the pensioners, and the masters of the robes, the jewel office, and the great wardrobe. For the most part these heads of sub-departments appointed all their subordinates.

Many of the great court officers thus had considerable patronage at their disposal. The lord chamberlain in particular disposed of dozens of honorific and financially attractive posts. He claimed the right not only to appoint all the servants on duty in the public rooms, including the gentlemen of the privy chamber and the ushers and grooms, but also all the king's physicians, surgeons and chaplains, the housekeepers, the officials of the office of ceremonies, the tradesmen and craftsmen engaged for the departments above stairs, the musicians, the watermen, the harbingers and all the other miscellaneous chamber servants including the principal painter and the Poet Laureate.[1] The only formal limitations on the lord chamberlain's sweeping claims to appoint most of the servants in his department seem to have been very minor ones. A number of lesser posts on the periphery of the chamber, including some that were only nominally court posts, were filled from outside the household;[2] but the bulk of the officers of his department were appointed (or at least the right of appointment was claimed) by the lord chamberlain.

The question is how much the heads of court departments freely exercised their rights of appointment, and it is a difficult question to answer. A number of places in the chamber were held by

---

[1] LC 3/13. Establishment of the lord chamberlain's department, 1727–33, with a list of 'places in the disposal of the Lord Chamberlain' at the end of the volume; and see LC 5/157, p. 188; *S.P. Dom.* 44/72, pp. 69–87.

[2] The post of comptroller of the accounts of the treasurer of the chamber, created in 1690 after the discovery of considerable frauds in the accounts of the department, was filled by a Treasury nominee (Baxter, *The Development of the Treasury*, p. 71); the secretaries of state seem to have appointed some at least of the messengers who acted as diplomatic couriers though they were still sworn into office by the lord chamberlain and could be dismissed by him, (Blenheim MSS. D 2/5; Add. MSS. 22221, fo. 251); similarly the master of the jewel office seems to have established a right to appoint the king's goldsmith (who dealt almost entirely with the jewel office) though it was a post under the lord chamberlain (*H.M.C. Townshend MSS.* p. 353); and the mayor and corporation of the City of London appointed their own sword bearer, who also appeared on the establishment of the lord chamberlain's department (*S.P. Dom.* 35/25, fo. 154).

patent[1] and the lord chamberlain's hold over appointments to these places was clearly more tenuous than over those that were appointed simply by virtue of his own warrants to a gentleman usher requiring him to swear the new entrant into office. The fact that the lord chamberlain found it necessary periodically to remind the signet office and the privy seal office of his rights, and to request that no grant for a chamber post be passed without his permission, suggests that lords chamberlain did not perhaps always enjoy their right.[2] But most chamber servants entered office by the lord chamberlain's own warrants.

Heads of other departments also appointed to places in their gift by their own warrants, and numerous examples can be found of the un-inhibited exercise of this patronage—by the lord steward[3] and the master of the great wardrobe,[4] for example. The duchess of Marlborough has left an account of how she disposed of the minor offices in her gift as mistress of the robes and groom of the stole which leaves no doubt that she filled the posts without reference to anyone. In *An Account of the Conduct of the Duchess of Marlborough*, published in 1742, the duchess merely lists the places in her disposal as mistress of the robes ('waiters, coffer-bearers, groom of the wardrobe, clerk of the robes, starcher, sempstress')[5] but there is a much fuller account in a manuscript version circulated among her friends while the duke and duchess were on the continent after she fell from favour at Anne's court. After describing how she disposed of the places of page of the back stairs to men recommended by her friends, she continues:

I gave the place of waiter in the Robes to Mr Curtis who married a woman that had served my children; I gave another place of the same kind to Mr Forster who was then in the service of the Duke of Marlborough and I made William Lovegrove coffer bearer who was also in the service of the Duke of Marlborough...I gave also a place of Coffer Bearer to Mr Woolrich and another place of Groom of the Wardrobe to Mr Hodges who were both

---

[1] Approximately seventy chamber officers held their posts by patent, including the physicians, surgeons and apothecaries, the musicians, wardrobe keepers, the sergeants at arms and the master of ceremonies. There is a list at LC 5/157, p. 188.

[2] See, for example, LC 5/157, p. 188.

[3] LS 13/261 (a book of appointments made by warrants from the lord steward).

[4] LC 3/33 (papers relating to appointments made by the master of the great wardrobe; mostly notes from the master to the clerk of the office notifying him of appointments).

[5] [N. Hooke], *An Account of the Conduct of the Dowager Duchess of Marlborough from her first coming to Court to the year 1710* (1742), p. 310.

servants in the family...Besides these I made Mrs Abrahal...the Queen's starcher and settled £100 a year upon her from the time of the Queen's first allowing me to regulate the office of the Robes...I gave also the place of Sempstress, to Mrs Rhansford...[1]

Of course the duchess was not an ordinary mistress of the robes. She had the power of a favourite to support her authority as a department head, but it seems clear that it was essentially as the latter rather than as the former that she made these appointments in her department.

Not only heads of departments but also a number of middle-ranking officers disposed of a few places under them entirely on their own authority. The clearest case is that of the four clerks of the board of green cloth who took turns to appoint the lowest servants in the kitchen and scullery—the door-keepers, turnbroaches, pankeepers and the like.[2]

On the other hand there is considerable evidence to suggest that the heads of court departments, and especially the lord chamberlain, whose authority extended over such a vast and decentralized collection of officials, did not always exercise their rights of appointment without interference or entirely on their own initiative. Such interference came from the king or, most commonly, from those close to him and with his support.

Direct interference by George I himself in the patronage of court officers was not common—at least there is not much evidence of it. One of his closest German advisers, Baron Bothmer, assured James Brydges at the beginning of the reign that in Hanover the king's rule was 'to leave to the several offices the disposition of all Employments which belong to their jurisdiction, or are dependent in any measure upon them, and that His Majesty never took it well when any other endeavor'd to interfere with them'.[3] Apart from one or two isolated

---

[1] From a copy made by Lady Cowper's daughter of 'An account of some matters of fact which relate to the Duchess of Marlborough's conduct at Court wrote by her Grace when abroad to some friends in England' (Panshanger MSS. Letterbooks, II, 91–2).

[2] LS 13/200: at the end of the book there are copies of certificates of appointment of men recommended by the clerks of the board of green cloth. And see LS 13/115, fo. 85 (minutes of the board of green cloth, 13 January 1719). 'Hester Lovett, necessary woman to the Board of Green Cloth, died this day and all four clerks gave her place to Jane Rowman. It was agreed that Mr Fielding should thereby not loose his right and turn to nominate a person to the next vacancy that shall happen.'

[3] HM, Stowe MSS. 57, vol. 10, pp. 259–60.

cases he apparently stuck to this, in so far as it applied to himself at least, in England. He seems to have appointed a confectioner to the household,[1] and on one occasion he apparently interfered in the patronage of the clerks of the green cloth by personally making an appointment to the lowly office of cartloader.[2] But such interference was rare in the department below stairs; indeed when, in the middle of the century, the duke of Rutland was 'directed or recommended' by George II to give someone a post that was in his disposal as lord steward, he resigned rather than submit to interference in his department that would, he protested, have meant his 'continuing with discredit and dishonour'.[3]

The lord chamberlain may, however, have suffered more in this regard than other heads of departments. Not all interference was as flagrant as is suggested by the case at the beginning of the reign of the lord chamberlain promising one man the post of king's printer, an office in his gift, only to discover that George I had given it to another.[4] But, since many of the servants in his department and in his gift were more personal to the king than those in other departments (except of course the bedchamber), the lord chamberlain could hardly expect always to select candidates at will, especially for such places as physician or surgeon to the person. The king's approval was therefore often sought for appointments even when the post was clearly in the lord

[1] The board of green cloth, investigating charges in 1716 against Charles Burroughs, a confectioner to the household, that he had publicly supported the Pretender, had said scandalous things about the royal family and in particular had used 'such indecent expressions concerning the King and Madam Kielmanseck [Kielmannsegge] as are not fit to be inserted', discovered that he had been appointed by the king himself only a few months before; or at least had been engaged 'by his Majesty's order to the Duke of Devonshire' who, as lord steward, had the right of appointment. Burroughs had accompanied the court to Hanover that summer, also on the king's orders to Devonshire. The king ordered him dismissed and sent home, and paid his wages to the day of his arrival in London—very lenient treatment which suggests that he was something of a personal favourite of the king's (LS 13/176, pp. 57–8). George was doubtless simply interested in the quality of his desserts; in a similar way he directed which of the three bakers was to make his own bread, though not in this case making an appointment (LS 13/115, fo. 90).

[2] In the list of appointments made by the clerks, Humphrey Wheeler is admitted as cartloader to the pantry, ewry and confectionery departments 'by His Majesty's direction' (LS 13/20: end of volume, d. 1 April 1725).

[3] Rutland to Newcastle, 28 May 1757, Chatsworth MSS. corresp. 1st ser. 140/14.

[4] Stowe MSS. 750, fos. 72–3.

chamberlain's gift. In 1723, for example, Newcastle, the lord chamberlain, wished to appoint Charles Jervas as principal painter following the death of Sir Godfrey Kneller. It was, or so he claimed,[1] his right to do so, but he did not make the appointment without first obtaining the king's permission. Indeed, it is clear he could not do so. Walpole wrote to Townshend, who was with the king in Hanover, 'The Duke of Newcastle begs you will not forget Jervas the painter. He has it much at heart to be dispatched'.[2] It was not until Townshend informed him that 'His Majesty approves of Mr Gervase [*sic*] to be the King's Painter'[3] that the appointment was made. Similarly, Newcastle sought permission to appoint a friend to the post of sergeant-at-arms, another place he claimed as part of his patronage.[4]

This was not of course, strictly speaking, a limitation of the lord chamberlain's rights since in both cases his candidates were appointed. But having to seek permission suggests a certain vulnerability to interference and it is clear that the lord chamberlain was on occasion reduced to giving formal approval to appointments made in practice by others. In August 1718, for example, the earl of Sunderland informed Newcastle that:

The King has been so good as to appoint Dr Goodman one of his physicians and has order'd me to acquaint your Grace with it that he may be putt upon the Establishment. I should not have mention'd anything of this kind when you was [*sic*] absent from Hampton Court, butt that I have had the King's promise ever since he came to the Crown and your leave to do it...you know I am no [page torn] nor frequent sollicitor and therefore I hope you will pardon this I have been so long engaged in.[5]

A Court officer with a vacant post at his disposal would often accept the recommendation of someone whom it would be unwise to offend—indeed one of the benefits of having posts to distribute was doubtless the pleasure of gratifying the great as well as clients—but it is clear that in the case of the appointment of Dr Goodman the lord chamberlain had no choice in the matter.

[1] LC 3/13. At the end of this establishment of the chamber, 1727–33, there is a list of 'places in the disposal of the Lord Chamberlain'.
[2] Coxe, *Walpole*, II, 290.   [3] Add. MSS. 32686, fo. 430.
[4] *H.M.C. Cowper MSS.* III, 118.
[5] Add. MSS. 32686, fos. 116–17. Dr Thomas Goodman entered office on 26 August 1718 (LC 3/7).

How normal such interference was or how often lords chamberlain sought royal approval of their appointments, it is very difficult to be certain. But it should not perhaps be over-emphasized. A suitor for the post of surgeon to the household who was trying to get Lord Cowper's support, told him that if he could 'make good interest to the King or Ld. Chamberlain I may get it still provided 'tis done quickly. What interest your Lordship has with the Ld. Chamberlain I cannot tell but hope tis good and then I shall be in some hopes...'[1] And certainly lords chamberlain filled a great many, and probably most, of the places in their department without referring their decisions elsewhere.[2]

II

Appointments to the most important places at court were made by the king. There were fifty or so posts that, though by no means strictly comparable, may be distinguished in terms either of honour and profit as being of the first rank. They were all in the king's gift.

How much George I was personally interested in appointments is difficult to discover since very little direct evidence has survived. He had a natural interest in diplomatic appointments[3] and it is well known that he was interested in improving the system of entry and promotion of army officers.[4] His interest in army appointments was not, however, in personalities, but in ensuring that the higher ranks were closed to all but experienced officers.[5] There is evidence of the king having personally

---

[1] Panshanger MSS. Bundle 'D', Francis Douce to Lord Cowper, 23 October 1714.

[2] For Lords chamberlain appointing to places in their department see, for example, Add. MSS. 33064, fo. 206; Coke (Melbourne) MSS. packet 106; LC 9/376, pt. 3 (a box including a book of warrants and orders signed by the lord chamberlain, 1734–45); LC 5/156–7 (*passim*) for the appointment of chaplains to the king; for another, promised, appointment as chaplain see *The Letter Books of the Earl of Bristol*, II, 380; LC 5/3, p. 28 (appointment of a master of the ceremonies; there is, however, some evidence that the secretaries of state had some say in the appointment of the master of the ceremonies, the officer responsible for the entertainment of foreign diplomats in London (see *C.T.B.* xiv, 125).

[3] D. B. Horn, *The British Diplomatic Service, 1689–1789*, p. 151.

[4] James Hayes, 'The Royal House of Hanover and the British Army, 1714–1760', *Bulletin of the John Rylands Library*, xl (1957–8), 328–57; Sir John Fortescue, *History of the British Army* (2nd ed., 1910), II, 29–31.

[5] Hayes, 'Royal House of Hanover'; Add. MSS. 32687, fos. 24–5; N.S.A., Cal. Br. Arch., Des. 24, England, 134 (newsletter of 8 March 1720 addressed to the Hanoverian

made appointments to places under the salt commissioners[1] and commissioners for wine licences[2] soon after coming to the throne. Of court appointments, it was said that James Craggs the younger was promised the post of cofferer to the Prince of Wales by George even before the death of Anne; Lady Mary Wortley Montagu thought that Craggs had had an affair with the countess of Platen who had introduced him to the Elector in Hanover.[3] According to another rumour Thomas Pulteney got the place of vice-chamberlain to the princess 'by speaking directly to the king himself',[4] but it seems clear that George did not often exercise his right of appointment personally. This was of course especially true at the beginning of the reign when a new court had to be established and his knowledge of those imploring jobs was extremely limited. Because the king often simply gave formal approval to appointments made by others, it cannot, however, be assumed that he was uninterested in the appointments. If instances of George I acting himself to make an appointment in his own gift, or to interfere in the patronage of others are rare, there is nevertheless a good deal of evidence to support the view that posts of any importance were filled only with his approval and that his approval was by no means given automatically. He refused to accept Charles Churchill, the illegitimate son of the brother of the duke of Marlborough, as a groom of the bedchamber to the Prince of Wales in 1714 because of his birth, even though Marlborough and the duke of Argyll, the prince's groom of the stole, spoke to the king in his favour.[5] Nor, in 1725, would he allow the post of out-ranger of Surrey to be given to the son of Lord King, the lord chancellor. Walpole was very anxious that Lord King's son should have the post but Townshend, who was with the king in Hanover, told him of George's reluctance to fill a place that might cause some interference in his hunting. 'Our master you know', he reminded Walpole, 'is very good, but he is

Secretary at War, Best, describing the new army regulations). The king made concessions to social rank in the Guards regiments but experience was also to be rewarded. Sunderland explained to the duke of Montagu in February 1720 that the king had refused to allow Colonel James O'Hara to purchase a troop of Guards because he believed that 'the troops of Guards must always be given to or allowed to be purchased by men of the first rank in England, or general officers of the oldest and longest service' (*H.M.C. Buccleuch and Queensberry MSS.* 1, 366).

[1] Add. MSS. 47027, fos. 367–8.   [2] *H.M.C. Egmont: Diary*, I, 19.
[3] Lady Mary Wortley Montagu, *Works* (1893), p. 129.
[4] J. J. Cartwright, *Wentworth Papers*, p. 432.   [5] *Ibid.* pp. 422, 423.

extremely nice in things of that nature.'[1] George demanded that a full report on the powers of the office be submitted to him by Francis Negus, the commissioner for the office of master of the horse. If that was satisfactory Townshend thought that their candidate 'may have it as soon as anybody'.[2] Walpole, who was in the country when Townshend's letter arrived, was sufficiently worried to request Negus not to submit a report until he got back to town.[3]

This is not, of course, of itself a very significant indication of George I's attitude to appointments. He was passionately devoted to the hunt and the fact that he was alarmed at the prospect of his pleasure being disturbed is understandable. But however minor an example, it does serve to illustrate that though George I may not have made many appointments of his own volition, he was nonetheless no cipher in the hands of his ministers. He was stubborn and he was strong. The following letter from Secretary Craggs to Lord Cowper, two men who must have known George I as well as any Englishmen in 1719, underlines the force of the king's personality, and his interest in appointments, very clearly. Cowper, who had in the previous year resigned as lord chancellor, had asked Craggs to press for the appointment of the earl of Essex as lord lieutenant of Hertfordshire. Craggs wrote to him on 9 November 1719 when the king was in Hanover:

...my own private opinion is that no recommendation would at this juncture engage the King to bestow these small marks of his favour upon the E. of Essex, which I imagined your Lordships acquaintance with your old Master's temper and thought did not leave you any more doubts than I have on that subject, and therefore I leave it with your Lordship whether you will have me make an application to H.M. upon his arrival [from Hanover] in your name...[4]

But even if George I was not totally uninterested in appointments in general, there is no evidence that he was especially concerned about the holders of household posts in the way that his son and great-grandson were. Ministers in George II's reign were reluctant to ask the king to dismiss members of his inner personal household who were opposed to the administration;[5] and George II complained when Newcastle, as

[1] Add. MSS. 32687, fo. 185.   [2] *Ibid.*   [3] *Ibid.* fo. 176.
[4] Panshanger MSS., corresp. bundle 'C'.
[5] In 1745, for example, when the Pelhams were negotiating with Pitt to get him into the ministry, he insisted as one of the conditions that two of Lord Granville's friends,

first lord of the Treasury, interfered in bedchamber patronage without his consent.[1] In the reign of George III, ministers were content to leave the disposition of important court places to the king.[2] If there is no evidence in George I's reign of any such royal insistence on personal control over household appointments it is because the king was consulted on all important appointments. It might also be said of course that George I had little reason to care deeply about court appointments since he had little to do with his English household servants. This was especially true of the first two years of the reign, but even after 1717, when he began to meet company regularly, he continued to maintain a German 'inner-court',[3] so that the personal character of his English private servants could not have meant as much to him as it did to George II. But it would be unwise to conclude from this that George I did not care at all about household appointments or that the court became the plaything of the politicians. On the contrary, appointments to important court posts as to other important posts were made in the closet, if not by the king himself then only with his approval.

The king's choice was all-important, but of course he was open to advice—advice which could come from many sources. In one department at least, the stables, the head of the department on occasion played some part in the filling of posts under him that were in the king's gift.[4] In 1723 the recommendation of the commissioner for the office of master of the horse, Francis Negus, seems to have been important in the

---

William and Edward Finch, be removed from their court posts. They were vice-chamberlain and groom of the bedchamber respectively and were therefore part of the 'inner' court, in personal service to the king. They had survived the fall of Granville in the previous year, 'doubtless', as Dr Owen says, 'because the ministers did not care to incur the King's wrath by insisting on the dismissal of his personal servants' (Owen, *Rise of the Pelhams*, pp. 247–8). When Pitt demanded their removal the Pelhams refused even to ask the king (*ibid.* pp. 285–6); and in the following year when other Granville supporters were removed from office, the Finches still survived. Newcastle said on this occasion that they obtained all the removals they wanted except 'the vice-chamberlain which the King begged us not to insist upon in such a manner and said he should take it so kindly if we did not do it, that in the opinion of every body it would have been indecent to have pressed it. As to Ned Finch, we all thought the Bedchamber could not be Attacked' (*English Historical Documents*, ed. D. B. Horn and Mary Ransome, x, 1714–83, p. 111).

[1] Yorke, *Hardwicke*, ii, 215–16.

[2] R. Pares, *George III and the Politicians*, pp. 144–6.

[3] See chapter 8. [4] *The Present State of the British Court* (1720), p. 58.

appointment of a page of honour. Negus wrote in November, when George I was in Hanover, probably to Lord Townshend, who was with the king:

I have not troubled his Majesty upon any things which have happened relating to the stables, because I did not think they were of such consequence but that they might wayt till his Majestys return for his orders, but hearing lately that his Majesty has been troubled with two solicitations for a Page of Honours place upon Mr Bloodworths[1] having a commission in the army, I take this opportunity to let you know how that matter past as farr as it came within my knowledge. Some little time before His Majesty left this place the Duke of Kingston spoke to me concerning Mr Villars[2] and desired I would recommend him to the King upon the first vacancy. I told his Grace that his Majesty had been already sollicited in favour of Lady Irby's son[3] and I believed would give it to him. For that I had at Mr Walpole's desire represented him to His Majesty as a young gentleman deserving his compassion and favour... whereupon I indeed understood that his Majesty gave his consent, and that I had leave so to informe Mr Walpole.[4]

The advice of heads of departments was not generally sought, however. Even if it had been, the decision was made by the king and this decision could be influenced by many people with access to him. Negus, in the example quoted above, may have been consulted and may have recommended Walpole's candidate, but that was not the end of the matter. Other contenders had a line to the king, and Walpole had to press Sir William Irby's claims in the closet; or rather, since the king was in Hanover, Townshend had to. Townshend wrote to Walpole in September 1723

I must beg your pardon that I do not send you the King's commands in relation to Sir Wm. Irby this post...I must acquaint you that since my writing to you on this subject, the Dutchess [of Kendal] pleads a prior promise made to one Willard. However I will certainly get it for Sir Wm. Irby if it can be done without disobliging her which I am sure you will not desire.[5]

---

[1] Thomas Bloodworth, page of honour 1714–24; commissioned in the Foot Guards 1724 (Dalton, *George I's Army*, I, 219, n. 23); member of Parliament for Bodmin 1741–7.

[2] ?Walter Villiers, page of honour, May 1724–7.

[3] For Sir William Irby, see above, p. 104.   [4] *S.P. Dom.* 35/46, fo. 86.

[5] Stowe MSS. 251, fo. 30. On 25 September Townshend wrote: 'I hope Sir Wm. Irby's business will succeed and that I shall get the Duchess to desist...' (Stowe MSS. 251, fo. 48). Irby was appointed in February 1724.

It is important, therefore, in considering how appointments to the leading posts were made to consider those who had habitual access to the closet. For the first few years of the reign at least, the dominant influence on the king came from the German ministers who accompanied him to England. These men—especially Baron Bernstorff, Baron Bothmer and Bernstorff's secretary, Jean Robethon—drew great strength in England from their initial monopoly of the king's favour. They had immense power, but no responsibility outside the court.[1] The extent of their influence on appointments was most noticeable at, though it was not confined to, the beginning of the reign, when a new court had to be established and when George I knew few Englishmen personally and it provides striking demonstration of the importance that such 'courtiers' could attain.

The Germans 'pretend to have nothing to do with the English affairs', Peter Wentworth wrote to his brother, the earl of Strafford, in October 1714, two weeks after George I arrived in England, 'yet from the top to the Bottom they have a great stroak in recommend[ing] Persons that are fit to serve his Majesty. Most, nay All the Addresses are made to Mons. Bothmar he having been so long in England is suppos'd to know all the English.'[2] The value of the Hanoverian ministers as channels to the king was not lost on place-hunters; Wentworth's judgement is abundantly supported by Bothmer's correspondence.[3] Bothmer was the Hanoverian envoy in London when Queen Anne died and during the next six weeks, while preparations for George I's journey were made, he was the principal link between Hanover and London. His letters to Bernstorff and Robethon during August and September are full of advice about filling posts in the new court and ministry. Many of those recommended were proposed of course by Englishmen, particularly by the Whig leaders—'our friends', as Bothmer called them—with whom he had been in contact since his arrival in England earlier in the year. Bothmer was the channel by which all applications were forwarded. He wrote to the king directly at first until he became afraid that he was pestering him too much. He then wrote only to his colleagues. Robethon kept a list of those Bothmer

[1] See chapter 7.
[2] Cartwright, *Wentworth Papers*, p. 427.
[3] Bothmer's letters to Hanover are among the Robethon papers in the British Museum, Stowe MSS. 222–32.

had recommended,[1] and Bernstorff sought the king's approval from time to time.[2] By this means most of the important changes and new appointments in the royal household were decided before George I arrived in England.

There were not in fact many changes made, at least in the household, and they were confined almost entirely to more important posts and involved reinstating Whigs who had been dispossessed by the previous Tory ministry.[3] Except for two of the four clerks, the entire board of green cloth was changed, but there were very few other removals in 1714 and those only of minor importance. There were, however, creations as distinct from changes, for there had naturally been no gentlemen or grooms of the bedchamber in the household of Queen Anne and these twenty important places had to be filled. There were many candidates— according to one estimate there were fifty for the eight grooms' places[4] —and Bothmer was at the centre of the pushing and intriguing competitors.[5] He suggested, or at least supported, some of the major appointments made in the department below stairs,[6] but it was in the filling of these vacant bedchamber posts that his advice seems to have been most influential. The duke of Grafton and the earl of Manchester asked for and got his recommendation and were appointed gentlemen of the bedchamber;[7] the earl of Dorset who carried the news of the queen's

[1] Stowe MSS. 227, fos. 294–5 (Bothmer to Bernstorff, 10/21 August 1714).

[2] 'Ayant pris la liberté d'écrire au Roy sur la disposition de quelque emplois icy, je n'ose pas m'adresser de nouveau immediatement a luy. Je prendray recours à vous Mr. pour un pareille sujet affin que vous puissiés en faire la proposition selon que vous le trouverés a propos' (Stowe MSS. 227, fo. 273: to Bernstorff, 6/17 August 1714). 'Je me donne l'honneur de vous écrire aujourdhuy une lettre et un p.s. touchant quelque emplois dont le Roy pourit desposer en faveur des personnes qui l'ont merité. Je crois que vous pourriés montrer l'une et l'autre a S.M. Je vous prie de me faire scavoir son intention ou même de me faire avoir ses orderes sur ce que je dois dire aux personnes qui m'ont parlé de ces emplois' (Stowe MSS. 227, fo. 277: to Bernstorff, another letter of 6/17 August 1714).

[3] Changes at court in 1714 are discussed at greater length below.

[4] Add. MSS. 31144, fo. 507.

[5] 'Je souhaite fort que vous veniés bientost', Bothmer wrote to Robethon in September, 'car les briques pour les charges et les voix [?] tenues aupres de moy pour des recommendations augmentent a measure que l'arrivée du Roy approche. Les gens disent que j'ay une liste de ceux qui pretendent aux charges longues comme le Mall' (Stowe MSS. 227, fos. 439–40).

[6] Ibid. fos. 273–6.   [7] Ibid. fos. 293–4, 319.

death to Hanover was given a bedchamber post as a reward for his journey, at Bothmer's suggestion;[1] and the earl of Lincoln, strongly supported by Townshend, was mentioned several times in Bothmer's letters to Bernstorff and Robethon as deserving of an appointment.[2] He too got a bedchamber place. At least four of the grooms appointed at the beginning of the reign—Dormer, Tyrrel, Honeywood and Ker— probably owed their places to Bothmer;[3] and it was rumoured that another groom, William Breton, got his place by bribing some of the German ministers.[4]

Bothmer's advice about bedchamber appointments seems to have been decisive in 1714. Not only were many of those appointed recommended by him, but it was also perhaps on his advice that the important post of groom of the stole was not filled immediately.[5] But the influence of the German ministers was not limited to household appointments or to the beginning of the reign, though there was naturally more scope for their suggestions in 1714 when there were more posts to be filled and when they virtually monopolized the king's ear. Surviving correspondence between Bernstorff and Lady Cowper[6] and between James Brydges (later earl of Carnarvon and duke of Chandos) and all the leading German courtiers[7] provides ample evidence of their continuing influence after 1714 and on other than household appointments.

[1] Stowe MSS. 227, fos. 317–18.   [2] Ibid. fo. 317.   [3] Ibid. fos. 293–4, 309–10, 337–40.
[4] Add. MSS. 31144, fo. 528.   [5] See above, p. 56.
[6] Lord and Lady Cowper became friendly with Bernstorff soon after his arrival in England and, with Lady Cowper acting as translator for her husband, a correspondence was established that proved beneficial to both sides. Bernstorff was able to get information about discussions at Cabinet meetings—from which he was debarred —and, after he left England in 1720 shorn of his power, he was able to keep in touch with English affairs by means of the Cowpers. On their side Lord and Lady Cowper found Bernstorff willing to urge the merits of their candidates for offices both ecclesiastical and civil. By Bernstorff's influence for example, Lady Cowper got Sir David Hamilton, Queen Anne's principal physician, retained in 1714 and also got him made physician to the Princess of Wales. Their advice on ecclesiastical promotions was also accepted, indeed it was solicited. Bernstorff's letters to Lady Cowper are among the Panshanger MSS. There are also transcripts of them in the letterbooks made by Lady Cowper's daughter. See Letterbooks, III, 135, 136, 153; V, 202, 203, 241–55, 266, 281–4; VI, 3–5, 71–8; and see Lady Cowper, Diary, pp. 12–13, 32.
[7] James Brydges established friendly relations with all the leading Hanoverian ministers in London. The strength of the friendship owed a good deal to his liberal purse and

Their meddling in appointments was not accepted by the king's English ministers without complaint. In September 1716 Townshend complained to Stanhope, who was in Hanover with the king, about Robethon's and Bothmer's interference in Scottish patronage.[1] Later in the summer, when it was clear that his position in the ministry was being undermined by a combination in Hanover of Sunderland and the Germans,[2] Townshend wrote more fully to Stanhope on this subject. All his and Walpole's troubles he blamed on their 'enemies about the King', and he concluded with this explanation of Bothmer's enmity towards them:

I am very sure that all these malicious insinuations to Walpole's and our prejudice arise from Bothmer, who has every day some infamous project or other on foot to get money; and these disappointments in these particulars are what he cannot bear, having nothing in his view but raising a vast estate to himself; and therefore he will never be satisfied till he has got the Ministry and Treasury into such hands as will satiate his avarice, at the expense of the King's credit, interest and service.[3]

It must be remembered of course that at this time Townshend desperately needed Stanhope's support in the closet and this doubtless added bitterness and exaggeration to his condemnation of Bothmer. But Townshend's was not the only complaint. When, for example, in June 1719 it was rumoured that another Hanoverian minister, Baron Görtz, was to return to England with the king, secretary Craggs wrote to Luke Schaub in Paris:

I have but one objection to Görtz's coming which is the filling of a new purse. It is incredible what prejudice all these sales of offices and other underhand dealings occasion to the King's Service; for to compleat our misfortune, I have remarked that there is no distinction of persons or circumstances.

he made a wise investment. By means of the Germans' influence Brydges got the promise of an earldom for his father, and when his father died before it could be conferred, he was himself raised to the earldom of Carnarvon in October 1714. He also got the deanship of Carlisle for his brother, and a reversion to the office of clerk of the hanaper for his son. He was himself offered a household post by Bothmer in 1714—either the comptrollership of the household or the treasurership of the chamber—which he declined (HM, Stowe MSS. 57, vol. 10, pp. 240–2; vol. 11, pp. 34–7, 52–3; vol. 12, p. 78; vol. 14, p. 321; C 66/3513/7).

[1] Coxe, *Walpole*, II, 93.
[2] J. H. Plumb, *Walpole*, I, 222–42; and see below chapter 7.
[3] Coxe, *Walpole*, II, 119.

Jacobites, Tories, Papists, at the Exchange or in the church; by land or by sea, during the session or in the recess, nothing is objected to provided there is money.[1]

Whether offices were sold as blatantly as this is not at the moment at issue here. Craggs' complaint is obviously exaggerated but it does suggest that English ministers not only resented the fact that their own patronage was diminished by German interference, but also that the patronage of the Crown was not perhaps being used in a way that might strengthen the administration. How much then did the ministers who carried on the king's business in parliament control or try to control appointments to court posts?

That it was in the interests of ministers to be the main channel to preferment needs little emphasizing. The 'favour of the closet' was as important to ministers as a stable majority in the House of Commons—indeed it was perhaps the necessary precondition of such a majority. Without it, without the full support and confidence of the Crown, ministers would be open to frustrations and rebuffs in the closet over policy, and open to desertions and weakening of support in Parliament.[2] One of the clearest indications of royal confidence was the ability to get jobs and honours for friends and supporters, or would-be supporters; it is a minor but significant point to notice in this regard that when the Pelhams returned to power after their joint resignation in February 1746, when, as Dr Owen makes clear, they possessed for the first time the confidence of both the king and the House of Commons, they demanded that the king should 'dispose of vacant Garters in such a manner, as to strengthen, and give a public mark of his satisfaction in, his administration'.[3] Influence on appointments to offices in the king's gift similarly gave evidence of royal support, and such evidence was particularly valued by rival factions within the same ministry struggling for supreme control over the king's affairs. There was bitter conflict over appointments, for example, between Walpole and Sunderland during the years 1720–22, on one occasion over the treasurership of the chamber.

The dispute was over the appointment of Charles Stanhope, Lord

[1] Add. MSS. 9149, fos. 143–4.
[2] This point is fully developed for a later period in J. B. Owen, *The Rise of the Pelhams* (1957).
[3] Quoted *ibid.* p. 299.

Stanhope's cousin. Stanhope, as secretary of the Treasury, had been implicated in the South Sea affair, accused of corruption and only narrowly acquitted in the House of Commons.[1] Forced to resign his office, Stanhope was promised the treasurership of the chamber which Henry Pelham vacated on his promotion to the treasury board in April 1721. This 'vindication' of Stanhope was urged by Sunderland, Carteret and Newcastle, and the king apparently agreed to make the appointment as soon as Parliament rose in the spring or early summer of 1721.[2] Walpole, however, argued that so soon after his acquittal by only three votes Stanhope's re-entry to office might inflame the House of Commons and revive criticism of the court and ministry. He counselled the king to delay the grant until the end of the 1721–2 parliamentary session, and George agreed that it would be wise to wait.[3] Stanhope was unwilling to wait so long. He petitioned the king on 21 August 1721 to grant him the office immediately because his reputation would suffer if he should 'appear to the world as thought by your Majesty unworthy of the honour you before intended me'.[4] Four days later he had an audience with the king and repeated his complaint. He wrote to Newcastle on 26 August:

I yesterday desir'd an audience of the King and represented to him the great uneasiness I was in, to the same purpose as in the letter I had sent him. He told me the world shou'd see he had a good opinion of me by his giving me the place which he had before promis'd me: and that a month or two's delay was of little consequence but that at present to do it was not proper for his affairs. I told him I suppos'd my friend Mr Walpole had suggested that to him at which he smiled, and call'd me back smiling to ask me if I cou'd get into Parliament, which Mr Walpole had suggested to him I cou'd not. I told him I thought I cou'd, if it was necessary for so short a time. Thus your Grace sees I am defeated for the present to my great mortification and the alarm of my Lord Sunderland's friends. But seeing the King determin'd in the point, and his otherwise gracious behaviour I have been persuaded to take the bitter pill as patiently as things of this nature can be by one who did not expect them.[5]

Stanhope was content to wait after this because, as Carteret said, the king 'spoke to him very kindly'.[6] This appointment (which was made

---

[1] J. Carswell, *The South Sea Bubble*, pp. 241–2; Plumb, *Walpole*, 1, 365–6.
[2] Add. MSS. 32686, fos. 183–4.   [3] *Ibid.* fos. 185–7.
[4] Add. MSS. 9150, fo. 56 (a copy of an English draft of a letter sent to the king in French).   [5] Add. MSS. 32686, fo. 191.   [6] *Ibid.* fo. 193.

as promised in March 1722) was not perhaps as direct a threat to Walpole's authority as first lord of the Treasury as has been suggested, but its postponement was clearly a victory for Walpole and was looked upon as such by Sunderland and Carteret.[1]

The importance to rivals for power of being able to influence appointments can be seen even more clearly in the period after Sunderland's death when Carteret tried to maintain intact the remnants of the Sunderland faction as a counter-weight to the Walpole–Townshend (and, now, Newcastle) group. The struggle between the two factions within the ministry is suddenly illuminated in the summer of 1723 when George I went to Hanover, taking with him both secretaries, Townshend and Carteret; the course of the conflict can be followed from one side at least in the letters that passed between Walpole and Newcastle, in London, and Townshend.[2] Walpole was particularly concerned that it should not appear in London that Carteret was dominating the king's councils or that the ministry was about to break up. 'The prospect of changes', he warned Townshend, 'always animate the discontented

[1] Plumb (*Walpole*, I, 366) has suggested that Walpole's authority in his own department was threatened by this appointment. As Owen has pointed out (*E.H.R.* LXXII, 1957, 331) the treasurer of the chamber was under the lord chamberlain's jurisdiction, not the Treasury's. This is quite true but that does not itself settle the question. The treasurership of the chamber was held by patent (see, for example, C 66/3535/7) and there seems to have been a dispute in 1721 if not about who had the right of appointment to the post, then about whether the secretary of state or the lords of the Treasury had the right to issue the warrant necessary to begin the grant-making process. Among the *State Papers, Domestic*, there is an undated and unsigned memorandum which can probably be assigned to this period. It reads: 'Pray send me a Md. of all ye Tr. of ye chamber you can find wch began in ye Secr: Off. for I find it will be disputed. Let me know too wch. arose in ye Treasury. Mr Pelham says his did' (*S.P. Dom.* 35/40, fo. 70; and see fo. 65 for a list of 'Treasurers of the Chamber arising in Secry. of State's office'). If the memorandum does belong to this period then the dispute between Carteret, one of the secretaries of state, and Walpole was clearly over more than just the timing of the appointment. Carteret certainly took the delay as a blow to his and Sunderland's position. Charles Stanhope in the letter quoted above spoke of the 'alarm of my Lord Sunderland's friends' and Carteret told Newcastle on 22 August 1721 that the King's decision had 'mortified Ld. Sunderland and me not a little' though in the same letter he reassures Newcastle that they have not 'lost any ground with ye King' (Add. MSS. 32686, fo. 185).

[2] Extracts from many of these letters are printed in Coxe, *Walpole*, II; and see on this Plumb, *Walpole*, II, ch. II.

and disaffected',[1] and the consequence, if changes seemed imminent, would be a weakening of their support in Parliament. The 'discontented' in 1723 were, most prominently, followers of Lord Sunderland who, unlike Newcastle, would not acquiesce in the domination of the administration by Walpole and Townshend. Lord Cadogan, master general of the ordnance and master of the robes, Lord Berkeley, first lord of the Admiralty, Lord Macclesfield the lord chancellor, the duke of Roxburgh, secretary of state for Scotland and Lord Carleton, lord president of the council, were prominent among those who followed Carteret within the ministry.[2] During the summer of 1723 they were busy spreading rumours of Walpole's impending eclipse and of Carteret's triumphs in Hanover. Walpole complained to Townshend that their enemies in London were boasting of their power and their favour at court. The king, he wrote, 'must be persuaded to make it very plain on one side or other'; if they were to retain the full support in Parliament of this dissident faction it would be necessary to prove their strength at court and their favour with the king. 'I am sure', Walpole wrote on this occasion, 'that 'tis impossible to have lord chancellor, or lord Berkeley, but by shewing them that we have the power...'[3]

The most striking demonstration of 'power' was the ability to influence the king's appointments to the court and administration. As Townshend told Walpole, after assuring him that the rumours that Carteret had entirely replaced him in the king's favour were false, 'The quickest and most effectual way for undeceiving people of all denominations in England, would be by obtaining some overt act in our favor.'[4] Thus, the conflict between the two factions in the ministry turned in good part during this summer on attempts to get rival candidates named to vacant posts, to create the appearance of power and thereby to suggest its substance. It was no easy task, as Townshend repeatedly complained, to keep the king 'steady' in Hanover where Carteret found allies among Germans, including Bernstorff, who were willing to help upset the ministry in the hopes of gaining or regaining influence over the king.[5] Throughout the summer the struggle over appointments continued.

[1] Coxe, *Walpole*, II, 265–6.
[2] C. B. Realey, *The Early Opposition to Sir Robert Walpole*, p. 117; Plumb, *Walpole*, II, p. 50; *H.M.C. Onslow MSS.* pp. 465–73.
[3] Coxe, *Walpole*, II, 276.   [4] *Ibid.* p. 255.
[5] See chapter 6.

On one occasion, after 'a fair battle before the King' over an appoint-ment to an expected vacancy as commissary-general of the army,[1] the king declared in favour of Townshend's candidate. This was a particularly sweet victory since the rival candidate was supported not only by Carteret but also by Cadogan, the master general of the ordnance, in whose province the vacancy fell.[2] Townshend warned Walpole on this occasion not to make this victory over their rivals 'a matter of triumph', adding, in a phrase that must dispel any lingering doubts about George I's part in making appointments or his concern for English affairs, 'the less we boast, the more we shall certainly have to boast of'.[3]

A vacancy among the gentlemen of the bedchamber, one of the most honourable and attractive of court posts, was also a subject of dispute during the summer; the details of the conflict provide further evidence that George I played a decisive part in appointments to court posts. Several candidates solicited the post including the duke of Rich-mond,[4] Lord Tankerville,[5] Lord Howard of Effingham[6] and the duke of Kent, who had a particularly strong claim in that he had been suc-cessively in the reign a gentleman of the bedchamber (1714–16), lord steward (1716–19) and lord privy seal (1719–20) and had been ap-parently promised a bedchamber post.[7] Walpole seems to have sup-ported Richmond initially but he soon cooled towards him when it became clear that Richmond was uninterested in his help.[8] But Walpole was removed from the important battlefield. In Hanover the bed-chamber place became another issue in the conflict between Townshend and Carteret. At the beginning of August, Carteret applied to the king in favour of his own candidate, Lord Glenorchy.[9] Townshend, who favoured Richmond, despite Walpole's reservations, sought to avoid

---

[1] It was thought that the holder, Sir William Strickland, was dying, though in fact he recovered.

[2] Coxe, *Walpole*, II, 273.   [3] *Ibid.* p. 274.

[4] Add. MSS. 32686, fo. 285.   [5] *Ibid.* fos. 287, 304.

[6] *S.P. Dom.* 35/66, fo. 14; Add. MSS. 32686, fo. 287.

[7] Stowe MSS. 251, fo. 38.

[8] Walpole told Newcastle that he had been visited by both Richmond and Cadogan and neither had mentioned the bedchamber post which meant, he concluded, that 'they have made their application directly themselves and will try it upon their strength' (Add. MSS. 32686, fo. 285).

[9] Stowe MSS. 251, fos. 23–4.

open disagreement and to avoid serious defeat by advising the king not to fill the vacancy until his return to England. This was accepted and, apart from a suggestion from Walpole that the duke of Kent might be given a pension of £3,000 a year in compensation if he was not given the post,[1] the matter rested, and no appointment was made.

George I had not perhaps played a very prominent part in the appointment of those in the first rank of court posts in 1714, but it seems clear that thereafter his was the most important voice in their selection. There is no evidence to suggest that ministers such as the first lord of the Treasury or the secretaries of state had established any claim to speak with particular authority in the filling of such places. In so far as they had access to the closet and the king accepted their advice, the leading ministers naturally had great influence on appointments, but their influence was maintained only by hard work.

III

In this discussion of who made appointments to court posts we have already gone some way towards answering the related question of why appointments were made, of how aspirants to office actually got jobs. The simplest answer to that question is: by bringing influence to bear on those who could make appointments. Who had to be influenced depended in part on the post that was sought. For a middle-ranking or a lower post the support of powerful friends naturally was helpful, but not always necessary. For a post of the first rank it is difficult to imagine anyone being successful without having at first or at least second hand the support of someone able to influence decisions in the closet.

Entry by patronage was not of course peculiar to the household departments in the eighteenth century. But the court was perhaps particularly open to the working of patronage if only because so few of the better and middle-ranking posts required anything in the way of

---

[1] Walpole's scheme was not well received in Hanover. Townshend wrote to him on 31 August (N.S.) 'The King does not at all relish the granting the Duke of Kent so large a sum as you mention, and as His Ma.ty never had the least thought or inclination towards giving Lord Glenorchy the place of Ld. of the Bedchamber, he does not at all enter into the notion of the Duke of Kents having any equivalent for it. Under these circumstances I did not think it proper to offer the blank warrant you sent me over, for fear of getting a negative put upon the whole, and I believe it will be best to leave that matter till the King's return' (Stowe MSS. 251, fos. 25–6).

'qualifications' in the sense of special training or competence. The only necessary qualification for the better posts was social 'quality'. That this was all-important requires little elaboration. A glance at the holders of posts of the highest rank testifies to the hold that the aristocracy had on the higher reaches of the court. In the reign of George I a total of 101 men held posts that may be distinguished as of the first rank in terms of honour. Of these, 53 were peers, 15 were sons of peers and at least 16 of the remainder were otherwise closely related to peers: a total of 84 men who were members of the peerage or closely related to it. Nor were social considerations unimportant for posts below the first rank and especially for those in the ceremonial departments above stairs. As has been seen in an earlier chapter, there were numerous members of gentry and even noble families among the servants in the public rooms, in the jewel office, the band of gentlemen pensioners and in other chamber posts. Supplicants for middle-ranking posts in the ceremonial departments are often found stressing their gentility and the fact that their income was sufficient to support them in the style necessary for the post.[1] Even in the department below stairs there is some evidence that social considerations were playing a more important part in recruitment than they had in the previous century.[2]

For posts for which some talent was necessary, 'ability' was sometimes urged in a candidate's favour. Steele promoted the (unsuccessful) application to the lord chamberlain of a man named Caulfield to be barge-builder to the king on the grounds that 'he is the only man on the River now in [the] Trade, who has himself built a Barge, and he has done many with great success'.[3] And Henry Foubert, equerry of the Crown stable in charge of the king's riding horses, got a reversion to his office granted to his nephew, Solomon Durrell, because he had 'with great pains and expense instructed and educated his nephew... so as to make him fit for the riding of our Horses'.[4] But 'ability' was not often a factor in appointment and it was never unmixed with patronage.

Special competence was not in any case normally required in the better and more honorific court posts, but if necessary it could be

[1] C(H)MSS. corresp. 2396e; and see above, p. 45.
[2] See above, p. 92.
[3] R. Blanchard (ed.), *Correspondence of Richard Steele*, p. 130.
[4] LS 13/260 (5 October 1721).

supplied by the employment of deputies. The cofferership, for example, was usually held in the early eighteenth century by a peer or by a would-be 'man of business'.[1] The drudgery of the office was borne by the cofferer's clerk, but the cofferers by George I's reign also employed deputies. 'Merit' seems to have been as important a consideration in their appointment as patronage. John Merrill who was deputy cofferer to William Pulteney (cofferer 1723–5) had had considerable experience in financial administration. He seems to have been in the army pay office by 1704;[2] by 1710 he was deputy to the paymaster of guards and garrisons[3] and by 1716 he was comptroller of army accounts when Pulteney was secretary at war.[4] In 1721 he was elected member of Parliament for Tregony in succession to Pulteney's brother, Daniel, and was by this time at least clearly attached to Pulteney. When William Pulteney became cofferer, Merrill came into the court post as his deputy.[5] Patronage and 'merit' seem to go hand in hand to explain his appointment, for Pulteney had a high opinion of Merrill's talents in financial matters if his sense of loss at Merrill's death in 1734 is any guide.

I have lost. . .the truest friend [Pulteney wrote to Swift in 1735] I may almost say servant, that ever man had in Mr Merril. He understood the course of the revenues, and the public accounts of the kingdom as well, perhaps better, than any man in it. It is utterly impossible for me to go through the drudgery by myself, which I used to do easily with his assistance. . .[6]

Merrill lost his place soon after his patron went out of office.[7] His successor, William Sloper,[8] was in office by 1726[9] under Lord Lincoln (cofferer 1725–8) and he remained deputy cofferer until his death in 1743.[10] Like Merrill, Sloper also had had a good deal of experience in financial affairs, having risen from a clerkship in the paymaster general's

---

[1] See above, chapter 3. [2] *C.T.B.* XIX, 46.
[3] *Ibid.* XXIV (index, sub. Merrill). [4] *Ibid.* XXX, 47.
[5] LS 13/115, fo. 130.
[6] F. E. Ball (ed.), *The Correspondence of Jonathan Swift* (6 vols., 1910–14), V, 281.
[7] He may still have been in office in September 1725 for in that month he was giving Pulteney information about the supposed use of the Sinking Fund for Civil List purposes (Plumb, *Walpole*, II, 128). He may have been dismissed for this.
[8] c.1669–1743; member of Parliament for Great Bedwin 1715–22, for Camelford 1722–7, for Great Bedwin again 1729–41, and for Whitchurch 1742–3.
[9] N.S.A., Cal. Br. Arch., Des. 24, England 141 (newsletter of 21 January/1 February 1726).
[10] Owen, *Rise of the Pelhams*, p. 50, n. 4.

office (by 1702) to the post of deputy paymaster general by 1711.[1] He remained in this post until 1721, serving, significantly, under Lord Lincoln who was joint paymaster-general 1715–20. Sloper lost his place in 1721 perhaps because of his independent stand in Parliament over the South Sea inquiry in which he was a member of the secret committee and one of the most adamant of Walpole's opponents.[2] It is not known by whose favour he returned to office as deputy cofferer to Lord Lincoln, but one may presume that his previous work under Lincoln was the important factor and that he owed his appointment simply to Lincoln's patronage.

Such acquaintance with a man who could himself dispose of places or who was in a position to influence those who did, was of course of inestimable benefit to an office-seeker. The attachment of a lesser man to a greater could provide the key to office for a man if his patron himself attained power. The careers of two other courtiers, Giles Earle and Thomas Archer, provide clear examples of this.

Giles Earle was so firmly attached to the duke of Argyll's interest that Walpole called him 'the Duke of Argyle's Erle'. In 1716 Earle spoke of having known Argyll well for twenty years and of having been a friend 'without design or reserve'. His career it would seem owed a good deal to Argyll's patronage. Argyll, having served with distinction under Marlborough, became ambassador to Spain in 1711, and governor of Minorca (1712–April 1714, October 1714–16). Earle, who also served in the army, became commissary of the musters in Spain in 1711 and commissary-general of the provisions at Port Mahon and in Minorca, 1712–16. When Argyll became attached to the Prince of Wales, serving as his groom of the stole from 1714 until the king forced his dismissal in 1716, Earle too attached himself to the prince's interest and was rewarded with the place of groom of the bedchamber (1718–20). In 1719 Argyll went over to the king and became lord steward (1719–25) and it was undoubtedly by his interest that Earle followed him to the king's court and to a post in the lord steward's department, becoming clerk of the green cloth in 1720. He retained this place until 1727.[3]

[1] *C.T.B.* xxv (index, sub. Sloper).
[2] Realey, *Early Opposition to Walpole*, pp. 24–5.
[3] Earle was member of Parliament for Chippenham 1715–22, Malmesbury 1722–7.
  In 1727 he became chairman of the committee on elections and privileges of the

Thomas Archer was the youngest son of a country gentleman and member of Parliament. He was educated at Oxford and after four years spent in foreign travel (1689–93) became a pupil and follower of John Vanbrugh. He became attached to the duke of Shrewsbury, for whom he built Heythrop in 1705. In the same year—possibly by Shrewsbury's influence—he got the post of groom porter at court which he retained to his death. Certainly Shrewsbury tried to advance him in other ways. He applied to Oxford in 1713 to get Archer appointed as comptroller of the works when Vanbrugh lost it, recommending him as the man with 'the best genius for building of anybody we have'. Archer failed to get this post, but in 1715 he got some monetary compensation in the form of an appointment as comptroller of the customs at Newcastle.[1]

Such 'clientage' also accounts for what was one of the commonest methods of entry especially at the lower levels of the court: transference from private to royal service. One of the clearest examples of this is the duchess of Marlborough's account of how she filled the office of the robes with her own and the duke's domestic servants.[2] But many other examples can be found of heads of court departments giving places in their gift to their own servants or to servants of their friends: a lord steward appointing one of his servants a groom of the buttery;[3] a master of the horse making one of his servants a yeoman saddler and store keeper;[4] a vice-chamberlain promoting his servant to be groom of the chamber;[5] servants of the nobility being found places as groom of the scullery, porter, messenger and musician.[6]

If 'ability' of a narrow kind was not often a factor in appointments especially to the better court posts, poverty, the needs for money to

House of Commons (until 1741) and subsequently commissioner of the Irish Revenues (1728–37) and a lord of the Treasury (1737–42) (Coxe, *Walpole*, II, p. 77; J. W. Croker (ed.) *The Correspondence of Lady Suffolk*, I, 11; Horn, *British Diplomatic Representatives*, 130; G.E.C., *Complete Peerage*; *D.N.B.*; Owen, *Rise of the Pelhams*, p. 21).

[1] *H.M.C. MSS. of the Marquis of Bath*, I, 231; *D.N.B.* (amended *B.I.H.R.* XIX, 38); M. Whiffen, *Thomas Archer*; *Complete Works of John Vanbrugh* vol. IV, *Correspondence*, ed. Geoffrey Webb, p. xxxix.

[2] See above, p. 134.   [3] LS 13/115, fo. 4.

[4] *C.T.P.* (1720–28), p. 478.   [5] Cowper (Melbourne) MSS. packet 106.

[6] Add. MSS. 45733, fos. 7, 17, 18; Add. MSS. 33064, fo. 206; Blenheim MSS. D 2/5; and see J. J. Hecht, *The Domestic Servant Class in the Eighteenth Century*, pp. 193–4; D. B. Horn, *The British Diplomatic Service*, pp. 220–1.

support penniless dignity, sometimes was. At the beginning of the reign, Lady Irby appealed to Lord Halifax, through Addison, to get her included among the women of the bedchamber to the Princess of Wales on the grounds that only through office could she be made 'easy in her fortune'.[1] This having failed, she pushed her son for court office, and when he was sixteen years old got him made a page of honour with Walpole's help. In supporting his candidate, Walpole took care to have him 'represented...to his Majesty as a young gentleman deserving his compassion and favour as being the remains of a worthy family fallen into decay....'[2] Similarly, in 1714 Lord Lincoln applied to Bothmer for a bedchamber post because he needed the money, and Bothmer recommended him successfully to the king on those grounds.[3] Also in the great distribution at the beginning of the reign, James Dormer, who was appointed a groom of the bedchamber, appealed to the king's generosity as a younger son and a general officer on half-pay who needed a post to support himself.[4] But Dormer had other points in his favour. His brother, Charles, had been a groom of the bedchamber to William III and had been killed at Almanza, and Dormer did not fail to point this out. Further, his mother was the daughter of Sir Charles Cotterell, a master of the ceremonies, whose son (and therefore Dormer's uncle) was master of the ceremonies in 1714; and Dormer's father had been assistant to the master.[5] He was therefore a member of a firm court connection and this may have been an influential factor in his appointment; certainly family and family connections played an important part in court recruitment.

Succession of father-to-son in court office or the succession of some other close relative was common, though more in the middle and lower ranks than in the higher. Such family succession took place in the early eighteenth century in the following court posts: knight marshal, cupbearer, groom of the privy chamber, groom of the great chamber, groom of the jewel office, housekeeper of Hampton Court, of Whitehall and of Westminster, ratkiller, watchman, riding surveyor of the stables, gentleman of the pantry and child of the scullery. In the office of master of the ceremonies one member of the Cotterell (later

[1] W. Graham (ed.), *The Letters of Joseph Addison* (1941), p. 302.
[2] *S.P. Dom.* 35/46. fo. 86.
[3] Stowe MSS. 227, fos. 317–18.   [4] *Ibid.* fos. 474–5.
[5] *D.N.B.* xii, 280 (Cotterell); xv, 245 (Dormer).

Cotterell–Dormer) family followed another through several genera-
tions.[1] One yeoman of the scullery resigned his post to his son-in-law
as part of his daughter's dowry.[2] At a much more exalted level the
duchess of Marlborough acquired a reversion to an office for her son-
in-law for the same purpose. This was a reversion to the mastership of
the great wardrobe, obtained by the son of the duke of Montagu in
1704 after his marriage to the duke of Marlborough's daughter.[3]

The Marlborough connection indeed acquired a widespread interest
in household offices and provides a good example of what G. E. Aylmer
has called a 'lateral' family connection in office, that is, 'family control
of several offices over a...limited period of time'.[4] The earl of Godolphin, son of the lord treasurer and son-in-law of Marlborough, was
cofferer of the household (1704–11, 1714–23) and later groom of the
stole (1723–35); he had been preceded in this latter office by the earl of
Sunderland, who was also Marlborough's son-in-law. The board of
green cloth, the governing committee of the household below stairs,
was fairly monopolized by members of the Marlborough connection
in the early eighteenth century. Apart from the coffership held by
Godolphin, three other relatives were on the board: Charles Godfrey,
Marlborough's brother-in-law,[5] was a clerk of the green cloth (1704–11,
1714–15); Hugh Boscawen (created Viscount Falmouth, 1720) the son
of Sidney Godolphin's sister, Jael, and husband of the eldest daughter
of Godfrey and Arabella Churchill's marriage, was comptroller of the
household (1714–20); and Edmund Dunch, who married another of
Godfrey's daughters by Arabella, was master of the household (1708–10,
1714–19). Another of Marlborough's sons-in-law, the duke of Bridgewater, had been in the household of the Prince of Denmark, and was,
after 1714, lord chamberlain to the Princess of Wales (1714–17) and
gentleman of the bedchamber to the king (1719–27). With another
son-in-law, Montagu, comfortably installed as master of the great
wardrobe for life, the accession of George I did a good deal to satisfy
what a contemporary called Marlborough's 'great appetite for offices

---

[1] LC 5/3; *D.N.B.* (Cotterell).   [2] LS 13/259, fo. 43.

[3] *H.M.C. Buccleuch and Queensberry MSS.* 1, 352, 356; W. King (ed.), *The Memoirs of
the Duchess of Marlborough* (1930), p. 304.

[4] G. E. Aylmer, *The King's Servants*, p. 81.

[5] He married Arabella Churchill, Marlborough's sister and James II's mistress. (*D.N.B.*
sub. Arabella Churchill).

for his relations';[1] it was said that the king himself expressed surprise at its magnitude and rebuked Marlborough for his zeal in soliciting jobs.[2]

Such family connections in court office were not unusual, though few were as widespread. There are some suggestions that it was not thought proper for one family to have too many places of the first rank at court; on occasion a father—generally a peer who could have some pretension to a place of honour in the royal household—can be found offering to stand aside on condition that his son be employed in the king's or the prince's court.[3] And of course the influence of family on office holding cannot be gauged by studying the household in isolation from other departments and offices in which gentlemen could with honour find employment. None the less even within the narrower scope of the household, family constellations existed at all levels. Several relatives of the duke of Newcastle, for example, were employed at court in George I's reign. Newcastle, as lord chamberlain (1717–24) engaged his second cousin, James Pelham, as his secretary in the lord chamberlain's office;[4] his brother, Henry Pelham, began his career in court office, as treasurer of the chamber (1720–2); and Newcastle's brother-in-law, the earl of Lincoln held several court posts.[5]

In the household below stairs it was quite common for sons to follow in their father's footsteps in a career in the department. But since the system of promotion by seniority was still fairly rigidly maintained, they very rarely were able simply to inherit their father's office but had to begin at the bottom and work their way up. It was by getting them a start on the promotion ladder that a father's influence could be helpful.[6] Wives of court servants often obtained places that could be held by a

---

[1] Add. MSS. 47027, p. 355.   [2] Cartwright, *Wentworth Papers*, p. 439.

[3] See, for example, *H.M.C. Carlisle MSS.* pp. 13–14.

[4] James Pelham (1683–1761) of Crowhurst, Sussex, son of Sir Nicholas Pelham of Carsfield Place, Sussex. Member of Parliament for Newark 1722–41, Hastings 1741–61. Secretary to the lord chamberlain 1720– ; secretary to the Prince of Wales 1728–37; deputy cofferer ?1744–54.

[5] Henry Clinton, earl of Lincoln (1684–1728) gentleman of the bedchamber to the Prince of Denmark, 1708; master of the horse to the Prince of Wales, September–November 1714; gentleman of the bedchamber to the king, 1714–27; cofferer 1725–8; joint paymaster-general of the forces, 1715–20; constable of the Tower, 1723–5.

[6] For example, Claud Arnaud and John Dissell, both master-cooks to George I, got their sons established in the department as children of the kitchen in this reign.

woman. Thus, Mary Lowman, the wife of Henry, clerk of the kitchen and housekeeper of Kensington, was keeper of the standing wardrobe at that palace and also laundress of the body linen; and Jane Gunthorpe the wife of George Gunthorpe, yeoman of the confectionery, was a laundress of table linen.

Even with the advantage of a relative at court or a patron in a position of influence, an office-seeker might still have to work hard to succeed. It was even more necessary of course for those without such a foot in the door to search for the favour of some man or woman of influence. Though he was not looking necessarily for a court post, Thomas Burnet, the third and youngest son of Bishop Burnet, provides a good example of a man whose advantages in 1714 did not immediately pay dividends, and who according to his own account had to search and work hard for favour. Burnet had helped himself by writing several whiggish pamphlets before 1714[1] which had brought him to Bernstorff's attention. At the beginning of the new reign he was introduced to Lord Halifax by Paul Methuen and to Bernstorff by Stanhope and with such 'visible hopes of Preferment' he was confident that his ambition would be gratified.[2] That was in October 1714. By December he was grumbling that 'praises are but damnd thin diet for a man who wants a place'[3] and he began on a career of office-seeking that was to last for nearly five years.

The author of the article on Burnet in the *D.N.B.* simply states that 'The Whigs, on their accession to power, rewarded him with the consulship at Lisbon'. But this disguises what was according to Burnet a long and troublesome struggle which involved a good deal of attendance at court. Perhaps he did not mind this as much as he protests he did but there can be no doubt that his struggle was genuine enough. In August 1717 he wrote to George Duckett 'I have been so divided between waiting upon his Majesty at Hampton Court and upon his ministers in London, that I have scarce had a leisure hour to write to a friend.'[4] At the same time he was confident that he would be given a

---

[1] *D.N.B.* VII, 410–11. His pre-1714 pamphlets included *Our Ancestors as wise as we: or Ancient Precedents for Modern Facts* which was an attack on the Tory government's treatment of Marlborough. In 1715 he wrote *The Necessity of Impeaching the Late Ministry.*

[2] D. N. Smith (ed.), *The Letters of Thomas Burnet to George Duckett*, p. 75.

[3] *Ibid.* p. 78.   [4] *Ibid.* p. 133.

place 'in one fortnight more'. But again he was to be disappointed. He continued to solicit, and to haunt the ante-rooms of the great. He even stayed at Hampton Court for the entire four months period of the king's residence there in the summer of 1717; and he never lost hope. There was no question, he told Duckett, but that his hard work would bear fruit; it was only a matter of time and dedication. He wrote to Duckett in September 1717:

As for the waiter's Place at Court, I confess I am pretty heartily tired of it; but I am satisfyed (notwithstanding the Common Cant that 'tis uncertain succeeding at Court) that if a man will but continually press on and solicit, provided he has any pretensions, he must gain his point at last; whether he will not be ruined before that come, he may judge, by Considering his Circumstances. If he can hold out five years, 'tis morally impossible he should not come into play.[1]

Burnet's 'pretensions' no doubt derived from the fact that he had written pamphlets and had helped to write a newspaper, *The Free-thinker*, for the government.[2] But apparently he lacked a powerful patron, someone willing to press his claims seriously and he had to continue his search for favour. In February 1718 he thought that at the end of the parliamentary session he would be given something,[3] but in the summer he was still soliciting. Compelled once more to spend a good part of the summer at Hampton Court where the king was again in residence, he was unable (because of 'this cursed Court attendance') to visit Duckett in the country.[4] In February 1719 he was looking forward to a more leisurely summer because he had heard that the king was going to Hanover.[5] However, before the king left, Burnet at last found his reward. In May he was appointed consul at Lisbon—'much a better thing than ever I asked'.[6]

Burnet's search for favour, while not resulting in a court appointment, must have been typical of those who sought posts at court without having the advantage of a well-placed relative or patron to urge their claims. It was an essential part of his campaign to spend a good deal of time at court (helping incidentally to swell the 'presence' when the king appeared in the drawing-room). Those who 'put themselves

---

[1] D. N. Smith (ed.), *The Letters of Thomas Burnet to George Duckett*, p. 135.
[2] *Ibid.* Introduction, p. xxxi; pp. 148, 155.
[3] *Ibid.* p. 142. [4] *Ibid.* p. 153.
[5] *Ibid.* p. 163. [6] *Ibid.* p. 170.

in the way' were more likely to gain favour and a post than those who were content to pursue their petitions from afar, or to rely on the influence of those who were not themselves at the centre.[1] Tenacity of purpose and determination to succeed were as important it would seem as the much-derided courtierly attributes, an ability to fawn and to flatter. Certainly Lady Cowper's brother, John Clavering, believed that he lost an opportunity to become a groom of the bedchamber because he had failed to annoy people sufficiently. He wrote to Lady Cowper in 1720:

I spoke to the Old Baron [Bernstorff] of Sir Wilfred Lawson's being made groom of the Bedchamber who seem'd much surpriz'd at it. I reminded him at the same time of the promise he got me...he promised to remember me and by what he say'd I really believe he would have got me declared if I had spoke to him before; he seemed to think I did not much desire it because I had not tormented him as other people do for all those things, for I really am the worst sollicitor for my self in the World.[2]

Lady Mary Wortley Montagu had a good deal to say to her husband in 1714 on this subject. If you want a good place, she advised him, you must not stand back, modest and self-effacing, afraid to ask. You must push others out of the way and go on asking until you get what you want. 'I don't say it is impossible', she wrote in September 1714, 'for an impudent man not to rise in the world; but a moderate merit, with a large share of impudence is more probable to be advanced, than the greatest qualifications without it.'[3]

In soliciting the favour of someone of influence, a place-seeker might simply offer gratitude in return, the recognition that he owed his position wholly to his patron.[4] Or he might offer something more substantial. It seems clear that favour was commonly purchased, though it is in the nature of things difficult to discover exactly how often a well-placed gratuity led to an appointment. Not all the evidence that survives is entirely trustworthy; much of it is little more than gossip retailed by

[1] Lord Chesterfield, writing from the Hague in 1729 agreeing to recommend a petitioner—the details are unimportant here—said that since the vice-chamberlain was supporting the candidate, he hoped his own support would be unnecessary 'as the recommendation of an absent person is commonly ineffectual' (*H.M.C.* 10th Report, App. pt. I, p. 154).   [2] Panshanger MSS., Letterbooks, v, 224–5.

[3] Lady Mary Wortley Montagu, *Works*, I, 214–15.

[4] See, for example, Add. MSS. 32686, fo. 173; Mrs A. T. Thomson (ed.), *Memoirs of Viscountess Sundon, Mistress of the Robes to Queen Caroline...* (2 vols., 1847), I, 317.

disappointed candidates or by people out of sympathy with the new reign.[1] But there is some reliable evidence of favour being stimulated by money or other gifts. Naturally, since they had a good deal of influence, much of this evidence especially from the early years of the reign, concerns the German courtiers. William Byrd of Virginia, who spent two years in London in George I's reign for purposes of business as well as pleasure, attended at court very frequently, partly at least because he wanted to be appointed governor of Virginia. He records in his diary in April 1719, that Lord Islay 'advised me to bribe the German [Bernstorff] to get the governorship of Virginia and told me he would put me in the way'.[2] More substantial evidence can be extracted from the correspondence and the accounts of James Brydges, duke of Chandos. His close understanding with the German ministers and court ladies was nurtured, if not entirely dependent, on his generosity to them. In August 1714 he gave Bothmer 250 lottery tickets;[3] in September, in order to induce Robethon to 'obtain a promise from His Majesty that Mr Nicholas Philpott[4] may succeed' his brother as cashier of the salt office, he sent via another German, Kreienberg, 'a small present of 400 Guineas for his [Robethon's] favour in compassing this matter'.[5] That was not all. Brydges was anxious further to express his appreciation for favours already, hopefully, received. The letter continues:

I must likewise entreat you will let me know whether if I should take the liberty of presenting him with 30 or 40 Lottery Tickets for his obliging care of my Brother (the only one I have now left) in the affair of the Prebend (for which I hope by this time the proper directions are given) he would take it amiss or not. I should think he ought not to refuse it considering there is nothing in it but what is very justifiable and besides that he has to do with one who I hope deserves the Character of a Man of honour.[6]

In October 1715, Madame Kielmannsegge was sent £3,000;[7] a little later Brydges gave a ring 'perfect in its kind' to her daughter.[8] Apart

---

[1] See, for example, *H.M.C. Stuart MSS.* II, 532; Add. MSS. 31144, fo. 528; Lady Cowper, *Diary*, p. 31.

[2] William Byrd, *London Diary*, p. 259.

[3] HM, Stowe MSS. 57, vol. 10, pp. 190, 219, 237–40.

[4] Philpott, Brydges explained, was an old friend who had helped him in Hereford.

[5] HM, Stowe MSS. 57, vol. 10, pp. 277–8.

[6] *Ibid.* pp. 277–8.   [7] *Ibid.* vol. 12, p. 165.   [8] *Ibid.* vol. 14, p. 343.

from other occasional gifts of wine and sweetmeats, Brydges's accounts suggest that between August 1715 and February 1720 he gave a total of £25,104 in cash to the Germans at court, distributed as follows: Madame Schulenberg, £9,500; Madame Kielmannsegge, £9,545; Bernstorff, £2,909; Bothmer, £1,350; Kreienberg £750.[1] This total is almost certainly too low since it includes nothing for Robethon who, as has been seen, was at least offered money, though it is conceivable that he did not take it.

The benefits that Brydges derived from this largesse have already been noticed.[2] But it would be a mistake to emphasize too much the willingness of the king's German courtiers to accept money in return for their influence, especially if it suggests that they were more venal than the English or that this was a peculiarly German vice. Influential English men and women were not above turning their positions to account; offers of bribes to influence the king's choice of court servants were received in 1727 by Mrs Howard and Mrs Clayton for example;[3] and at different periods of the eighteenth century the secretaries of the lord steward and of the lord chamberlain were discovered selling the natural influence that their places afforded.[4]

It was safer and less complicated of course for a place-seeker to purchase a vacant post immediately from the person who had the right to fill it, than to try to buy the influence of a middleman. The duchess of Marlborough suggests that such sale of offices was common at William III's court and at Anne's, and she records instances of a gentleman usher paying £800 for his place and of grooms of the stole selling the posts of page of the backstairs for 1,000 guineas.[5] She herself sold two such places at Anne's court (before Anne succeeded to the throne) for £400 each.[6] But she claims that she sold no others though she was many times offered presents after procuring a post for someone. When she got Thomas Maul made a groom of the bedchamber to the Prince of Denmark, for example, he, 'knowing what was usual in such cases sent

---

[1] C. H. Collins Baker and M. I. Baker, *The Life and Circumstances of James Brydges, First Duke of Chandos*, p. 112, n. 1.

[2] See above, p. 145.

[3] *Suffolk Correspondence*, I, 102; Mrs A. T. Thomson (ed.), *Memoirs of Viscountess Sundon*, I, 317.

[4] LS 13/117, p. 5.

[5] Panshanger MSS Letterbooks, II, pp. 89, 90.

[6] William King (ed.), *The Memoirs of the Duchess of Marlborough*, p. 217.

a message to me, desiring leave to make me a present'; again, she was offered £500 by Lord Delawarr when she helped to get him made groom of the stole to the Prince. These presents she refused. In her 'Account' written after she left Anne's court to answer criticisms of her conduct while in office, she repeatedly claims that she sold very few places, many fewer than she might have. If she had been guilty of selling titles and places her best defence in any case, she added, was that 'it was usual and customary' for people in her position to do so.[1] Indeed, the duchess claimed credit for encouraging the royal warrant of 29 June 1702 to the board of green cloth which ordered that everyone who came into a post in the department below stairs must swear on oath that they had not in any way paid for the place.[2]

Whether this order had any more effect than the existing laws against the sale of offices[3] it is difficult to know, but there does seem to have been a general decline in the purchase of court posts, especially perhaps of those at the highest level. No evidence has been found of any of the major court posts being bought and sold in George I's reign. Certainly men who lost major court posts were sometimes given monetary or other compensation, and this is in a sense purchase by the king in order to reward another man. But of the direct treating between two individuals for one of the posts of the first rank, such as had taken place in the later seventeenth century and in Anne's reign for bedchamber posts, for the mastership of the horse and the post of lord chamberlain,[4] no trace has been found. The only exception is the post of master of the great wardrobe which the duke of Montagu tried and failed to sell in 1719 and for which the duke of Chandos made inquiries of him.[5]

Below the first rank in the period 1700–40 there is evidence that the following posts were obtained by purchase: housekeeper of Kensington, corporal of the yeomen of the guard, lieutenant, standard-bearer and

---

[1] William King (ed.), *The Memoirs of the Duchess of Marlborough* pp. 217–18; Panshanger MSS. Letterbooks, II, 95.

[2] Panshanger MSS. Letterbooks, II, 94.

[3] K. W. Swart, *The Sale of Offices in the Seventeenth Century* (The Hague, 1949), pp. 50–1.

[4] *H.M.C. MSS. of the Duke of Sutherland*, p. 186; *H.M.C. MSS. of Sir H. Ingilby*, p. 369; J. P. Kenyon, *Robert Spencer, Earl of Sunderland*, p. 24; Burnet, *History of his Own Time* (Oxford, 1823), V, 140. Dartmouth's note (but see Cartwright, *Wentworth Papers*, p. 134).

[5] HM, Stowe MSS. 57, vol. 16, pp. 179–80; Blenheim MSS. D 2/2.

gentleman of the band of pensioners, porter of St James's, messenger and groom baker.[1] In a number of other cases there are strong suggestions that the sale of offices was taking place, but no definite proof. In the book of appointments to chamber places, for example, the 'surrender' of a post is clearly distinguished from vacancies caused by death, promotion or removal, and 'surrender' might or might not indicate sale when the person who succeeds is not related to the retiring holder.[2] And in the department below stairs a few cases have been found of a court servant resigning his place to someone, which also might indicate a sale.[3]

In would seem that entry to the better posts at court in the reign of George I was less commonly accomplished by purchase than it had been a hundred years earlier[4] or even a generation earlier, though in the absence of more positive evidence any conclusion must be tentative. But purchase, even when it can be definitely established, was never by itself a sufficient agent. The purchaser had to be sworn into office and had to receive a certificate of entry before he could be paid.[5] In the case of the under-officers of the yeomen of the guard and of the band of gentlemen pensioners—which explains why a number of cases of purchase are known—the warrant of appointment had to be signed by the king, though the right of appointment was in the captain. After obtaining the captain's permission to buy a place it was then necessary to get the king's. The influence of someone able to accomplish this had to be sought, as the following letter from the duke of Montagu, when captain of the band of gentlemen pensioners, to Walpole indicates:

Forgive me troubling you with this in relation to the officers of the Band of Pensioners. I took the liberty some time ago to tell you that Sir Samuel Garet, the Lieutenant had agreed with Sir William Winn the Standard Bearer to resign his place of Lieutenant to him, and that Mr Newton a gentleman of very good family and estate had agreed with Sir Willlam Winn to succeed him as Standard Bearer. They are perpetually speaking to me to get the affair finished and I am unwilling to trouble you about it as often as they

---

[1] Add. MSS. 20101, fos. 15–16; *H.M.C. Cowper MSS.* III, 20; LS 13/176, p. 81; Pegge, *Curialia*, pt. II, 95. LS 13/117, p. 5.

[2] LC 3/63–4.   [3] E.g. LS 13/115, fo. 23.

[4] Aylmer, *The King's Servants*, ch. 3, pt. I.

[5] In the household below stairs such certificates had to be approved by the board of green cloth (see, for example, LS 13/115, fo. 56; LS 13/116, fo. 31).

would have me, but as the last time I spoke to you about it you said you had no objection to it and that the reason you had not spoken to the King was that you had really forgot it, and not willingly forgot it, I beg you will speak about it by which you will oblige these Gentlemen and save a great deal of sollicitation and trouble to

Your Obedient
Humble Servant
Montague[1]

IV

It has been suggested that entry by purchase was probably less common in the reign of George I than it had been in the previous century. In any case money by itself was not enough to provide entry to court posts, and certainly not to posts of the first rank or to the more honorific places of the second rank in the chamber. For these posts purchase could only be successful in conjunction with patronage, with the influence of a man able to get the necessary approval which meant in some cases the king's approval.

Once in office a man might expect to find opportunites more readily available for promotion or for transference to a better post through merit ot favour. But there was in fact little movement within and almost none between court departments though there were two exceptions to this. The first concerns the department of the household below stairs in which below the level of clerk of the board of green cloth, an established system of promotion by seniority was still in part maintained; the second concerns the very highest posts in all departments.

Changes in the most important posts were in general very frequent.[2] The duke of Grafton's long tenure as lord chamberlain (1724-57) was the exception rather than the rule. In George I's reign of under thirteen years there were, for example, four lords chamberlain, four lords steward and two grooms of the stole in office; and among slightly less important places, there were three treasurers of the chamber, three comptrollers of the household, three cofferers and eleven holders of the four clerkships of the green cloth. Transference at this level between one court post and another was common, amounting in most cases to promotion. To give a number of examples: the duke of Kent moved

[1] C(H)MSS., corresp. 2396e; for two similar requests see: *S.P. Dom.* 35/68, fo. 360; C(H)MSS. corresp. 3258.

[2] The subject of tenure in court office is dealt with below, pp. 173-80.

from gentleman of the bedchamber to lord steward in 1716; the earl of Godolphin from cofferer to groom of the stole in 1723; Francis Negus from commissioner for the office of master of the horse to master of the buckhounds in 1727; and promotion from the comptrollership of the household to the treasurership—a change which brought no increase in emoluments but which meant removal from a relatively busy post to a virtual sinecure—was a regular occurence.[1] If transference back and forth between these and posts outside the household is considered, the mobility in the first rank of court posts is even more striking. There was frequent movement from the court to a place of 'business': Newcastle moved from the lord chamberlainship to become secretary of state (1724); Carteret to a similar place from the bedchamber (1721); the duke of Bolton moved from the lord chamberlainship to the lord lieutenancy of Ireland (1717); Henry Pelham (treasurer of the chamber 1720–2) and Giles Earle (clerk of the board of green cloth 1720–34) both transferred from their court posts to a seat on the treasury board. The list could easily be extended. Nor was the movement all in one direction; a number of examples can be found of men moving from places more clearly in the administration to high court office.[2] Further a number of men held court and administrative posts simultaneously.[3] Thus, though not all men wished to take advantage of this, court office could provide a springboard for the politically ambitious as well as a resting place for the weary; certainly it would be a mistake to make a rigid distinction between courtiers and 'men of business' in this period.

The system, of very old lineage, by which promotion was regulated in the household below stairs has been mentioned previously in connection with the organization of the department. As was seen then, the original system which had contemplated that all posts below master of the household, including cofferer and clerk of the board of green cloth, would be filled by promotion from below, had been perverted by the early eighteenth century. The clerkships of the green cloth were no

[1] See above, p. 70.
[2] Duke of Grafton, lord lieutenant of Ireland to lord chamberlain (1724); Charles Stanhope, secretary of the Treasury to treasurer of the chamber (1722, after some delay; see above, p. 147); Sir John Hobart, a lord of trade to treasurer of the chamber (1727); earl of Holdernesse, first lord of trade to gentleman of the bedchamber (1719).
[3] See below, p. 250.

longer filled from among the senior clerks of the various offices in the department; and indeed the household ordinances, in what was a remarkably swift recognition of the real situation, no longer after 1701 enjoined as they had done previously that these posts and the cofferership should be filled from below.[1] This cut off the possibility that a man starting in a low place could rise by slow stages to a very senior and lucrative position, a seat on the board of green cloth and perhaps a knighthood. Nevertheless, it was still contemplated that if the plums of the department were now out of reach, the clerkships of the various offices, in no way mean positions, would still be open to promotion. But even at this level, however, promotion by seniority did not work as automatically in 1714 as it had earlier.

There were two distinct ladders of promotion within the department: one designed essentially to train a competent clerical staff for the more important offices; the other occupied by those who did the work of the offices. The two major clerical posts were the clerkships of the kitchen and spicery which, with the clerkship of the avery in the stables were next below the clerks of the green cloth. The other household offices to have clerks were, in descending order of importance, the acatry, poultry, bakehouse, woodyard, scullery and pastry. As it worked originally,[2] the system of promotion in the clerical rank provided that men, having served first as an assistant clerk in the accounting house, should serve through the hierarchy, beginning as a clerk of the pastry and moving up as vacancies occurred to become clerk of either the kitchen, the spicery or the avery and eventually from there to become a clerk of the green cloth. Not only was this top rank inaccessible in the early eighteenth century, but also the lower clerkships were not always filled by such strict promotion. And, further, they were sometimes being combined under the one man. The old system was not entirely defunct. John Shaw who came into the household in January 1705 as a groom of the accounting house, that is as an assistant clerk, was promoted to yeoman of that office in April. In 1707 he was made clerk of the woodyard, spicery and pastry, and in May 1713 he moved up to become clerk of the poultry and bakehouse.[3] So far (apart from the fact that he held several posts at once) this was perfectly orthodox

[1] LS 13/43.   [2] Newton, *Tudor Studies*, pp. 242, 254–5.
[3] All information about appointments and promotions in the household below stairs is taken from the warrants of appointment, recorded in LS 13/258–61 (for 1702–27).

promotion. But Shaw never got any further. Whereas John Price had been promoted from clerk of the poultry and bakehouse to a joint-clerkship of the acatry in 1707, Shaw never made this jump. When a vacancy occurred in the acatry in 1716 it went to another man, Charles Tuckwell, who had not previously held a household post. The career of James Eckersall further illustrates that household promotion was no longer working as smoothly as it once had. Eckersall entered the department as a doorkeeper of the kitchen in 1692, not therefore on that ladder of promotion that led to the clerical ranks. But for some reason— either because of his ability, or the favour of a clerk of the office, or perhaps both—he was in 1708 brought forward and made a clerk of the kitchen extraordinary to serve in the place of James Clark, the first clerk of the kitchen, who was 'indisposed by his great age'. His warrant of appointment justified this on the grounds that he had been 'bred these sixteen years past in the office, and [was] well-instructed in the Duty, Method and Practice of a Clerk of the Kitchen'.[1] In 1709 Eckersall was appointed second clerk when James Clark died and Lowman was promoted. Both he and Lowman remained clerks of the kitchen for life. In a similar case in 1722 a clerk extraordinary was appointed to perform Lowman's duties when he too became too old and infirm to do them himself. In this case Lowman was allowed to recommend his successor and he chose Edward Arnold, who had been his personal clerk and was not even officially on the household establishment.[2] Though there was still a certain amount of promotion by seniority, numerous other cases could be cited of clerks being appointed in the middle of the promotion ladder from outside the household altogether. Once this began to happen the old promotion system was bound to break down, for if some offices could function with an untrained clerk at their head, others, and notably the kitchen, could not; this is perhaps why men who came into their first post in the department as clerks of the acatry, for example,[3] tended to stay there and why the kitchen began to recruit its clerks from its own junior, and trained, men.

The other promotion ladder or ladders in the household below stairs

[1] LS 13/258, pp. 65–6.
[2] LS 13/260 (royal warrant to the lord steward, 17 November 1722).
[3] Three clerks (actually joint-clerks) of the acatry were appointed during George I's reign—Charles Tuckwell (1716–18) James Bret (1718–22) and Sir Anthony Wescombe, Bt. (1722–7)—and for all of them it was their initial household appointment.

provided not for movement from one office of the department to another but simply for promotion between the non-clerical posts in each office. In most offices this meant beginning as a groom and rising by seniority through that rank to become a yeoman of the office, though some offices had a higher level—gentleman or sergeant, and, in the kitchen, master cook—and the kitchen also had several lower than groom—child, scourer, turnbroach and doorkeeper. With only a few exceptions[1] the system of promotion by seniority in these offices was still operating in the department. Promotions from groom to yeoman regularly took place as vacancies occurred; and in the kitchen—where the beginning of the promotion ladder was at the level of child and not below—the master cooks of George I's household had all worked up through the ranks, having been many years in the department.[2] This regular succession was sometimes interrupted at a change of sovereign because of the necessary amalgamation of two courts, but the general pattern was not unduly disturbed by this.

There was by comparison very little regular promotion in the chamber. In only one post was promotion automatic when a vacancy occurred above; the assistant gentleman usher in the presence chamber invariably became a gentleman usher when the senior usher died or retired. In the reign of George I there was only a handful of other promotions, all of them isolated cases not apparently following or creating a precedent. Of course not everyone who had a chamber post would be interested in promotion; the carvers, cupbearers and sewers of the eighteenth century were, as often as not, men whose main work and interests lay elsewhere and who occupied these sinecures perhaps partly for the honour, partly for the salary and as insurance against the future, and for whom promotion to a post that required their attendance would not be welcome. For those seeking it, promotion in the chamber was no easy matter; it seems likely that patronage, family influence and favour were as important in securing a promotion as an original appointment. The duchess of Marlborough wrote of a page of the bedchamber who 'had risen to this employment from being a footman, and without money';[3] it is difficult to know which is more astonishing, the fact

---

[1] Several gentlemen of the buttery had not worked their way up to that post.
[2] Claud Arnaud, snr., who became a master cook in 1725 had, for example, entered the office as a child of the kitchen in 1692.
[3] W. King (ed.), *The Memoirs of the Duchess of Marlborough*, p. 217.

that he had not eased his way with money or that he had moved at all.

The difficulties of promotion in the chamber—though this is at a fairly high level—are perfectly illustrated by the case of Peter Wentworth who seems to have devoted a good part of his life to trying to make his way at court. He was the brother of Thomas Wentworth, earl of Strafford who was in such odium at the beginning of the reign of George I for the part he played in the Treaty of Utrecht. Wentworth had been appointed an equerry to Queen Anne, a position which, because the salary was only £250 after taxes and fees were paid, had never satisfied him. At the beginning of the new reign he was full of hope of being promoted to groom of the bedchamber and of achieving this, surprising as this may seem, mainly by his brother's influence. Strafford, who was recalled as Ambassador Extraordinary to the United Provinces on 20 November 1714,[1] and who was as concerned about his own future as his brother's,[2] agreed to present Wentworth's request to the king at The Hague when George I arrived there on his way to England.[3] Neither this, nor the duke of Shrewsbury's support, nor, after the king arrived, that of some of his German ministers, was sufficient, and Wentworth remained an equerry.[4] He then tried to get appointed a groom extraordinary, that is, in effect, to get the post in reversion, but this also failed. He had spoken about this, he told his brother on 2 November, with Baron Görtz, the Hanoverian treasurer in London.

I desired he would speak that I might be made Groom Extraordinary and that the Establishment might not be exceeded, I might continue my Salary as Query to the King and the Pention I have as servant to the late Prince of Denmark. He promised he wou'd, but I have no great faith in success, because he told me he shou'd see me at Court at noon where I did not fail to meet him but he said nothing to me. I did not make much up to him for fear people shou'd take notice for the cry is already that too much is done by Forreigners.[5]

Three days later Görtz told him that the king had 'said I must be

---

[1] Horn, *British Diplomatic Representatives*, p. 160.
[2] See, for example, his letters in September to Dartmouth and Argyll (Add. MSS. 22211, fo. 37; 22221, fos. 77–8).
[3] Cartwright, *Wentworth Papers*, p. 416.
[4] Add. MSS. 31144, fo. 507; Cartwright, *Wentworth Papers*, p. 433.
[5] *Ibid.* pp. 433–4.

content yet awhile with what I am'.[1] In letters very much like those Burnet wrote to Duckett, Wentworth kept his brother informed throughout this reign and into the next of his continuing search for promotion. He spent a good deal of time at court, more apparently than his place demanded. In August 1717 he said that

my time is still spent half between London and Hampton Court, having every time some repeated promise that some thing shall be done for me.[2]

At George I's death, he had to make way as equerry for those who had served the Prince of Wales, but he was compensated with a similar place in the queen's court. He even became her secretary and had, as he said in 1729, 'honours and favours heaped upon me', but, he still complained, 'no money yet'.[3] Ease and affluence continued to elude him despite the fact that he was diligent in his attendance and service, despite the fact that whenever he got a chance he put himself 'in sight of the King and Queen, well powdered, when the weather would permit me'.[4] There is little wonder that his son should declare that 'the Summett of my Ambition is to be Easy and Quiet from a long attendance as my father has had at Court'.[5]

Apart from the very highest posts and, to some extent, the household below stairs, there was very little movement from one post to another at court. Having come into an office in the chamber and its offshoots a man would almost certainly remain in it until he died or was removed. How long he might expect to remain in it—his security of tenure— is a subject we must turn to now.

V

By far the greatest number of places in the royal household were held 'during pleasure', the pleasure, in the case of the greater posts, of the king, and in the case of the bulk of middle and lower ranking places, of the head of the department. Dismissals could be effected simply by notification of the withdrawal of pleasure and the issuance of a warrant of appointment to another man. There were very few posts at court that were granted with absolute security of tenure, that is for life or for a

[1] Cartwright, *Wentworth Papers*, p. 436.
[2] Add. MSS. 22227, fo. 23.
[3] *Ibid.* fo. 82.
[4] Add. MSS. 31145, fo. 13.
[5] Add. MSS. 22229, fo. 217.

term of years. Among the former were the following posts: knight marshal of the household, housekeeper of Whitehall and of Kensington, master of the revels, surveyor of the gardens and waterworks, keeper of the lions in the Tower;[1] among those granted for a term of years: printer (30 years) and bookseller (40 years).[2] Two other offices, clerk of the wardrobes and knight harbinger, were granted in George I's reign 'during good behaviour',[3] not as precarious a tenure as 'during pleasure' perhaps, but still not as secure as those granted for a number of years or for life. But these few exceptions apart, the generality of those who got court posts were not ensured of permanence.

Tenure 'during pleasure' was not equally insecure for all men. Below the first rank there seem to have been few dismissals while the sovereign lived. For those in the higher posts however, and especially for peers and members of Parliament in office, there was inevitably political involvement and this was bound to introduce a certain precariousness into their tenure of office. So long as the administration had the king's confidence it was natural that those who served him at court would also serve him in Parliament by voting for the ministry. Lord Berkeley of Stratton seemed to hold the doctrine that such loyalty was only due from those who were being paid; those with only honorary places, he seemed to believe, were freed from it. He advised Lord Strafford in November 1714, when Strafford was unsure whether he should ask the king for a pension: '...I am thinking that if you still pres't to be of the bedchamber supernumerary without pension, it would show an inclination to the service, a disinterestedness, and leave you at full liberty in Parliament...'[4] But normally, he implies, courtiers who were paid

---

[1] Patent Rolls: C 66/3513/6, C 66/3552/8, C 66/3553/16, C 66/3559/24, C 66/3561/9, C 66/3562/20.

[2] C 66/3513/6, C 66/3520/13. [3] C 66/3548/3, C 66/3552/4.

[4] Cartwright, *Wentworth Papers*, pp. 434–6. Just as curious a notion was advanced by Carnarvon in 1718. He seems to suggest in the following letter written to Lord Harcourt on 10 September, that only if the king's ministers were instrumental in getting a man a favour granted was political obligation due to them; the same favour from the king, granted without their help, brought no such obligation. His 'affair'—which could only be the grant of his dukedom—was almost completed, he wrote, and he continued: As this Mark of the King's Favour comes immediately from his own goodness, without such an intervention of his Ministers as will lay Me under the obligation of an entire dependence upon them, and an absolute resignation of myself to their Measures' (HM, Stowe MSS. 57, vol. 15, pp. 333–4).

were not at liberty to vote freely. Of course, whether dismissal followed political disloyalty would depend on whether ministers could persuade the king of its necessity. In George I's reign there seem to have been few bonds of affection between the king and his courtiers, bonds that under George II occasionally protected courtiers who did not wholeheartedly support the administration.[1] George I, however, was not a vindictive man[2] and there were very few dismissals from political motives in his reign. Conyers Darcy, one of the commissioners for the office of master of the horse, was dismissed in June 1717 because he had consistently opposed the government in Parliament;[3] and the duke of Grafton and the earl of Dorset were both dismissed from their bedchamber posts in July 1717, following Walpole's resignation.[4] In February 1716 Sir John Walter, a Tory, member of Parliament for the City of Oxford, was dismissed from the clerkship of the green cloth he had obtained in 1711, also for opposing the government.[5] There were, of course, other removals—as has been seen earlier there was a good deal of mobility in this first rank of court posts—but there were few men removed in anger[6] and who were not compensated either with a peerage, like

---

[1] See above, p. 140.

[2] The following remark in a letter of Townshend to Stanhope in September 1716 after the duke of Argyll had been forced to vacate his post in the prince's household earlier in the year, gives some indication of this: '...his majesty may remember, that upon his shewing us the list of the duke of Argyle's creatures and dependants given him by the duke of Roxburgh, he was pleased to declare, that such of them against whom the want of zeal or skill in their business could not be objected, should keep their places...' (Coxe, *Walpole*, II, 93). See also Newcastle's remark in 1723 that 'the King was always good to those who had got into his service' (Add. MSS. 32686, fo. 269).   [3] *H.M.C. Polwarth MSS.* I, 271.

[4] *S.P. Dom.* 35/9/39 and 41; for the split in the ministry of which these dismissals were a result see below chapter 7.

[5] W. R. Williams, *The Parliamentary History of Oxfordshire*, p. 125.

[6] Lord Guernsey, who resigned his place of master of the jewel office in March 1716, was perhaps on the verge of being dismissed. He had voted, along with his father, Lord Aylsford, and his uncle, Nottingham, in favour of the lords condemned for their part in the Rebellion of 1715, for which Nottingham had been dismissed as lord president of the council and Aylsford as chancellor of the duchy of Lancaster. In reporting the dismissals to his brother, Walpole wrote that 'all the trouble we have had in favour of the condemned lords arose from that Corner'; and Lady Cowper recorded in her diary that the king was very angry about this opposition from men in his service (N.S.A., *Cal. Br. Arch.*, Des. 24, England 123, newsletters of 13 March, 5 April, 1716; Coxe, *Walpole*, II, 51; Lady Cowper, *Diary*, p. 84).

Boscawen, or with a pension, like Radnor.[1] Also, a little political in-discretion did not necessarily bring dismissal. Consistent opposition could not be overlooked, but occasional lapses often were. Lord Lons-dale, for example, voted against the government several times in November 1718 and January 1719 (on one occasion while he was actually in his week of waiting as gentleman of the bedchamber) without losing his place.[2]

Below the first rank there was much greater security of tenure while the sovereign was living. When a new court was established at the beginning of a reign, as we shall see presently, there was little security for some lower servants against exclusion, especially if, as was usually the case, the new sovereign had had a household as heir to the throne, the members of which had to be accommodated. But apart from this important exception, dismissals of middle and lower ranking servants in the chamber and in the household below stairs were not common. In the appointment books of the lord chamberlain's department,[3] in which the cause of a vacancy is always noted, only two cases of dis-missal are recorded for the whole reign. In the household below stairs the dismissal of a confectioner for saying slanderous things against Madame Kielmannsegge has already been noted.[4] But in this depart-ment too dismissals were infrequent. And the case of Edward Phillips, a messenger to the accounting house, suggests that the lord steward and the board of green cloth were in fact extremely reluctant to dismiss anyone at all.[5]

[1] *H.M.C. Polwarth MSS.* II, 566–7.

[2] Add. MSS. 33064, fo. 178; *H.M.C. Portland MSS.* V, 570.

[3] LC 3/63–4, for George I's reign.

[4] Above, p. 136.

[5] Phillips's main work was to wait outside the room in which the board of green cloth met—and in which the clerk on duty worked—to be ready to carry messages. In November 1723 he was suspended from his office 'for his dilatory and negligent performance of a message he was to carry from the Board to the Hon. Giles Earle, Esq.' No details are given, but it is clear that this particular indiscretion was only one of Phillips's many sins. When in April 1724 this suspension was removed it was only lifted under the following conditions, which hint at the comprehensiveness of his former evil practices:
'In the duty of your office you are here as messenger only, and are not to exhort, demand or receive fees from any persons whatsoever when you are sent with messages, orders or petitions from this office.
Neither are you for the future to interfere with the chamber keeper [of the Green

The establishment of a new court at the beginning of a reign did not endanger equally the jobs of all those who had served in the previous sovereign's household. The heir to the throne's household was inevitably smaller than the royal household to be established and since the Prince of Wales did not have any yeomen of the guard, or gentlemen pensioners or sergeants at arms, or numerous other servants to be found in the main court, those in these positions were not as insecure at the end of a reign as the deceased monarch's bedchamber servants or his cooks, who might have to give way to the prince's servants. Changes were very easy to effect at the beginning of a new reign. By an Act of Anne's reign,[1] all public officers, including household servants, were to continue in office for six months after the death of a sovereign unless sooner removed by the next successor. But all household servants had to be reappointed to office and had to be sworn in again in the new reign, so that a positive act of dismissal was therefore unnecessary; the post could simply be given to another. How extensive such removals were depended in part on the size of the heir to the throne's household and doubtless the extent to which he felt himself committed to reward those who had served him as heir. Infrequently, as in 1714, the new monarch had not had a household—that is, an English household— as heir to the throne and this meant that the setting up of a new court did not involve many dismissals from the old. The establishment of the new households in 1714 and 1727, provides ample illustration of the different ways in which the demise of a sovereign could affect the tenure of court servants.

In 1714 only those in the first rank of court posts were seriously disturbed by the change of sovereigns. The mistress of the robes and all

Cloth] in his office, by claiming any share in fees that are his; neither are you to wait at the door unless you are called thereto.

And at all times for the future you do behave yourself with sobriety, honesty and diligence.'

Phillips was further warned not to be absent without leave, and was reinstated. Within a year he was in trouble again, having sold information to a man that the board of green cloth had given permission to his creditors to proceed against him; for this the board asked the lord steward to dismiss him 'as this, my Lord, is betraying the greatest trust that can be reposed in the said Phillips'. The lord steward agreed, and Phillips was finally dismissed. But clearly dismissals were not undertaken lightly (LS 13/115, fo. 125; LS 13/176, pp. 213, 219).

[1] 6 Anne, c. 3.

the ladies and women of the bedchamber of course lost their places, and there were twelve other changes in the first rank, nine of them outright dismissals. For the most part these changes involved the reinstatement of Whigs who had been displaced by Anne's last ministry.[1]

Below the first rank there were very few changes. Four of the pages of the bedchamber were replaced, two of the new pages being men who had served William III and had been displaced in 1702. Bernard Granville, the brother of Lord Lansdowne, lost his place as carver, but none of the other servants attached to the public rooms was disturbed. A few of Queen Anne's more personal servants were removed,[2] and a number of lower servants in the stables lost their places, but altogether there were only roughly twenty changes among middle- and lower-ranking servants in the chamber and its offshoots and about ten in the stables; in the household below stairs there were some readjustments of personnel, but no dismissals.

The changes in the household in 1714 were almost entirely political in nature. George I took over Queen Anne's household largely intact. There was a purge of Tories in high places but the purge was not very

[1] The duke of Devonshire, who had been lord steward 1707–10 was brought back in the place of Earl Paulet; the earl of Cholmondeley, treasurer of the household 1708–13, who had lost his place for speaking against the Peace of Utrecht in the council replaced Lord Lansdowne as treasurer (Swift, *Journal to Stella*, ed. H. Williams p. 656; Add. MSS. 17677 HHH, fo. 423); the earl of Godolphin, who had been cofferer 1704–11 and who had lost his place to Lord Masham, was reinstated in it; Edmund Dunch, master of the household 1708–10 came back into that office in place of Sir William Pole; and Charles Godfrey, clerk of the board of green cloth 1704–11, came back in place of Charles Scarborough. With Sir John Stonehouse being replaced by Hugh Boscawen, the entire board of green cloth, except for two clerks, was replaced at the beginning of the new reign, most of the changes resulting in the reinstatement not only of Whigs and former officers but also of relatives of the duke of Marlborough. There were a few other changes. The duke of St Albans who had also lost the post of captain of the band of gentlemen pensioners in 1712 for speaking against the ministry was reinstated, replacing the duke of Beaufort. (*H.M.C. Dartmouth MSS.* p. 309; Add. MSS. 17677 HHH, fo. 395). The earl of Radnor replaced Lord Delawarr as treasurer of the chamber, but Delawarr received another post—a tellership of the Exchequer—in compensation. The only other changes in the first rank in 1714 involved three of Queen Anne's equerries: one, William Duncombe, lost his place, and two, George Fielding and William Breton, were both promoted to the post of groom of the bedchamber.

[2] Three physicians and her laundress of the body linen, sempstress, starcher and yeoman of the robes.

thorough and there was no attempt to remove lower servants appointed during the late ministry.

In 1727, at the accession of George II, there were many more changes in the household, especially below the first rank, caused by the amalgamation of the prince's court and the late king's. Changes were not unexpected by contemporaries. When news of the death of George I reached England, there was not, according to Lord Hervey,

a creature in office, excepting those who were his [George II's] servants as Prince, who had not the most sorrowful and dejected countenance of distress and disappointment, so there was not one out of employment who did not already exult with all the insolence of the most absolute power and settled prosperity.[1]

Among the more personal servants the changes were naturally most striking. All eight of the prince's gentlemen of the bedchamber and six of his seven grooms, found employment in those positions in the new court. The size of the bedchamber establishment was at the same time reduced from George I's seventeen gentlemen (and one supernumerary) and ten grooms, to twelve and nine respectively. Fourteen of George I's gentlemen and all ten grooms were thus displaced.

Others of the prince's personal servants were rewarded with places in the new court. Augustus Schutz, a favourite who had come over from Hanover in the prince's entourage in 1714 and who had served him as master of the robes, displaced Walpole's son-in-law, Lord Malpas, from that post in the royal household. Malpas became a lord of the Admiralty and, in 1728, master of the horse to the Prince of Wales. Another favourite, the earl of Scarborough came in as master of the horse, having served George II as Prince of Wales in that office; Francis Negus was compensated with the mastership of the buckhounds, vacant at George I's death. There were further changes in the higher ranks of the stables. Two of the prince's pages of honour and three of his equerries displaced an equal number of those who had served George I. The only changes on the board of green cloth was the substitution of three of the prince's clerks for three of George I's clerks. The only change, apart from the mastership of the robes, among important chamber places was the replacement in the treasurership of the chamber of Charles Stanhope by Sir John Hobart who was the father of Henrietta Howard, later countess of Suffolk, George II's mistress.

Some of these changes in the first rank of court posts in 1727 may have

---

[1] Hervey, *Memoirs* (ed. Sedgwick), pp. 25–6.

been stimulated by political motives. Walpole, it was widely believed,[1] forced the dismissal of the earl of Berkeley from his post as first lord of the Admiralty so that Berkeley's further dismissal from the bedchamber may have been politically inspired. But it seems clear that the generality of changes in the first rank in 1727, unlike those in 1714, were not at root political but can be explained quite simply as the result of the grafting of the prince's household on to the household already in existence.

It was clearly for this reason that there were many more changes below the first rank in 1727 than there had been at the beginning of George I's reign. Whereas the number of servants displaced at Anne's death was about twenty in the chamber, ten in the stables and none in the household below stairs, in 1727 the corresponding figures were, roughly, fifty, thirty and thirty. Of these 110 new servants in 1727, at least seventy can be identified as having served George II as the Prince of Wales.

Not all of those displaced from the royal household in 1727 were entirely unprovided for. Two gentlemen ushers, Henry Sauniers and Mark Anthony Saurin, who gave way to two of the prince's ushers, found places in the queen's court; and Francis Coxeter who lost his place as a quarter waiter, became an usher to Princess Louisa. Another quarter waiter who was displaced, Langham Edwards, came back to court in 1728 as a groom of the privy chamber.

There was of course a good deal of continuity in personnel between one reign and the next, even when the heir to the throne's court had to be grafted on to the main court, because the permanent royal household was so much larger than the ephemeral one set up for a Prince of Wales. Long careers in the household were not unusual, indeed they were more the rule than the exception. The end of a reign brought a certain period of insecurity for many servants, more especially for those in posts that were duplicated in the heir's household. And the death of a sovereign was sufficiently unsettling to make Lord Dartmouth's dictum applicable to all levels of the court and not just to the first rank: 'nobody', he wrote in October, 1714, 'ought to look upon a place at Court (especially in England) as a settlement for life'.[2] But most court servants managed to weather the storm at the end of a reign and managed to survive to enjoy the fruits of office. What those fruits were—the value of court office—forms the subject of the next chapter.

[1] Hervey, *Memoirs* (ed. Sedgwick), p. 27; H.M.C. T.W. Webb MSS. p. 683; H.M.C. Portland MSS. VII, 449–50.   [2] Add. MSS. 22211, fo. 39.

6

THE VALUE OF OFFICE

I

In no other way are such eighteenth-century handbooks as Chamberlayne's *Magnae Britanniae Notitia; or, The Present State of Great Britain* more inaccurate or misleading about the household than in the matter of the value of offices. This is because for only very few offices was the established wage or fee—which is all that Chamberlayne could include—the only income. In some cases the allowance paid by a household treasurer or by the exchequer may have provided the bulk of a court officer's income but most often it was only a part, and sometimes a small part, of it. The difference could be quite striking. The fixed salary (including a payment known as board-wages) of the cofferer and of a clerk of the board of green cloth, for example, was £500 each, whereas the true value of these posts was closer to £3,000 and £1,000 a year respectively. Similarly a treasurer of the chamber could expect to receive a yearly sum close to five times that of his fixed allowances of £469; and, to take a less important but perhaps more typical case, the post of yeoman of the jewel office was probably worth more than double the stated salary of £107 a year. Almost all court office-holders at all levels, enjoyed further benefits of several kinds which, as these examples suggest, could increase substantially the profits of an office. These benefits could include one or more of the following: a pension, board-wages, diet at court, lodgings or money in lieu of them, travelling wages, a 'livery'—either clothes or material or a money payment—and fees and perquisites of various kinds.

The annual stipend of court offices consisted in some cases simply of a wage or fee, in others, of this plus board-wages. Board-wages were paid by the cofferer to many officers in the departments under the lord steward and lord chamberlain who had previously enjoyed the right to dine at court. A hundred years earlier an allowance of 'diet' had been for numerous officers a major part of the emoluments of office and also one of the major items in the annual expenditure of the

Crown.[1] At the Restoration such entertainment on a lavish scale was continued[2] but such was the burden on the royal finances that retrenchments were soon necessary. By 1668 only court servants who came regularly into waiting were given a diet;[3] and board-wages, a fixed payment, was paid to those whose right to dine at court had been taken away. In George I's reign many of those who came regularly into waiting still dined at court during their week or month of duty, but this right was now confined to these servants.[4]

Many officers in the lord chamberlain's department and the great majority of those under the lord steward received board-wages in the eighteenth century in the place of a diet at court. The amounts of course varied greatly—from £1,360 a year paid to the lord steward down to £23 a year paid to the pages of the presence—but the board-wages paid in the eighteenth century were not simply a strict equivalent for the value of the diet lost. They did not always conform, as the diet itself had,[5] to the rank of the officer concerned. Rather board-wages were now essentially part of the fixed salary, and it seems clear that they were a means of bringing an ancient fee up to date and of ensuring that this fee and the board-wages together reflected the rank of the office. Thus the ancient fee of the lord chamberlain was £100 a year, that of the master of the robes was £50 and that of the groom of the stole £33. 6s. 8d. By the eighteenth century these men received board-wages of £1,100, £400 and £966. 13s. 4d. respectively, so that, in all essentials, their annual salaries were £1,200, £450 and £1,000 each. Board-wages were also used to equalize the ancient fees of offices of roughly the same rank. The treasurer and the comptroller of the household, for example, were paid board-wages sufficient to give them each a salary of £1,200 a year, though they had previously enjoyed a similar 'diet' and their old wage or fee remained at £123. 14s. 8d. and £107. 17s. 6d. respectively. And the old wages of the cofferer (£100) the master of the household (£66. 13s. 4d.) and the clerks of the board of green cloth (£44. 6s. 8d.) were all raised by the addition of board-wages, to £500 a year each; the clerks of the green cloth, that is, received more in board-wages than

---

[1] Aylmer, *The King's Servants*, p. 168.
[2] LS 13/31 (household establishment, 1662).
[3] LS 13/35 (household establishment, 1668).
[4] LS 9/115–124 ('Books of Fare').
[5] Aylmer, *The King's Servants*, p. 168.

the first two, though their allowance of diet at court had only been half that of the cofferer and the master.[1]

That board-wages were not simply a strict money equivalent of a previous 'diet' is most clearly underlined by the fact that many of those who still dined at court were paid board-wages as well. In their case too, this was a supplementary payment which increased what was generally a very low fee and also made the resulting salaries correspond more than they had to equivalent ranks. Thus the posts of gentleman usher daily waiter and gentleman usher of the privy chamber were by the eighteenth century roughly equal in terms of honour. In the sixteenth century, however, when the privy chamber had been more like the private apartments of the eighteenth century, the post of usher of the privy chamber had been correspondingly more honorific than those of the less private presence chamber, and the sixteenth-century wage, still paid in George I's reign, had reflected this difference: the ushers in the privy chamber received £150 a year and those in the presence £20 a year. But the addition of board-wages brought these offices closer together in value, as, by the eighteenth century, they were in honour. For the ushers in the privy chamber were given only £50 in board-wages, to make their salary £200 a year, while those in the presence chamber had £130 and an annual allowance therefore of £150.

Board-wages in the eighteenth century were paid in most cases not only in lieu of dinner and supper at court but also in lieu of another allowance that had once been even more widely enjoyed among court servants than diet;[2] this was a daily allowance of bread, beer, and wine known as 'bouge' of court. In George I's reign 'bouge' was still delivered out of the appropriate household offices, in accordance with the limits laid down by the establishment, to the king's table and to the tables of those servants who dined at court. The first clerk of the kitchen and the first master cook each had a daily allowance of a loaf of bread, a gallon of beer and a bottle of claret (the clerk and the cook actually in waiting had a separate allowance)[3] but normally 'bouge' was delivered to groups of officers, rather than to individuals. Thus the eleven men who dined at the gentlemen ushers' table also received daily eighteen manchets and twelve loaves, eight gallons of beer and ten

[1] LS 13/31, p. 3.
[2] Aylmer, *The King's Servants*, p. 170.
[3] LS 13/44.

bottles of wine;[1] and the yeomen of the guard got twenty-eight loaves and twenty-one gallons of beer. A number of servants below stairs who were not allowed a diet were still in receipt of this daily allowance.[2] But the scale on which these allowances were provided in the eighteenth century—both the amounts and the number of servants who enjoyed them—was very much reduced from what it had been a century earlier. The difference in scale can be seen perhaps most clearly by a comparison of the allowances for wastage—the amounts the offices which distributed the 'bouge' were allowed to claim in their accounts as wastage each day—in both periods. In the period 1627–30 this was set at 200 loaves, 240 gallons of ale and twenty-four gallons of wine;[3] in 1714 the maximum waste allowed was six loaves, six gallons of beer and five bottles of wine a day.[4] The vast majority of those who had previously been given 'bouge' and a diet as part of the emoluments of office were by the eighteenth century given a fixed allowance of board-wages instead.

Some of the more important officers received a further supplementary payment from the Crown. Thomas Coke, vice-chamberlain to Queen Anne and George I, had two such payments above his wages and board-wages of £559: £600 paid at the exchequer, and a further £1,000 which Anne gave him 'in consideration of his constant waiting and attendance on her person and the extraordinary expense occasioned him thereby'. This had been paid in Anne's reign out of the privy purse, 'to avoid it being a precedent', but George I continued it in the form of a pension, and since Lord Hervey had a similar grant during part of his tenure as vice-chamberlain to George II, it seems to have become a settled part of the salary of the post.[5] Some lords chamberlain also had a pension from the Crown. Shrewsbury had £2,000 while in the office, and Grafton had £3,000. But these may have been given for particular considerations in each case and not simply to increase the salary of the post,[6] for the duke of Newcastle does not seem to have

---

[1] There were complaints from time to time that this 'bouge' was not always shared equally; in 1719 a complaint was made to the lord chamberlain that much of the bread and wine provided for the gentlemen ushers' table was 'sent away to private lodgings and houses whereby his Majesty's Servants who have a right to eat there are deprived of their allowance' (LC 5/157, p. 210).

[2] LS 13/44.   [3] Aylmer, *The King's Servants*, p. 170.

[4] LS 13/44.   [5] C(H)MSS. 45/50; T 1/181/35; *C.T.B.* xxx, 290–1.

[6] Shrewsbury's pension was perhaps in compensation for his having lost the offices of lord treasurer and lord lieutenant of Ireland at George I's accession; a contemporary

enjoyed a pension or any supplementary allowances as lord chamberlain; this was perhaps one reason why he was rejoicing, a year before he became secretary of state, of 'some prospects I have had of exchanging my place for one infinitely more profitable'.[1] Two other great court officers, the groom of the stole and the master of the horse, commonly received a substantial pension to supplement a fixed allowance of wages and board-wages. Anne's master of the horse seems to have received an extra £4,000 a year.[2] As for the grooms of the stole, Portland under William III, and the duchesses of Marlborough and Somerset under Anne, had £2,000 a year from the exchequer. George I gave his two grooms, Sunderland and Godolphin, £4,000 a year, to make their total salary £5,000 and the office one of the most profitable as well as most honourable at court.[3]

Such large supplementary allowances were never enjoyed by more than a few courtiers of the first rank, but the salaries of most court servants were enhanced in several other ways. One of these was the provision of lodgings at court. Lodgings were generally enjoyed by court servants as a right inherent in particular offices and not simply as a favour from the Crown. The duke of Montagu, master of the great wardrobe, in complaining to the lord chamberlain about a room having been taken from him at Windsor, spoke of his right to have lodgings there, as he had lodgings at Hampton Court and in Whitehall.[4] In 1720, the yeoman of the scullery was said to enjoy lodgings 'by virtue of his office, custom and My Lord Steward's warrants'.[5] And in 1719 the lord chamberlain wrote to the housekeepers to remind them 'that no person shall be permitted to have lodgings...who are not by their places entitled thereto'.[6] Not all court servants were given lodgings, but the great majority of these who came regularly into waiting—in all departments and of all ranks—were provided either with an apartment or with a money composition in its place. Indeed the fact that a man

thought he had asked for it on these grounds (Cartwright, *Wentworth Papers*, p. 421). In Grafton's case his status as the son of one of Charles II's bastards may have been a more important factor than the office he held.

[1] Quoted by S. H. Nulle, *Thomas Pelham-Holles, Duke of Newcastle: his early political career, 1693–1724* (1931), p. 165.   [2] T 1/124/39.

[3] C(H)MSS. 45/39; Blenheim MSS. D 1/38.

[4] H.M.C. *Buccleuch and Queensberry MSS.* I, 217.

[5] LS 13/115, fo. 102.

[6] LC 5/157, p. 247.

came into waiting seems to have been the crucial point in determining whether he would have lodgings or not.[1] Particular sets of rooms became attached to particular jobs. In 1717, when Sir William Forester retired as a clerk of the board of green cloth and in recognition of his twenty-eight years in that post was allowed to keep his lodgings in Whitehall 'for the rest of his life', the succeeding clerk, William Coventry, was thereby deprived of lodgings and was given an allowance of £80 a year instead.[2]

Lodgings of course varied in size. Some of the lesser servants, especially in the household below stairs, had only a room or two attached to their places of work.[3] But most lodgings consisted of several rooms—sometimes, as in the case of the master of the horse's lodgings at Hampton Court, as many as nine—with a kitchen and often a cellar and garrets and other additions;[4] they were often large enough to house the officer's family and his own servants as well. In London very few of these apartments were in the king's residence, St James's Palace, which was far too small to accommodate all those who had a right to lodgings. At the end of Anne's reign, the lord chamberlain and vice-chamberlain, the master cooks, and another fifteen or so officers had apartments in St James's.[5] But the great majority were lodged elsewhere: in Somerset House,[6] in the great mews at Charing Cross, where most of the officers of the stables including the equerries were lodged,[7] or scattered about in Whitehall, in apartments in the buildings of the old palace not destroyed in the fire, or in houses raised in the ruins. Many of these houses in Whitehall were held by court officers or leased from the Crown on very favourable terms. James Heymans, for example, had a house in the privy garden at £10 p.a. rent, and Patrick Lamb, the master cook, a house in the 'pastry yard' in Whitehall at a rent of 6s. 8d. a year.

---

[1] In 1716 a surveyor general of Crown lands successfully petitioned for a grant of lodgings on the grounds that he was a servant 'in constant attendance' (*C.T.B.* xxx, p. 105).

[2] LS 13/260 (royal warrants to the board of green cloth, 17 April and 20 September 1717).

[3] LC 5/202, pp. 218–23 (a list of lodgings in Whitehall in May 1713); LS 13/115, fo. 3.

[4] LC 5/202, pp. 195–201, 218–23, 339–44 (lodgings at Hampton Court, Whitehall and Somerset House).

[5] *H.M.C. Cowper MSS.* III, 110–11.

[6] LC 5/202, pp. 339–44.

[7] LS 13/260 (royal warrant dated 3 August 1724); *C.T.B.* xxx, pp. 121, 252.

A number of other houses in Whitehall had been built privately by officers on ground leased from the Crown.[1]

Not all those who were given apartments actually occupied them. In 1713 at least seven court officers, including three ushers, rented their apartments or houses in Whitehall and another officer, Somerset English the yeomen of the woodyard, lived in only part of his apartment and rented the rest.[2] But even if they were not thus turned to account, free lodgings must have been a considerable benefit to many, and must have done much to enhance the salaries especially of lesser servants.

Few court officers seem to have had lodgings provided at Kensington, and when the court was in residence there servants in waiting—at least those in the household below stairs—were given an extra daily allowance. These so-called 'travelling wages', which ranged from 3s. a day for a clerk to 1s. 6d. a day for a menial servant,[3] must be considered as another, though small, addition to the salaries of those court servants who came regularly into waiting. They were also paid to servants in all departments when the court was at Hampton Court or Windsor. Lodgings for most servants were provided there,[4] and further, some officers were given lodging and stabling allowances for the days on which they actually travelled to these palaces; the gentlemen pensioners, for example, had 13s. 4d. a day, and the equerries 22s. a day to cover the cost of their journeys. Though not all of those who travelled to Hampton Court or to Windsor enjoyed this, those who were in waiting in the country had the kind of 'travelling wages' that the servants of the household below stairs were given for their service at Kensington, that is a daily allowance above their salary while in waiting. The scale of these allowances for the officers and servants of the chamber varied between 7s. 6d. a day for a physician, and 6s. 8d. for a gentleman pensioner, down to 1s. 6d. for a musician; below stairs a clerk of the green cloth got 5s. a day and the other servants were paid at the same rate as at Kensington.[5]

[1] LC 5/202, pp. 218–23; N.S.A., Hannover 92, Schr. IIIA, No. 11X (a list of Crown leases in Whitehall (c. 1717). Some of the apartments in Somerset House may also have been held on lease, for Sir Charles Dalton, a gentleman usher, left his lodgings there to his nephew in his will (P.C.C. *Potter*, fo. 309).

[2] LC 5/202, pp. 218–23; N.S.A., Hannover 92, Schr. IIIA, No. 11X.

[3] LS 13/175, fo. 40.

[4] LC 5/202, pp. 195–201 (lodgings at Hampton Court).

[5] LS 8/55, fos, 1–3, 7. (household creditor, 1718); *C.T.B.* xxx, 322–3; LC 5/157, pp. 88–90.

'Travelling wages' did not provide a very large additional salary. Most servants were in waiting only part of a summer. And in George I's reign at least, the court did not go to the country every year since the king went to Hanover on six occasions.[1] Even when the court spent the whole summer in the country the extra allowances were not large for the majority of servants. In 1717, for example, George I spent almost four months at Hampton Court and a fortnight at Newmarket. During this period, the king's physician, who was in waiting every day, and who had the most generous allowance of travelling wages, 7s. 6d. a day, earned an extra sum of £45 and the two gentlemen ushers who shared the duty, added £22 and £13. 15s. respectively to their yearly salaries. But most servants in the chamber and household below stairs were richer by only £5 or £10.[2] Some individuals may have been grateful for these travelling wages, and particularly servants who had small annual allowances and who did more than their share of duty during the summer, but on the whole, and especially when averaged over the reign, they added only a pittance to court servants' income; and of course the cost of the journey to the country meant that these wages were not in any case pure profit.

Many servants of all ranks and in all departments received another small, though regular, payment: an allowance of clothes, or material or sometimes a money composition in its place. Some of this was delivered out of the office of the robes, and the stables provided a uniform for the coachmen and footmen and the other servants of the department who wore the king's livery. But most livery payments were made by the great wardrobe. This office provided many officers of the chamber and household below stairs, including the lord chamberlain, with one or two 'parcels' of material a year to an established value, paid sometimes in money, but most often in kind. It was in most cases not a large payment. The master of the great wardrobe's own livery was valued at £106. 13s. 4d., the lord chamberlain's £66. 16s., and the pages of the bedchamber got two issues worth together £46. 16s. 4d. But most liveries were between £10 and £20; again, as with travelling wages, only a small addition, and of particular benefit mainly to the lesser servants.[3]

[1] A number of English servants were always taken on these journeys but they were paid travelling wages for the journey only.

[2] LS 8/55, fo. 7; LC 5/157, pp. 88–90.

[3] *C.T.B.* XXIX, pp. cxciv–cxcvii; LC 9/347; C(H)MSS. 45/18/8.

II

The settled allowance of many court posts was thus supplemented by the Crown in a number of ways. But the most valuable source of supplementary income was not, at least directly, paid by the Crown and was irregular in amount. This was income from fees and perquisites. Fees provided the bulk of the income of a number of officers, but even when they were not so proportionately important, fees must often have been valued because salaries were rarely paid on time; delays of a few months were common and when the Civil List was in debt payments were sometimes a year or more behind. Many fees and perquisites must have been more regular in receipt than salaries and when court payments were so long delayed, must have been a sheer necessity for numerous men who had no other income than that derived from office.

Fees and perquisites were claimed by a great number of officers in all departments and at all levels. Perhaps the most valuable was the commission, known as poundage, that household treasurers took on the money they handled. The cofferer of the household, for example, collected 6d. in the pound on purveyors' bills and on the wages and board-wages paid in his office.[1] On the basis of the average annual expenditure of the office in George I's reign, the cofferer's poundage must have been at least £2,010 a year. With other small benefits and his wages and board-wages of £500 it is clear that the office was worth close to £3,000 a year gross, as a well informed observer estimated in George I's reign.[2] Of course this would be reduced by certain taxes and fees.[3] A new cofferer in 1754, George Lyttelton, thought that his place was 'good for £2000 a year' (and was enough incidently, that in three or four years it 'ought to build my new house without my being obliged to borrow').[4] Such an income of course helps to explain why an office lacking the honorific quality of many other court posts—it was only 'an office of profit', as one noble place-hunter rather apologetically admitted in 1728[5]—was held by two peers in George I's reign.

---

[1] LS 13/175, p. 107; LS 13/115, fo. 88; LS 13/116, fo. 3. The officers of the board of green cloth were not charged this cofferer's fee on their salaries; this was a considerable exemption, for, including the cofferer's own wages and board-wages, their salaries amounted to £6860 a year.

[2] Add. MSS. 17677 KKK 7 (L'Hermitage to the States General, 12 June 1725).

[3] See below, pp. 202–4.   [4] Quoted in Wiggin, *A Faction of Cousins*, p. 149.

[5] Add. MSS. 20105, fo. 36 (Lord Sussex to Mrs Clayton, 12 September [1728]).

After 1723 the deputy cofferer was also allowed by the board of green cloth to take a poundage of one per cent on all money issued on the cofferer's account. This created a lucrative minor place, for 1 per cent on all issues (including in this case the wages of the board of green cloth) would be worth close to £900 a year. The cofferer's clerks and a number of minor clerks in the household below stairs were also allowed to take poundage from the purveyors. The clerks of the acatry, buttery and woodyard received one penny per pound from the purveyors who supplied their offices; and the clerk of the kitchen's clerk was allowed a similar poundage from the purveyor of beer. These fees were of course petty compared to the cofferer's and his deputy's; they varied in 1714, from about £8 to the clerk of the kitchen's clerk to about £40 a year to the clerk of the poultry.[1]

A household purveyor who had already paid about £70 for his annual contract[2] was therefore obliged to pay close to 4 per cent of the value of his bill in household fees; and on top of that the purveyors paid a further 2½ per cent to the cofferer for Exchequer fees.[3] Not unnaturally the purveyors passed this burden on to the Crown in the form of higher prices. In the last year of Anne's reign the board of green cloth decided that it would be cheaper if the Crown paid these fees directly; it was thought that the purveyors 'might have no pretence for extravag[ant] prices' if fees were allowed in the accounts of the household.[4] In Christmas quarter 1713 this was done. But it proved to be too great a direct burden on the royal finances and this system did not survive the queen. In George I's reign the purveyors again paid household fees; that is to say the Crown continued to pay them, but indirectly.

Other household treasurers were also in receipt of poundage. The treasurer of the chamber seems to have taken over 5 per cent—over double that taken by the cofferer—on most bills and salaries paid in his office, though on some smaller salaries—the £40 to a yeoman of the guard, for example—he took less than 1 per cent. But the higher rate was much more common; and, indeed, in a calculation of the treasurer's poundage made by his clerks in 1720 for the benefit of the new treasurer, Henry Pelham, the total yield works out at 5½ per cent. On a computed

[1] LS 13/175, pp. 107–8. [2] *Ibid.* p. 110.
[3] Sir William Beveridge (and others), *Prices and Wages in England from the Twelfth to the Nineteenth Centuries*, p. 334. [4] LS 13/175, pp. 107–10.

expenditure of £34,727 his poundage was estimated to be £1,928,[1] since the real expenditure of the office averaged close to £40,000, the treasurer of the chamber's poundage in George I's reign must have been closer to £2,200. Out of this he had to pay £200 a year to his deputy who was not authorized to take fees. As in the case of the cofferer's fees, those taken by the treasurer of the chamber on salaries were paid by the servants, whereas at least some of the poundage taken on bills was paid by the Crown sometimes in the form of higher prices, occasionally directly as part of the bill.[2]

The master of the great wardrobe had in 1674 given up his right to levy a poundage of 12½ per cent on the purveyors' bills in return for a fixed salary of £2,000 for himself and £200 for his deputy;[3] and the clerk of the office was also, after 1702, paid £300 a year by the Crown in lieu of a poundage of 2½ per cent.[4] Notwithstanding, the master continued to extract a poundage from some purveyors and, since there was virtually no check on great wardrobe accounts, the purveyors in turn could not be prevented from passing this on to the Crown.[5] The master had the best of both worlds therefore, and while the duchess of Marlborough's suggestion that the post was worth £8,000 a year when she procured its reversion to her son-in-law[6] is doubtless exaggerated, the master clearly had some opportunities to increase his salary in an office with an annual expenditure of £23,000 over which there was so little outside control. The commissioners of the land tax for Westminster thought in 1712 that he probably made an extra £1,000 a year in fees and increased the duke of Montagu's assessment accordingly; but the master's deputy swore on oath that Montagu made no more than an extra £300 a year.[7]

[1] P.R.O. 30/26/113.   [2] *C.T.B.* xxvi, 455; LC 5/157, p. 159.
[3] *Ibid.* xv, 206.   [4] *Ibid.* xviii, 381.
[5] See above, chapter 4.
[6] W. King (ed.), *The Memoirs of the Duchess of Marlborough*, p. 304.
[7] LS 13/234, fo. 5. Paymasters also had the opportunity of using their balances in hand for their own purposes. That this was done occasionally is suggested perhaps, though it is not proved, by the evidence of a man who received, as executor to a deceased deputy treasurer of the chamber, '£15,000 of public money when it was not thought there was a shilling in the office'. By taking up offers of bills at a great discount he might he thought, have obtained a considerable estate with this money (*C.T.P.* 1708–14, p. 456). All paymasters who imprested money had *some* opportunity to use it privately, but no evidence has been found of them doing so in George I's reign.

Except in the household below stairs, the benefits of poundage were not felt much below the highest level in 'paying offices'. But both in these and in many other offices, court servants took fees for performing the service of the office, fees that were paid by the Crown, by the public or by other court servants. A few examples may serve to indicate their variety.

Generally speaking, whenever an office issued a warrant or a debenture, by virtue of which a household treasurer issued money, the clerks of the office received a fee for performing the service. The staff of the lord chamberlain's office, for example, collected a fee for issuing warrants requesting payments by the treasurer of the chamber and for those ordering goods or services from the great wardrobe and jewel office; these fees were paid either by the beneficiary of the warrant, or by the Crown as a charge in the accounts of an office. Further fees were collected whenever a man entered a chamber post, for every new servant had to obtain a warrant of appointment in order to receive his wages and for this he had to pay a fee to the clerks of the lord chamberlain's office and to the office keeper. In the 1780s these lord chamberlain's 'office fees' were apparently charged at three rates: £12. 14s. 6d. from such officers as a gentleman of the bedchamber and captain of the yeomen; £6. 14s. from middle-ranking officers such as a groom of the jewel office and sergeant at arms; and £3. 17s. 9d. from lesser servants like the waiter of the robes and the musicians.[1] No fee-books seem to have survived from the early eighteenth century but there is some evidence to suggest that the scale in George I's reign was very close to that in force in 1780.[2] It has proved impossible to attempt even an estimate of what these fees were worth in George I's reign, and in any case, it is unknown how they were shared among the clerks or if the lord chamberlain and his secretary benefited from them. The absence of any evidence suggests perhaps that the lord chamberlain himself did not take a share of the office fees; but his secretary may have. The secretary's salary was only £60 a year and this was hardly commensurate with the social position of the men who held the post. When Sir John Stanley retired as secretary he was given a pension of £400 a year and it is possible that this reflected the true annual value of the post and

---

[1] LC 9/376, pt. 1 (rough account books, including a book of fees paid in the lord chamberlain's office, *c.* 1780–1800).

[2] LC 5/3, p. 28 (office fees paid by a master of the ceremonies in 1715).

that the secretary could expect to make a good deal in office fees every year.[1]

In addition to these fees for warrants and certificates, a new office holder had to be sworn in, and in most cases he was required to pay a fee for this too. Some of the more important officers of the chamber including the vice-chamberlain, the officers of the yeomen and pensioners, and the gentlemen and grooms of the bedchamber, were sworn in by the lord chamberlain himself, but the greatest number were sworn in by the ushers on duty in the presence chamber. The lord chamberlain did not apparently collect a fee for this service, but the ushers did. The ushers' 'swearing fee' varied with the status of the officer sworn, from 5 guineas for a gentleman usher of the privy chamber down to 1 guinea for a waterman. These fees are also difficult to estimate accurately because the size of the fee received from every chamber servant is not known, nor the principle of distribution; the first usher may have taken more than the second and so on. But, assuming an equal distribution, it has been calculated very roughly that these fees probably were worth somewhere in the range of £20–£40 a year on average to each of the four ushers. At the beginning of a reign, when all office holders, new or continuing, had to be reappointed, swearing fees were lucrative. Each usher received perhaps £150 in 1714 and 1715; but over the reign they probably made only £25 or £30 a year.[2]

Similar fees, charged whenever the office performed a service, were collected in the jewel office. Whenever gold or silver plate was delivered out to those officers entitled to it, or to a private person as a gift from the Crown, or whenever a new knight of the garter received the insignia and ribbon of the order, or a waterman a badge, a fee had to be paid. This fee, which varied with the cost of the delivery, was shared by all the officers of the jewel office except the master. On 1000 oz. of plate delivered to an ambassador the office fee was £22. 10s. 9d., and was paid by the Crown; in most other cases these fees were paid by the individual.[3] In 1782, when the jewel office was suppressed, it was calculated that the fees in the office had averaged £540 a year since

[1] For Stanley see above, p. 25.
[2] This estimate is based on the scale of 'swearing fees' charged in the late eighteenth century. As with 'office fees', there is some evidence to suggest that a similar rate was in force in George I's reign (LC 9/376, pt. 1; LC 5/3, p. 28).
[3] *C.T.B.* XXIII, 460.

1760; since they were shared equally among the four officers under the master—a clerk, two yeomen, and a groom—they received £135 a year each.[1] There were only three officers in George I's reign (there was only one yeoman) so that, assuming that they collected fees on the same order as later in the century, their salaries must have been increased by about £180 a year each.

Office fees were also taken in the great wardrobe,[2] in the treasurer of the chamber's office[3] and in the household below stairs. The cofferer's clerks received a fee of £43 a year, paid by the Crown, for keeping office accounts,[4] and further fees from office-holders who were paid by the cofferer. To be paid wages or board-wages by the cofferer an officer would also have to pay a fee to the under-clerks of the board of green cloth for entering the certificate in the household accounts, another to the clerk of the kitchen for the debenture, and another to the door-keeper of the office, as well as the cofferer's own poundage and his clerks' fee for issuing the money.[5] The under-clerks of the board of green cloth extracted a fee from the purveyors for transcribing their contracts, and another for entering their bills in the book of comptroll-ment;[6] and all of the clerks of the sub-departments below stairs charged the purveyors £1 or £2 a year for the office debentures without which the purveyor could not be paid.[7]

These fees collected for performing the work, and generally the clerical work, of an office were further supplemented in some depart-ments, and especially below stairs, by fees on certain goods, by per-quisites in kind or by a money composition in lieu of these rights. The clerk of the spicery benefited particularly from these fees. He claimed the right to a percentage in kind of all the goods delivered out of his office: a fee on linen sent to the ewry, one ounce per pound on wax candles, two ounces per pound on tallow candles and percentages on all groceries and spices.[8] The board of green cloth was obviously aware

---

[1] LC 5/114 (not paginated; An account of the salaries and fees of the officers of the Jewel Office...', 1782).

[2] C.T.B. XXIII, 460; LC 9/376, pt. I.   [3] C.T.B. XXVI, p. 455; LC 5/157, p. 159.

[4] LS 1/60.

[5] Blenheim MSS. D 1/36, D 1/38 (Sunderland's receipts for board-wages paid at the cofferer's office, 1719 and 1720).

[6] LS 13/175, pp. 107–10.

[7] LS 13/115, fo. 88; LS 13/175, pp. 107–10.

[8] LS 13/115, fos. 13, 20, 21, 28, 68.

that such fees, taken by the man who controlled the office, could not but encourage poor stewardship. The clerk's fees were scrutinized at board meetings on several occasions in 1715, and at one meeting the increasing cost of the spicery office was discussed in conjunction with the clerk's fees and an attempt was made, according to the minutes, 'to regulate the same'.[1] But nothing came of this threat, if it was such, for the clerk of the spicery was taking the same fees in 1760.[2] The officers of the pantry[3] and the clerk of the acatry[4] also had fees on goods delivered out of their offices, in each case a money composition in lieu of a previous right to perquisites in kind; and the cooks claimed such perquisites as all lambs' heads, and the fat and dripping from roasts.[5]

Such perquisites of 'remains' as the cooks claimed were also common in other offices both in the lord steward's department—in the ewry, for example[6]—and above stairs. The ushers of the chamber and their servants took candle ends daily[7] and the servants who laid the table, the table 'deckers', for the gentlemen of the bedchamber and other court tables had the right to the remains of wine at these tables.[8]

Valuable perquisites rather like 'remains' also enhanced the salaries of some of the greatest court officers. Furniture 'unfit for the King's use' was the perquisite of the lord chamberlain;[9] and at the death of a sovereign the furniture of some of the public rooms whatever its con-

---

[1] LS 13/115, fo. 10.

[2] Bray MSS. 85/2/3 (a description of the household in 1760).

[3] The officers of the pantry shared a money fee, charged on the accounts of the bakehouse, which was the equivalent of two ounces on every twenty-three ounce loaf of bread delivered out of the pantry (LS 13/175, fo. 20).

[4] The clerk of the acatry was allowed by the board of green cloth in 1715 to continue to take a fee of 6s. 8d. per case of veal delivered into his office. This was paid by the Crown and charged in the account of incidental household expenses. It seems to have been worth between £150 and £200 a year to the clerk (LS 13/176, p. 32; LS 13/90; LS 1/60).

[5] LS 13/115, fo. 41.

[6] The gentleman of the ewry had a fee on every yard of material bought for tablecloths or napkins (LS 1/60); all the servants of the office had the right to claim for their own use worn cloths and napkins. It is clear that these rights were frequently abused (see above, p. 94).

[7] Blenheim MSS. F 1/65.

[8] Mrs A. T. Thomson (ed.), *Memoirs of Viscountess Sundon*, I, 240. In the late eighteenth century a 'table-decker' to the gentlemen of the bedchamber was said to have made £700 or £800 a year out of remains of wine (Bray MSS. 85/2/3).

[9] LC 3/13 (note at end of volume).

dition was his too.[1] The groom of the stole and the master of the horse also laid claim to some of a deceased sovereign's goods; the first had the right to take the furniture and hangings of some of the private rooms and the plate in use there; and the carriages and other equipage, but not the horses, were the master of the horse's perquisite. In 1714, however, Anne's groom of the stole, the duchess of Somerset, accepted £3,000 for relinquishing her pretensions to some of the furniture of the private apartments[2] and the commissioners for the office of master of the horse probably did so too for a money fee.[3]

All of these fees on goods handled in an office and perquisites of 'remains' were open to abuse. This was especially true of those taken in the household below stairs for many of the men claiming such fees were not only the accountants of the offices but also in some cases the purveyors too.[4] The right to purvey goods was doubtless in itself a source of profit for some household officers but the opportunities were obviously heightened when the man supplying the goods was responsible for checking his own honesty and when on top of that he also collected a fee on the goods he supplied. As has been seen, the board of green cloth in George I's reign made a determined effort to prevent fraud, but perhaps the only remedy, so far as the abuse of fees was concerned, was the withdrawal of the right to take them in return for an increased salary. The clerks of the green cloth had themselves given up a right to certain 'remains' in 1703 for a fixed sum of £438 a year 'to encourage them to execute their offices with care and frugality'.[5] A number of other officers had been similarly encouraged, but as has been seen, many more retained the right to these fees, doubtless to their own benefit and the Crown's impoverishment.

One other major source of fees remains to be discussed: fees of honour. These were fees paid to certain officers in all departments, according to a fixed schedule, by archbishops and bishops upon their appointment or translation, by knights of the garter and knights bachelor upon receiving the honour and by new peers or men promoted in the peerage.[6] They varied both with the degree of honour conferred and

[1] LC 5/156, pp. 26, 50, 139. [2] C.T.B. xxix, 237; LC 5/156, p. 57.
[3] C.T.B. xxx, cxci. [4] See chapter 3.
[5] LC 13/258, fo. 17.
[6] For the fees due for these various honours see John Chamberlayne, *Magnae Britanniae Notitia* (25th ed., 1718), pp. 94–8; C.T.B. xxxii, 259–60, 468–9.

with the rank of the officer receiving the fee. The four gentlemen ushers of the presence chamber shared a fee of £20 from a duke, £15 from a marquis, £10 from an earl and so on down to £5 for the creation of a knight bachelor, whereas the four pages of the presence shared fees for similar honours ranging from £3 down to 10s. These fees were most often paid by the recipient of the honour, though on occasion they were paid by the Treasury.[1] Not surprisingly, since they would be essentially private accounts, no full record of fees of honour received in the household seems to have survived. There is, however, a rather scrappy account of these fees received in 1715, which suggests that they were paid in a lump sum to one chamber servant who distributed them and kept a receipt book.[2] Since both the scale of fees and the number of honours granted are known, a calculation of their possible value, and an annual average can be calculated for George I's reign.[3] An estimated value appears in the table forming the appendix to this chapter. In the absence of more extensive records of such fees, this calculation must remain theoretical since it is not known whether the fees were always collected. An annual average of possible fees taken also conceals the fact that some holders of an office must have benefited more than others; at the beginning of a reign their annual value, for example, would be higher than at other times. But it at least provides a clue to the possible range of these fees. Some of the middle-ranking chamber servants made perhaps £30 a year in fees of honour, and one or two individuals such as the sergeant porter and the knight harbinger probably made more, though the lower servants of the lord steward's department and the footmen could only hope to increase their income by a pound or two a year from them.

[1] C.T.P. (1708–14), pp. 393–4.
[2] E 407/136 (a book of receipts for fees of honour, 1715).
[3] In calculating the figures contained in the appendix, the following sources have been relied on: *The Handbook of British Chronology* (2nd ed.), ed. by Powicke and Fryde, pp. 202–66 (for the appointment and translation of archbishops and bishops in George I's reign); W. A. Shaw, *The Knights of England* (2 vols., 1906) (for K.G.s and knighthoods); A. S. Turberville, *The House of Lords in the Eighteenth Century* (1927), App. A (for peerages).

III

Certain other occasional benefits besides fees and perquisites enhanced the value of court posts. Some of the greater officers had a right to a quantity of plate, valued at £400, out of the jewel office, which, though it was only on loan, was generally not returned.[1] A number of lesser servants received an annual Christmas or New Year's present from the king and from courtiers,[2] and some men—the pages of the bedchamber, the porters and footmen and perhaps others—could expect to receive some tips from the greater court officers and the public.[3] Other benefits were essentially negative in that they provided protection and immunity against some distasteful duty or forced service. Household servants, for example, were freed from the duty of serving on juries or holding local offices or from serving in the militia.[4] The seamen who worked for the king's purveyors of fish and on the boats bringing the king's wine from France, and even those who worked on the Thames for any royal purveyor, were protected against impressment into the navy.[5] Other rights were more positive but not directly monetary. The gentlemen ushers could invite friends to dine at their court table, for example.[6]

[1] LC 5/202, p. 12, and see above, chapter 2. Many household officers, including some in such middling posts as page of the bedchamber and clerk of the kitchen, received a gift of plate from the jewel office at the christening of their children (LC 5/156, pp. 250, 360; LC 5/157, pp. 62, 63, 87).

[2] George I distributed between £250 and £300 every year to a number of lesser servants including the footmen and musicians. There is an account of these at N.S.A., K.G., Cal. Br. 22, XIII, Anhang no. 3. For gifts from a nobleman to household servants at Christmas and New Year in 1698 see G. S. Thomson, *Life in a Noble Household*, pp. 354–5.

[3] Charles Cathcart, a gentleman of the bedchamber to the Prince of Wales, records in his diary giving tips of four and a half guineas to the pages of the bedchamber and a half guinea to their valet and to the necessary woman of the bedchamber; one may presume that such tips in the prince's household were common also in the king's (Cathcart MSS., Journal A/11, 2 February 1715; A/12, 9 January 1718). Whenever the king visited Hampton Court or Kensington, the permanent servants there seem to have been tipped out of the privy purse—the housekeeper £10 and the lower servants smaller amounts (N.S.A., K.G., Cal. Br. 22, XIII, Anhang no. 3, vols. XIX and XX). The watermen were also given 'drinking money' whenever they rowed the king on the river (*ibid.* vol. XX).

[4] LS 13/115, fo. 36; LS 13/176, pp. 16–18, 133.

[5] LS 13/176, pp. 76, 95–6, 111, 116–17, 235–6, 238.

[6] When, in 1760, no ushers' table was provided, they got £30 a year each in lieu of the right to invite guests to dine at court (Blenheim MSS. F 1/65).

And the lesser servants of the court were attended by the household physician and received medicine from the household apothecary, both at the king's expense.[1]

Though they were not an addition to the monetary value of offices, the practice of paying a small pension to retired or discarded servants or their widows no doubt increased the attraction of court jobs. There was neither a 'retirement age' nor a settled pension system, and it by no means followed automatically that a man would get a pension on leaving a court post. This doubtless encouraged men to stay on in office long after they were capable of doing the work and either hire a deputy, a practice that was discouraged, or simply ignore their duties. But, although there was no established system, pensions were paid both by the cofferer and by a separate paymaster of pensions to a great number of old servants who petitioned for the king's bounty. Chamber servants, musicians for example,[2] were sometimes granted a pension on leaving the court, but pensions were most commonly granted to servants of low rank in the household below stairs and the stables (or their widows) most of whom could present a genuine case of need. Occasionally an officer of some standing was given a pension. In 1714, for example, Charles Scarborough was given £400 a year on being removed as a clerk of the board of green cloth at George I's accession[3] and the widow and two children of another clerk, Robert Wroth, were granted £100 a year each when Wroth died in 1720.[4] Occasionally an officer in the household below stairs was allowed to 'retire' in office, to continue to enjoy the fruits of office without doing the work. In the case of Henry Lowman, a clerk of the kitchen who was allowed to 'retire' in this way, his work was done by a man whose only reward was a reversion to the post.[5]

Most genuine pensions were paid to the lowest servants of the household and of the stables. As has been said, not all apparently benefited;

---

[1] *C.T.B.* xxx, 485; LS 13/260 (royal warrant of 29 June 1724 granting 10s. a day to the physician of the household for expenses since 'he is obliged to attend the household servants who live dispersedly in Westminster, London and other places...').

[2] LC 5/156, p. 314.

[3] LS 13/260 (warrant dated 16 February 1715); T 1/207/15.

[4] LS 13/260 (warrant dated 11 June 1720); the daughter of another clerk, Sir William Forester, was given £200 a year 'in consideration of her father's long and faithful service', several years after he retired (LS 13/260, warrant dated March, 1722).

[5] See above, p. 170.

and even if a pension was granted, it was never necessarily for life. Since they were on an establishment, pensions could easily be removed if the establishment was recast, and old servants' pensions were therefore vulnerable, especially at the change of sovereigns when all establishments came to an end. In 1714, however, George I was still paying pensions to twenty-seven men who had been employed by Charles II, James II or William III and who had been turned out in 1702, and to 126 servants (or their widows and children) who had been granted a pension during the previous four reigns. The pensions ranged from £10 to £200, but generally speaking they were well under £50 a year.[1] A large number of George I's lesser servants were retired in his reign with a small pension, 'in consideration', as the grant to two men who had served as grooms of the stable for forty and thirty-five years explained, 'of their long service, for their support in their old age'.[2] And even more common were grants of small amounts to widows of men who died in office. The board of green cloth informed the lord treasurer in 1706 'that when any of the sworn servants under my lord Steward have left a widow and children in great necessity, they have usually had pensions granted them suitable to the employment the deceased held'.[3]

These grants were all paid by the Crown as part of the household or the pensions establishment, but on occasion a new servant was made to pay part of his salary to the man he replaced. Four new messengers in 1724, for example, were each required to pay £35 a year out of their fixed salary of £45 (they made most of their money in bills for their services)[4] to their predecessors who had been retired on account of their age.[5] Other office holders who could not expect their widows to receive any royal bounty sometimes made arrangements among themselves to provide some limited provision for them. The yeomen of the guard agreed in 1704, for example, that each would contribute 10s. (making about £50 in all) to the widow of a deceased yeoman.[6] But this was

---

[1] LS 13/44 (establishment of the household, 1714).

[2] LS 13/260 (royal warrant dated 1 January 1719). And other warrants of 29 January 1717 and 29 April 1720.

[3] LS 13/175, fos. 45–6; and see LS 13/115, fo. 27; LS 13/260 (royal warrants dated 27 June 1716, 8 February 1717, 24 January 1718, 19 February 1726, 2 January 1727—each containing the names of several widows of royal servants granted small pensions).

[4] See above, pp. 120–1.   [5] LC/158, pp. 268–9.

[6] S. Pegge, *Curialia*, pt. III, p. 79.

obviously very limited both in amount and in scope and generally speaking, only the lowest household servants—though large numbers of these—could hope that at their retirement or death some provision would be made for themselves or their widows.

IV

So far in this chapter we have been concerned to examine the various ways in which the fixed allowance of court posts was supplemented. But even if all the elements making up court salaries could be calculated accurately—and, by their nature, many of them cannot—the true value of office to the individual courtier might still not be determined because of another practice: pluralism, the combining of offices. Some court posts, including those of the first rank like gentleman of the bedchamber and minor sinecures like carver and cupbearer, were often held by men whose main sphere of activities lay elsewhere than at court.[1] In many cases it is clear that the court post, even a bedchamber post, was simply a lucrative and honourable addition to a more important job. On the other hand, some men in court posts held another at court or elsewhere, which may be regarded as providing a supplementation for an essentially household income. Some court posts indeed seem always to have been held in conjunction with another. The first master cook, for example, always enjoyed the place and profits of first yeoman of the pastry office; when the place of first master cook was temporarily suspended in 1715 to make way for a German cook, the post in the pastry office was suspended too.[2] There was a good deal of this sort of pluralism below stairs. The yeomen of the accounting house were usually also under-clerks of the board of green cloth; two or three clerkships of the sub-offices were combined permanently in one man; and the right to act as a purveyor granted to a number of servants in the department was also tied to the holding of a particular office and was a form of pluralism. Above stairs there are few examples of places being permanently joined, though the under-housekeeper of St James's was usually also a page of the bedchamber. But both above stairs as well as below numerous cases can be found of a more temporary pluralism. Henry Lowman, the first clerk of the kitchen was also housekeeper of Kensington Palace and his wife, Mary, was wardrobe keeper there as well as being mistress laun-

[1] See pp. 36, 250.   [2] See above, p. 84.

dress to the king. An usher, Thomas Brand, also held the minor place of embellisher of letters, another was also under-housekeeper of Somerset House while two others, Sir Edward Lawrence and Leonard Pinkney, were collectors of the customs at Shoreham and Newcastle respectively. At least one other court officer, Thomas Archer, the groom porter, also held a place in the customs at Newcastle. Another usher held his place with a commission in the yeomen of the guard. Below stairs, a clerk of the acatry in George I's reign was also a yeoman of the scullery; and in the stables, Michael Stedholme combined the clerkship of the office with the post of surveyor of the highways.

For some court servants there were opportunities to increase their income by working outside the court. The master cooks and other kitchen servants who took turns in waiting at court could and often did, with the permission of the board of green cloth, work privately in the houses of the nobility.[1] Another form of pluralism, especially common among officers of the first rank and chamber servants in middling ranks, was the holding of a court post with a commission in the army or navy. Some examples of this in George I's reign have been noted in earlier chapters, and a number of other cases of this and other forms of pluralism involving court officers will be found in the salary table at the end of this chapter.

V

In the appendix to this chapter an attempt is made to present estimates of the salaries of a select number of court officers. In some cases it is relatively easy to calculate an officer's total salary for not all benefited from the diverse sources of income that have been discussed above, and for other posts there are available contemporary estimates of their value, some of which are authoritative. But most often an exact calculation is impossible and many of the estimates in the salary table are only informed guesses.

It is necessary to make another point about these salary totals. They are of gross salary only. That is, they do not take into account the several official deductions that were made from court salaries largely because these are even more difficult to estimate accurately than the salaries themselves. Nor, of course, can the expense of office be calculated, and it is clear that the style of life necessarily maintained by some

---

[1] LS 13/116, fo. 78.

officers, especially those of the first rank, meant that there might be little financial benefit accruing to their family or estate through their office-holding. Deductions from salaries and the expense of office could make a considerable difference to the value of a court office. Occasionally the amount of the deductions from a particular salary is known and this is noted in the table. But since no attempt has been made to calculate the net salaries of all offices, it is necessary to say something in more detail here about the three main deductions made in George I's reign: the land tax, the Civil List tax and fees.

The palaces of Whitehall and St James's formed a unit for land tax purposes. They were assessed to produce a certain sum annually, depending on the prevailing rate, and commissioners, who were generally members of the board of green cloth, with the addition of a number of other household and chamber officers, determined the individual assessments on salaries and houses.[1] In the war years 1704–10, household servants paid at the following rates on their wages and board-wages: 3s. in the pound on salaries over £100; 2s. 8d. in the pound on salaries between £40 and £100; and on those below £40, 1s. 4d. in the pound.[2] In George I's reign, however, the assessments were generally lower than this. The earl of Sunderland, in February 1722, paid at the rate of 2s. 9d. in the pound on £4,000 of his wages as groom of the stole,[3] but in 1716 at least, many household servants, including some whose income was in the £100 to £150 range, and including the groom porter at £550 a year, seem to have paid only 9d. in the pound.[4] The land tax was in some cases stopped at source, that is deducted by the household treasurer, and paid by the clerks of the office to the receiver; the clerks of the treasurer of the chamber, for example, paid £2,588 to the receiver in 1716. But it was also paid to him individually, or so the receiver's accounts for the same year suggest.[5]

Another deduction from household servants' wages was made after

[1] W. R. Ward, *The English Land Tax in the Eighteenth Century* (1953), pp. 7, 27–8; the land tax commission for Whitehall and St James's always included the clerks of the board of green cloth; a number of chamber officers, including a yeoman of the removing wardrobe and the master of ceremonies, served on it too from time to time. The clerks of the commissioners were usually two of the under-clerks of the green cloth. The commissioners met in the green cloth office at St James's (LS 13/234 —minutes of the commissioners' meetings, 1709–53.)

[2] *C.T.P.* (1708–14), p. 213.   [3] Blenheim MSS. D 1/38.

[4] LS 13/232, pp. 24–31.   [5] *Ibid.*

1721 for the Civil List tax. This was first imposed in 1721 for the purpose of funding a loan of £500,000 to pay the Civil List debt.[1] It was at the uniform rate of 6d in the pound on all salaries paid by the Crown and was deducted by the office issuing the salary which then paid it to the receiver.[2]

In an earlier section of this chapter the fees charged by paymasters and their clerks were discussed as an addition to their salaries. Now the other side of the equation must be emphasized, that is that household servants whether paid by a household treasurer or by the exchequer, had to pay several fees in order to get their money, and this must obviously be taken into account as a deduction from their salary. These fees were probably in the neighbourhood of 5 per cent at the cofferer's office and 7½ per cent at the treasurer of the chamber's and these offices paid the bulk of household salaries. When to this is added a land tax varying perhaps between 4 per cent and 15 per cent and, after 1721, a Civil List tax of 2½ per cent, the possible range of deduction from the wages paid at court must have been 12–25 per cent. Sunderland's £5,000 as groom of the stole was reduced by almost £1,000 (i.e. 20 per cent) by taxes and fees; and the treasurer of the chamber's £2,689 was reduced in 1720 by £586 (c. 22 per cent) by taxes, fees and the salary paid to his deputy, or by £386 (14 per cent) without counting this salary.[3]

Though in the case of the land tax assessments the commissioners for Whitehall and St James's may have taken into account income from fees and perquisites in determining individual rates,[4] the deductions for the civil list tax and for office fees were of course only on the fixed court wage paid by the Crown. The more a man made in fees and perquisites, therefore, the less, as a proportion of his whole court income, would be the deductions.

Besides these official deductions, some officers had to meet other substantial calls on their salaries for the wages of clerks or deputies. In some cases the Crown paid the wages of an officer's deputy or of servants needed for the work of an office. The master of the great wardrobe, for example, received an extra £200 a year for his deputy;[5]

[1] See above, chapter 4.   [2] Blenheim MSS. D 1/38.
[3] *Ibid.*; P.R.O. 30/26/113 (1).
[4] See, for example, the commissioners' attempt to raise the master of the great wardrobe's assessment on the basis of his possible income from fees, above, p.   .
[5] *C.T.B.* xv, 206.

and, at a much lower level, Somerset English, the yeoman of the wood-yard and purveyor of wood and coal, was given £5 a year to pay for a man to deliver fuel to court lodgings.[1] Other deputies and clerks, like the deputy cofferer, were paid entirely by fees. But not all officers could provide for necessary servants in either of these ways. The treasurer of the chamber paid the first clerk of his office, who was also his deputy, £200 a year out of his own salary.[2] The treasurer, of course, levied a considerable poundage and this wage represented less than a tenth of the profits of the office. Other court officers were much harder hit in paying their servants or clerks. The housekeepers of royal palaces were responsible for maintaining a small staff of servants to clean and look to the general upkeep of the palace, especially when the court was not in residence. They had to do this out of their salary which was paid, in most cases, 'in lieu of bills',[3] and as a result their quite substantial wages (varying between £200 and £350) must have been seriously decreased. The under-housekeeper of St James's claimed that the wages of necessary servants cost him £40 a year out of his salary of £100.[4]

One other factor tending to reduce the financial value of office must be touched on here: the expense of living at court. 'Drawing-rooms' and balls filled the courtier's life, even in George I's reign. For office holders of the first rank, who were 'courtiers' as well as court 'officers' and whose right and duty it was to take part in this social life, it must have been very expensive to maintain over a long period the necessary style of life. There is a good deal of evidence that some officers found it difficult to meet what Lord Hervey called the 'necessary expenses incurred by dangling after a Court'.[5] One of the prince's ushers in 1736 claimed that he spent more than his salary 'in supporting the character of a Gentleman' and a little later he complained that the prince's ushers 'are obliged to live beyond our posts'.[6] It is perhaps to be expected that the household servants of the Prince of Wales would be particularly hard hit since their salaries were generally much lower than those paid in the king's household while their attendance both on the prince and the king could not have been much less expensive. But the expense of office in the king's court was well understood too; James Brydges, who

---

[1] LS 1/60. [2] P.R.O. 30/26/113 (1).
[3] See above, chapter 2. [4] C(H)MSS. 45/33.
[5] Hervey, *Memoirs* (ed. Sedgwick), p. 208.
[6] Add. MSS. 22229, fos. 144–5, 162–3.

could well afford it, gave as his reason for refusing an offer of the comptrollership of the household in 1714 'the attendance that Post and also the expense it requires'.[1]

Those of the greater court officers like the lord chamberlain and lord steward, who were expected to help the king entertain distinguished visitors by maintaining a table at their own expense when the court was in the country, and who had to support a large staff of personal servants as a consequence, must have genuinely needed the large pensions that were usually attached to these posts.

The expense of living in London for a good part of the year was doubtless no minor consideration, though of course this was not only the practice of court officers. One particular financial burden must have been especially heavy for those who had to attend regularly at court: the cost of providing themselves with suitable clothes. Anyone who went often to a 'drawing-room' or to a court ball had this expense of course, but for those whose office made it obligatory for them to appear regularly at court it must have been especially burdensome. Good clothes were expected at all times, but on several occasions in the year, on days of celebration, the expense incurred was particularly heavy. On such days as the king's birthday or the prince or princess's birthday, on the anniversary of the accession and of the coronation, it was expected that courtiers would appear in new and especially fine clothes. The more the clothes cost, the greater was the compliment. Spencer Cowper explained to Lady Cowper in 1722 that his daughter could not go to court for the Princess of Wales's birthday because of the expense, 'for', he said, 'I think it better not to attempt without doing it as it ought to be'.[2] Lady Cowper herself had been advised by the duchess of Marlborough in 1715 to let the princess know that she had made new clothes for the birthday even though she was prevented from going to court by Lord Cowper's illness.

...since you have made clothes [wrote the Duchess of Marlborough] and everybody in the World knows your present circumstances [i.e. Lord Cowper's illness] it will be just as well to put them on the first day you can easily wait upon the Princess, and shew her how fine you were to have been. She will have more time to take notice of them than she would have today and to do more now is carrying a compliment too far.[3]

[1] HM, Stowe MSS. 57, vol. 11, pp. 34–5.
[2] Panshanger MSS., Letterbooks, vol. 6, p. 46.   [3] *Ibid.* vol. 3, p. 127.

It was perhaps natural that courtiers strove to out-do one another in their compliments and it was observed in 1722 that men's court dress was becoming extremely ornate. Mrs Sarah Osborn described to her brother the celebration at court for the king's birthday. There was a large attendance, she wrote,

and most people very fine, but I believe the gentlemen will wear petty-cotes very soon, for many of their coats were like our Mantuas. Ld. Essex had a silver tissue coat, and pink colour lutestring [i.e. lustring] wascote, and several had pink colour and pale blue padesway [padausoy] Coats, which look'd prodigiously effeminate.[1]

Such finery must obviously have been expensive. In George II's reign, Hervey said, none of the king's servants made a fortune under him, or indeed made 'more than just what defrayed the annual expenses of birthday clothes' and other necessary expenses.[2] If this is exaggerated, it does serve to emphasize that clothes would be a large item for any courtier. Later in the century Lady Louisa Stuart reckoned that 'Fifteen of sixteen hundred a year would not do much for two people who must live in London and appear in fine clothes at St James's twice a week'.[3] It was said in 1736 that the duke of Montagu had spent £400 on his clothes for the wedding of the Prince of Wales;[4] and, if this was perhaps an extreme case, Charles Cathcart, a member of the prince's household spent over £30 on new clothes for the king's birthday in 1715.[5] A place-hunter sought the post of groom of the bedchamber to the Prince of Wales despite the fact that 'the sallery...[is] not very great and the Birth day Cloaths...[are] expensive'.[6]

The financial burden on courtiers may have discouraged some, as it did Spencer Cowper's daughter, from going to court on these occasions of special celebration. When Queen Caroline in 1736 'desired people would not make fine clothes' for her birthday, 'but reserve them for the Prince's wedding', Egmont thought that the crowd at court for her birthday celebration was, in consequence, much larger than was usual.[7] By the same token it was a boon to tradesmen. In Anne's reign, Vice-

---

[1] E. F. D. Osborn (ed.), *Political and Social Letters of a Lady of the Eighteenth Century*, p. 23.

[2] Hervey, *Memoirs*, p. 208.

[3] Rosamund Bayne-Powell, *Eighteenth Century London Life*, p. 60.

[4] *H.M.C. Egmont MSS. Diary*, II, 264. [5] Cathcart MSS., *Diary*, II, 264.

[6] Add. MSS. 32687, fos. 262–3. [7] *H.M.C. Egmont MSS. Diary*, II, 240.

Chamberlain Coke received a petition from the mercers, weavers and silkmen of London asking him to encourage the queen to have court balls 'on her birth night and other public occasions, which are certainly the greatest support to ours and almost all other trades'.[1] London tradesmen complained that their business suffered if the court stayed too long in the country for the summer,[2] and the journeys to Hanover were also unpopular for this reason.[3]

The court also went into mourning on the death of European crowned heads and of members of the English royal family, however distant, and this too required a special and precise form of dress.[4] There can be no doubt that the buying of clothes must have put a certain strain on some court officers and especially on those officers of the chamber below the first rank whose attendance was required but whose salaries were not large. Soon after George I's accession, the members of the band of gentlemen pensioners petitioned the treasury board for their arrears of salary on the grounds that in 1714 they had had to buy new clothes for Queen Anne's birthday, mourning clothes for her funeral and 'rich clothes' for George I's coronation.[5] And such men as the gentlemen ushers and the chamber grooms must surely also have spent a good part of their income on necessary expenses of office.

Even for those of the first rank whose salaries were larger, such expenses must have reduced the profits of court office perceptibly. And it is well to keep such expenses in mind, as well as the official deductions for taxes and fees, when considering the profits of office which are summarized, for selected posts, in the table that follows.

[1] *H.M.C. Cowper MSS.* III, 184.   [2] See below, p. 275.
[3] When George II decided to celebrate his birthday in Hanover in 1736, Horatio Walpole remarked sarcastically that this was 'an admirable scheme to satisfy the mob and tradesmen in England' (*H.M.C. Buckingham MSS.* p. 3).
[4] *H.M.C. Savile MSS.* p. 125.   [5] *C.T.P.* v (1714–19), 52.

APPENDIX: The Emoluments of Selected Court Offices.

(1) Lord chamberlain's department

Officer	Salary or fee (£)	Diet and/or board-wages (£)	Other income: purveyance; bills; pensions; livery (liv.); other office (attached to court post) (£)	Travelling wages (trav.) and lodgings (lodg.)	Perquisites and fees (hon. = fees of honour) (£)	Total (£)	Other offices held (not attached to court post); army and naval officers
Lord chamberlain	100	1,100 b.w.	Pension 2,000 (1714), 3,000 (1726); plate valued at 400; 67 (liv.)	Lodg.	Furniture at d. of sovereign 24 (hon.); ? sale of offices	1,291–4,291+	—
Vice-chamberlain	667	493 b.w.	Pension 1,000 (1706–27)	Lodg.	—	2,160	—
Treasurer of the chamber	469	—	—	—	Poundage c. 2220	2,689 (reduced in 1720 by 586 for taxes, fees and salaries)	—
Gentleman usher, daily waiter	20	130 b.w. and diet	1st usher also usher of the Black Rod	Trav., lodg.	Swearing fees c. 30; hon. c. 30	210+ (Black Rod 410+)	—
Groom of the privy chamber	20	53 b.w. and diet	40 liv.	Lodg.	c. 31 (hon.) ? candle ends ? tips	144+	—
Master of the robes	1,240	—	—	—	—	1,240	(Cadogan) general, and col. of a regt.; master-general of the ordnance; ambassador to Holland

Officer	Salary or fee (£)	Diet and/or board-wages (£)	Other income: purveyance; bills; pensions; livery (liv.); other office (attached to court post) (£)	Travelling wages (trav.) and lodgings (lodg.)	Perquisites and fees (hon. = fees of honour) (£)	Total (£)	Other offices held (not attached to court post); army and naval officers
Yeoman of the robes	380	—	—	—	c. 15 (hon.)	395	—
Master of the ceremonies	300	—	100 in lieu of earlier payments	—	—	400	—
Master of the jewel office	50	400 b.w.	(1758) 700 from exchequer	Lodg. or 80 in lieu	—	450–530; (1758) 1,230 gross, 955 net	—
Yeoman of the jewel office	107	—	—	—	Office fees 135 (1782)	? 242	Joint receiver-general of the excise
Knight harbinger	209	—	Payments on bills	Trav.	c. 63 (hon.)	272+	—
Groom porter	550	—	Bills for supplying fireplace irons to court apartments	—	c. 9 (hon.) profits from court gambling; fee for licensing gaming houses	559 + (too low)	Comptroller of the customs at Newcastle (1714)
Master of the great wardrobe	100	—	2,000 in lieu of fees	Lodg.	Poundage and measurage (?) at least 300 (1712) probably much more; 107 liv.	2,507 (too low)	—
Clerk of the great wardrobe	25	—	300 in lieu of fees (1702–) 34 liv.	—	? poundage	359+ ?	—

(2) The bedchamber

Groom of the stole	33	967	Plate valued at 400; 4,000 at Exchequer. ? Sale of offices	Lodg.	Furniture in private apts. at d. of sovereign (worth 3,000 in 1714)	5,000+. Deductions for taxes and fees in 1719 and 1721, 989	1st lord of the Treasury, 1719–21
Gentleman of the bedchamber	1,000	Diet when court in the country	—	Lodg.	—	1,000	See pp. 250–1
Groom of the bedchamber	500	Diet when court in the country	—	Lodg.	—	500	7 army officers; 1 envoy to Prussia
Page of the bedchamber	3	77 b.w. and diet and bouge; 365 in lieu of diet (1725)	1 always underhousekeeper of St James's (100, perhaps 40 net) 47 liv.	Lodg.	17 (hon.); gratuities, perhaps c. 120 p.a. ?	144 min. (perhaps c. 264); in 1726 509 min. without diet	—

(3) Lord steward's department

Lord steward	100	1,360 b.w.	Plate valued at 400	Lodg.	Query fees, and sale of offices	1460+ (c. 1782; 1,540 at exch. total 3,000; reduced to 2,456 by taxes and fees)	—
Treasurer of the household	124	1,076 b.w.	Plate valued at 400	Trav. and lodg.	—	1,200+	—
Comptroller of the household	108	1,092 b.w.	Plate valued at 400	Trav. and lodg.	—	1,200+	(1717–20) joint vice-treasurer of Ireland (3,000) and warden of the Stanneries
Master of the household	67	433 b.w.	Plate valued at 400; 438 p.a. in lieu of fees; 20 p.a. for a clerk; 80 in lieu of lodgings	Lodg.	—	958–1,038	—

14-2

Officer	Salary or fee (£)	Diet and/or board-wages (£)	Other income: purveyance; bills; pensions; livery (liv.); other office (attached to court post) (£)	Travelling wages (trav.) and lodgings (lodg.)	Perquisites and fees (hon. = fees of honour) (£)	Total (£)	Other offices held (not attached to court post); army and naval officers
Cofferer	100	400 b.w.	—	Trav. and lodg.	Poundage c. 2010	2,510 (est. 3,000 in 1725)	(1725–7) gentleman of the bedchamber
Clerk of the board of green cloth	44	456 b.w.	438 in lieu of fees	Trav. and lodg.	Swearing and certificate fees c. 15; fee at Christmas 5	958; 1 clerk at least got 80 in lieu of lodg. (i.e. 1,038)	—
1st clerk of the kitchen	44	206 b.w. bouge and diet when in waiting	—	Trav. and lodg.	Fees for issuing debentures for b.w.; illicit perquisites (?)	250+	Housekeeper
Clerk of the spicery	16	84 b.w.	—	Trav. and lodg.	Fees on linen bought, on groceries and wax candles	100+ (prob. closer to 200)	—
Clerk of the acatry	7	113 b.w.	6. 13s. 4d. in lieu of lodgings	Trav.	Fee of 6s. 8d. per case of veal (worth 150–200 a year); fee for debentures (c. 35 in 1713); 20 a year for writing the office creditor	c. 332–382	1 yeoman of scullery (1725) and deputy commissary-general of Guards and Garrisons (1726); 1 clerk to the clerks of the green cloth (1714)

Office							
Clerk to the clerks of the board of green cloth	50	—	Extra allowance of 1s. a day (18. 9s.); 20 a year in lieu of wine and 14. 7s. 6d. in lieu of venison	Trav.	Fee for writing creditors 6; fees from purveyors on signing contracts; poundage on land tax (?); fees for issuing certif for b.w.; for entering bills (c. 14 in 1713)	113+ (low); est. in period 1754–82 by one of them to be worth at least 215	1714 the four under-clerks were also respectively the clerks of the woodyard, of the poultry and a yeoman of the accounting house; two of them were clerks to the commissioners of land tax for Whitehall and St James's
Yeoman of the accounting house	5	78 b.w. and bouge	—	Trav.	—	83+	1 clerk to the clerks of the green cloth; 1 deputy treasurer of the chamber (1710–)
2nd master cook	11	109 b.w. diet	50 in lieu of lodgings; 40 liv.	—	Perquisites in kind	210 (min.)	—
Yeoman of the bakehouse	5	45 b.w.	Share of contract to supply bread	Trav.	—	50 (min.) and profits of contracts	—
Yeoman of the scullery	5	45 b.w.	Contract to supply charcoal	Lodg.	—	50 (min.) and contract	—
Gentleman of the buttery	11	49 b.w.	Contract to supply cider	Trav. and lodg.	c. 20 (hon.); fee for ale debentures (? 3 p.a.)	83 (min.) and contract	(1721–?) army officer

APPENDIX (*cont.*)

Officer	Salary or fee (£)	Diet and/or board-wages (£)	Other income: purveyance; bills; pensions; livery (liv.); other office (attached to court post) (£)	Travelling wages (trav.) and lodgings (lodg.)	Perquisites and fees (hon. = fees of honour) (£)	Total (£)	Other offices held (not attached to court post); army and naval officers
Gentleman of the ewry	11	49	—	—	c. 5 (hon.); fees on all new tablecloths and napkins (c. 15 in 1715–16); share of worn linen, 50 a year for providing rose water for king	130 (?)	—
(4) The stables							
Sergeant porter at St James's	11	109	—	Lodg.	Tips (?)	120+	Naval officer
Master of the horse	67	1,200 b.w.	Use of royal foot-men and horses; carriages at d. of sovereign; plate valued at 400; pension 4000 p.a. (Anne's reign)	Lodg.	? sale of offices	1267+ (5,267+ with pension)	—
Commissioner for master of the horse	800	—	—	Lodg.	? sale of offices	800	Avenor (1715–27); gentleman of the horse (1715–17)
Equerry	300	Diet when in waiting	—	Trav. and lodg.	—	300	4 army officers
Page of honour	260	Diet when in waiting	—	Trav.	—	260	—

PART II

7

THE COURT IN POLITICS

I

For most court servants the attraction of office must have been quite simply that it provided their livelihood. Below the first rank there could not have been many men who were not largely dependent on their court income, and even some of the greater officers must have found the ready cash provided by their court posts an essential foundation of their style of life. But the value of some offices, and especially those of the first rank, cannot be measured simply in terms of their emoluments. They also conferred honour and distinction; and they could open the way to the acquisition of further honours and even of power and public eminence, for it was still possible to move from court office to high position in the administration. Further, even without moving to a post that brought him directly into the 'public business', a courtier still had at least potentially some possibility of influencing the distribution of patronage and the formulation of policy because the king remained the active head of the administration and the ultimate source of authority. The court was still at the centre of the political world.

Nothing could be further from the truth than that George I abdicated his power to the Whig ministers in 1714. Throughout the reign his opinion was decisive in the important affairs of government: the formulation of foreign policy, the appointment and dismissal of ministers and the distribution of the patronage of the Crown. Of course it was obvious by 1714 that Parliament could not be ignored. Its co-operation was essential to the functioning of the government and no set of ministers could last if they could not lead Parliament and get the king's business done. But ministries were much more imposed on Parliament by the king than on the king by Parliament; and provided that he chose politicians who could function effectively in the major departments of the administration and in Parliament, the king determined the composition of the government and its policy.

Stable administrations were founded therefore only on the twin pillars of court and Parliament. And the leadership of such administrations fell only to those who could win the support of both the king and the House of Commons. If one of these necessary supports crumbled the ministry could not last for long. The House of Commons had to be carefully managed therefore; the friends of the government had to be organized, and debates had to be properly staged. But the ministers of the Crown had also to be courtiers. The king had constantly to be played, his wishes consulted, his prejudices pandered to, and those who were close to him had to be watched carefully. It was essential for ministers that they be able to build up and maintain in Parliament a strong following of men who enjoyed places or pensions or other marks of the royal favour, and who owed these benefits to the ministers' influence with the king. It was essential to the ministers not only to influence the king's will in order to make supporters happy; it was perhaps even more important that they make their influence visible, that they make it obvious to the political world that they were secure in the king's confidence. When, during their struggle with Carteret for the leadership of the ministry in 1723, Walpole and Townshend hoped to get some 'overt act' in their favour they had in mind the appointment of one of their candidates for a post.[1] This demonstration of interest would make it plain where the king's confidence lay; it would give heart to their friends and help to win to their side all those who hoped to be favoured in the future with some part of the king's bounty. Whether they had rivals in the ministry or not, ministers who wanted to dominate and lead a stable administration had to make the attractive power of government work in their favour. Their band of followers would thereby be enlarged, their hold on the government and their control of Parliament would be further secured and the king would come to depend more and more on them. In turn he would be the more willing to accept their nominations for posts in the household and administration and so the ministers' power would grow in an ever-widening circle.

But even ministers who were firmly in the king's favour could not rest content and take it for granted. Their recommendations about policy and appointments would be the more easily accepted if they were sensitive to the king's every mood and whim; and if they could so act on him that he was more conscious of being followed than led. It was

[1] See above, p. 150.

this that made the court an important political institution, for those who surrounded the king could be either very helpful or very obstructive to the king's ministers. They could indeed be highly dangerous, for a minister could still be toppled by an intrigue at court. It seems clear, for example, that Townshend was dismissed from the secretaryship in 1716 in good part because his enemies dominated the closet and put the worst possible gloss on his actions and motives.[1] Even if the threat was not often so basic as this, the king's ministers would obviously find the task of leading the administration much harder if their advice about appointments and the general distribution of patronage was forever being parried by counter advice from a hostile source close to the king. As George II was once moved to say, 'A Prince who will be well served in this country must free his minister from all apprehension at court, that his minister may give all his attention to the affairs of his master'.[2] On the other hand, a friend at court could smooth the ministers' path by acting as an intermediary with the king. If the ground could be prepared and unpalatable advice given in small doses, the king would be the more receptive to his ministers' advice when it was presented in the closet. It is well known that Queen Caroline helped Walpole in this way in George II's reign; one of the objects of this chapter is to show, what is less well known, that the duchess of Kendal acted this part very ably in the last five years of the reign of George I.

The character of politics and the place of the court in politics in George I's reign were determined to a considerable extent by the fact that the king was a foreigner who came to England in the prime of his life with an entourage that included ministers and advisers whom he had worked with and trusted for years. These men were officially in England to help the king-elector manage the affairs of Hanover. But in the early years of the reign, as was perhaps inevitable, he accepted their advice on all his concerns, English as well as Hanoverian. Since these men could not accept responsible offices in the English government, their advice could only be 'unofficial'. With regard to English affairs they were little more than courtiers, if not typical courtiers, in that they had power without responsibility, and their successful interference in English domestic and foreign affairs serves to make strikingly clear the continued importance of the court as a focal point of political power. This is the subject of this chapter. It is hoped to illustrate the continuing

[1] See below, pp. 224–33.   [2] Hervey, *Memoirs*, p. 151.

importance of the court as a political institution by means of a number of examples or 'case studies' of how superior interest in the closet could buoy up or undermine and frustrate an administration. First it is necessary to introduce the Hanoverian ministers who played such a large part behind the scenes in this reign.

II

When George I came to England in 1714 he brought with him about ninety ministers, courtiers and servants. Of these, fifteen were members of what came to be known as the Hanoverian Chancery in London, the office through which the king-elector conducted the affairs of his German dominions. For George retained in his own hands the conduct of the most important aspects of Hanoverian affairs—foreign and military policy—and, though the privy councillors he appointed in 1714 to exercise authority in his absence were naturally charged with day-to-day domestic business, all important decisions were made in London and quarterly accounts of revenue and expenditure were forwarded to the elector for his inspection. To conduct his Hanoverian business, the elector brought to London two ministers of state, two officers of his exchequer and the councillors of war, of justice and of the embassies. These ministers, together with their secretaries and clerks, had an office at St James's; two of them were lodged permanently at court and the remainder lived very close by—in Arlington St., Duke St., Little Ryder St., Germain St.—in furnished houses rented before the king's arrival by the envoy in London, Johann Caspar von Bothmer.[1]

By the terms of the Act of Settlement, the Germans were prohibited from holding office or taking a title in England. But, though they were officially in London as ministers for Hanoverian affairs, forced to work at a distance because the Elector resided in the more important of his dominions, no law could prevent them giving the king advice on

---

[1] N.S.A., K.G., Hannover 9, Secreta Domus, III, 6; Stowe MSS. 227, fos. 366–71, 389–90, 423–9, 435–6; A. W. Ward, *Great Britain and Hanover* (1899), pp. 51–63; Rudolph Grieser, 'Die Deutsche Kanzlei in London, ihre Entstehung und Anfänge, *Blätter fur Deutsche Landesgeschichte* (1952), pp. 153–68. Baron Johann Caspar von Bothmer (1656–1732) was in the service of Duke William of Celle from 1682. He held a series of diplomatic posts, in Berlin, Vienna, Paris and The Hague. In 1705, on the death of Duke William, he entered the Elector's service and went to London as ambassador in 1710.

English as well as Hanoverian affairs if he allowed it. On foreign affairs they could scarcely avoid advising George as king as well as Elector. But, beyond that, their position at court, their proximity to the sovereign and the reliance he placed on them, gave these Hanoverian ministers a great opportunity to influence decisively the exercise of the power that the sovereign still possessed. This was not lost on politicians, place-hunters and foreign ministers in England. As soon as it was apparent that Queen Anne was dying, Baron Bothmer had become the centre of an excited crowd of politicians hungry for office and of hangers-on hoping to pick up a crumb in the great change that was anticipated. On 30 July, two days before the queen died, there was a 'great meeting' at Bothmer's house; and on the following day there were so many people in his house, he complained, he could hardly find privacy enough to write his reports to Hanover.[1] When Anne died, Bothmer played a leading part in the proclamation of George I. He led a committee of the Council to the queen's closet in Kensington, burned the private papers in her cabinet, and removed the gold plate. Bothmer was the centre of attention. He was courted by ambassadors, by politicians (including Lord Oxford) and, to judge by his correspondence with colleagues in Hanover during August and September about setting up the new court and ministry, by everyone with hopes of a job.[2] He was not, however, the most important Hanoverian minister in the new reign even though he seems to have known more about England than any other of the elector's ministers in 1714. The most important of the German ministers in the new reign accompanied the king to England in September 1714—Baron Andreas Gottlieb von Bernstorff.

Bernstorff had been in the Elector's service as a minister of state since 1705; before that he had served Duke William of Celle in a similar capacity.[3] His knowledge of Imperial and Northern affairs was extensive, his personality dominating. It was clear immediately to every-

---

[1] Stowe MSS. 227, fo. 250; Cartwright, *The Wentworth Papers*, p. 408.

[2] Stowe MSS. 227, *passim* Add. MSS. 17677 HHH, fo. 335; Add. MSS. 20101, fo. 13; Cartwright, *The Wentworth Papers*, p. 408.

[3] W. Michael, *England under George I*, I, *The Beginnings of the Hanoverian Dynasty* (1936), pp. 103–4; Ward, *Great Britain and Hanover*, pp. 71–6. Baron Andreas Gottlieb von Bernstorff (1649–1726) was born in Mecklenburg-Schwerin. He was in the service of Duke William of Celle until 1705 when he moved into the Hanoverian administration, of which he became the head in 1709.

one in England that he was George I's leading minister and councillor,[1] and it was clear too that he was not unwilling to add English affairs to his cares of office. Lord Carnarvon's comment in 1716 that Bernstorff was 'the first and only minister the King relies on' was only slightly exaggerated.[2]

Bernstorff was particularly influential in the early years of the reign in the formulation of foreign policy. He enjoyed the able assistance of Jean Robethon, a French Protestant refugee who had served William III before entering the Hanoverian service, and who came to England as councillor of the embassies and George I's private secretary.[3] Robethon and Bernstorff were both devoted, hard-working, professional statesmen of long experience. They were not much troubled about nice distinctions between English and Hanoverian spheres of action; the Robethon correspondence and the diplomatic correspondence of Lord Polwarth, the British Minister to Denmark, 1716–21, both testify to the enormous extent to which British interests were confused with Hanoverian and the use that Bernstorff made of British power and British agents.[4] The Germans were of course passionately interested in the affairs of the North, where the declining power of Sweden and the ambitions of the threatening and enigmatic Russia were matters of the first consequence for Hanover. The value of a British fleet in the Baltic and the importance of Lord Polwarth, the leading British diplomat in the area were not lost on them. On his first going to Copenhagen in June 1716 Polwarth received private instructions from Bernstorff, in Robethon's hand, in addition to those from the English secretary.[5] Throughout his career there, Polwarth wrote more fully and more confidentially to the German than to the English ministers and he also sent Robethon copies of his correspondence with the secretary of state for the North. In

---

[1] Michael, *England under George I*, I, 104, quoting a report of Bonet of February 1715.

[2] HM, Stowe MSS. 57, vol. 14, pp. 177–8.

[3] J. F. Chance, 'Jean de Robethon and the Robethon Papers', *E.H.R.* XIII (1898), 55–70. Robethon left France soon after the Revocation of the Edict of Nantes and became secretary to Baron L. J. S. von Schütz, the Hanoverian ambassador in London. In 1698 he became private secretary to William III and in 1701 he joined the service of Duke William of Celle in a similar capacity. In common with Bothmer, Bernstorff, and other members of the Celle civil service, he moved to Hanover in 1705; he became private secretary to the Elector.

[4] Stowe MSS. 222–32; *H.M.C. Polwarth MSS.* I and II.

[5] *H.M.C. Polwarth MSS.* I, 32–3.

return, Robethon kept him much more fully informed about events, foreign and domestic, than did the English secretary.[1]

The German ministers often had a hand in domestic matters too. In December 1714 the Prussian Resident in London, Frederick Bonet, reported that the government of the country was controlled by Marlborough, Townshend, Bothmer and Bernstorff; and he thought that of the quadrumvirate the English ministers were distinctly in second place.[2] On one occasion during the rebellion in 1715, dispatches from Scotland were opened at Bernstorff's house by the secretaries of state; and Bernstorff was apparently able to keep Lady Cowper more fully informed of the latest news of the campaign (in which she had a great interest because her cousin, Thomas Forster, was one of the leading rebels) than could her husband, the lord chancellor.[3]

The friendship which very quickly developed between Bernstorff and Lord and Lady Cowper proved indeed to be beneficial to both sides, for through the lord chancellor Bernstorff got the one kind of information that he might have had difficulty obtaining: decisions of the Cabinet, from which, as a foreigner, he was excluded. Lady Cowper recorded in her diary in October 1715—a passage which the editor of the printed version thought it wise to suppress:

There was at this time some misunderstandings in the Cabinet Council. B[aron] Bernstorff desired me to get information of it from my Lord Cowper who by me gave B. Bernstorff a faithful Account of every thing that was useful for him to know. It was an employment I was not fond of, but as it was at the request of B. Bernstorff and that I thought he was right in getting all the information he could I consented to it and so did my Ld. Cowper.[4]

In many matters both great and small the Germans were the most direct channel to the king and were employed as such by English ministers and courtiers. As late as August 1717 papers were presented to the king by Bernstorff and Bothmer on behalf of a secretary of state.[5] And on one occasion, even the king's sempstress, Mrs Stocken, who had petitioned the board of green cloth for an increase in her salary was 'referred to Count [*sic*] Bothmer to apply to his Majesty'.[6] The

[1] See, for example, *H.M.C. Polwarth MSS.* 1, 124.
[2] Michael, *England under George I*, 1, app. p. 374.
[3] Panshanger MSS. Letterbooks, III, 196; Lady Cowper, *Diary*, p. 57.
[4] Panshanger MSS. Lady Cowper MS. Diary.
[5] *S.P. Dom.* 35/9, fo. 320.   [6] LS 13/115, fo. 47.

king did meet his English ministers and courtiers, of course, both in private and, until 1717, in the Cabinet. But in the early years of the reign he naturally relied heavily on the men whose ways he was used to and whose judgement he trusted. Also George was handicapped in his relations with English ministers both by his inability to speak their language and by an ignorance of English conditions so profound in 1714 that he did not even know the ranks of the peerage.[1] The German ministers' great influence in this situation was perfectly natural. They were of course supremely vulnerable. But so long as the king gave them his countenance the English ministers were in some measure dependent on them. In the course of disputes apparent at the beginning of the reign, English politicians to some extent competed for the king's favour through his Hanoverian advisers. The Germans did not cause these disputes, but their interference in them was of considerable importance. The danger of falling foul of them and thereby running the risk of losing the king's favour was illustrated clearly in the political crisis of 1716–17, which resulted in the dismissal of Townshend from the secretaryship and ultimately in a split among the Whig politicians.

III

Divisions among the Whig leaders had been apparent to contemporaries from the beginning of the reign. The earl of Oxford—not, of course, a disinterested observer—found in November 1714 'Germans and whigs divided amongst themselves'. The 'two parties', he told a friend, 'now hang out their colours in battle array. Nothing but the fear of the Tories keeps them from outraging each other.'[2] The leading figures in the new ministry were Townshend and Stanhope, the secretaries of state; Halifax, first lord of the Treasury; and Marlborough, captain-general. In the background were Lord Nottingham, the lord president, Robert Walpole, paymaster for the first year of the reign, and the duke of Argyll, who was established in an advantageous position at court as groom of the stole to the Prince of Wales. But perhaps the most important man in the second rank of power, because he was the most discontented, was the earl of Sunderland, Marlborough's son-in-law. He had been a secretary of state in Anne's reign and, according to Bothmer, he had expected to be given the seals again in 1714. Being

---

[1] Stowe MSS. 227, fos. 423–9.   [2] *H.M.C. Portland MSS.* v, 501.

fobbed off with the post of lord lieutenant of Ireland left him greatly embittered and not unwilling to see a general change in the ministry.[1]

From the beginning of the new reign, therefore, there was an element of instability in politics. After the election of 1715, which gave the administration a predominance in the House of Commons, the Whig leaders were free to indulge in intrigues against each other; as Lord Cowper observed in 1716, 'when either party is uppermost there is a struggle for power by ambitions to monopolize it'.[2] The main struggle within the ministry after 1714—not the only one, but the one of most interest here—centred around the attempt by Sunderland and the followers of Marlborough to displace lord Townshend. The German ministers played a major part in the success of this intrigue.

Lord Sunderland became lord privy seal in 1715 following the death of the marquess of Wharton. It had not, however, satisfied his ambition. He coveted the post of secretary of state, unfairly in his view given to Townshend whom the representative of the Spencers considered as little better than a Norfolk squire.[3] In the spring of 1716, Sunderland, aided by his father-in-law, Marlborough, and by their close friend William Cadogan, seems to have entered into a scheme with the Germans to change the ministry. Some of the German ministers were not unwilling to help. By 1716 they were becoming dissatisfied with Walpole and Townshend who seem to have opposed more violently than other ministers the Hanoverians' interference in English affairs.[4] Nor was Townshend's position at court strengthened when he earned the hatred of one of the ladies who had accompanied the king to England, Madame Schulenberg. She had recently been created duchess of Munster in the peerage of Ireland but she blamed Townshend for her failure to get an English title.[5]

By the early summer Walpole believed that his and Townshend's positions in the ministry were threatened by this alliance of Sunderland and some of the German ministers.[6] Lady Cowper, too, got hints of the

---

[1] Stowe MSS. 227, fos. 309–12, 406–8; *H.M.C. Onslow MSS.* pp. 508–9.

[2] Panshanger MSS. Lord Cowper MSS.: 'notes for a conference with Baron Bothmer, 31 Dec., 1716.'

[3] *H.M.C. Onslow MSS.* pp. 508–9; Plumb, *Walpole*, I, 223.

[4] Lady Cowper, *Diary*, pp. 107–11.

[5] Coxe, *Walpole*, II, 59. Ehrengard Mesuline von der Schulenberg was created duchess of Munster in 1716 and duchess of Kendal in the peerage of England in 1719.

[6] Coxe, *Walpole*, II, 58–9.

intrigue against them.[1] It was a blow to them, therefore, when George I
left in July for his first visit to Hanover, taking with him Bernstorff,
Robethon, the duchess of Munster and secretary Stanhope. And it
became even more ominous when Sunderland, upon a pretext of going
to Aix for his health, joined the king in Hanover later in the summer.
Before he went, according to Lady Cowper, Sunderland had visited
Marlborough several times at Bath 'for his instructions' and to plan
'the great Things that were to be done when the King came over'.[2]

With so many of their enemies ranged against them in Hanover,
Walpole and Townshend could only hope that Stanhope would support
them in the closet. Since their official letters and dispatches were subject
to censorship and perhaps distortion by Bernstorff before reaching the
king, Townshend attempted to keep an unprejudiced line open by
means of a private correspondence between Stephen Poyntz, in London,
and Stanhope. These letters, Poyntz told Stanhope, were 'not to be
communicated to any body, but to his Majesty only, and that with all
imaginable precautions of secrecy'.[3] The correspondence was established,
but it was not enough to save Townshend. Before the king left Hanover,
in December 1716, Townshend learned that the seals had been taken
away from him. He was offered the lord lieutenancy of Ireland, and
under great pressure from all sides, he accepted, to preserve a façade of
Whig unity. But he chafed under his disgrace—and, though the Irish
post was not in itself a mean one, disgrace it obviously was—and within
four months his barely concealed opposition brought his dismissal.
When this occurred, in April 1717, many of his friends in the ministry,
including Walpole, resigned with him, and there followed a period of
deep and bitter political division.

The reason for Townshend's demotion in December, 1716, is not
entirely clear, and it would be unfair—particularly perhaps to George I
—to suggest that the intrigues of his enemies at court were solely to
blame. For, however numerous his enemies, the king still had to be
convinced that Townshend was a liability as secretary, and George I
was not the kind of man who could be easily gulled into believing this
without evidence. It is important to recognize, therefore, that Townshend had, in eighteenth-century parlance, given his enemies a 'handle',
indeed two 'handles'. And they were both particularly powerful in

---

[1] Lady Cowper, *Diary*, pp. 118–22.   [2] *Ibid.* p. 122.
[3] Coxe, *Walpole*, II, 55–6.

that they concerned subjects dear to the king's heart: foreign affairs, and the conduct of his son, the Prince of Wales.

Townshend made it clear that he disapproved of the turn that English foreign policy took in the summer of 1716. Difficulties arose in particular over the treaty with France that was negotiated in Hanover by Stanhope and the Abbé Dubois. For three months after this treaty had been agreed to, its formal signature at The Hague was delayed because the full powers necessary to authorize the British envoy's signature were not forthcoming from London. This was interpreted in Hanover as a deliberate attempt by Townshend to delay and if possible to prevent the ratification of the treaty. As the summer passed, and the king, Bernstorff and Stanhope became increasingly impatient to have the treaty formally concluded, there can be no doubt that Townshend's position at court gradually weakened.[1]

The king and the ministers in Hanover were particularly anxious to conclude the French negotiation so that they could turn their full attention to the problems of the North. In that troubled area, where wars had raged sporadically since 1683, Hanover had always had a deep and natural interest, an interest considerably increased by the elector's claim to the Swedish territories of Bremen and Verden. In 1716 a new complication developed for Hanover in the North as a consequence of the movement of Russian troops into Mecklenburg, a territory adjacent to Hanover.[2] This caused considerable alarm. Russian expansion into the Baltic was one thing, but the presence of Russian troops in Germany could not be lightly tolerated. In 1716, therefore, the king and his Hanoverian advisors cast about for support against the Czar, and their thoughts naturally turned towards the resources of England and to her navy in particular. This raised the difficult question of the extent to which the king-elector should be allowed to use the resources of his kingdom in the interests of his electorate, and in its discussion Townshend further alienated the Hanoverians. Bernstorff in particular was anxious for the English fleet

---

[1] For this negotiation, George I's policy and Townshend's disapproval, see Michael, *England under George I*, I, ch. XII, and Basil Williams, *Stanhope*, ch. VIII. And see Coxe, *Walpole*, II, pp. 86–90, 100–8, 110–15, 126–8, 129–35.

[2] Williams, *Stanhope*, pp. 234–6; J. F. Chance, *George I and the Northern War; a Study of British-Hanoverian Policy in the North of Europe in the Years 1709–1721* (1909), pp. 105 ff.

in the Baltic under Sir John Norris to join immediately with the Danish fleet to deliver if necessary a crushing blow against the Czar to discourage Russian designs in Germany.[1] There seems no doubt that in the previous year Bernstorff had managed to get British naval support for Hanover and her allies against Sweden—who was still England's nominal ally—without the English ministers being fully aware of it. On that occasion the fleet had been sent to the Baltic under Norris ostensibly to protect English merchantmen against privateers. But Norris had been given orders privately by Bernstorff that if necessary he was to act in a positive and aggressive way against the Swedish fleet. In the end England and Sweden did not clash, but it was only avoided by the narrowest of margins and a detachment of eight English warships did aid Sweden's enemies to some extent.[2] In 1716 Bernstorff envisaged even more positive support from the fleet and the king asked Stanhope how far he 'could venture to give orders' to Norris.[3] Townshend rebelled when he got wind of this. He had opposed England's involvement in 1715[4] and he did so again a year later. It seemed to him purely a Hanoverian affair in which British policy and the fleet should not be concerned. He wrote privately to Stanhope in September:

My chief design is to beg of you not to consent to Sir John Norris staying [in the Baltic] any longer than the first of November, nor to the king's engaging openly in the affair about the Czar.[5]

On the other hand, Lord Sunderland told Townshend in November that he believed England's interests to be at stake in the North; it was 'the old Tory' notion, he wrote, 'so justly exploded since the Revolution' that 'England can subsist by herself, whatever becomes of the rest of Europe'.[6]

It seems clear that there was a definite difference of opinion between Stanhope and Sunderland on the one hand and Townshend on the other about Britain's interests in the North and about the extent to which the king-elector should be allowed to use the diplomatic and naval resources of Britain in the service of Hanover. Stanhope and

[1] Coxe, *Walpole*, II, 84.
[2] Williams, *Stanhope*, p. 232; J. F. Chance, *George I and the Northern War*, pp. 82-97; Brian Tunstall (ed.), *The Byng Papers* (Navy Records Society), III, (1932), xxxix.
[3] Coxe, *Walpole*, II, 84.
[4] Michael, *England under George I*, I, 322.
[5] Coxe, *Walpole*, II, 85. [6] *Ibid.* p. 128.

Sunderland were clearly more willing to follow the Hanoverian lead in foreign policy. Certainly Stanhope saw much more quickly than did Townshend the necessity and virtue of the Anglo-French alliance following the death of Louis XIV; and in the affairs of the North he and Sunderland were not unduly alarmed when George, as was natural, did not make a fine distinction between the interests of his two countries. Perhaps because they were more conscious of the necessity of parliamentary support, Townshend and Walpole were more cautious. The exact nature of the differences between the two sides is of secondary concern here, however. Townshend took the narrow view, his opponents a broader, more 'European', view of the problem; Townshend thereby presented Sunderland and his Hanoverian enemies with a powerful weapon to use against him with the king.

Nor was it the only one they could find. For it was further insinuated that summer that Townshend and Walpole were forming an alliance with the Prince of Wales and encouraging him in unfilial behaviour; and this was the subject about which, after foreign affairs, the king felt most passionately.

The king and his son had not been on good terms when they came to England in 1714, and the popularity that the prince had won since then, limited though it was, did nothing to bring them closer together.[1] When the king decided to go to Hanover in 1716, he made plain his dislike of his son by casting about for an expedient to prevent the prince being made regent with full power in his absence. Various schemes were devised to this end only to be found unacceptable, until the king finally conceded him the position of regent but with authority so restricted that it was virtually an empty title.[2] Just before the king left the prince suffered the further indignity of having his groom of the stole (and his favourite adviser), the duke of Argyll, removed from his service by the king's order. Argyll had been for years a fierce opponent of the Marlborough faction, especially of Cadogan and Marlborough himself, and his dismissal from the prince's service seems to have been a product entirely of their fear that he would have too much power as chief adviser of a regent, even a regent without authority.[3]

These were deliberately wounding blows and the prince was naturally humiliated and furious. When the king left, and the prince moved with

[1] See below, pp. 262–3. [2] Plumb, *Walpole*, I, 225.
[3] Michael, *England under George I*, I, 221–2.

229

his family to Hampton Court, he seemed determined to hurt his father in return. The centre of power had no doubt moved with the king, but the prince was still heir to the throne and he could provide an effective rallying point for all those, Whigs and Tories alike, who could not hope to find favour during the present reign. When, therefore, the prince and princess moved to Hampton Court and began to live in a style previously unknown to the reign, their court was immediately crowded with opponents of the administration. Tories and dissatisfied Whigs, including Argyll, flocked to Hampton Court during the summer and the prince did nothing to discourage them; on the contrary.[1] The king learned regularly of the prince's activities from Bothmer who had been left in England for just this purpose.[2]

Entertaining and encouraging the king's enemies was bad enough in itself, but it was further reported during the summer that the prince and Argyll were planning to maintain an interest in the next Parliament independent of the ministry.[3] This could only drive a deeper breach between the king and prince. And, among other things, it placed Townshend and Walpole in an extremely difficult position. They were forced in the ordinary course of business to be in regular attendance on the prince, for, powerless or not, he had to be kept informed and he had to sign papers. Townshend and his family resided at Hampton Court during the summer, and Walpole went down twice a week.[4] Given the atmosphere there they were open to the charge (which was duly made by Bothmer, or so Townshend believed)[5] that they too were in league with the prince and Argyll. There is, indeed, some evidence that Townshend and Argyll were coming together for mutual support against the ambitions of the Marlborough faction. The Dutch Resident in London, L'Hermitage, who was a very well-informed observer, was writing about such an alliance in the spring of 1716.[6] But whether it was true or not the insinuation provided Townshend's enemies in Hanover with another weapon. How powerful it was is indicated by Walpole's spirited defence of their conduct at Hampton Court in his letters to Stanhope. He wrote in December:

[1] Coxe, *Walpole*, II, p. 61. [2] Lady Cowper, *Diary*, p. 121.
[3] Coxe, *Walpole*, II, 60, 61, 64. [4] *Ibid.* p. 66; Lady Cowper, *Diary*, p. 121.
[5] Coxe, *Walpole*, II, 66.
[6] A. R. Heinsius Correspondence, no. 1970; L'Hermitage to M. D'Alonne, 22 May 1716.

What is given out here and publish'd from letters from among you in regard to the prince, I cannot but take notice of, and will stake my all upon this single issue, if one instance can be given of our behaviour to the prince but what was necessary to carry on the king's service; and we never had a thought but with a just and due regard to the King as our King and master; and as for any secret intimacies or management undertaken with the two brothers [Argyll and the Earl of Islay, his brother], if there be the least handle, or one instance can be given of it, call me for ever villain; if not, think as you please of those that say or write this.[1]

Lord Cowper, the lord chancellor, was also clearly aware of the difficulties of their situation. In December, 1716, he scribbled a sheet of notes for a 'conference with Baron Bothmer', the main reason for which was to urge him to 'use his int[erest] with [the] K[ing] to command reconciliation and to reject new schemes to gratify amb[ition] and make one sub[ject] m[aste]r of the rest'. In the course of the conversation, Cowper proposed to make the point that 'the representing us here as too much with [the] Prince [is] a mere artifice to get the K[ing] on their side'.[2] Cowper was very careful to go to the prince's court as infrequently as possible that summer.[3]

It is impossible therefore to be sure of the real reasons for Townshend's disgrace in 1716. He had enemies, English and German, near the king who were working for his dismissal even before he gave them such powerful weapons by his intransigence over foreign policy and his alleged intrigue with the prince and Argyll. But in what proportion these were the causes of Townshend's removal cannot be known with any certainty because the decision lay with the king, and George I's own opinions are entirely unknown. In his letters to Walpole after the event, Stanhope naturally emphasized the king's displeasure with Townshend's conduct, and though he agreed that the Germans had spoken against him, he implied that the suspected intrigue at Hampton Court was the main cause of the king's anger.[4] But if the king was himself so violently angered by his conduct as to dismiss him as secretary of state, why was Townshend left with a seat on the Cabinet

[1] Coxe, *Walpole*, II, 144.
[2] Panshanger MSS. Lord Cowper's MSS. (notes for a conference with Baron Bothmer).
[3] Panshanger MSS. Letterbooks, IV, 264–5.
[4] Coxe, *Walpole*, II, 140.

and why was Walpole urged to remain in the ministry?[1] If for the sake of Whig unity, as seems most likely, the whole affair savours of an intrigue skilfully managed; Townshend was removed from the centre of power—to make room for Sunderland or someone amenable to his and the Germans' influence—without splitting the Whigs in Parliament. Townshend and Walpole, not unnaturally, saw the events in these terms, and they blamed the enmity of the Hanoverians and of Sunderland for all their difficulties. After his dismissal, in December 1716, Townshend had no doubt who was responsible. In a letter to a Dutch friend he rehearsed what he called the supposed reasons for his disgrace, and continued

...though these are the topics given out by my enemies, I am far from thinking that they are the true and original causes of my disgrace. I believe the duchess of Munster, Mr Bernstorff, and Mr Robethon could give a much more exact and authentic account of the real causes that produced this event.[2]

During the summer, as complaints from Hanover had mounted against them, Townshend had often expressed similar views to Stanhope, the only man near the king he could trust. He was sure, he wrote in October

That no service which Mr Walpole, or you, or I can ever render to his Majesty, will be sufficient to screen and support us against the false and malicious suggestions of our enemies...I can struggle no longer against the difficulties which our enemies about the king create us every day.[3]

This surely is the crux of the whole affair. The great advantage that their rivals had over Townshend and Walpole was that they could argue their case against them without fear of contradiction. While the king was in Hanover, Townshend was unable to defend himself, unable to influence the exercise of the royal will. This is one of the most important aspects of the journeys that the first two Hanoverian kings indulged in so frequently. Whenever the king left England, the ministers in London were to some extent at a disadvantage. In Hanover the king was open to influence not easily controlled even by the English ministers in attendance, and the Germans who were important at St James's were doubly so at Herrenhausen. On the occasion of every

[1] Coxe, *Walpole*, II, p. 141. Walpole's brother, Horace, declared many years later that the king was not won over to Sunderland's and the Germans' side until they convinced him that Walpole would not resign if Townshend were disgraced (*ibid.* p. 161).   [2] *Ibid.* p. 161.   [3] *Ibid.* p. 117.

royal journey, therefore, the king was no sooner gone than the ministers remaining in London began to plead for his return. On 9 August 1716, just three weeks after the king had left London, Walpole told Stanhope that he knew of no remedy to the great problems caused by rumours of divisions in the ministry 'but the king's return'. It was an opinion expressed frequently in London during the summer.[1] Townshend and Walpole were faced in 1716 not only by these normal hazards of the king's absence, but also by the determined and dangerous opposition of the Germans and the enmity of one of the English ministers in attendance. They were excluded from and thereby defeated in the closet.

Lord Cowper was convinced that the ostensible reasons for Townshend's removal were mere window dressing. The object of those who accomplished it, he told Bothmer just before it occurred, was 'to get the K[ing's] power to place and displace'; and they would get Townshend removed, he thought, 'by shewing it nec[essar]y to some end they undertake'.[2] Townshend's doubts about the French treaty and Northern policy were, of course, used by his enemies to undermine him; and the suspicion that he had encouraged the prince might have weighed heavily with the king. But if Townshend had had friends in Hanover these problems might easily have been minimized. As it was he had only enemies near the king and the problems were emphasized.

In the reign of Elizabeth I, an historian has said, 'absence from Court was perilous to faction-leaders. It gave opponents the opportunity of poisoning the Queen's mind with malicious stories.'[3] Townshend's dismissal in 1716 suggests that it was no less perilous in the reign of George I.

IV

Townshend did not accept his disgrace in good spirit. As lord lieutenant of Ireland he gave only lukewarm support to the administration in Parliament in the spring of 1717; in April, as a consequence, he was dismissed. On the following day a considerable number of his friends, including Walpole, Pulteney, Methuen and Orford, resigned with him.[4] The administration was reconstructed around Stanhope and Sunderland.

---

[1] Coxe, *Walpole*, II, pp. 64, 76, 80–1, 82, 93–4.

[2] Panshanger MSS. Lord Cowper's MSS. (notes for a conference with Baron Bothmer).

[3] J. E. Neale, 'The Elizabethan Political Scene', *Proceedings of the British Academy*, XXXIV (1948), 14. [4] Plumb, *Walpole*, I, 241–2.

It was a ministry composed for the most part of pro-Hanoverians, or at least of men who had not objected as emphatically as had Townshend and Walpole against the extent to which English policy was conditioned by Hanoverian interests. As a result, Bernstorff's influence in England was even greater than ever. And his freedom of action was perhaps further increased because this administration was much more distracted on the parliamentary front than its predecessor had been. When the disaffected Whigs began an open, harrassing opposition, and especially when they got the support, numerical and moral, of the Prince of Wales after December 1717, following the split in the royal family, the ministers were often hard-pressed in Parliament.[1] And until they were sure of themselves in Parliament they could not afford any weakening of their support at court. At first, then, Stanhope and Sunderland seem to have acquiesced in and perhaps even welcomed the co-operation of Bernstorff. There was formed what Wolfgang Michael has called a 'dual régime', and a régime so dominated by German influence that he goes on to suggest that the early years of the ministry could well be called a period of foreign domination. Bernstorff, he says, 'became unbending and deaf to everything that did not suit his aims. His decisions were said to be the sure and infallible oracle which was obeyed and from which there was no appeal.'[2] 'Through the great credit that he had with the king', the Prussian envoy reported to his government, 'Bernstorff held the ministers in dependence.'[3]

Michael may have exaggerated, but there is no doubt that, in foreign affairs especially, Bernstorff's opinion carried great weight. There is evidence that in 1718, with the king's approval, he guided—or at least worked along with—the English secretary. In May Robethon told Polwarth that

His Majesty said this morning to M. de Bernstorff that he thought it best that General Bothmer [the Hanoverian representative in Copenhagen] should follow the King of Denmark to Holstein and that you should remain at Copenhagen...I shall speak on the matter to Mr Stanhope and ascertain his mind. He will inform you of his Majesty's wishes.[4]

[1] Plumb, *Walpole*, VII; A. S. Foord, *His Majesty's Opposition, 1714–1830* (1964), pp. 61, 92–4.
[2] Michael, *England under George I*, II, *The Quadruple Alliance* (1939), pp. 269, 272.
[3] Quoted by S. H. Nulle, *Thomas Pelham-Holles, Duke of Newcastle*, p. 118.
[4] *H.M.C. Polwarth MSS.* I, 500–1.

Getting Stanhope's opinion, it seems, was as much a formality as the letter he would write to Polwarth. In August of the same year, Robethon and Secretary Craggs were 'working together' at Hampton Court and Polwarth was informed that while the court was in the country he need not send the German Chancery copies of the letters he wrote to the English secretary.[1]

The English ministers were to an extent, then, dependent on Bernstorff as a channel to the king and they seem to have welcomed the alliance. So long as his and their ideas ran parallel all would be well. But Stanhope and Sunderland were not men to allow Bernstorff to influence or direct English policy in opposition to their broad aims. And as his influence increased and, as happened, his ideas more and more ran counter to theirs, so this 'double ministry' ran into difficulties and there developed a great struggle behind the scenes. While the administration fought off the challenge of a well-directed opposition in Parliament in 1719, the English ministers were engaged in another battle that was perhaps even more crucial to their political survival, a battle with Bernstorff at court.

In October 1718 the German and English ministers came into conflict over the details of Northern policy.[2] And early in the next year the Germans seem to have opposed the Peerage Bill behind the scenes, presumably out of a conviction that anything that reduced the king's influence reduced theirs.[3] But it was not until the court moved to Hanover in the summer of 1719 that things came to a head. During that summer Stanhope was immersed in the complicated affairs of the North, trying to establish a basis for a settlement in an area torn by more than twenty years of war.[4] English interests no less than Hanoverian favoured peace and a stable settlement in the Baltic, for, apart from the enormous commercial importance of the area, only recently had a threat of Swedish aid to the Pretender been frustrated.[5] And there was too the ominous power of Russia to be reckoned with. Having gobbled up Sweden's Baltic territories and sent troops into Mecklenburg, she posed now a direct military threat to Poland, Prussia, Hanover

[1] *H.M.C. Polwarth MSS.* I, p. 572.   [2] *Ibid.* pp. 632–3.
[3] Add. MSS. 32686, fo. 150; Panshanger MSS. Letterbooks, v, 266; N.S.A., Hannover MSS, Des. 92, IIIA, no. 8 (a paper in Bothmer's hand on the folly of the Peerage Bill, n.d.)   [4] Williams, *Stanhope*, ch. XIII.
[5] *Ibid.* pp. 246–7; Michael, *England under George I*, I, pp. 303–8.

and other German states. She was also a threat to English trade in the Baltic. It was to England's advantage to have the Northern scene stabilized as quickly as possible.

In the negotiations that took place among the various powers follow- ing the death of Charles XII in 1717, Stanhope was one of the leading architects of a settlement. One of his main preliminary aims was to detach Prussia from a Russian alliance only recently and hastily con- tracted after the incursion of the Czar's troops into Mecklenburg. Stanhope regarded Prussia as an essential ally, both against Russia and as a means of bringing pressure for a settlement to bear on Sweden. But he discovered that the negotiations for an alliance with Prussia, which were the key to his general plan, ran counter to the ideas of some of the German ministers, and especially of Bernstorff. Relations between Hanover and Prussia were not cordial in any case because there was considerable personal hostility between George and his son- in-law, Frederick William. But beyond that the Hanoverians remained firmly convinced that Hanover's best interests were served by an alliance with Austria. Bernstorff did what he could, therefore, to frustrate the negotiations with Prussia. Moreover, while the Anglo-Prussian talks were in progress Hanover entered a defensive alliance with Austria and Saxony designed to guarantee the integrity of Poland against the obvious ambitions of Russia and Prussia to carve up her territory.[1] Although this treaty, which was signed in January 1719 in Vienna, was a purely Hanoverian affair and George had joined the alliance only as Elector and without consulting his English ministers, the treaty had been largely negotiated by the English ambassador in Vienna[2] at Bernstorff's direc- tion. One of its secret clauses, moreover, committed the English fleet to operations in the Baltic in support of the allies. But undoubtedly, from the English ministers' point of view the most disastrous aspect of this alliance was the further breach it caused with Prussia and the damper it put on the negotiations then in progress. And Bernstorff continued to harrass the negotiations as much as possible. Stanhope wrote to Sunderland in July: 'Your lordship will have perceived by my late letters to Mr Craggs how much industry hath been used here to break us with Prussia.'[3]

[1] Michael, *England under George I*, I, pp. 227–33.
[2] Francois Louis de Pesmes, Seigneur de St. Saphorin, British Minister in Vienna, 1718–27.   [3] Blenheim MSS. D 1/33, Stanhope to Sunderland, 6 July 1719.

It was all the more galling to the English ministers that Bernstorff's hatred of Prussia, and his objections to an alliance with her, sprang in good part from a personal motive. He owned three villages in Mecklenburg adjacent to the border with Brandenburg over which Frederick William of Prussia had claimed sovereignty.[1] Bernstorff seems to have allowed this to colour his thinking on foreign policy, though he justified his ideas on the grounds that the emperor would not be pleased if Hanover and Prussia formed too close an alliance.[2] But it seemed to the English ministers that Bernstorff could have no real objection to the alliance apart from his three confiscated villages. He had, so secretary Craggs thought, no policy of his own with regard to Northern affairs. Craggs wrote to Lord Stair, the English ambassador in Paris, in April 1719:

By a long observation, and really applying it to the very best of my judgment, I have discovered that old Bernsdorf is an old woman: he keeps certain ministerial appearances of gravity and wisdom, which at bottom are no better than an arrant stupidity...Without comprehending what is right or wrong, without having any general system of affairs—nay, without having so much as formed a scheme of his own for his German affairs—he lets everything moulder and crumble away without doing anything or suffering anybody else to attempt it. The worst of all is, that the king has not made the same discovery which I think I have, and in these Northern affairs we can neither get forward nor backward.[3]

It was a very important triumph for the English ministers when George I did 'discover' during this summer in Hanover Bernstorff's real intentions and the barrenness of his policy. By July Stanhope had won the invaluable support of Madame Schulenberg (who had recently been created duchess of Kendal in the English peerage) and even that of Robethon, who seems to have deserted his old master at this time.[4] And when he asked Sunderland to consider 'whether we should endeavour to get him [Bernstorff] left here when the king returns',[5] Stan-

---

[1] Williams, *Stanhope*, p. 366. [2] *Ibid.* p. 370.
[3] J. M. Graham, *Annals and Correspondence of the Viscount and the First and Second Earls of Stair* (2 vols., 1875), II, 399–400.
[4] *H.M.C. Polwarth MSS.* II, 121; Blenheim MSS. D 1/33, Stanhope to Sunderland, 6 July 1719; Panshanger MSS. Letterbooks, VI, 74–8: Lady Cowper to Bernstorff, [?April] 1722.
[5] Blenheim MSS. D 1/33, Stanhope to Sunderland, 6 July 1719.

hope was clearly feeling more sure of his ground. Four days after he wrote this he moved to bring the whole question of policy towards Prussia into the open and have it debated before the king. He won a major victory. He informed Craggs that they had

at last got a complete victory over the old man. The King has twice, in council, before all his German Ministers, overruled him with an air of authority in relation to our negotiation with Prussia. One of these rebukes ought to be the more sensible to him, as it concerned the three villages you have so often heard of.[1]

For the next two months the struggle continued behind the scenes as Stanhope fought to break Bernstorff's superior interest with the king. 'The old man', he wrote in August, "grows worse and worse, I think I gain ground upon him daily with the king who is extremely good to me.'[2] He got additional support when Sunderland joined him later in August—having obtained permission from the king through the duchess of Kendal[3]—arriving in Hanover for the second time in the reign to destroy a minister's reputation. His credit with the king—clearly demonstrated earlier in the year when George appointed him his first groom of the stole, and remarked on by a well-informed contemporary in November[4]—could only have strengthened Stanhope's hand in the last stages of his struggle with Bernstorff. The fruits were dramatic and decisive, for the English ministers won in October a victory greater perhaps than they expected. The king not only criticized again and in the strongest terms Bernstorff's opposition to the Prussian negotiations, he also went on to prohibit him or any other German minister from interfering ever again in English affairs, or even to speak to him about English affairs. At a stroke Bernstorff was powerless; and the Prussian treaty was concluded without further trouble.[5]

The English ministers were jubilant. Newcastle, the lord chamberlain, who did his share to spread the news in England, reveals in one of his letters how much the ministry had felt the taunt that they governed only by Bernstorff's sufferance. 'The World', he said, 'will now be

[1] Mahon, *History of England*, II, App. p. lxxx.
[2] Blenheim MSS. D 1/33, Stanhope to Sunderland, 3 August 1719.
[3] *Loc. cit.*
[4] HM, Stowe MSS. 57, vol. 16, p. 393, Chandos to Mrs Dartiquenave, 29 November 1719.
[5] *H.M.C. Carlisle MSS.* p. 23; Add. MSS. 32686, fo. 149v.

convinced how scandalous those reports were that this Administration were supported by the Germans.' He goes on none the less in the same letter to reveal the shakiness of a ministry that depended to some extent on the Germans as intermediaries with the king. While the Germans had had great influence with George I, he confessed, the administration had always been in danger that Bernstorff might have 'destroyed it and betrayed them [the ministers] to the Prince and his Party'.[1]

Bernstorff may not have contemplated trying to change the English ministry before but now that his power was at an end this must have seemed the only way to its recovery. After he returned to England in November, he entered into an intrigue to destroy the administration and replace the leading ministers with Walpole and Townshend. He succeeded only in increasing his own impotence. Instead of destroying the ministry he strengthened it, for his intrigue, having been revealed in mysterious circumstances to Sunderland and Stanhope, stimulated the reunion of the whig politicians and a reconciliation in the royal family, both effected in the spring of 1720 without his knowledge.[2] Without the king's favour, and with the leading politicians united against him, Bernstorff was now of no account in England, and in the summer of 1720 he accompanied the king to Hanover and never returned. He kept in touch with English affairs through Lady Cowper,[3] and he looked forward to regaining his pre-eminent position, but the period of his influence was over.

By this repudiation of his Hanoverian advisors in 1719 the king clearly intended for the future to place more direct reliance on his English ministers. Perhaps, as an historian has speculated, 'for the first time George I realized his duty towards England'.[4] It was natural that after five years he would be more used to English ways and more at ease with English ministers, especially since he had entertained lavishly and lived very much a public life since 1717.[5] He must also have recognized by 1719 the talent of Stanhope, and he had clearly demonstrated his trust in Sunderland by making him his groom of the stole.

On the other hand there were still certain difficulties of language and temperament preventing a free and easy *rapport* between the king and

[1] Add. MSS. 32686, fo. 88.   [2] Plumb, *Walpole*, I, 282–92.
[3] See their letters in 1721 and 1722 in Panshanger MSS. Letterbooks, v, 202, 203, 241, 269, 281–2; VI, 3–5, 71–8.
[4] Michael, *England under George I*, II, 255.   [5] See chapter. 8.

English ministers. Not all of his ministers spoke French fluently and, despite a story told in his old age by Horace Walpole that his father communicated with the king in Latin, there is evidence that George I did not readily understand spoken Latin.[1] Even without a language difficulty, George I was not always easy to deal with. Though he kept himself well informed about foreign affairs—he read all the diplomatic correspondence and he was the first to complain when an ambassador's reports were not detailed or frequent enough[2]—he disliked being troubled too much by his ministers outside the two or three hours he set aside each day for business. And if it was true, as the Imperial ambassador suggested in 1726, that the king liked to receive information and advice 'by other hands than by his ministers',[3] this must have presented them with another difficulty. How did the English ministers, then, secure the closet after the preponderant influence of the German ministers had been removed, the influence which, for a price, had secured the closet against rivals? How, in the later years of the reign, did the ministers try to ensure that hostile advice did not reach the king? What follows is not intended to answer that question fully but to suggest only that one factor was of considerable importance to Robert Walpole's hold on power during the last five years of the reign: the support of a lady of the court who was very close to the king, Ehrengard Mesuline von der Schulenberg, duchess of Kendal.

V

George I brought two ladies to England in 1714: Fraulein von der Schulenberg and Sophie Charlotte von Kielmannsegge, the wife of the Hanoverian master of the horse. Both ladies were widely regarded as the king's mistresses though some contemporaries and some historians have speculated that Kielmannsegge was probably his half-sister, and Schulenberg his wife by a morganatic marriage.[4] It is not of crucial

---

[1] Bernstorff offered his services in 1717 as an interpreter when Lord Cowper wanted to speak to the king about an appointment because, as he told Lady Cowper, 'le Roy ne pouvant pas tout a fait entendre ce que Myl. lui dit en Latin ou en Anglais' (Panshanger MSS. Letterbooks, IV, 240.)

[2] Add. MSS. 9151, fo. 120; Stowe MSS. 231, fo. 122.

[3] Coxe, *Walpole*, II, 507.

[4] Kielmannsegge was the daughter of Countess Platen, who had been the mistress of George I's father, the Elector Ernst August and, though it has never been clearly

importance. Both ladies were high in the king's regard and this was sufficient to ensure that their friendship was thought to be worth cultivating. But if the king had married the duchess of Kendal, to give her English title, it would help to explain why she surged ahead of her rival in England and became in the last five or so years of the reign a very important figure in politics.

The malicious Lady Mary Wortley Montagu thought that the attraction between Kendal and the king was one of like, and weak, minds. The duchess, she says,

was so much of his temper that I do not wonder at the engagement between them. She was duller than himself, and consequently did not find out that he was so; and had lived in that figure at Hanover almost forty years (for she came hither at threescore) without meddling in any affairs of the Electorate.[1]

It may well be that the duchess had not found scope for political activity in Hanover, but in England her proximity to a monarch whose favour was so crucial to politicians and place-hunters made her so valuable an ally that the temptations to interfere in political matters were irresistably strong. She had ample opportunity to speak to the king, especially when, soon after his arrival, he formed the habit of taking his supper in her apartment every evening. The kind of help she could give to the English ministers is indicated by Stanhope's reply to Sunderland's request that the king's permission be obtained for his proposed journey to Hanover in August, 1719. 'I have mentioned to the Dutchess your lordships coming over', Stanhope wrote, 'and she

established, several writers have assumed that she was a product of this union (Fritz Genzel, "Studien zur Geschichte des Nordischen Kriegs, 1714–20" (unpublished thesis, Bonn University, 1951), p. 16; Imbert-Terry, *George I*, p. 147; Lewis Melville, *The First George in England and Hanover*, II, 23 ff.). On several occasions during the reign it was rumoured that the marriage of the king and Madame Schulenberg would be publicly acknowledged. It never was. Horace Walpole thought in later life that they probably had been married, and he has been followed in this by some historians (H. Walpole, *Reminiscences written...in 1788*, ed. Paget Toynbee (1924), pp. 25–6; Genzel, p. 16). Wolfgang Michael found no evidence in continental archives that the marriage took place (*England under George I*, I, p. 81). As Edward Calamy notes in his memoirs, 'How matters really stood between his Majesty and the Duchess of Kendal will remain, for the most part, a secret, until the great ones are pleased to make discoveries' (Calamy, *Own Life*, p. 494). What he meant by 'for the most part' remains a mystery.

[1] Lady Mary Wortley Montagu, *Works*, p. 127.

has promised and judges it most proper to open it herself first to the king.'[1] As the Prussian envoy said of another favour she did for the ministry in the following February, Kendal often 'broke the first ice' with the king.[2]

There are indications that Kendal was of some political importance at various times in the early years of the reign. Townshend thought, for example, that her anger with him in 1716 had much to do with his disgrace; and it is clear that Stanhope valued her assistance in his struggle with Bernstorff in 1719. References to her political activities during the first eight years of the reign are, however, scattered and sparse compared to the period after 1722. After the establishment of the Walpole ministry she looms large in the correspondence of Townshend, Newcastle and Walpole. She became an invaluable intermediary for them with the king, and though her assistance does not, of course, explain Walpole's success, her management of George I and her help in securing the closet undoubtedly helped to establish and maintain Walpole's strong and stable administration.

The old notion that Walpole rose to power in 1720 on a wave of popularity, hailed as the saviour of his country after the disasters of the South Sea speculation, has recently been corrected.[3] Walpole and Townshend were little more than junior members of the administration when they came back into office in June 1720. The ministry was still dominated by Stanhope and Sunderland, and it was only the death of these men—the first in February 1721, the second in April 1722—that made it possible for the brothers-in-law to grasp the leadership of the government. Even then they were not without rivals for the king's favour, for many of Sunderland's followers retained office after his death and showed little desire to shift their allegiance to his arch-enemy, Walpole.[4] Of these men the most outstanding was unquestionably Lord Carteret who had recently become secretary of state in the place of the younger Craggs. Carteret was only thirty-one when he was given the seals but he had already enjoyed the experience and the *éclat* of the highly successful diplomatic mission to Sweden in 1719 and 1720 upon

---

[1] Blenheim MSS. D 1/33, Stanhope to Sunderland, 3 August 1719.
[2] Blenheim MSS. D 1/33, Wallenrodt to Sunderland, 18/19 February 1720.
[3] Plumb, *Walpole*, I, chh. 8 and 9; C. B. Realey, *Early Opposition*, pp. 1–34.
[4] *H.M.C. Onslow MSS.* p. 465; for the Sunderland faction in 1721 see Realey, *Early Opposition*, pp. 56–7.

which the settlement of Northern problems had been founded. This success, his ability to speak fluently four European languages, including German, and his extensive knowledge of Northern and Imperial politics, brought him quickly into the favour of George I.[1] After Sunderland's death he was Walpole's most serious rival with the king. And his personal charm, his talent and the followers he inherited from Sunderland made him a formidable rival indeed. There was little wonder, then, that when the king announced his intention to go to Hanover in 1723 and to take Carteret with him, his fellow-secretary, Townshend, remembering no doubt his troubles in 1716, took alarm and managed to be included in the party.

In Hanover—where, Townshend discovered, 'factions and intrigue are natural and in fashion'[2]—Carteret waged a vigorous campaign to oust Townshend from the king's favour. He did not lack allies. Bernstorff was still in touch with English politics and was looking for just such an opportunity to help destroy a ministry in order to make another that might accept his guidance. He and Carteret were quickly working together.[3] Carteret acquired another valuable ally in the countess of Platen, a favourite of the king's of long standing; and he tried to win over other Germans, including an old friend of Sunderland's, Madame de Wendt.[4] Newcastle, in London, said bravely that Carteret's friendship with Bernstorff and the countess of Platen would not help him much.[5] But this was whistling in the dark, and all of Townshend's correspondence from Hanover provides its contradiction. From the beginning Townshend was made aware that Carteret and Bernstorff would stop at nothing to ruin his reputation with the king. It was, he confessed to Walpole, a very bewildering situation; it was no easy task in Hanover

for a stranger to behave himself inoffensively: however, I am very sure I have lost no friend, and I think I have made no enemy; tho' it is not a very agreeable situation to be eternally upon ones guard from all quarters.[6]

But Townshend was no tyro. He was able to neutralize much of the initial support that Carteret had won among the women at court by

[1] Coxe, *Walpole*, I, 177–80.   [2] *Ibid.* II, 261.
[3] Add. MSS. 32686, fos. 265–6.
[4] Coxe, *Walpole*, II, 258–61; Townshend to Walpole, n.d. (the original is dated 6 August 1723, n.s. in Stowe MSS 251, fos. 17–23).
[5] Add. MSS. 32686, fo. 266.   [6] Coxe, *Walpole*, II, 261.

persuading Walpole—who was in an advantageous position for this sort of game at the head of the Treasury—to provide several of them, including Platen and Madame de Wendt, with gifts of money or payments on their pensions.[1] And he was not above using 'evidence', provided by Walpole, that Carteret had had dealings with Tories during the past session of Parliament in an effort to discredit him.[2] But above all else Townshend depended that summer on the support of the duchess of Kendal. Through all the complications and involutions of intrigue and counter-intrigue that fill Townshend's letters to Walpole and Newcastle, the importance of her friendship is constantly reiterated. She is 'the good duchess and...fast friend' to whom 'we have sworn an eternal and inviolable attachment'.[3] She helped Townshend win a number of tactical victories. For example, though she disliked the man, Townshend depended on her influence to persuade the king to take Marshal Hardenberg into the Hanoverian ministry and to take him to England as his chief advisor for the affairs of the electorate. Hardenberg, who had been in England since 1714 as marshall of the court, the Hanoverian equivalent of lord steward, was an innocuous man. It was precisely for this reason that Townshend pressed for his elevation in the ministry; 'at least he will serve to exclude some more dangerous person from being brought over to England', he told Walpole.[4] 'I am glad', Newcastle wrote to Walpole when he heard the news, that 'the Dutchess and Lord Townshend have got the Marshall into the Ministry, which will seem to the world like a victory on our side and prevent any mischief done us.'[5] There is no doubt that Kendal had been the principal instrument of this appointment. She urged the king over and over again to make it, and, indeed, she so persisted in it against his initial hostility that, as Townshend said, she 'strained her interest, perhaps further than was advisable'.[6]

The alliance of Townshend and the duchess seems to have strengthened as the summer progressed, undoubtedly because Kendal discovered that she, too, needed help against her own rivals. The duchess enjoyed a

---

[1] Stowe MSS. 251, fos. 17–23, 37, Townshend to Walpole, 6 August, 17 September 1723. These letters were printed by Coxe in *Walpole*, vol. II, but he omitted the passages dealing with the bribes.

[2] Coxe, *Walpole*, II, 265.

[3] *Ibid.* I, 182; Add. MSS. 9150, fo. 98.   [4] Coxe, *Walpole*, II, 271.

[5] Add. MSS. 32686, fo. 339.   [6] Coxe, *Walpole*, II, 271.

pleasant and profitable position in England as the king's leading favourite. It is probably not true, as some historians have believed, that Kendal was given the emoluments of the office of master of the horse, one of the richest of court posts,[1] but she had a pension from the king[2] and opportunity to add to it in various ways. And she had undoubtedly used her position to line her pockets as much as possible.[3] Kielmann-segge, Robethon and Bernstorff had done so too, but in the 1720s Kendal was without serious rivals in England for the major share of the king's favour from which everything else flowed. It was therefore a matter of crucial importance to her that Carteret cultivated the countess of Platen so assiduously, and especially when it was rumoured in the summer of 1723 that he was hoping to persuade her to return to England with the king.

Platen was younger and more attractive than the duchess of Kendal. She had been a favourite of the king's for many years[4] and Carteret had from the first seen in her a useful counter-weight to the duchess who acted so much in concert with Townshend. It was well known in England that he paid her much attention during the summer, and, though the story was denied, it was widely believed that Carteret had urged

[1] Coxe thought that Kendal had been given the salary of this office (*ibid.* 1, 84) and he has been followed by Melville, Imbert-Terry and others. They were perhaps misled by the fact that the mastership was in commission during the reign (except for the first year when it was held by the duke of Somerset). It was put into commission not in order that the duchess might enjoy the profits, but to save money. The saving (£1,645 per annum) appears in the household accounts. (C(H)MSS. 45/5). The office had also been in commission during the last two years of Anne's reign.

[2] I have not been able to verify that it was £7,500 a year as the Imperial ambassador said in 1726 (Coxe, *Walpole*, II, 509).

[3] She helped, for example, to procure the dukedom of Chandos in 1719 for James Brydges, earl of Carnarvon, and in the following year she received at least £9500 from him (C. H. and N. I. Baker, *The Life and Circumstances of James Brydges*, p. 112, n. 1); it seems likely too that she received something in 1717 for helping to get the Garter for Newcastle; and it was said that Kendal received £11,000 for her help in getting Bolingbroke permission to return to England (Hervey, *Memoirs*, p. 13; Coxe, *Walpole*, I, 209). In common with other Germans and some English ministers Kendal seems to have been handsomely bribed during the South Sea fraud. She also made a considerable sum out of the patent to manufacture copper coinage for Ireland which she was granted by the king and which she sold to William Wood (see Plumb, *Walpole*, II, 67–8).

[4] Lady Mary Wortley Montagu, *Works*, pp. 128–9.

the countess to return with the king. Townshend had attempted to minimize Carteret's advantage by cultivating the countess himself as much as possible, and through Walpole, he was able to do her a number of favours. He wrote to his brother-in-law in August:

I make no secret here of owning my attachment to our friend the Dutchess, yet I endeavour to live on as good terms as I can with the Countess of Platen, from whom I have received great civilities...I am most obliged to you for your readiness in paying the arrears of the Pension I wrote to you about, which has had a very good effect.[1]

It could only have been to Carteret's advantage, however, if Platen went to England. Townshend all along thought it unlikely that she would,[2] but he none the less worked hard to ensure that she did not. In November he was able to assure Kendal that the king would not permit Platen to cross to England.[3]

If it had not been clear before, Townshend and the duchess of Kendal both discovered in Hanover in 1723 how much mutual benefit there was in their alliance. In threatening both their interests, Carteret only succeeded in bringing them closer together. And Townshend, having been forced out in 1716 because he lacked a defender at court, succeeded in 1723 in defeating another intrigue against him, partly at least because he found a very powerful ally there. Throughout the summer Townshend was able to demonstrate to those who were sensitive to such things that his influence with the king was unimpaired by the way that vacant posts were filled.[4]

Carteret's threat had only been parried, of course. While he remained a secretary of state and the leader of a sizable group within the ministry he was obviously not beaten. But he had gained nothing on his rivals, and even his friends lost hope of driving them out when his campaign to weaken them at court failed so obviously.[5] And in April 1724, within a few months of the return from Hanover, his failure was made apparent to all, for Walpole and Townshend were by then strong enough with the king to get Carteret sent to Ireland as lord lieutenant. Newcastle, an old Sunderlandite, but now an ardent follower of Walpole, was given the seals. Though enemies remained within the

---

[1] Stowe MSS. 251, fo. 25.
[2] Coxe, *Walpole*, II, 267.
[3] *Ibid.* p. 287.
[4] See above, pp. 149–52.
[5] Realey, *Early Opposition*, p. 132.

administration, Carteret's and later dismissals deflated their ambitions,[1] and the triumvirate of Walpole at the Treasury and Townshend and Newcastle as secretaries of state assumed a firm grip on the ministry. There was obviously much truth in Newcastle's boast in May 1724 that 'ever since the king's accession to the throne, he never had ministers that were so thoroughly without any competitors with him as those at present'.[2]

Secure in Parliament, with the opposition in disarray, with their rivals in the ministry subdued, and free of the overweening influence of a powerful German minister, the leadership of Townshend and Walpole was firmly established after 1724. The stability of the administration depended on their ability to get the king's 'business' done, but it is important to remember that it depended as much on their security at court as on votes in Parliament. And to keep the king 'steady' they continued to rely very heavily on the duchess of Kendal. Foreign observers had no doubt that much of the ministry's strength depended on her friendship.[3] The French—who had ignored her in a detailed report on the English court drawn up for a new ambassador in 1719[4]— thought it worth their while to try and buy her friendship in 1724. Count Broglie told Louis XV in July that he was 'convinced that she may be advantageously employed in promoting your majesty's service'; to which the king replied:

There is no room to doubt that the duchess of Kendal, having a great ascendency over the King of Great Britain, and maintaining a strict union with his ministers, must materially influence their principal resolutions. You will neglect nothing to acquire a share of her confidence, from a conviction that nothing can be more conducive to my interests.[5]

It is perhaps exaggerated to say that the duchess influenced the government's 'principal resolutions', but she did act as a link between the king and his ministers, making an initial approach to him about

---

[1] Roxburgh was dismissed as secretary for Scotland in 1725, for example, after as thorough a job of character assassination by Townshend in Hanover, as had been performed on Townshend himself in 1716 (*ibid.* pp. 141–2.)

[2] Add. MSS. 9152, fo. 3. For the circumstances surrounding Carteret's removal from the secretaryship see Plumb, *Walpole*, II, ch. II.

[3] Coxe, *Walpole*, II, 300, 301, 509–10.

[4] Michael, *England under George I*, II, 319–24.

[5] Coxe, *Walpole*, II, 301, 304.

delicate subjects, relaying his opinions, preparing the ministers for meetings in the closet and so on.[1] Walpole said himself of Kendal that she was 'in effect, as much Queen of England as any ever was; that he did everything by her'.[2] And Hervey thought that during George I's reign Walpole was always to some extent dependent on Townshend because the duchess preferred to deal with him.[3]

In the next reign, Walpole developed very close ties with Queen Caroline. She proved to be an even abler manager of the king than Kendal had been, so that during the greater part of his twenty-year ascendency Walpole was freed from much worry about one of the indispensible bases of his power through the friendship of two women who 'possessed the king's ear'. His abilities as an administrator and 'parliament man' have perhaps obscured for historians the necessity of such support in the reigns of the first two Georges. This is not to deny the obvious importance to a ministry of Parliamentary management. But the ministry's ability to control Parliament was in many ways secondary to and dependent on their ability to control the monarch. As Walpole said in 1716, 'Nobody can carry on the King's business if he is not supported at Court.'[4] Ministers could not afford to ignore the court. Their foremost concern had to be to secure, as Walpole did with the help of the duchess of Kendal and Queen Caroline, the primary base of their power, the king's closet.

[1] See, for example, Add. MSS. 9156, fo. 29.
[2] Lady Cowper, *Diary*, p. 132.   [3] Hervey, *Memoirs*, p. 84.
[4] Coxe, *Walpole*, II, 59.

APPENDIX TO CHAPTER 7

A NOTE ON THE SIZE OF THE HOUSEHOLD
GROUP IN PARLIAMENT

It is difficult to estimate accurately the contribution that household patronage normally made to the support of the king's government in Parliament because the evidence is defective. Reports of debates are scanty and division lists are almost non-existent: there are only three known division lists for the Parliament of 1715–22, and none at all for that of 1722–7.[1] Such evidence as there is suggests, not surprisingly, that those who took the king's money normally voted in support of his administration in Parliament. Eight members of Parliament with posts at court voted for the Septennial Bill (1716), and none against; nine voted for the repeal of the Schism Act (1719), and none against; and six voted for the Peerage Bill (1719) and one, Sir Richard Steele, voted against. What *is* surprising perhaps is not that household servants voted for the administration in these divisions, but that there were so few of them. Since it seems often to be assumed that the household provided the king's ministers with a phalanx of supporters in both Houses it may be worthwhile asking how many peers and members of Parliament held posts at court in this reign in order to consider the extent to which the patronage available in the household was used for political purposes.

The court was of course the natural habitat of the peerage and peers dominated the first rank of court posts. The four major officers—the lord chamberlain, lord steward, groom of the stole and master of the horse—were invariably peers, as were in George I's reign the gentlemen of the bedchamber. A number of other honourable and profitable places were often held by peers. In George I's reign a total of fifty-three peers had posts at court, the number in office at any one time varying from twenty (in 1715) to twenty-seven (in 1720 and 1721).[2]

---

[1] Mary Ransome, 'Division Lists of the House of Commons, 1715–1760', *Bulletin of the Institute of Historical Research*, XIX, pp. 1–8.

[2] On 31 December of each year during the reign the totals of peers in court office was as follows: 1714, 21; 1715, 20; 1716–18, 21; 1719, 26; 1720–21, 27; 1722, 26;

These peers all held posts of honour but their sphere of action was not thereby limited to the court. Some of them held 'posts of business' along with the court post and a few were concerned with the making of national policy at the highest level. Sunderland as groom of the stole in 1721–2 is the prime example of such a man in this reign. But, in a less obvious way, the duke of Newcastle also made his office, the lord chamberlainship, into more than just a court post. After the death of Sunderland, with whom he had been associated in his early years, Newcastle turned to Walpole and became an important member of the Townshend–Walpole group in its struggle with Carteret within the ministry. During the summer of 1723, when both secretaries accompanied the king to Hanover, Newcastle, though still only lord chamberlain, helped to fill the gap in the administration in London. For a few weeks, while Walpole was in Norfolk, he was in full charge. He corresponded with Townshend in Hanover and with Walpole at Houghton and obviously worked extremely hard and with already well-developed thoroughness. When Carteret was forced out of office in the following year, Newcastle had established a strong claim to succeed him, even though, unlike most secretaries of state under the first two Georges, he had had no diplomatic experience abroad.[1]

Such movement from the court to the administration—and indeed movement in the other direction—was not uncommon. Nor was it uncommon for a courtier to hold his post in conjunction with a place of 'business'. The thirty-one men who were gentlemen of the bedchamber during the reign, to take them as a convenient group to study for this purpose, provide a number of examples. The earl of Berkeley (first lord of the Admiralty, 1717–27), the earl of Lincoln (paymaster of the forces, 1715–20), the earl of Stair (ambassador to France, 1715–20), lord Carteret (ambassador to Sweden, 1719–20), the duke of Portland (governor of Jamaica, 1721–6), were all gentlemen of the bedchamber

---

1723–24, 25; 1725, 24; 1726, 23. (In 1725–7 two peers held two court posts each.) The increase in 1719 was due mainly to the creation in that year of four new gentlemen of the bedchamber.

The largest total of peers in office, 27 in 1720–1, was made up of: lord chamberlain, lord steward, groom of the stole, seventeen gentlemen of the bedchamber, master of the great wardrobe, treasurer of the household, cofferer, master of the robes, captain of the band of pensioners, captain of the yeomen, master of the hawks.

[1] S. H. Nulle, *Thomas Pelham-Holles, Duke of Newcastle*, pp. 151, 154–6; D. B. Horn, *The British Diplomatic Service*, p. 106.

during their tenure in the more active place. For them the court post was of distinctly secondary interest, but it provided a sizable addition to their salary as well as the prestige and honour of the king's personal favour.

If not engaged in administrative or diplomatic work, most of the other gentlemen of the bedchamber enjoyed further honours of all kinds. The earl of Lincoln gave up the paymastership in 1720, but he was later constable of the Tower (1723–5) and cofferer of the household (1725–8) while remaining a gentleman of the bedchamber throughout the reign; the earl of Leicester was lord warden of the Cinque Ports (1717–28), captain of the yeomen (1725–31), and a bedchamber man (1717–27); the duke of Dorset, a gentleman of the bedchamber, 1714–17, was warden of the Cinque Ports at the same time. The earl of Orkney, who was already governor of Virginia and colonel of a Guards regiment when George I came to the throne, became in 1714 governor of Edinburgh Castle and a supernumerary gentleman of the bedchamber; he was advanced to the full appointment in 1716 when the duke of Kent was promoted to the lord stewardship. Indeed, George II gave as his reason for not continuing Orkney in the bedchamber in 1727 that he enjoyed sufficient places without it.[1] Very few of the peers who occupied a bedchamber post did not enjoy some further benefit, either of salary or honour, from the Crown. To mention only a few more examples: of the thirty-one gentlemen of the bedchamber, four were created knights of the garter while holding the post, four were created knights of the Bath when that order was revived in 1725, four were colonels of regiments, and twelve were lords lieutenant. In 1734 Lord Hervey thought that Lord Pembroke had strong pretensions to the office of master of the horse because he had served George II as prince and king 'twenty years in the bedchamber without any other preferment than a regiment'.[2]

The gentlemen of the bedchamber were not untypical of other peers in court office. There was, it seems clear, a concentration of preferments and honours in relatively few hands; it is, indeed, a concentration so striking that it suggests the weakness of patronage as the sole means of building a parliamentary majority. In 1720 approximately 15 per cent of the members of the House of Lords held posts at court. This was a sizable group; it was, relatively, much larger than the household group

[1] Cathcart MSS. A/15 (1 August 1727). [2] Hervey, *Memoirs*, p. 251.

in the House of Commons. But more peers could perhaps have been attached to the government if court posts had been distributed with more care or with more of an eye to simple political advantage. It seems clear that the influencing of as many votes as possible could not have been the only concern of the king and his ministers when vacancies were filled at court.

Much the same could be said about those posts that could be held by members of the lower House. Only nine courtiers were members of Parliament in 1714.[1] At the elections in 1715 all but two of these men were re-elected[2] (though two changed seats)[3] and a further four courtiers entered the House,[4] making a total of eleven court members of Parliament when the new Parliament assembled. The number steadily increased. During the Parliament that sat from 1715 to 1722, five courtiers entered the House,[5] and ten members of Parliament got court posts,[6]

[1] William Cadogan, master of the robes (Woodstock); Heneage Finch, Lord Guernsey' master of the jewel office (Surrey); Hugh Boscawen, comptroller of the household (Penryn); Edmund Dunch, master of the household (Boroughbridge); Sir William Forester, clerk of the board of green cloth (Wenlock); Sir John Walter, clerk of the board of green cloth (Oxford City); Sir Richard Steele, surveyor of the stables at Hampton Court (Stockbridge); Richard Lockwood, gentleman of the privy chamber (Hendon); Sir Thomas Read, gentleman of the privy chamber (Cricklade).

[2] Forester and Lockwood.

[3] Dunch sat for Wallingford and Steele for Boroughbridge in the new Parliament.

[4] William Ker, groom of the bedchamber (Dysart Burghs); Conyers Darcy, gentleman of the horse, avenor and clerk martial and a commissioner for the office of master of the horse (1715–17), master of the household 1719–30 (Newark); Thomas Catesby, Lord Paget, captain of the yeomen (Staffordshire); William Hucks, brewer of the household (Wallingford).

[5] Francis Negus, commissioner for the office of master of the horse, 1715–27 (member of Parliament for Ipswich, 1717–32); Robert Wroth, clerk of the board of green cloth, 1715–20 (Guildford 1705–8, 1710–11, 1717–20); Henry Berkeley, equerry and gentleman of the horse, 1714–36 (Gloucester 1720–34); Philip Cavendish, sergeant porter, 1705–43 (Beeralston 1721, St Germans 1722–7, Portsmouth, 1734–43); Owen Buckingham, gentleman of the privy chamber, 1714–20 (Reading 1708–13, 1716–20).

[6] James Brudenell, master of the jewel office, 1716–30 (Chichester 1713–15, Andover 1715–34, Chichester 1734–46); William Feilding, clerk of the board of green cloth, 1716–24 (Castle Rising 1705–23); William Coventry, clerk of the board of green cloth, 1717–19 (Bridport 1708–19); Sir Robert Corbet, clerk of the board of green cloth, 1720–35 (Shropshire 1705–10, 1715–22); Giles Earle, clerk of the green cloth, 1720–34 (Chippenham 1715–22, Malmesbury 1722–47); Robert Bristow, clerk of the board of green cloth, 1720–37 (Winchelsea 1708–37); Henry Pelham, treasurer

which more than offset the three who died,[1] the four who were dismissed[2] and the three who retired from the House of Commons.[3] In March 1722 when the Parliament was dissolved, sixteen members held court posts.

At the general election of 1722 seven more courtiers entered Parliament[4] and only one of the previous court members, Sir Robert Corbet, did not return to the House. In the course of that Parliament, which sat until George I's death in 1727, a further ten members of Parliament were given posts at court[5] so that, despite decreases due to death and removals,[6]

of the chamber, 1720–2 (Seaford 1717–22, Sussex 1722–54); Paul Methuen, comptroller of the household, 1720–5 (Devizes 1708–10, 1713–14, Brackley 1715–47); Sir Wilfred Lawson, groom of the bedchamber, 1720–3 (Boroughbridge 1718–22, Cockermouth 1722–37); Sir Brian Broughton, gentleman of the privy chamber, 1718–24 (Newcastle-under-Lyme 1715–24).

[1] Dunch (1719); Wroth (1720); Buckingham (1720).

[2] Lord Guernsey (1716); Walter (1716); Lord Paget (1715); Steele (?).

[3] Cadogan was made a baron in 1716; Boscawen gave up his court post on being made a viscount in 1720; Coventry inherited the earldom of Coventry in 1719 and also retired from his court place.

[4] James Tyrrel, groom of the bedchamber, 1714–27 (member of Parliament for Boroughbridge 1722–42); Henry Pulteney, equerry, 1714–17 (Hedon 1722–34, 1739–41, Hull 1744–7); Henry Aylmer, equerry, 1714–27 (Rye 1722–7); William Charles Van Huls, clerk of the robes and wardrobes, 1700–22 (Bramber 1722); Peter Campbell, gentleman of the buttery, 1721–?51 (Buteshire 1722–7, Elgin Burghs 1728–34, Buteshire 1734–41); James Pelham, secretary of the lord chamberlain, ?1720–61 (Newark 1722–41, Hastings 1741–61); Richard Lockwood, gentleman of the privy chamber, 1714–27 (Hendon 1713–15, London 1722–7, Worcester 1734–41).

[5] Charles Stanhope, treasurer of the chamber, 1722–7 (Milbourne Port 1717–22, Aldborough 1722–34, Harwich 1734–41); John Merrill, deputy cofferer, ?1723–5 (Tregony 1721–7, St Albans 1733–4); William Pulteney, cofferer, 1723–5 (Hedon 1705–34, Middlesex 1734–42); Robert Herbert, groom of the bedchamber, 1723–7 (Wilton 1722–68); Richard Sutton, clerk of the board of green cloth, 1724–7 (Newark 1708–10, 1712–37); Daniel, Lord Finch, comptroller of the household, 1725–30 (Rutlandshire 1710–30); William Sloper, deputy cofferer, ?1725–1743 (Great Bedwin 1715–22, Camelford 1722–7, Great Bedwin 1729–41, Whitchurch 1742–3); Viscount Malpas, master of the robes, 1726–7 (East Looe 1724–7, New Windsor 1727–33); marquis of Hartington, captain of the gentlemen pensioners, 1726–31 (Lostwithiel 1721–4, Grampound 1724–7, Huntingdon 1727–9); Richard Swynfen, gentleman of the privy chamber, 1720–7 (Tamworth 1708–10, 1723–6).

[6] William Feilding died in 1724; Van Huls died soon after his election to Parliament in 1722; Broughton died in 1724. Henry Pelham was promoted to the treasury board

the court group increased until at the end of the reign it numbered twenty-four.

Thus, between 1715 and 1727 the court group in the House of Commons varied between eleven and twenty-four. Altogether, forty-three members of Parliament held a post at Court during the reign. At least nine of these men were also army officers[1] and one, Philip Cavendish, was a naval officer.

Thirty of these forty-three members of Parliament held posts that may be described as being of the first rank, either because they were posts of honour like groom of the bedchamber or, like the post of clerk of the board of green cloth, the salary made the post very attractive. Very few of the posts held by members of Parliament can be called sinecures. Apart from the few gentlemen of the privy chamber, only the places held by Steele, Cavendish and Campbell—surveyor of the stables at Hampton Court, sergeant porter and gentleman of the buttery—seem to have required neither attendance nor effort. Certainly men in court posts were not by definition sinecurists. Many of them devoted a lot of time to their court duties and, in addition, a few— the comptroller of the household, for example—seem to have played a certain role in the ministry's work in Parliament.[2] And, as in the case of the peers, there was always movement of men between court posts and posts of 'business'. In the House of Commons as in the House of Lords there was no rigid and lasting division among government supporters between courtiers and 'men of business'.

The maximum number of members of Parliament holding court office in George I's reign, twenty-four, seems to have been rarely exceeded in the eighteenth century. In 1701 there were thirteen members

in 1722; Lawson surrendered his place in 1723, William Pulteney his in 1725; Merrill was replaced, probably in 1725; Swynfen was out of his court place by 1726.

[1] Ker, Tyrrel, Wroth, Sutton, Negus, Berkeley, Henry Pulteney, Peter Campbell, Cadogan.

[2] The comptroller of the household acted as a link between the House of Commons and the king. On many occasions during the reign, the comptroller brought messages from the king and carried messages and petitions from the Commons to the palace. Instances of this are noted in the reports of L'Hermitage to the States General (Add. MSS. 17677 KKK2, fo. 491 (1 March 1718), KKK4, fo. 109 (28 February 1721) KKK6, fo. 397 (1 December 1724) and in newsletters sent to Hanover (Cal. Br. Arch. Des. 24, England 129 (18 February 1718) and England 134 (6 May 1720).

of Parliament with court posts;[1] in 1742 seventeen;[2] in 1761 the total climbed to about forty-two,[3] but this was quite unusual and it has been explained as the result partly of the amalgamation of two courts and partly of the efforts of the duke of Newcastle to find enough places for his dependents;[4] by 1782 the number had again declined to around twenty-four.[5]

Considering the number of places available this was not a large number of court members of Parliament. John Robinson, later in the century, put the number of court posts that members of Parliament could accept, socially and legally, at about sixty,[6] and this was probably conservative. A total of twenty or so members of Parliament with court posts does not therefore seem excessive, especially considering that the Prince of Wales's household in 1715 included twenty-two. The court group in both Houses increased steadily during George I's reign, but it seems clear that the patronage available in the household was not disposed as single-mindedly, or as easily, to yield immediate political advantage as some accounts of eighteenth-century politics would have one believe; there were certainly fewer members of Parliament holding offices at court than there might have been. Perhaps the reason is to be sought partly in the nature of the posts themselves. Not many were strictly 'political' posts. Almost all required some attendance of the holder and many brought a man into close contact with the king. Perhaps the offices on the board of green cloth, from the treasurer down

[1] R. Walcott, *English Politics in the Early Eighteenth Century*, App. 1.

[2] J. B. Owen, *The Rise of the Pelhams*. Dr Owen lists (p. 50, n. 4) fourteen 'courtiers', but he includes seven men—including the master of the mint, the lyon king at arms, and the surveyor of the king's lands—who, by the rather narrow definition of 'the court' employed in this study, should be excluded; clearly it is a matter of definition. On the other hand there are two members of Parliament among the 'men of business' who also held court posts (p. 48, n. 1), seven among army and naval officers (p. 51, n. 5) and one (the secretary of the lord chamberlain) whom Dr Owen includes with the sinecurists (p. 51, n. 1) though not all of these men were strictly 'courtiers', the number of members of Parliament with court posts in 1742, and the figure which should be compared with those given here for George I's reign, is seventeen.

[3] L. B. Namier, *England in the Age of the American Revolution* (1930), pp. 260-1.

[4] I. R. Christie, 'Economical Reform and "The Influence of the Crown", 1780', *Cambridge Historical Journal*, XII (1956), 146.

[5] I. R. Christie, *The End of North's Ministry*, p. 186.

[6] W. T. Laprade (ed.) *The Parliamentary Papers of John Robinson, 1774–1784*. Camden Third Series, vol. XXXIII. Royal Historical Society, 1922. pp. 9–11.

to the four clerks, and the headships of the main departments and sub-departments, except the bedchamber, could change hands easily with political changes. But the personal places in the stables and the bed-chamber clearly could not in the early eighteenth century. And even if the king made such posts available for political purposes, not all members of Parliament would be anxious or socially qualified to do such service. But perhaps the main reason why there were not more members of Parliament with posts at court is simply that the mass of patronage that was available to the Crown could not always be wielded for direct political purposes—to influence directly the parliamentary vote—because, as was said in an earlier chapter, there were many other forces besides the pull of immediate political advantage playing on those who made appointments at court.

8

THE CHARACTER OF COURT LIFE

I

When George I entered his capital for the first time, on 20 September 1714, the city was in darkness and the great crowds assembled along the Strand and elsewhere on the way to St James's Palace were not given the satisfaction of seeing the king.[1] This was a characteristic, if unplanned, gesture, for there was dominant in George I's character an extreme shyness of crowds and a dislike of formality. Though his inability to speak English undoubtedly heightened his discomfort in his new kingdom, it was not simply English crowds and English ceremony that he disliked; whenever he travelled the routes were always so arranged to avoid civic receptions if possible. The arrival in London may not indeed have been unplanned, for, on his way to England in 1714 the king wanted to arrive at The Hague at two o'clock in the morning in order to avoid 'much embarrassment and a great crowd of people'.[2] He always avoided grand receptions whenever possible; when it was learned that the Dutch were preparing a reception for the king on his way to Hanover in 1716 the Hanoverian representative at the Hague was instructed to inform the Dutch government that the king was travelling incognito and had not the slightest desire to be met with the honours befitting his rank.[3] In England, George never acquired interest in the trappings of royal power. He never courted popular acclaim and only rarely showed himself to his people. He travelled infrequently and never without purpose, trying always to slip unnoticed from one place to another. It was often impossible of course. When the king passed through a village, the church bells were rung and flowers were strewn, but the king obviously would have preferred silence and deserted streets. In 1723 on his return from Hanover, Townshend informed Walpole that the king wished 'that there may

[1] *H.M.C. Portland MSS.* v, 495.
[2] N.S.A., K.G., Hann. 9 Secreta Domus, III, 6.
[3] N.S.A., K.G., Hann. 92, Domestica, 34b.

be as little concourse of noisy attendants at his landing or on the road to London as possible. If he should pass through the city or the park [Townshend continues] anything of that kind would be more excusable, tho' it is what he desires entirely to avoid.' It was presumed by those who had to plan his reception on the same occasion that he would land south of the river, at Margate or Gravesend, rather than at Harwich, because he could thereby avoid passing through the city of London.[1]

George I treated his courtiers little better than the rest of his subjects during the first two and a half years of the reign. The arrangements of his private life had been simple in Hanover and they remained so in England. The king wanted to take advantage of very few of the innumerable rights and courtesies to which he was entitled; and he was not, for example, dressed formally in leisurely stages by peers of the realm as he might have been. English gentlemen and grooms of the bedchamber came into waiting, but their formal services were not required, for, besides his Hanoverian ministers, George brought with him to England his personal household servants who met the king's simple needs in the private rooms of the state apartments.

This 'inner' court was not as large as is sometimes imagined. Nor, as is sometimes assumed, did his German servants occupy posts on the English establishment. A. W. Ward, for example, thought that the court was full of Germans; but many of the men he calls 'German domestics' were men who, while German in origin, had been household servants in England for many years by 1714.[2] George *did* bring a large number of servants in 1714. There were about seventy-five in England at the beginning of the reign, including gentlemen of the bedchamber, pages, footmen, two physicians, two surgeons, two trumpeters, a tailor and a complete kitchen staff.[3] But many of these servants returned to Hanover in 1715[4] and more remained there after the king's visit in the next year. In December 1716 Bothmer thought that the king would return with 'only those servants who are necessary' and, a month later, events apparently having confirmed this belief, he

[1] Coxe, *Walpole*, II, 294; S.P. Dom. 35/46, fo. 86.
[2] A. W. Ward, *Great Britain and Hanover*, p. 49.
[3] N.S.A., K.G., Hann. 9, Secreta Domus III, 6; for the kitchen staff see above, p. 84.
[4] Add. MSS. 17677, III, fo. 288.

told Robethon, who was in Hanover, that 'it will give great comfort here that the King brings so few people with him this time'.[1] After 1716 it seems that there were never more than about twenty-five Hanoverian servants in England apart from the chancery staff.[2] About ten of these served in the king's kitchen; the others included two pages, four grooms of the chamber, eight footmen and an apothecary.

This seems a very modest household; none of the servants was 'unnecessary', except perhaps the curious character often referred to as the king's 'young Turk', Christian Ulrich Jorry, a dwarf. Ulrich was kept around the court presumably to provide some amusement for the king. He was certainly highly favoured. Many of his clothes—or costumes—were made by the king's tailor; he was taught English and painting; he was given servants and companions, and all at the king's expense.[3] He was not so highly favoured, though, that he escaped punishment when he attacked first one of the countess of Portland's maids and then a footman who tried to defend her. The king ordered him to be tried by the board of green cloth and, when he was found guilty, put into solitary confinement on bread and water for fifteen days.[4] While he behaved himself, though, he seems to have been well provided for in England. And he was an important enough part of the court to be included among the painted figures on the great staircase at Kensington done for George I by William Kent.[5]

Several of the other Germans were more than simple domestic servants. The two pages seem to have been particularly important to the king's functioning in England. From 1724 to 1727 at least, George paid for English lessons for them. They were also given two copies of Chamberlayne's *Magnae Britanniae Notitia; or, The Present State of Great Britain*, a contemporary description of the country which included lists of office-holders, army and naval officers and so on. And from 1724 to the end of the reign, the king's pages received three English newspapers. This could not have been simply for their own amusement.

[1] Stowe MSS. 229, fo. 339; Stowe MSS. 230, fos. 1-2.
[2] N.S.A., K.G., Cal. Br. 23, Finanzsachen no. 5 (accounts of salaries paid to the Hanoverian household in London).
[3] K.G., Cal. Br. 22, XIII, Anhang no. 3, vols. XVI-XXIII, *passim*.
[4] Earl of March, *A Duke and his Friends: the Life and Letters of the Second Duke of Richmond* (2 vols., 1911), p. 89; N.S.A., Cal. Br. Arch. 24, England 139 (newsletter of 5/16 June 1724); LS 13/115, fos. 121, 126.
[5] Margaret Jourdain, *The Work of William Kent* (1948), p. 72.

It seems obvious that they were paid to keep in touch with English affairs and to provide the king with a private source of information.[1] This would seem to cripple the notion that George I did not care about English affairs.

Two other members of the king's inner household who were particularly close to the king, his two Turkish grooms of the chamber, Mehemet and Mustapha, had caused a considerable stir when they arrived in 1714. They had been taken into the king's service in 1686 when George was campaigning in support of the emperor against the Turks. Mehemet and Mustapha are sometimes pictured as little more than slaves, but nothing could be farther from the truth. They had both risen high in the elector's service, Mehemet in particular. Having taken the Christian faith and been christened Ludwig Maximilian Mehemet, he was ennobled by the emperor in 1716 as Ludwig von Königstreu. He married the daughter of a wealthy Hanoverian and by her had two children, one of whom became a captain of cavalry in the Hanoverian army.[2] In England, as well as being a groom of the king's chamber and keeper of the closet (and perhaps the closest servant to the king), Mehemet was also in fact though not in name, keeper of the privy purse. In this reign about half of the £30,000 a year provided for the privy purse was used to pay the expenses of the German court in London.[3] This was technically illegal but it could never be discovered because the privy purse was private and the expenditure did not have to be accounted for. The forms were observed. Caspar Frederick Henning, the official keeper of the privy purse, received the money out of the exchequer but he passed it on immediately to the Hanoverian household treasurer, Frederick Butemeister.[4] This man paid the salaries and the other fixed charges, but the king's tailors' bills, his theatre subscriptions and his many other necessary expenses were paid by Mehemet who kept the accounts books and preserved the receipted bills.[5] Thus,

---

[1] N.S.A., K.G., Cal. Br. 23, Finanzsachen, nos. 5, 6, 7, *passim*, for the bills for English lessons, books, and newspapers.

[2] N.S.A., Cal. Br. Arch. 23, Des. 15, M, 138, papers relating to M. Von Königstreu.

[3] N.S.A., K.G., Cal. Br. Arch. 23, Finanzsachen, nos. 5, 6, 7.

[4] N.S.A., K.G., Cal. Br. Arch. 23, Finanzsachen no. 7, an account of money delivered by Henning to Butemeister, 1726.

[5] These receipts are in N.S.A., K.G., Cal. Br. Arch. 22, XIII, Anhang no. 3 ('Hofhaltung Quittungen'). Among other occasional expenses were lodgings for Hanoverian officials visiting London. One such man, a Captain Theise, had to leave in a hurry

though the Germans were prevented by the terms of the Act of Settlement from occupying posts on the English establishment, their salaries were still in this way paid by English money. When Mehemet died in 1726, Mustapha took his place. Both men were highly favoured by the the king. They had apartments near his; and Mehemet's mother and Mustapha's son, who were both in England, were also well provided for.[1]

The existence of this inner German court in London allowed George I the more easily to indulge his preference for privacy and informality. In reports to the King of Prussia in January 1715 and July 1716, Frederick Bonet emphasized that George appeared to his new subjects to be living in seclusion.[2] He rose early but did not emerge from his bedchamber until noon, when he went into the closet adjoining it to receive his ministers and other visitors. These audiences often lasted until three o'clock,[3] and then the king retired once more into his bedchamber to dine alone. In the late afternoon he usually walked alone in the gardens of St James's. During the early weeks of the reign the king dined often at the houses of the Whig nobility,[4] and about twice a month he went to the opera or the theatre. But for the most part he seldom left the palace at night and if he did it was without fanfare.[5] Occasionally he joined the princess's evening parties for a half hour but never to join the card games, and if not otherwise occupied (which he rarely was) he spent the evening at Madame Schulenberg's apartment where his supper was served.[6] All the evidence from 1715 and 1716 suggests that George I fully deserves the reputation he so firmly enjoys of a recluse who 'lived a retired life in the bare palace of St James's'.[7]

and left the following letter for his landlady, Jane Shewbridge: 'Mrs Schonbritz... ken present dis bil how leis in dis lettre to Mr Mehemet: ay hope you will receive aynii tinck.' She was paid by Mehemet (K.G., Cal. Br. Arch. 22, XIII, Anhang no. 3, vol. XXIV).

[1] LS 13/145, fos. 95, 121; Wren Society, *Publications*, VII, 218; *H.M.C. Stuart Papers*, II, 141.

[2] Extracts from these reports are printed in Michael, *England under George I*, I, 372–80.

[3] Algemeen Rijksarchief (The Hague), Heinsius Corr. no. 1867, L'Hermitage to Heinsius, 18 December 1714.

[4] J. J. Cartwright, *Wentworth Papers*, p. 425; Add. MSS. 22202, fos. 186, 189; Add. MSS. 17677 HHH, fos. 413, 415, 425, 427, 472; *Verney Letters of the 18th Century*, II, 16–17; *The Diary of the Earl of Bristol*, p. 62.

[5] Add. MSS. 22202, fo. 189.   [6] LS 13/115, fos. 81, 85, 93.

[7] Michael, *England under George I*, I, 84.

And it is hardly surprising that people were complaining in 1716 that the court lacked that certain majesty and nobility which encouraged reverence for the sovereign.[1]

The king was able to remain in the background partly because of the stability of the government, but mainly because the Prince and Princess of Wales on the other side of the palace were very much in evidence. They were keenly interested in display and their court contrasted sharply with the king's. Lord Hervey, who knew court life intimately, observed later that 'the pageantry and splendour, the badges and trappings of royalty, were as pleasing to the son as they were irksome to the father'.[2] Both the prince and princess were dressed and served in form by their bedchamber servants, and, though they too had brought Hanoverian servants with them in 1714, they did not neglect the services of their English attendants.[3] Their apartments were much more open and lively than the king's during the first years of the reign for they strove to attract the fashionable world to their court. During the first winter the princess held an evening drawing-room twice a week, and also gave a series of balls at Somerset House and St James's.[4] The king was content to let them take the lead. If the princess entertained, there was less necessity for him to do so; he could enjoy his privacy and emerge from his apartments only when the mood struck him, not when etiquette demanded it. It was perfectly clear when they arrived that the king disliked his son[5] and perhaps he was jealous of the limited popularity that the prince and princess acquired; in 1730 Walpole said that 'the late King did not like that his son should be preferred to him'.[6] But so long as their social activities remained politically harmless, so long that is as the prince's servants and guests were unwavering in their devotion to the administration, he would no doubt have remained in the background, allowing them to lead court social life.

By the summer of 1716, however, when George I returned to Hanover for the first time, it was becoming clear that this condition could not be maintained for long. The prince had been deliberately

---

[1] Bonet, quoted in Michael, *England under George I*, I, p. 380.

[2] Hervey, *Memoirs*, p. 66.

[3] Lady Cowper, *Diary*, p. 19; Cathcart MSS. Journal A/11 (21 November 1714, 23 February, 1 June, 9 July 1715).   [4] Add. MSS. 17677 III, fos. 26, 65, 73.

[5] Bonet, quoted in Michael, *England under George I*, I, 378.

[6] H.M.C. *Egmont MSS. Diary*, I, 85.

humiliated, first by the dismissal of Argyll, his groom of the stole, and then by the king's refusal to allow him to assume a regency with full power; social success the king might allow his son, but control of the Crown's patronage he would never consent to. And when the king left for Hanover and the prince and princess removed to Hampton Court, the prince seemed anxious to humiliate or to hurt his father in return. He lived in great style at Hampton Court, dining in public and making progresses, and the obvious attempt to point the contrast between their courts could not have pleased the king much. But it was the news that the prince was welcoming opponents of the administration to his court and planning to maintain an independent group in Parliament in the next session, all of which was reported so avidly to Hanover that summer, that drove the serious breach between them and made their quarrel much more than a personal one. When the king returned from Hanover the hostility between father and son was open and avowed, and their relations steadily worsened during 1717.

In the session of Parliament held immediately after the king's return, the prince's supporters began ostentatiously to sympathize with the opposition, even voting against the government on occasions.[1] In April, when they had abstained in a vote on supply which the ministry carried by only four votes, a member of the king's court spoke of this as evidence of 'a division or coolness between the King and Prince, the one visibly espousing it with all his vigour, and the other, if not as apparently discouraging it, at least giving no help in the success'.[2] By May a Jacobite spoke of the prince, only a little prematurely, as the head of the opposition.[3]

This obvious hostility in the royal family was both deepened and made considerably more significant by the split among the Whig politicians that had occurred simultaneously. The reconstruction of the ministry following the dismissal of Townshend and the resignation of his friends in April 1717 had weakened considerably its support in Parliament. On several occasions in April and May the new administration had been hard pressed to maintain a majority in the House of Commons. In this situation the prince's independent action was very serious. The split among the Whigs and the prince's hostility to his father's ministers both produced a drastic change in the political scene in the spring of

[1] A. S. Foord, *His Majesty's Opposition*, p. 101.
[2] *H.M.C. Polwarth MSS.* I, 211–12.   [3] *H.M.C. Stuart Papers*, V, 543.

1717, therefore. The change had a drastic effect on George I's life. The king was forced to become more active in support of his administration and it seems clear that he decided or was persuaded that he could no longer allow his son's court to outshine his own. Both to overawe the prince, therefore, and to give visible support to his ministers, George I was forced to emerge from his habitual and preferred seclusion and replace his son as the leader of the social world.

Immediately after his return from Hanover, the king's life was little different from what it had been previously. He did not grace many public or even court functions with his presence and to those outside his immediate circle he seemed as cold and withdrawn as ever. 'The King locks himself up as formerly', reported one of his grooms of the bedchamber in February 1717.[1] But when, in July, the court moved to Hampton Court for the summer, the king seemed to become transformed, for he began to take an active and apparently enthusiastic interest in court life. A few days after the king left St James's the bishop of Lichfield reported to a friend that London

is now very empty since the Royal family went to Hampton Court, where the public manner in which the king lives, makes it the rendezvous not only of the Ministers and great men but of the people of all ranks and conditions. He dines openly and with company every day and the novelty of the sight draws a mighty concourse. After so long a reserve we may easily imagine how great a constraint he puts upon himself.[2]

The king continued to live in this novel way while he remained at Hampton Court. Every day he dined in public. Fifteen or more guests were invited by the gentleman of the bedchamber in waiting from among the foreign ambassadors, peers and 'other persons of distinction'. The gentleman and groom of the bedchamber in waiting also sat at the king's table, for, unlike Charles II, George I did not dine 'in state', waited on by his noble attendants on bended knee.[3] Visitors to the court were allowed to watch the spectacle and the king was not at all shy at these dinners. Most of his guests undoubtedly spoke French without difficulty, and Sir Gustavus Hume, a groom of the bedchamber who

[1] H.M.C. Polwarth MSS. I, 176.
[2] Chatsworth MSS. corresp. 1st series, 93/5.
[3] Boyer, Political State, XIV, (1717), pp. 83–4, 349–52; LS 13/260, royal warrant to the lord steward, 26 August 1717; Add. MSS. 17677 KKK2, fo. 268; John Macky, A Journey through England (4th ed., 1724), I, 198–9.

was often present, thought that 'the freer the conversation the more to the King's mind'.[1]

He did not dine as formally as he might have, but it is obvious that the king had radically and consciously altered the pattern of his life; he had never before dined with his courtiers let alone before visitors. And besides dining in public at Hampton Court in 1717, he came out of his apartment much more often than he had ever done before and mixed more freely with his court. Once or twice he held a morning *levee* for the gentlemen of the court; occasionally in the early afternoon before dinner he held court in the drawing-room,[2] and in the evening he mixed freely and regularly with visitors. On Sundays and Thursdays —the public days—the court was crowded with visitors and on these evenings there were assemblies at which the king invariably appeared.[3] On Thursdays the court was particularly crowded because throughout the summer the king met the Cabinet on that day. Stanhope and Sunderland were both in residence at court, and those other ministers who were not came up from town for the day. By the end of the summer there were so many people permanently in residence at Hampton Court that an assembly, or drawing-room, was held every evening except Sunday. The audience chamber, a room that had been built for this purpose, was found to be too small for all the company and in September the tennis court was fitted up for these assemblies by the board of works.[4] When the weather became colder they were transferred to the Cartoon Gallery in the palace, which was 117 feet long and ran the whole length of the state apartments. Balls were also held there several times a week, and occasionally a concert; if there were no other diversions, there were always card tables and a billiard table set up in the Gallery. The king joined these parties every evening at about ten and stayed until after midnight 'with', a visitor wrote, 'a constant serenity in his countenance and universal affability to all about him'.[5]

During the summer the king also indulged his passion for hunting both near Hampton Court, and on several occasions, in Windsor Forest.

[1] *H.M.C. Polwarth MSS.* I, 320–1.
[2] *The Letters of Thomas Burnet to George Duckett, 1713–1722*, ed. D. N. Smith (Oxford, 1914), pp. 139–40.
[3] *H.M.C. Polwarth MSS.* I, 320–1.
[4] *H.M.C. Cowper MSS.* III, 186; LC 5/157, pp. 102–3.
[5] Smith (ed.), *Burnet Letters*, p. 139; and see Add. MSS. 17677 KKK2, fo. 351; *H.M.C. Portland MSS.* V, 538, 539.

After one hunt at Windsor he dined at Lord Ranelagh's house at Cranbourne where a great number of people from the neighbourhood came to get a glimpse of him. They were not disappointed, for they were all invited in and the king dined in the midst of a great crowd of people. George also dined that summer at Lord Orkney's country house and at Cleremont with the duke of Newcastle.[1]

II

There can be no doubt that the political situation had encouraged this striking change in George I's behaviour. The Sunderland–Stanhope ministry had been under considerable pressure at the end of the previous session of Parliament. The ministers desperately needed more support before they faced Parliament again and, it seems clear, they enlisted the natural attractiveness of the king's court. A lively and brilliant court, if not necessarily inducing all those attracted to it to support the king's government wholeheartedly, would perhaps help to make the dynasty and the ministry more popular, and make opposition to it appear merely factious. George I's ministers perhaps suggested this to him; certainly they were hopeful that his affability at Hampton Court would have good results. Early in the summer the bishop of Lichfield thought that by dining in public with company the king would 'enter into a degree of intimacy with the nobility above what could be arrived at in the cabinet or drawing-room'.[2] This hope is often echoed in the correspondence of secretary Addison with Lord Stair in Paris. 'The king obliges the nobility and others very much at Hampton Court by inviting them to sit down with him at table', wrote Addison in September; a little later he thought that the king had 'gained many hearts by his affable and condescending way of life'.[3] James Craggs, the secretary at war, told Stair in September that the king must show the dissident whigs that

...they must come into his measures, and not he into theirs; and if you'll have my poor opinion, his steadiness and visible proofs of his being determined has had that effect to a vast degree and will to a greater.[4]

[1] Add. MSS. 17677 KKK 2, fos. 293, 308; *H.M.C. Polwarth MSS.* I, 371.
[2] Chatsworth MSS. corresp. 1st series, 93/5.
[3] J. M. Graham, *Annals of Stair*, II, 25, 28.
[4] *Ibid.* p. 38.

The campaign to win support for the ministry became even more obvious when the king went to Newmarket in October for the race meeting. He instructed his gentleman of the bedchamber to invite everyone to dine with him in turn—except Walpole and Townshend—and, Lord Cadogan reported to Stair, he 'behaved himself with great ease and skill to everybody...He was particularly civil to the dukes of Devonshire, Rutland, Grafton, my Lord Orford and Mr Methuen... you can't imagine the good effect his presence seemed to have every-where.'[1] Friends of Walpole and Townshend were cultivated therefore while they themselves were publicly snubbed. Cadogan thought in sum that the journey had had 'un effet merveilleusement bon et n'aura pas peu chagrinné et surpris le Faction'.[2] James Craggs agreed that by appearing at Newmarket the king had done 'great good'; and he hoped that now it would 'not be so difficult, against another time, to make him take a progress'.[3]

The new conviviality of the court did not end when the king returned to London in November 1717. He began immediately, and for the first time in the reign, to hold an evening drawing-room three times a week at St James's.[4] An even more striking change was the establish-ment of a public table at court. Such a table, known as the 'green cloth table' because it was presided over by the clerks of the board of green cloth, was not usually maintained in town. It was commonly kept only in the country where opportunities for dining outside the court were limited; it was designed, as Swift said of a similar table in 1711, 'to entertain foreign ministers and people of quality who come to see the queen and have no place to dine at'.[5] George I had supported such a table at Hampton Court in the summer of 1717[6] at which as many as fifty guests had dined at once. But it was most unusual for a public table to be maintained in town, and the one kept at St James's in the winter of 1717–18 was an important part of the effort to make the court more attractive. A contemporary thought indeed that it was aimed

[1] J. M. Graham, *Annals of Stair*, II, p. 41.
[2] Blenheim MSS. D 1/33, Cadogan to Sunderland, 22 October 1717, n.s.
[3] Graham, *Annals of Stair*, II, 41.
[4] Add. MSS. 17677 KKK2, fos. 366, 370; *H.M.C. Portland MSS.* v, 546, 549.
[5] H. Williams (ed.), *Journal to Stella*, p. 328.
[6] *H.M.C. Portland MSS.* v, 568; *Burnet Letters*, pp. 139–40.

directly at bolstering the ministry in Parliament. Arthur Onslow wrote
later of the years of political crisis between 1717 and 1720:

Among other methods used by the Court to secure a majority, chiefly in the
House of Commons, a magnificent public table, at vast expense to the King,
was kept at St James's House in Parliament time, for the entertainment of the
members.[1]

The table, established about 21 November and maintained until
5 April 1718, continued as long as Parliament was in session. Onslow
believed that though 'many [Members of Parliament] came often,
others seldom, and some out of curiosity to see it; of which last were
a few who were in opposition to the party then in power', the public
table 'produced very little effect for the purpose designed by it'. It was
none the less a striking indication—especially as it cost over £700 a
month—that George I and his ministers felt very keenly the threat to
the administration posed by the opposition of the Townshend and
Walpole Whigs. It is an indication too of their belief that an attractive
court that gave visible proof of the king's determination to support his
ministers could be an effective weapon in combatting this opposition.

The motives and the compulsion behind George I's changed attitude
to his court in 1717 were thus doubtless at heart political. There was,
too, that other more personal influence, inextricably tied to this, working on the King himself: his hatred and fear of the Prince of Wales.

In the spring of 1717 the prince had made no attempt to hide his
dislike of the ministry and relations between father and son had become
steadily worse during the year. The king's treatment of his son during
the summer did not improve matters. When the court was at Hampton
Court, the prince and princess were kept in the background. They were
not allowed to dine in public[2] and the prince was never invited to the
king's table. In striking contrast to the early months of the reign, it was
not in the princess's drawing-room that court entertainment was to be
found but in the king's. The king was determined, it seems clear, to
impress his son with a sense of his social inferiority, to deter him from
becoming even more independent and openly giving succour to the
king's enemies. If they had been in Hanover, the king was later to say,
he would have known what to do with his son. In England, as much
as it was against his nature and inclinations, he could only enter into

[1] *H.M.C. Onslow MSS.* p. 509. [2] *H.M.C. Polwarth MSS.* 1, 320–1.

competition with him. For the prince was essentially independent of his father. His annual income of £100,000 was part of the king's Civil List, but though it was granted to the prince by Letters Patent it had been in effect guaranteed to the prince by Parliament at the beginning of the reign. There had indeed been a move by the Tories in the House of Commons during the Civil List debate in May 1715 to separate the prince's revenue of £100,000 a year from the king's £600,000. The court party opposed this because they saw it as 'a design to divide the royal family by lessening the next heir apparent's dependence on the King', and it was defeated. None the less, though the Civil List of £700,000 was granted to the king, it was well understood in Parliament that £100,000 of this was for the prince.[1] Of course what Parliament had granted it could easily take away, and the prince was occasionally afraid that his Civil List allowance might be reduced; but to revoke a grant made by Letters Patent and upon parliamentary security might easily have inflamed the House of Commons, and, as one man observed, would have made 'a world of persons uneasy who have tenures from the Crown secured the like way'.[2] It would have been too drastic and it was never attempted.

Besides having financial independence, the prince maintained his own household separate from the king's; he engaged and controlled his own servants, and, though the king had forced him to dismiss Argyll, if the prince wanted to be stubborn and if his servants were willing to depend solely on his patronage, his household could not be compelled to support the government.

There was, therefore, beneath the personal distaste the king and prince felt for each other a deeper current of conflict. The prince's financial self-sufficiency gave him real independence which frustrated and infuriated the king but it also shielded him against the worst effects of his father's anger. Undoubtedly, George would have preferred to have beaten a sense of duty into his son; he had already sentenced his faithless wife to life imprisonment. But things were not so simple in England. There he could only check his son in a way that was entirely distasteful to him: he began in 1717 what was virtually a competition for popularity. The king's ministers may have urged him to attend the

---

[1] *P.H.* VII, 59. The prince had besides about £20,000 a year from the lands he held as Prince of Wales.
[2] Add. MSS. 47028, p. 441.

race meeting at Newmarket in October, and certainly they valued his presence there, but, according to secretary Addison, the king really 'took the sudden resolution of being present at the diversion of that place' because he heard that the Prince of Wales intended to go.[1]

At Hampton Court, while the king entertained freely, the prince was kept in the background and on the rare occasions when they met they were both extremely formal and curt.[2] In these circumstances their relations could only worsen and it was hardly surprising that a trivial incident at the end of the year provoked a major crisis which resulted in the prince and princess's expulsion from the palace.

The immediate cause of the quarrel was a disagreement about the choice of a godfather to the son born to the princess early in November 1717. The king insisted, against the prince's objections, on his right to name his lord chamberlain, the duke of Newcastle. They also quarrelled about the child's name. The prince was forced to submit, and this further humiliation enraged him so much that at the christening of the young prince on 28 November he could not contain his anger. He insulted the lord chamberlain and, Newcastle thought, challenged him to a duel. This led first to the prince's confinement in the palace (guarded by a detachment of yeomen of the guard) and then on 2 December to his expulsion from St James's. The prince and princess found a temporary home at Lord Grantham's house until, early in 1718, their court was established permanently at Leicester House.[3]

The king's immediate actions show how deeply he had resented the prince's independence, and how much he feared its consequences in the future. Within days of the prince's expulsion, there were rumours current that the king would insist as a condition of reconciliation that the prince accept his recommendations for appointments to his household, 'to take into his family', as a newsletter writer said on 5 December, 'only such as the king shall name or approve'.[4] Two weeks later it was

---

[1] Graham, *Annals of Stair*, II, 26.

[2] *H.M.C. Polwarth MSS.* I, 320–1; *H.M.C. Portland MSS.* V, 541.

[3] There are many accounts of the scene at the christening and of the subsequent events. Secretary Addison sent an account to all British Ambassadors and representatives abroad; this is printed in Graham (ed.), *Letters of Addison*, pp. 394–5. Horace Walpole included the account of the affair he was given by Lady Suffolk, who was present at the christening, in his *Reminiscences*, ed. by Paget Toynbee, pp. 105–7. Other accounts are in *S.P. Dom.* 35/10, no. 15; *H.M.C. Polwarth MSS.* I, 404–5; *H.M.C. Stuart Papers*, V, 273–5.   [4] *H.M.C. Portland MSS.* V, 545.

thought that not only would the king press this demand but that he would also insist that the prince give him control of his annual income of £100,000.[1] These reports were correct in substance. On 21 January the judges were asked to give their opinion as to whether the king could revoke the prince's right to his £100,000 and his right to name his own servants.[2] The attorney-general, Sir Edward Northey, who was himself a moderate Tory and a hold-over from Anne's last ministry, informed Sunderland towards the end of January that it was his opinion that in both cases the king could not revoke the prince's right.[3] Northey was removed from office in March 1718 but the prince's control over his income and his servants was never attacked directly. His submission in these matters remained for a long time a condition of their reconciliation as far as the king was concerned.[4] And, indirectly, attacks were made on the foundation of the prince's independence, his Civil List income. When the prince was expelled the palace, the king had kept his children. In January 1718 he demanded that the prince give him £40,000 a year for their maintenance and education. The prince replied that he would be only too happy to support them under his own roof.[5] This having failed, the king apparently threatened to get the money by Act of Parliament and as a preliminary he consulted the judges again on his right to educate his grandchildren; but nothing came of it.[6] The prince's hold on his income and on his right to appoint his own servants remained unshaken. But he was obviously aware of the seriousness of the threat to his independence. When he came to the throne in 1727 he refused to allow his son and heir, Frederick, more than £50,000 a year, even though Parliament had made the same provision for the Prince of Wales as in 1714.

[1] *H.M.C. Portland MSS.* v, p. 549; *H.M.C. Stuart Papers*, v, 335.
[2] One of the prince's servants was allowed to appear before them to argue his case (Panshanger MSS. bundle 'S', Sunderland to Cowper, 23 January 1718).
[3] Blenheim MSS. D 1/34.
[4] Panshanger MSS. Letterbooks, v, pp. 119–20, 'Conditions d'Accomodement, Jan. 1718'.
[5] Add. MSS. 9133, fos. 39–40; Add. MSS. 17677 KKK 2, fo. 446.
[6] Add. MSS. 47028, p. 442; Panshanger MSS. Lord Cowper MSS. bundle 'S', Sunderland to Cowper, 23 January 1718.

III

The enemies of the king and the ministry were naturally overjoyed at the split in the royal family. The Jacobites were of course delighted[1] and looked for the imminent collapse of the dynasty. So too were the Tories, who even if they were supporters of the Hanoverian house, had little hope of preferment under George I. Charles Cathcart, one of the prince's grooms of the bedchamber, recorded in his diary at the end of December that the new court was crowded with Tories.[2] But the prince's court became the focal point not only of a generalized and vague opposition to the government; much more important, it soon became the centre of the specific and vocal opposition of Walpole and Townshend and other dissatisfied Whigs.[3] And the split in the royal family not only hardened existing political divisions: its effects were felt throughout the fashionable world, for within a few days the king let it be known through the vice-chamberlain and the master of ceremonies that anyone who paid court to the prince would not be welcomed at St James's.[4] Thus the courts became, even more than they had been previously, two hostile camps. Attendance at either was a declaration of allegiance to one side or the other—to the king and the government or to the prince and the opposition.

In 1737 there was a similar quarrel in the royal family and a similar separation between the courts of George II and his son Frederick, Prince of Wales. On the king's birthday in that year Lord Hervey observed,

those that were in the king's service, or espoused his cause in the quarrel with his son, piqued themselves on contributing to make up the crowd on this first showday after the separation of the Courts, and by these means the drawing-room, to the great satisfaction both of the King and Queen, was much fuller than ever it has been on any other 30th of October [George II's birthday] since the first after his Majesty's accession to the Crown.[5]

A similar rivalry between the courts of the reigning monarch and the heir to the throne had helped to encourage the transformation of

---

[1] *H.M.C. Stuart Papers*, v, 274.
[2] Cathcart MSS. Journal A/12 (December 1717).
[3] See J. H. Plumb, *Walpole*, I, ch. 7.
[4] Add. MSS. 17677 KKK 2, fo. 422; Add. MSS. 47028, p. 441; *H.M.C. Portland MSS.* v, 545, 550.
[5] Hervey, *Memoirs*, p. 854.

George I's court in 1717. After the separation of their courts, in 1717 as in 1737, the rivalry increased, for on both occasions the prince became the leader of an active opposition and performed, as a historian has said, 'the constitutional equivalent of heading an insurrection against his father who was thereby exposed to the danger of being taken prisoner by his son'.[1] With the prince's friends now aiding the opposition in Parliament, the king's administration was under greater pressure than ever. In February 1718 Lord Carnarvon said that the breach in the royal family was 'of the first consequence for the administration'; the ministers, he predicted, 'will have a very troublesome time'. And as a new session opened in October of that year the Princess of Wales predicted that because the prince's friends and the Tories were 'firm', the ministers could look forward to a 'painful session'.[2] In 1718 and 1719 the ministry was indeed harrassed by a motley but effective opposition under the titular leadership of the Prince of Wales and the tactical leadership of Robert Walpole, and on several occasions the government was defeated in Parliament. In 1719 the opposition enjoyed a resounding triumph in defeating the Peerage Bill.[3] In these circumstances it was now more necessary than ever that the king's court should be more attractive than the prince's. Court society, having been forbidden to go to Leicester House, had to be entertained at St James's. The competition noticed in 1717 was therefore intensified in 1718. The king's court became even brighter and livelier, and remained so until the quarrels in the Whig party and in the royal family were resolved and George I was allowed to follow once more the dictates of his heart.

In the winter of 1717–18 the king held an evening assembly in the drawing-room of St James's three times a week, and the clerks of the green cloth again presided over a public table to which court visitors were invited. When the court moved to Kensington in April 1718 the king again met company often. To encourage visitors, the road through St James's Park was opened to 'all coaches without distinction'; normally only the highly favoured were given the key to the gate and permission to drive a coach in the park. At Kensington a visitor said, 'the ladies say they [have] never see[n] so much company and every body fine, the King very obliging and in great good humour... [at

---

[1] Hervey, *Memoirs*, introduction, p. xxxiii.
[2] HM, Stowe MSS. 57, vol. 13, p. 93; Panshanger MSS. Letterbooks, v, 93.
[3] Foord, *His Majesty's Opposition*, pp. 60–3, 92–4; J. H. Plumb, *Walpole*, I, 278–81.

night] all the garden illuminated and music in it and dancing in the Green House and the long Gallery'.[1]

In August the king moved to Hampton Court for the remainder of the summer and until the end of October there was entertainment on such a scale there that even the novelty of 1717 paled in comparison. The king again dined in public (he had not at St James's and Kensington) and appeared every evening at the assemblies held in the tennis court or in the Cartoon Gallery of the palace. Again the clerks of the green cloth entertained as many as fifty or sixty guests to dinner every day.[2] But this year there were further attractions. In 1717 only three or four musicians had been permanently in residence at Hampton Court; in 1719 there were twenty, and at least twice a week there was a ball in the Music Room in what had been formerly the princess's apartment.[3] And there were plays for the first time, in direct competition with the prince. In August the prince and princess prepared a theatre in their summer house at Richmond and engaged a troupe of players. The king would not be outdone. He gave immediate orders that a theatre be erected in the Great Hall at Hampton Court. Steele's company was brought up from Drury Lane Theatre, and between 23 September and 25 October they performed seven times.[4] This alone meant an extra charge on the treasurer of the chamber's establishment of £575. How much the entertainment in 1717 and 1718 added in total to the household expenses is very difficult to calculate precisely because the accounts do not lend themselves to that kind of analysis. But it was anticipated in 1717 that the extra food ordered for the king's, the bedchamber and the green cloth tables would cost close to £600 a week;[5] and it was estimated that the summer's entertainment in 1718 added about £15,000 to the expenditure of the department below stairs alone.[6] On top of that, extra servants had to be sworn in to deal with 'the increased business in his Majesty's kitchen'.[7]

Competition between the courts in 1718 went so far as to encourage

[1] Panshanger MSS. Letterbooks, v, 24–5, Mrs Allanson to Lady Cowper, 29 May 1718.

[2] Add. MSS. 47028, p. 499; Add. MSS. 17677 KKK 2, fo. 73; LS 13/115, fos. 79, 80; H.M.C. Portland MSS. v, 568.

[3] LC 5/157, p. 190; LS 13/115, fo. 81.

[4] N.S.A., Cal. Br. Arch., Des. 24, England 129 (newsletter of 26 August/6 September 1718); LC 5/157, p. 154; J. Blanchard (ed.), Correspondence of Steele, p. 130 n.

[5] LS 13/260, royal warrant to the lord steward, 26 August 1717.

[6] C(H)MSS. 45/5, p. 1.   [7] LS 13/115, fo. 80.

a race back to London at the end of the summer. When the court was in the country the tradesmen of London—not only household purveyors, but all those who depended on the custom of the nobility and other courtiers—suffered a loss of business. A contemporary thought that this was why the king returned from Hampton Court a month earlier than in 1717. The trade of London always suffers when the royal family is absent, a newsletter-writer (probably a secretary in the Hanoverian chancery in London) explained to his correspondent in Hanover, and the king therefore decided to return before the prince and 'thereby gain the affection' of the citizens.[1] But, though the court returned earlier than usual from the country, the entertainments were not discontinued. Three times a week the king held an evening assembly in the drawing-room at St James's. The public table was again maintained. And at least once a week during the winter of 1718–19 there was a ball at court.[2] Indeed there was so much unaccustomed entertainment that some of the servants in the department below stairs complained of the overwork.[3] Perhaps they had in mind particularly the extra work arising out of the court balls; they were obviously not entirely dignified affairs for at the conclusion of one of them the vice-chamberlain informed the board of green cloth that 'the room where the Side Board was kept' was so 'stained with claret [that] it was necessary to provide Sayl cloth against another Ball to prevent the like damage'.[4]

IV

George I spent the summers of 1719 and 1720 in Hanover—perhaps in part to avoid having to live so public and distasteful a life as he had found to be necessary in 1717 and 1718. Between these visits—during the winter of 1719–20—the pattern of life at St James's was much as it had been during the previous two winters; there were again regular drawing-rooms and balls and a public table was again kept at St James's. But when the king next remained in England during the summer, in 1721, and the court moved to a country palace, the character of court life resembled that of 1715 rather than 1717 and 1718. Once more he

[1] N.S.A., Cal. Br. Arch., Des. 24, England 129 (newsletter, 28 October/8 November 1718).
[2] LS 13/115, fo. 85; William Byrd, *London Diary*, p. 204.
[3] LS 13/115, fo. 87.   [4] LS 13/115, fo. 97.

withdrew as much as possible from the public eye. He could not retire entirely from court life after 1720 because his and the prince's courts remained separated even after their reconciliation and he had to appear regularly in his own drawing-room at least. But after 1720 it is clear that as much as he could he retired into the background. There is no evidence in the household accounts or in contemporary correspondence or in the reports of men like L'Hermitage, the Dutch Resident in London, who had so avidly reported the king's activities in 1717 and 1718, that he ever again entertained on the scale that had been necessary during the years of political crisis. In the second half of the reign the king never dined in public and the balls and plays that had been so striking a feature of court life between 1717 and 1720 were never repeated on such a scale. The special provision for the entertainment of guests, the green cloth table, was discontinued at St James's after 1721.

The reason for George I's withdrawal is not hard to find: he preferred to lead a less active life and after 1720 there was no reason why he should not follow his own preferences. For in April 1720 the split among the leading politicians had been resolved when Walpole and Townshend forced their way back into the ministry;[1] in the next few years the struggle for power went on behind the scenes, not in Parliament. At the same time, and as a necessary prelude, the king and the prince had been brought together and what passed for a reconciliation effected. They were not henceforward on good terms but the prince did at least refrain from leading the opposition to his father's ministry. George was thus freed from the necessity of making a particular effort to support his ministers and of competing with his son's court, and he was able for the future to live as quietly and simply as he desired.

It would not be easy to show what effect the efforts to improve court life between 1717 and 1720 had had on his administration's fortunes in Parliament. On a narrow front, it has been seen that Onslow doubted that the green cloth table, for example, had changed any votes in the court's favour. But it need not be doubted that both the king and his ministers saw the value, perhaps the indispensability, of an attractive court and a gracious monarch in the face of an opposition based on Leicester House. The ministers were certainly convinced of the value of the king's activity at the least as providing powerful evidence of his support and of his confidence in them.

---

[1] Plumb, *Walpole*, I, pp. 282–5; Michael, *England under George I*, II, pp. 302–6.

More positively, the king's activity must have contributed to what one can only call the defeat of the Prince of Wales. The prince did retain control over the appointment of his own servants (and the king was still insisting on his right to name them as late as February 1719 as a necessary condition of a reconciliation).[1] But for a Prince of Wales defeat was always bound up with a triumph in opposition. If the 'outs' were successful they would be taken in, as they were in 1720, but their leader, the prince, could not join a government. And so he would be 'deserted'. But also one senses that in 1720 the prince's personal position was particularly weak. He came back very quietly and caused the administration and his father no further trouble. Of course the reconciliation among the politicians removed the sting from the prince's court and he was undoubtedly pulled along in the wake of stronger forces. But there are suggestions that, contrary to the common assumptions about the 'brilliance' of Leicester House as compared to St James's, his court had been distinctly second rate. There is no way of knowing whether this troubled him very much, and the evidence for it is not in any case overwhelming, but there are suggestions in the journal of Charles Cathcart, an officer of the prince's bechamber, and in other correspondence, that the prince's court attracted very few people outside their immediate 'family' during the years of separation when court society was forbidden to attend the prince and when George was making such an effort to attract them to St James's.[2] Immediately following the reconciliation between the king and the prince it was noticed that 'la cour de S.A.R. [Son Altesse Royalle] augmente tous les jours'.[3] Two months later, Lord Cowper said that he had not talked much recently with the prince and princess, because 'the company is now so much more than used to be last year, that they have not so much time to bestow as they then had'.[4] This social respectability, if one can call it that, was all the prince had to gain by the reconciliation. His servants could look forward to a lot more; to those interested in an army career, for example, the split in the royal family was disastrous. For all the prince's servants, the reconciliation opened up again the lush pastures of royal patronage so firmly closed during the past three years. This may

[1] Cathcart Journal, A/12, 1 February 1719, report of a conversation with Robethon.
[2] Cathcart MSS. A/12.
[3] N.S.A., Cal. Br. Arch., Des. 24, England, 134 (newsletter 8 April 1720, n.s.).
[4] Panshanger MSS. Letterbooks, v, 226.

have played some part in the prince's meek return. But the king's determination to better his son—his efforts to increase the natural attractiveness of the court—must have been important too. Lord Hervey reminded Frederick, Prince of Wales, a few years later how poorly his father had fared in competition with George I's court. He told Frederick, when he was contemplating opposition,

I can remember when your father had the misfortune to quarrel with your grandfather, and notwithstanding he had many people of the first rank, quality, understanding, character, and consideration of this kingdom in his party; notwithstanding one of his own servants was in the chair of the House of Commons; and notwithstanding he had a revenue of £120,000 a year independent of the King, I can remember in a little time how poor a figure his opposition to the Court made, how weary both he and his adherents were of it...and how little it availed him in any one article.[1]

George's activity makes nonsense of the view expressed by Count Broglie in 1724, and repeated in one form or another about the first Hanoverian king ever since, that he never cared about England or English problems and looked upon the country 'as a temporary possession, to be made the most of while it lasts'.[2] His extraordinary efforts between 1717 and 1720 to make his court the undisputed centre of political life surely gives the lie to that. His own inclinations certainly did not encourage these exertions, as the character of court life both before 1717 and after 1720 indicates. The drabness of court life in the second half of the reign was made possible because the administration was freed from the pressure they had known when Walpole and his friends were ever ready to seize an opportunity to unite Tories and independents against the government; and because the prince was generally quiescent.[3] The king undoubtedly found it to his taste. It underlines most clearly the magnitude of the effort he had made in support of his administration during the years of political crisis. It underlines too the fact that the court was still a most important political institution in the early eighteenth century.

[1] Hervey, *Memoirs*, p. 303.   [2] Coxe, *Walpole*, II, 303.
[3] Foord, *His Majesty's Opposition*, p. 116.

APPENDIX

OFFICES IN THE
ROYAL HOUSEHOLD IN THE
REIGN OF GEORGE I

I. THE CHAMBER AND OFFSHOOTS

Lord chamberlain
Vice-chamberlain
Treasurer of the chamber
Comptroller of the accounts of the treasurer of the chamber
Secretary to the lord chamberlain
4 clerks

Privy Chamber

48–72 gentlemen
4 gentlemen ushers
4 grooms

Presence chamber

4 cupbearers
4 carvers
4 gentlemen sewers
4 gentlemen ushers,
  daily waiters
1 assistant usher
8 gentlemen ushers,
  quarter waiters
8 sewers of the chamber
4 pages
1 chamber keeper

Guard chamber

10 grooms

Ceremonies

Master
Assistant to the master
Marshall

8 sergeants-at-arms
4 sergeants-at arms
  attending officers
Poet laureate
Historiographer
Groom porter
Knight harbinger
6 yeomen harbingers
Master of the buckhounds
2–3 physicians to the
  person
2 apothecaries to the
  person
2 surgeons to the person
1 apothecary to the
  household
1 surgeon to the house-
  hold
11 housekeepers and
  under-housekeepers
Goldsmith
Jeweller
Watch maker
Principal painter

Miscellaneous

Master of the barges
48 watermen
Master of the musick
24 musicians
Keeper of the
  instruments
Instrument maker
Organ maker
Sergeant trumpeter
12 trumpeters
1 kettle drummer
4 drum majors
4 drummers
6 hautboys
Locksmith
Rat-killer
Mole-taker
Strewer of herbs
Card maker
Barge builder
Writer and embellisher
Mathematical instrument
  maker
Oculist

Appendix

Revels

Master
Yeoman
Comptroller

Removing wardrobe

Yeoman
2 grooms
3 pages
1 clerk
6 standing wardrobe
 keepers

Band of pensioners

Captain
Lieutenant
Standard bearer
Clerk of the cheque
2 paymasters
Harbinger
Axe keeper
40 gentlemen

Yeomen of the guard

Captain
Lieutenant
Ensign
Clerk of the cheque
4 corporals
100 yeomen (incl.
 8 ushers)

Miscellaneous (cont.)

Keeper of the pictures
Joiner
Latin secretary
Painter in enamel
Keeper of the library
Bookseller, bookbinder
 and stationer
Master of the tennis
 court
40 messengers
2 clerks of the cheque
7 messengers attending
 officers
Decypherer
Chemist
Anatomist

Embroiderer
2 cabinet makers
Dentist
Oar maker
Tuner of the organs
Coffer maker
Glover
Cutler
Drugster
Gunsmith
Keeper of the private
 armoury at Westminster
Printer
Keeper of the lions in
 the Tower
Harpsichord maker
Chocolate maker
Gilt leather seller
Furrier
Maker of optic glasses
Engraver of the seals

Chapel royal

Dean
Clerk of the closet
Closet keeper
48 chaplains
Gentlemen and boys of
 the choir

Great wardrobe

Master
Deputy master
Clerk
c. 30 tailors and arras-
 workers

Jewel office

Master
Yeoman
Groom
Clerk

Robes

Master
Yeoman
3 grooms
2 waiters
1 page
1 brusher
c. 15 tradesmen

Appendix

II. THE BEDCHAMBER

Groom of the stole
11–17 gentlemen of the bedchamber
8 grooms of the bedchamber
6 pages

2 coffer bearers
2 necessary women
Sempstress and starcher
Laundress

III. THE HOUSEHOLD BELOW STAIRS

The board of green cloth:
    Lord steward
    Treasurer of the household
    Comptroller of the household
    Master of the household
    Cofferer
    4 clerks (and 4 under-clerks)

Accompting house

2 yeomen
2 grooms
1 messenger
2 chamber keepers

Spicery

1 clerk
1 under-clerk

Confectionery

2 yeomen
1 groom

Ewry

1 gentleman
1 yeoman
1 groom

Larder

2 yeomen
3 grooms

Pastry

1 clerk
2 yeomen
2 grooms
1 furner
1 salsaryman

Cellar

1 gentleman
3 yeomen
2 grooms
1 yeoman of the ice
  house
2 wine porters

Kitchen

2 clerks
2 under-clerks
2 master cooks
6 yeomen
5 grooms
6 children

8 turnbroaches
2 scourers
2 door keepers

Acatry

2 joint-clerks
1 sergeant
1 yeoman of the salt
  stores

Poultry office

1 clerk
1 yeoman
2 grooms

Scalding house

1 yeoman
2 grooms

Woodyard

1 clerk
1 yeoman
2 grooms

281

Appendix

Scullery

2 yeomen
2 grooms
1 servant
2 children
2 pan keepers
2 pages

Bakehouse

1 clerk
1 yeoman
2 grooms
1 bread bearer

Pantry

1 gentleman and yeoman
2 grooms

Buttery

1 gentleman
1 yeoman
3 grooms

———

Gentleman harbinger
4 harbingers

2 yeomen cart takers
2 groom cart takers

2 officers of the hall

1 yeoman of the
  almonry
1 groom of the almonry

Clerk of the verge
Coroner of the verge

Knight marshal
6 marshal's men

Sergeant porter
4 yeomen porters
3 groom porters
3 other porters and
  watchmen

2 wine porters

IV. THE STABLES

Master of the horse
Gentleman of the horse
Avenor and clerk martial
6 equerries
2 equerries of the crown stable
4 pages of honour
Governor to the pages

Surveyor general of the highways
Surveyor of the stables
Surveyor of the stables at Hampton Court
Riding surveyor of the stables

Clerk of the avery
Clerk of the stables

16 footmen
6 coachmen
6 postilions
6 helpers
13–18 grooms
1 bottle groom
4 chairmen

Master of the stud
3 grooms of the stud

Saddler and storekeeper
Esquire saddler
Yeoman saddler
Marshall farrier
Sergeant farrier
Yeoman farrier
2 groom farriers
Coach maker
3 purveyors
5 stable keepers
1 mews keeper
2 porters
Sergeant of the carriages
Yeoman of the carriages
Gentleman messenger
2 yeomen riders
Gentleman armourer

BIBLIOGRAPHY

I. MANUSCRIPT SOURCES

1. PUBLIC RECORD OFFICE

(i) *Lord Steward's Department*

LS 1/58–71 Incidental expenses, 1714–27.

LS 4/21–31 'Pedes Parcellarum', August 1714–25; a monthly, half-yearly and yearly account of the expenses of each office for both ordinary and extraordinary expenditure.

LS 8/51–64 'Creditors', 1714–27; annual account of extraordinary expenditure.

LS 9 Kitchen books.

LS 9/37 'Diets', 1707, 1714, 1716, 1717; daily totals of ingredients used in the kitchen.

LS 9/41–5 'Diets', 1713–27 (broken series).

LS 9/56–9 'Diets', green cloth table 1717–21.

LS 9/73–7 Kitchen ledgers, 1714–20; quarterly account of board-wages paid by the cofferer.

LS 9/114–22 'Books of fare'; daily menus for all court tables including the king's.

LS 13 Miscellaneous Books.

LS 13/22 Contracts, 1715–27; annual contracts made by the board of green cloth with purveyors.

LS 13/44 Establishment, 1714; the established expenses of the cofferer's office.

LS 13/88 Judicial proceedings of the palace court, 1689–1730.

LS 13/90 Acatry ledger, 1715–23.

LS 13/95 Buttery, pantry and cellar ledger, 1710–16.

LS 13/115 Minutes of the meetings of the board of green cloth, 1714–26.

LS 13/116 The same, 1726–60.

LS 13/122 Board of green cloth orders on petitions, 1714–47.

LS 13/176 Entry book of records, board of green cloth, 1714–27.

LS 13/177 The same, 1727–46.

LS 13/193 New rules for making up the accounts of the household below stairs, early George III.

LS 13/200 Certificate book recording the admission into office of all servants paid by the cofferer, 1714–27.

LS 13/232 Receipt of land tax paid to the receiver for the palaces of White-hall and St James's, 1715–36.

LS 13/234 Minutes of the meetings of the commissioners for the land tax in Whitehall and St James's, 1709–53.

LS 13/260 Entry book of warrants of appointment, 1714–27 (king's).

LS 13/261 Entry book of warrants of appointment, 1714–27 (lord steward's).

LS 13/268 Wine book, issues and remains, 1720–33.

LS 13/277 Treatises on the household, Edward I–Charles II; a copy made in 1765.

LS 13/281 Notebook of John Secker (secretary to the lord steward) 1766–83.

(ii) *Lord chamberlain's department*

LC 3/7 Establishment of the chamber and bedchamber, 1714–27.

LC 3/8 Another, *c.* 1719–24.

LC 3/33 Papers relating to the appointment of servants in the great wardrobe by the master, 1660–7, 1689, 1709–48.

LC 3/63–4 Entry books of warrants of appointment to places in the chamber and bedchamber, 1714–33.

LC 5/3 A book of extracts from the notebooks of Sir Clement Cotterell Dormer, master of the ceremonies (1710–58).

LC 5/46 Copies of warrants received by the great wardrobe, 1715–37.

LC 5/72 The same, 1714–18.

LC 5/109 Entry book of lord chamberlain's warrants received by the jewel office, 1710–31.

LC 5/127–8 Lord chamberlain's warrants to the jewel office, great wardrobe, etc. (originals) 1714–27.

LC 5/156–8 Entry books of lord chamberlain's warrants, 1714–27 (with indexes).

LC 5/196 Household ordinances, Charles II and James II.

LC 5/202 Precedents book of the lord chamberlain's office, 1697–1738.

LC 9/44 Jewel office, delivery book, 1698–1732.

LC 9/47 Jewel office, account book, 1702–28; quarterly accounts of goldsmiths' work.

LC 9/145–57 Great wardrobe, yearly accounts, 1714–27. Latin. Accounts of deliveries by tradesmen into the great wardrobe which duplicate the totals in the declared accounts of the office; and accounts of liveries delivered out of the office.

LC 9/206–7 Great wardrobe, entry books of receipts for liveries delivered out of the office, 1715–32.

LC 9/286–7 Great wardrobe, entry books of tradesmen's bills, 1716–29.

LC 9/376, 3 parts Rough account books, including an account of fees taken in the lord chamberlain's office at the end of the eighteenth century.

Bibliography

(iii) *State papers*

S.P. Dom. 35   State Papers, Domestic, General, George I. 76 vols.

(iv) *Treasury papers*

T 1/181–266   Treasury board papers, 1714–28.

T 30/4–7   Yearly accounts; revenue and expenditure, 1710–30.

T 38/180   Civil List expenditure, 1714–17.

T 38/196   Payment of Civil List debt, 1721.

T 38/197   Civil List debt at death of George I, 1727.

T 38/507   Second report of Thomas Gilbert on reforms in the household, with a list of persons claiming compensation for offices abolished, 1782.

T 38/523   A collection of papers relating to the treasurer of the chamber's office, 1689–1717; including a comparison of the establishment of the office in the reigns of James II, William III, Anne and George I.

T 48/91   Lowndes papers; Civil List accounts, income, expenditure and debts, at various dates, William III–George I.

(v) *Declared accounts*

E 351/1874–84   Cofferer, 1714–25.

AO 1/410/151–412/161   Treasurer of the chamber, 1714–27.

AO 1/2055/40–2056/43   Master of the robes, 1714–26.

AO 1/2368/145–2371/158   Master of the great wardrobe, 1714–27.

AO 1/1446/28–1447/33   Master of the horse, 1714–27.

AO 1/2448/148–2050/161   Paymaster of the works and buildings, 1714–27.

(vi) *Exchequer of receipt*

E 407/57 (4)   Poultry office book, 1716.

E 407/136   Fees of honour, 1715–16.

(vii) *Miscellaneous Papers: gifts and deposits*

P.R.O. 30/26/113 (1–12)   Henry Pelham MSS., household papers 1720–48; including an abstract of the establishment of the treasurer of the chamber, June 1720, with a calculation of the treasurer's fees.

P.R.O. 30/26/114   An account book of John Holbeck, deputy treasurer of the chamber, Christmas 1719–June 1720.

2. BRITISH MUSEUM

(i) *Additional manuscripts*

Add. MSS. 9148–97   Coxe Papers.

Add. MSS. 17677   Transcriptions from the Dutch archives at The Hague of correspondence and papers relating to England, 1576–1764; especially Add. MSS. 17677 HHH–KKK 9, the reports of the Dutch Resident, L'Hermitage, to the States General, 1714–27.

Bibliography

Add. MSS. 20101   Papers relating to the palaces of Kensington and Hampton Court, 1699–1756.

Add. MSS. 20102–5   Correspondence of Charlotte Dyves, Lady Sundon, 1713–36 (many of these letters were printed by Mrs A. T. Thomson, see below, section II).

Add. MSS. 22202, 22211, 22217, 22220–3, 22225–9, 31139–49   Correspondence of Thomas Wentworth, earl of Strafford (selections printed by J. J. Cartwright, see below, section II).

Add. MSS. 22625–9   Correspondence of Henrietta Hobart, countess of Suffolk (most of the letters were printed by J. W. Croker, see below, section II).

Add. MSS. 29464–6   An account of the expenses on the Civil List, 1714–96; vol. I, 1714–28.

Add. MSS. 32686, 32687, 33045, 33064   Newcastle MSS.

Add. MSS. 47027–33   Letter books of John Perceval, 1st earl of Egmont, 1712–31.

(ii) *Stowe MSS.*

Stowe MSS. 222–32   Robethon correspondence.

Stowe MSS. 246–7   Letters to James Craggs (the younger) 1711–20.

Stowe MSS. 251   Fos. 1–74, correspondence of Townshend with Walpole, Newcastle and others, 1723 (some printed in part by Coxe in *Walpole*, II).

Stowe MSS. 306   Fos. 92–7, 'An account of places in the gift of the lord steward...' n.d. (but *c.* 1782(?)).

Stowe MSS. 562   Household ordinances, Charles II.

Stowe MSS. 563   Bedchamber ordinances, 11 June, 1689. (A copy made in 1736.)

(iii) *Egerton MSS.*

Egerton MSS. 3350   Bedchamber ordinances, 17 May 1684.

3. CAMBRIDGE UNIVERSITY LIBRARY

Cholmondeley (Houghton) MSS. The papers of Sir Robert Walpole temporarily deposited in the Cambridge University Library. There is little personal correspondence of importance, but the following series have been very helpful for this study:

C(H)MSS. 45/1–63   Treasury papers, mainly 1710–40, relating to the household; establishments, accounts, notes on salaries and debts etc.

C(H)MSS. 46/1–66   Papers relating to the Civil List funds, 1699–1742; accounts of the yield of the funds, payments made on the Civil List, etc.

Bibliography

4. HERTFORDSHIRE RECORD OFFICE

Panshanger MSS. The correspondence and papers of Lord and Lady Cowper. A very valuable collection which includes letters from the Princess of Wales, Bernstorff and the Duchess of Marlborough, as well as Lady Cowper's MS. diary.

5. BLENHEIM PALACE

D 1/23–38, D 2/1–11 Correspondence and papers of Charles, 3rd earl of Sunderland, mainly 1714–22.

E/50 A small packet of letters and papers relating to the quarrel in the royal family, 1717.

F 1/12 The duchess of Marlborough's papers relating to the office of the robes.

F 1/13 Two MS. volumes of bedchamber ordinances of William III.

F 1/65 Estimates of the income of some places under the lord chamberlain, 1762.

6. CHATSWORTH MSS.

The manuscripts of the dukes of Devonshire: correspondence, Ist series.

7. MELBOURNE HALL, DERBYSHIRE

Coke (Melbourne) MSS. The MSS. of Thomas Coke, vice-chamberlain 1706–27. The most important letters and papers relating to the household were printed in Historical Manuscripts Commission, 12th Report, Appendix, part III, *The MSS. of the Earl Cowper*, vol. III, but the commissioners excluded a number of items that were of some help for chapter 2. The manuscripts are now owned by the marquess of Lothian.

8. CATHCART MSS.

The property of Lord Cathcart: inspected, in 1959, when they were on loan to the Historical Manuscripts Commission. Papers of Charles Cathcart, groom of the bedchamber to George, Prince of Wales, including twenty-four volumes of his diary in French. There are also eighteen volumes of a clear copy of the diary, also in French. The diary is mainly a social record but it contains numerous entries relating to the work of the Prince's grooms and it has helped to clarify many points. The diary dates from 1709 to 1739, with breaks. The volumes most used in this study are those relating to George I's reign, viz: A/11 (9 November 1714 to 19 August 1715); A/12 (26 December 1717 to 12 March 1719; 1 August 1720 to 12 April 1721); A/14 (1 October 1725 to 25 June 1727). Volume A/13 (for March–October 1725) is missing, but its entries are preserved in two volumes of the copy (A/34–5).

Bibliography

9. GUILDFORD MUNIMENT ROOM

Bray MSS. 85/2/3   A bound volume of papers relating to the board of green cloth in the seventeenth and eighteenth centuries collected by William Bray, an under-clerk of the green cloth, 1760–1806.

10. SHROPSHIRE RECORD OFFICE

Apley Castle Documents   A paper describing the allowances and fees of a clerk of the board of green cloth in 1714.

11. HENRY E. HUNTINGTON LIBRARY, SAN MARINO, CALIFORNIA

Stowe MSS. 57/3–36   The letterbooks of James Brydges, earl of Carnarvon (1714), duke of Chandos (1719). Out-letters 1709–30. Volume 20 (c. 1721) is missing.

12. NIEDERSÄCHSISCHES STAATSARCHIV, HANOVER (N.S.A.)

(i) *K.G. (König Georg: the Royal archive; papers of George I)*

K.G., Hannover Brief Archiv, designation 9, Secreta Domus, III, 6   Includes papers relating to the king's journeys between Hanover and England, 1714–27, and some accounts of payments to the German court in London from the privy purse.

K.G., Hannover Brief Archiv, designation 92, 34b: Akten der Londoner Kanzlei   Arrangements for the king's journeys between Hanover and London, 1716, 1719, 1720.

K.G., Calenberg Brief Archiv, 23: Finanzsachen no. 5; Englische Kassenrechnung   Accounts of the expenses of the Hanoverian court in London: nos. 1 and 2, 1714–18 (missing); nos. 3, 1719–21; no. 4, 1721–3 (missing) no. 5, 1723–5; no. 6, 1725–6; no. 7, 1726.

K.G. Calenberg Brief Archiv, 22, XIII, Anhang no. 3, Hofhalts Quittungen   Receipts for items purchased for the king; vols. XVI–XXVII (1714–26).

(ii) *Calenberg Brief Archiv, designation 24, England*

No. 123   Zeitungen aus London, 1714–16; newsletters in French to Hanover written by Kreienberg, a minister in the Hanoverian Chancery in London; occasionally written by Jean Robethon.

No. 128   Berichte und Zeitungen aus London, 1717; many written by Robethon.

Nos. 129–32   Zeitungen aus London, 1717–21.

No. 134   Zeitungen aus London, 1720.

Nos. 136–41   Zeitungen aus London, 1721–26.

(iii) *Calenberg Brief Archiv, designation 15, Privatakten*   Including (15M) some papers relating to Mehemet von Königstreu.

Bibliography

(iv) *Hannover, designation 91* Papers of a number of Hanoverian statesmen, including (no. 54) a diary of Johann Phillip von Hattorff, who came to England in 1714 as a member of the Chancery staff, describing the journey and including a long and detailed account of George I's coronation.

13. ALGEMEEN RIJKSARCHIEF, THE HAGUE Correspondence of Anthony Heinsius, including a number of letters from L'Hermitage in London.

II. PRINTED SOURCES

Unless otherwise noted, all books were published in London.

1. OFFICIAL

Redington, Joseph (ed.). *Calendar of Treasury Papers*, 6 vols. [1557–1738]. (*C.T.P.*)

Shaw, W. A. and others (eds). *Calendar of Treasury Books*, 31 vols. [1660–1719]. (*C.T.B.*)

Shaw, W. A. (ed.). *Calendar of Treasury Books and Papers*, 5 vols. [1727–45].

2. HISTORICAL MANUSCRIPTS COMMISSION REPORTS (H.M.C.)

Buccleuch (Montagu House) MSS. 1 (1899).
Buckinghamshire MSS. Fourteenth Report, appendix IX (1895).
Carlisle MSS. Fifteenth Report, appendix VI (1897).
Clements MSS. Various Collections, vol. VIII (1913).
Cowper MSS. vol. III, Twelfth Report, appendix III (1889).
Egmont MSS. Diary, I–III (1920, 1923).
Lord Montagu of Beaulieu (Montagu) MSS. (1900).
Onslow MSS. Fourteenth Report, appendix IX (1895).
Polwarth MSS. I–III (1911, 1916, 1931).
Portland MSS. V–VII, Harley MSS. III–V (1889, 1901).
Rutland MSS. vol. II, Twelfth Report, appendix V (1889).
Savile MSS. Eleventh Report, appendix VII (1888).
Stuart MSS. I–VII (1902–23).
Townshend MSS. Eleventh Report, appendix IV (1887).

3. MEMOIRS, CORRESPONDENCE, ETC.

Ball, F. E. (ed.). *The Correspondence of Jonathan Swift*. 6 vols., 1910–14.
Blanchard, Rae (ed.). *The Correspondence of Richard Steele*. 1941.
Cartwright, J. J. (ed.). *The Wentworth Papers, 1705–1739, selected from the private and family correspondence of Thomas Wentworth, Lord Raby, created in 1711 Earl of Strafford*. 1883.

Bibliography

Chamberlayne, John. *Magnae Britanniae Notitia; or, The Present State of Great Britain.* 24th ed., 1716; 25th ed., 1718; 26th ed., 1723; 27th ed., 1726; 28th ed., 1727.

Cole, G. D. H. (ed.). Daniel Defoe, *Tour Through the Whole Island of Great Britain.* 2 vols., 1927.

A Collection of Ordinances and Regulations for the Government of the Royal Household...from King Edward III to King William and Queen Mary. The Society of Antiquaries, 1790 (*Household Ordinances*).

Cowper, Spencer (ed.). *The Diary of Mary, Countess Cowper, Lady of the Bedchamber to the Princess of Wales, 1714–20.* 1865.

Coxe, William. *Memoirs of the Life and Administration of Sir Robert Walpole, Earl of Orford.* 3 vols., 1798 (vols. II and III, correspondence).

Croker, J. W. (ed.). *Letters to and from Henrietta, Countess of Suffolk and her Second Husband, the Hon. George Berkeley, from 1712 to 1767.* 2 vols., 1824.

Graham, J. M. (ed.). *Annals and Correspondence of the Viscount and the First and Second Earls of Stair.* 2 vols., 1875.

Graham, W. (ed.). *The Letters of Joseph Addison.* 1941.

Hervey, John, Lord. *Some Materials towards Memoirs of the Reign of George II,* ed. R. R. Sedgwick. 3 vols. 1931.

Hervey, S. H. A. (ed.). *The Diary of John Hervey, First Earl of Bristol.* Wells, 1894.

The Letter Books of John Hervey, First Earl of Bristol. 3 vols. Wells, 1894 (Suffolk Green Books, no. 1).

(Hooke, N.) *An Account of the Conduct of the Duchess of Marlborough.* 1742.

King, W. (ed.). *The Memoirs of the Duchess of Marlborough.* 1930.

Macky, John. *A Journey through England.* 4th ed., 1724.

Matthews, W. (ed.). *The Diary of Dudley Ryder, 1715–16.* 1939.

Montagu, Lady Mary Wortley. *Letters and Works.* 2 vols. 1887.

Newman, A. N. (ed.). *The Parliamentary Diary of Sir Edward Knatchbull, 1722–1730.* Camden Third Series, vol. XCIV, 1963.

Saussure, Cesar de. *A Foreign View of England in the Reigns of George I and George II.* 1926.

Smith, D. N. (ed.). *The Letters of Thomas Burnet to George Duckett, 1712–22.* Oxford, Roxburghe Club, 1914.

Swift, Jonathan. *Journal to Stella,* ed. H. Williams. 2 vols., 1948.

Thomson, Mrs A. T. (ed.). *Memoirs of Viscountess Sundon, Mistress of the Robes to Queen Caroline...* 2 vols., 1847.

Verney, Margaret, Lady (ed.). *The Verney Letters of the Eighteenth Century.* 2 vols., 1930.

Walpole, Horace. *Reminiscences written...in 1788,* ed. Paget Toynbee. Oxford, 1924.

Bibliography

Webb, Geoffrey, and Dobree, Bonamy (eds.). *The Complete Works of Sir John Vanbrugh.* 4 vols., 1937–8.

Wright, L. B. and Tinling, M. (eds.). *William Byrd of Virginia, the London Diary, 1717–21.* New York, 1958.

III. SELECTED SECONDARY WORKS

Aylmer, G. E. *The King's Servants. The Civil Service of Charles I, 1625–42.* 1961.

Baker, C. H. Collins and Baker, M. I. *The Life and Circumstances of James Brydges, First Duke of Chandos.* Oxford, 1949.

Baxter, Stephen B. *The Development of the Treasury, 1660–1702.* 1957.

Beveridge, Sir William, and others. *Prices and Wages in England from the Twelfth to the Nineteenth Centuries.* Vol. I, *Price Tables: mercantile era.* 1939.

Binney, J. E. D. *British Public Finance and Administration, 1774–1792.* Oxford, 1958.

Carlisle, Nicholas. *An Enquiry into the Place and Quality of a Gentleman of the Privy Chamber.* 1829.

Carswell, John. *The South Sea Bubble.* 1960.

Chambers, E. K. *The Elizabethan Stage.* 4 vols., 1923.

Chance, J. F. *George I and the Northern War; a Study of British–Hanoverian Policy in the North of Europe in the Years 1709 to 1721.* 1909.

Chance, J. F. *The Alliance of Hanover; a study of British Foreign Policy in the last years of George I.* 1923.

Clark, D. M. *The Rise of the British Treasury.* New Haven, 1960.

Curling, J. B. *Some Account of the Gentlemen at Arms.* 1850.

Dalton, Charles. *George the First's Army, 1714–1727.* 2 vols., 1910–12.

Elton, G. R. *The Tudor Revolution in Government. Administrative Changes in the Reign of Henry VIII.* 1959.

Foord, A. S. *His Majesty's Opposition, 1714–1830.* 1964.

Grieser, Rudolph. 'Die Deutsche Kanzlei in London, ihre Entstehung und Anfänge', *Blätter für deutsche Landesgeschichte* (1952), pp. 153–68.

Hecht, J. J. *The Domestic Servant Class in Eighteenth Century England.* 1956.

Hennell, Sir R. *History of the King's Bodyguard of the Yeomen of the Guard.* 1904.

Horn, D. B. *The British Diplomatic Service, 1689–1789.* 1961.

March, Earl of. *A Duke and his Friends: the Life and Letters of the Second Duke of Richmond.* 2 vols., 1911.

Michael, Wolfgang. *Englische Geschichte im achtzehnten Jahrhundert.* 5 vols., Leipzig, 1896–1945. (The first three volumes deal with the reign of George I. Volumes I and II have been translated into English under the titles: *England under George I. The Beginnings of the Hanoverian Dynasty* (1936); *England under George I. The Quadruple Alliance* (1939).)

Bibliography

Myers, A. R. *The Household of Edward IV*. 1959.

Newton, A. P. 'Tudor Reforms in the Royal Household', in R. W. Seton-Watson (ed.). *Tudor Studies*. 1924.

Nulle, Stebelton H. *Thomas Pelham-Holles, Duke of Newcastle; his early political career, 1693–1724*. Philadelphia, 1931.

Owen, J. B. *The Rise of the Pelhams*. 1957.

Pegge, Samuel. *Curialia: or an Historical Account of some Branches of the Royal Household*. Vol. I in three parts: I, Obsolete office of Esquire of the King's Body, Gentlemen of the Privy Chamber; II, Account of the Band of Pensioners; III, Account of the Yeomen of the Guard. 1791.

Plumb, J. H. *Sir Robert Walpole. The Making of a Statesman*. 1956.

Plumb, J. H. *Sir Robert Walpole. The King's Minister*. 1960.

Realey, C. B. *The Early Opposition to Sir Robert Walpole*. Kansas, 1931.

Ward, A. W. *Great Britain and Hanover*. 1899.

Woodsworth, Allegra. 'Purveyance for the Royal Household in the Reign of Queen Elizabeth', *Transactions of the American Philosophical Society*, vol. xxxv, pt. I. Philadelphia, 1945.

Wren Society Publications. Vol. VII, *The Royal Palaces of Winchester, Whitehall, Kensington and St James's*. 1930.

Younghusband, Sir G. *The Jewel House*. 1921.

INDEX

Index

Berkeley, James, 3rd earl of (first lord of the Admiralty and gentleman of the bedchamber), 59, 150, 180, 250

Berkeley of Stratton, William Berkeley, Lord, on political obligations of office holders, 174

Bernstorff, Baron Andreas Gottlieb von, 56, 57, 85, 143, 160, 162, 163, 164, 221–4; access to Cabinet discussions, 223; influence on English policy of, 222, 227–8, 234–8; friendship with Lady Cowper, 145, 223; his villages in Mecklenburg, 237–8; deserted by Robethon, 237; conflict with Stanhope in 1719, 236–8; repudiated by George I, 238; attempts to undermine government, 239; leaves England, 239; allied with Carteret in 1723, 243

Betton, Wriotesly, 33 n.

birthday, king's, celebration of at court, 12–13, 206

black rod, gentleman usher of the, value of the post, 41

Bloodworth, Thomas, 103 n., 142

Board-wages, 85, 181–4

Bolingbroke, Henry St John, viscount, 245 n.

Bolton, Charles Paulet, 2nd duke of, 24 n., 168

Bonet, Frederick; on English court, 261; on Hanoverian ministers, 223

bookseller, 280; tenure of, 174

Boscawen, Hugh (later viscount Falmouth), 70, 158, 176, 178 n., 252 n., 253 n.; accompanies George I to Hanover, 69

Bothmer, Baron Johann Caspar von, 56, 85, 135, 157, 163, 164, 220–4, 231; importance of at Anne's death, 221; and establishment of new court, 143–5; influence on appointments, 59, 143–6; English complaints about his influence, 146; reports to Hanover on Prince, 230; on size of Hanoverian court, 258–9

'bouge' of court, 183–4

Brand, Sir Thomas, Kt., 42 n., 202

Bray, William, 89; description of household below stairs by, 96; on under-clerks of green cloth, 97

Brent, Humphrey, 34 n.

Bret, James, 170 n.

Breton, William, 62, 103, 145, 178 n.

Bridgewater, Scroop Egerton, 5th earl and 1st duke of, 60 n., 158

Bristol, John Hervey, earl of, 41

Bristow, Robert, 74 n., 252 n.

Brocas, Thomas, 35 n.

Broglie, Count, on George I, 247, 278

Broughton, Sir Thomas, Bt., 34 n., 253 n.

Brown, Edward, 63

Brudenell, James, 122, 252 n.

Brumpstead, Charles, 53

Brydges, Sir Brook, Bt., 33 n.

Brydges, James, earl of Carnarvon and duke of Chandos, 29, 45 n., 165, 245 n.; on Bernstorff's dominance, 222; on the breach in royal family, 273; on comptrollership of the household, 69; on expense of court life, 205; on Hanoverian courtiers, 145; bribes Hanoverians, 163–4; his household, 19; on political obligations of office holders, 174 n.

Buck, Sir Charles, Bt., 34 n.

buckhounds, master of the, 279

Buckingham, Owen, 33 n., 252 n., 253 n.

Burnet, Thomas, seeks office, 160–1

Burroughs, Charles, 136 n.

Bute, Lady, on drawing-room, 15

Butemeister, Frederick, 260

buttery; officers and work of, 89, 282; clerk of, fees taken by, 190; gentleman of, value of the office, 213

Butts, Robert, bishop of Norwich, 5

Byrd, William, of Virginia, 163; visits court, 14 n.

Cabinet, and great household officers, 4

cabinet maker to household, 280

Cadogan, William (later earl), 3, 64, 150, 151, 229, 252 n., 253 n., 267

Campbell, Peter, 92, 253 n., 254

card maker, 279

Carleton, Henry Boyle, Lord, 150

Carmichael, Archibald, 103 n.

Caroline, Queen, 173, 207; on privacy of the Civil List, 116 n.; and Walpole, 219, 248; as Princess of Wales, 13, 127, 262, 263, 268, 270, 274

carriages, sergeant and yeoman of, 282

cart takers, 282

Carteret, John, Lord (gentleman of the bedchamber, lord lieutenant of Ireland, secretary of state), 58, 59 n., 148, 150, 151, 168, 250; struggle with Walpole and Townshend, 149–52, 242–7; lord lieutenant of Ireland, 246

Index

Goodman, Thomas, appointment of as physician, 137

Görtz, Baron, 146, 172

Grafton, Charles Fitzroy, 2nd duke of, 267; gentleman of the bedchamber 59 n., 144; dismissed, 175; lord chamberlain, 4, 24 n., 167; pension as, 184; lord lieutenant of Ireland, 168

Granville, Bernard, 178

Grassineau, James, 37 n.

Grave, Lambert de, 63

great chamber, grooms of, 37, 279; duties of, 43

great wardrobe, work of, 25, 50–1; supplies furniture to Hanoverians and prince, 127; liveries supplied by, 50, 188; its independence, 122; its reputation for wastefulness, 123; expenditure under George I, 112; heavy expenses in at beginning of reign, 112; difficulties of controlling expenditure of, 122; reforms attempted before 1714, 124; Treasury and reform of, 124–6; expenditure of limited, 127–8; weakness of Treasury control, 122–3; reforms after 1728, 124–5; its abolition suggested, 128–9

master of the, 51, 280; accounts of, 111, 123; appointments made by, 134; as a paymaster, 110; fees taken by, 191; livery payments to, 188; value of the office, 191, 210; duchess of Marlborough on value, 191; and see Montagu

deputy master of, 51, 280; value of the office, 204

clerk of the, 51, 280; value of the office, 191, 210

comptroller of, 124–5

surveyor of, 125

green cloth, board of: composition, 66; changes at accession of George I, 144; office of, 77 n.; meetings, 77; attendance, 67; and household establishment, 79–80; and control of household expenditure, 80–1; and regulation of allowances to servants, 80; control of deputies by, 82; and discipline below stairs, 82–3; attempts to prevent fraud, 93–5; fees in household scrutinized by, 195; judicial work of, 77–8; regulation of offices below stairs by, 79–83; vigilance of, 81; decline of under George II, 96–7; George III on, 97

clerks of, 66, 67, 74–5, 281; appointment of, 73–4; and accounts of household offices, 95–6; their patronage below stairs, 135; accept salary in lieu of fees, 196; value of the office, 181; 182–3, 212; as commissioners for land tax, 203 n.; as J.P.s, 78

under-clerks of, 75–6, 281; as clerks of land tax commission, 203 n.; fees of, 194; value of the office, 213

green cloth table, 267–8; expense of, at Hampton Court, 274; at St James's, 275; discontinued, 276; Onslow on, 267–8

Greswold, Henry, 34 n.

groom porter, 52, 279; value, 210; and see Thomas Archer

groom of the stole, 17, 281; rights and duties of, 56; independent of lord chamberlain, 54, 56; and Cabinet, 4; post held by royal favourites, 56; George I leaves vacant, 56–7; Sunderland appointed, 57, 238; struggle over vacancy, 58; rights of appointment in bedchamber, 132, 134; selling posts, 164; board-wages and fee of, 182; pension paid to, 185; perquisites claimed by, 196; receives plate from jewel office, 50; value of the office, 211

guard chamber, 6–10

Guernsey, Heneage Finch, Lord, 252 n., 253 n.; resignation of, 175 n.

gunsmith, 280

Gunthorpe, George, 160

Gunthorpe, Jane, 160

Hackett, Lisle, 35 n.

Halifax, Charles Montagu, Lord, 157, 160, 224

Hall, officers of, 282; reduced in number, 18

Hamilton, Sir David, 145 n.

Hampden, John, 103 n.

Hanoverian chancery in London, 220

Hanoverian court in London, 141, 258–61; paid from privy purse, 260–1; courtiers, and sale of favour, 163–4; pages of given English lessons, 259–60; and see Mehemet, Mustapha

Hanoverian ministers in London, 9, 219, 220, 223–4, 225–6; allowances from great wardrobe and household below stairs, 127; and English foreign policy, 221, 222, 227–9, 234–5; and see Bernstorff, Bothmer, Robethon

Index

harbinger, gentleman, 25, 48, 282; knight, 48, 279; conditions of appointment of, 174; value of, 210; yeoman, 48, 279
Hardenberg, Marshall, 244
Hardwicke, earl of, on Sunderland as groom of the stole, 57
Harold, Anthony Grey, Lord, 60 n.
harpsichord maker, 280
Hartington, William Cavendish, marquis of, later duke of Devonshire, 253 n.
Harvey, Gideon, 34 n.
hautboys, 279
Hawley, Henry, 34 n.
Henning, Caspar Frederick, 36, 260
Herbert, Lord, 60
Herbert, Robert, 62 n., 253 n.
Hervey, Carr, Lord, 41
Hervey, John, Lord, 4, 5, 179; on contrast between George I and his son, 262; on expense of 'birthday clothes', 207; on expense of court life, 205; on import-ance of Kendal, 248; on London tradesmen and the court, 13; on quarrel in royal family, 272, 278; salary of as vice-chamberlain, 184
Heymans, James, 93, 186
Hickman, Nathaniel, 33 n.
historiographer, 279
Hobart, Sir John, 179
Hodges, Charles, 64, 134
Holdernesse, Robert Darcy, earl of, 60 n.
Honeywood, Philip, 62, 145; deprived of his regiment in 1710, 62 n.
household, royal: structure of, 17; reduc-tion in size in 17th century, 17–18; size under George I, 18–19; functions of, 1–2; and central government, 1, 2, 48–51; expenditure of, 112–18, ch. 4, passim; and the Treasury, 118–19, 122–6; establishments of, 119–21; ordinances of, of 1539–40, 28, 70–2, 76; ordinances of James II and Charles II, 38; bedchamber ordin-ances of William III, 11, 54, 56, 64; posts of first rank in, changes frequent in, 167–8; reforms of in sixteenth century, 1–2, 28, 70–2; retrenchments in, 127–31; servants' servants, 19; value of offices in, 5–6, 209–14, ch. 6, passim; paymasters of, see household, cofferer of; chamber, treasurer of; great wardrobe, master of; robes, master of; master of the horse; gentle-men pensioners, paymaster of; privy purse, keeper of

household below stairs: structure and func-tions of, 17, 66, 83; number of ser-vants in, 18; list of offices in, 281–2; reduction in size, 84; rights of ap-pointment in, 132; clerkships of offices held together, 88, 90, 201; establishments of, 77, 119–20; ex-penditure in under George I, 112–13; expenditure in and court entertain-ment, 113, 274; control of expendi-ture in, 120; attempted retrenchment in, 128; fees collected in, 194; promo-tion in, 168–71; purveyance in, 76–7, 90–1, 93; orders forbidding sale of offices in, 165; *and see* green cloth, board of; acatry, accounting house; almonry; bakehouse; buttery; cellar; confectionery; ewry; kitchen; pantry; pastry; poultry; scalding house; scul-lery; spicery
household, cofferer of, 2, 66, 67, 281; work of enlarged by Tudors, 28, 70–1; under George I, 71–2; declared accounts of, 111; expenditure of, 112; an 'office of profit', 189; as a pay-master, 110; pensions paid by, 199; board-wages paid to, 182–3; fees col-lected by, 189; value of the office, 212
deputy cofferer, work of, 72–3; fees taken by, 190; value, 73; cofferer's clerks, fees taken by, 190
household, comptroller of the, 66, 67, 69–70, 281; and parliament, 254; receives plate from jewel office, 50; value of the office, 182, 211
household, master of the, 66, 67, 70, 281; value of the office, 182–3, 211
household, treasurer of the, 66, 67, 281; value of the office, 50, 182, 211
housekeepers, 46–7, 279; salaries of, 205; of Whitehall, tenure of, 174; of Kensington, tenure of, 174; purchase of, 165
Howard of Effingham, Thomas Howard, Lord, 151
Howard, Charles (later earl of Suffolk), 62 n.
Howard, Henrietta (later countess of Suffolk), 164, 179
Howe, Emanuel, 103 n.
Hucks, William, 252 n.
Huls, William Charles van, 53, 253 n.
Hume, Sir Gustavus, Bt., 61 n., 62 n.; on George I's conversation, 264–5
Hutt, John, appointed to new post in great wardrobe, 125

Index

St James's (*cont.*)
rebuilding of, 9–10; servants lodged there, 9 n., 185–7, 220
sale of offices, 164–6
Sambrooke, Sir Jeremy, Bt., 33 n.
Sanderson, Sir William, 41 n., 42 n.
Sands, Henry, 42 n.
Saunders, Jeffrey, 44 n.
Sauniers, Henry de, 42 n., 180
Saurin, Mark Anthony, 42 n., 180
Saussure Cesarde, visits court, 14 n.
Scalding house, officers and work of, 90, 281; abolished under George III, 96; fraud in, 94–5
Scarborough, Charles, 178 n.; pension paid to, 199
Scarborough, Richard Lumley, earl of, 100, 179
Schaub, Luke, 146
Schism Act, repeal of, 249
Schulenberg, Ehrengard Mesuline von der, duchess of Munster and duchess of Kendal, 164, 240–1, 261; allowances at court, 80 n., 85; Broglie and Louis XV on her importance, 247; failure to get English title, 225; importance of, 219; granted fixed sum in lieu of supplies from household below stairs, 127; and a household appointment, 142; supports Stanhope, 1719, 237, 241–2; supports Townshend and Walpole, 1723, 242, 244–6; her profitable position in England, 245; and South Sea Bubble, 245 n.; Walpole on importance of, 248; and 'Woods Patent', 245 n.
Schutz, Augustus, 64, 179
scullery, officers and work of, 90, 282, clerk of, 73, 169; yeomen of, 282; right to lodgings, 185; value of the office, 213
secretaries of state, receive plate from jewel office, 50
secretaries to embassies receive plate from jewel office, 50
Selkirk, Charles Hamilton Douglas, earl of, 59 n.
sempstress and starcher, 281
Septennial Bill, 249
sergeant porter, 52
sergeants-at-arms, 45, 279; purchase of office of, 45 n.
sewers of the chamber, *see* presence chamber
Seymour, William, 44 n.

Shaw, John, 75 n., 169
Sherrard, Brownlow, 42 n.
Sherrard, Sir Richard, 35 n.
Shewbridge, Jane, 261 n.
Shrewsbury, Charles Talbot, duke of, 24 n., 45 n., 156, 172; pension as lord chamberlain, 184
Skipworth, Sir George Bridges, Bt., 34 n.
Sloper, William, 72, 154–5, 253 n.
Somerset, Charles Seymour, duke of, 101
Somerset, duchess of, 64, 196; pension as groom of the stole, 185
Somerset House, servants' lodgings at, 186
South Sea Bubble, 245 n.
Speaker of the House of Commons, receives plate from jewel office, 50
spicery, 90; clerk of, 73, 169, 281; fees collected by, 194–5; value of the office, 212; under-clerk of, 281
Spiesmaker, Luder, 75 n.
stables, officers and work of, 17–18, 98–104, 282; list of offices in, 282; clerk of, 99, 282; expenditure in for extraordinaries under George I, 112; financial arrangements of, 98–9; reduction in servants of, 18; livery allowances in, 188; purveyors, 104, 282; rights of appointment in 141–2; surveyors of, 104; *and see* avenor; avery, clerk of; carriages; equerries; farrier; master of the horse; pages of honour
Stair, John Dalrymple, earl of, 59 n., 250
standing wardrobes, keepers of, 47, 280
Stanhope, Charles, 29 n., 179, 253 n.; appointment as treasurer of the chamber, 147–9
Stanhope, James, Lord, 146, 160, 224, 241, 265; foreign policy of, 1716, 227–9; accepts Bernstorff's influence in England, 234; Northern policy of, 236; conflict with Bernstorff over foreign policy, 235–9
Stanley, Sir John, Bt., 25 n., 192
state apartments: in sixteenth and seventeenth centuries, 6–8; at Hampton Court, 8; at Kensington, 10; at St James's, 9–10; at Whitehall, 8
Statham, Sir John, Kt., 35 n.
stationer, 49; bills of, 120
Stedholme, Michael, 202
Steele, Sir Richard, 26, 104, 153, 252 n., 253 n., 254; theatre company of, performing at Hampton Court, 274; votes against Peerage Bill, 249
Stocken, Mrs, 223

304